D0219804

A Brief History of Economic Thought

The evolution of economic thought can be traced back from its beginnings in classical antiquity up to the present day. In this book, Professor Alessandro Roncaglia offers a clear, concise and updated version of his award-winning *The Wealth of Ideas*, studying the development of economic thought through perspectives and debates on the economy and society over time. With chapters on prominent economic theorists, including William Petty, Karl Marx, and John Maynard Keynes, as well as on other important figures and key debates of each period, Roncaglia critically evaluates the foundations of the marginalist–neoclassical (scarcity–utility) approach in comparison to the Classical–Keynes approach. A comprehensive guide to the history of economic thought, this book will be of value not only to undergraduate and postgraduate students studying economic thought but also to any readers desiring to study how economics has evolved up to the present day.

ALESSANDRO RONCAGLIA is Professor of Economics at Sapienza University of Rome. He is a member of the Accademia Nazionale dei Lincei, Editor of *PSL Quarterly Review* and *Moneta e Credito*, and was previously President of the Società Italiana degli Economisti. His numerous publications, translated into various languages, include *The Wealth of Ideas*, also published by Cambridge University Press (2005).

A Brief History of Economic Thought

Alessandro Roncaglia
Sapienza University of Rome

CAMBRIDGE
UNIVERSITY PRESS

CAMBRIDGE
UNIVERSITY PRESS

University Printing House, Cambridge CB2 8BS, United Kingdom

One Liberty Plaza, 20th Floor, New York, NY 10006, USA

477 Williamstown Road, Port Melbourne, VIC 3207, Australia

4843/24, 2nd Floor, Ansari Road, Daryaganj, Delhi – 110002, India

79 Anson Road, #06–04/06, Singapore 079906

Cambridge University Press is part of the University of Cambridge.

It furthers the University's mission by disseminating knowledge in the pursuit of education, learning, and research at the highest international levels of excellence.

www.cambridge.org
Information on this title: www.cambridge.org/9781107175334
DOI: 10.1017/9781316798416

English translation © Alessandro Roncaglia 2017

This publication is in copyright. Subject to statutory exception and to the provisions of relevant collective licensing agreements, no reproduction of any part may take place without the written permission of Cambridge University Press.

First published in English by Cambridge University Press 2017 as *A Brief History of Economic Thought*
Originally published in Italian as *Breve storia del pensiero economico* by Manuali Laterza and © Gius. Laterza & Figli 2016

Printed in the United Kingdom by Clays, St Ives plc

A catalogue record for this publication is available from the British Library.

Library of Congress Cataloging-in-Publication Data
Names: Roncaglia, Alessandro, 1947– author.
Title: A brief history of economic thought / Alessandro Roncaglia.
Description: New York : Cambridge University Press, 2017.
Identifiers: LCCN 2017020505| ISBN 9781107175334 (hardback) | ISBN 9781316627365 (paperback)
Subjects: LCSH: Economics – History. | BISAC: BUSINESS & ECONOMICS / Economic History.
Classification: LCC HB75 .R646 2017 | DDC 330.1509–dc23
LC record available at https://lccn.loc.gov/2017020505

ISBN 978-1-107-17533-4 Hardback
ISBN 978-1-316-62736-5 Paperback

Cambridge University Press has no responsibility for the persistence or accuracy of URLs for external or third-party internet websites referred to in this publication and does not guarantee that any content on such websites is, or will remain, accurate or appropriate.

Contents

Preface

With *The Wealth of Ideas* (Roncaglia 2005), published more than a decade ago, my aim was to present my own reconstruction of the history of economic thought, on the lines drawn by Piero Sraffa in his writings (i.e. opposing the Classical to the marginalist approach) but with some significant differences, such as re-evaluation of Adam Smith as compared to David Ricardo, greater attention to the themes concerning the interpretation of society beyond the theory of value and a reformist view of the capitalist economy. I have also tried to locate and illustrate similarities and differences inherent to each approach – classical and marginalist – and to assess the position of somewhat anomalous authors like Marshall, Keynes, Schumpeter and Sraffa himself.

The book enjoyed a favourable reception and was also utilized as a textbook in various languages and countries. However, I became aware that its proportions stood in the way of both perception of its main theses and its use as a textbook or an introductory text for non-economists on a discipline that concerns us all. Hence the decision to prepare a drastically simplified and shortened version. In particular, apart from passing over some aspects of lesser importance, I cut out nearly all references to the secondary literature (which remain available to the interested reader in the *editio maior*). The new book also gave me the opportunity for thorough revision and a number of minor changes and some rewriting, including extensive revision of the final chapter, with hints at a new interpretation of recent trends in economics that I plan to develop fully in my next book.

I hope in this way to provide an introduction to the history of economic thought that might also help the reader understand the current economics debate. Underlying the debate there are quite often, hidden from sight but still very significant, different approaches to economics, and not only different opinions on policy. What is now considered the mainstream approach, supported by many as the only truly scientific approach or even as the only one *tout court*, is but one, and possibly not the best, of the various approaches developed in the course of time.

Thanks are due to Giuseppe Laterza and to Philip Good, who encouraged me on this venture; to Nerio Naldi and Nicholas Theocarakis, who read and commented on a preliminary draft of this work; to Carlo D'Ippoliti and Aldo Montesano for comments on the final chapter; to the many careful readers of *The Wealth of Ideas* who sent me their comments; and to Graham Sells for carefully revising my (Italo-)English style. Finally, I am always in debt to Paolo Sylos Labini and Piero Sraffa for their teachings.

1 Introduction: The History of Economic Thought and Its Role

> To understand the others: this is the historian's aim.
> It is not easy to have a more difficult task.
> It is difficult to have a more interesting one.
>
> (Kula 1958, p. 234)

1.1 Why the History of Economic Thought Is Considered Useless: The Cumulative View

The history of economic thought (HET) is essential for anyone interested in understanding how economies work. Thus – I maintain – economists, precisely as producers and users of economic theories, should study and practise the history of economic thought. This thesis is opposed to the now prevailing consensus. Most contemporary economists are convinced that HET is not necessary for the progress of research, which, rather, requires work on the theoretical frontier.

This anti-HET attitude relies on a *cumulative view* of the development of economic thought, according to which economic analysis displays a progressive rise to ever higher levels of understanding of economic reality. The provisional point of arrival of today's economists – contemporary economic theory – incorporates all previous contributions.[1]

The cumulative view is connected to positivism or, more specifically, to a simplified version of logical positivism, the so-called *received view*, which found a considerable following as from the 1920s: scientists work by applying the methods of logical analysis to the raw material provided by empirical experience. To evaluate their results, objective criteria for

---

[1] An illustrious and indeed radical example of this position is offered by Pantaleoni 1898. According to him, the history of thought must be 'history of *economic truths*' (ibid., p. 217): 'its only purpose ... is to relate the origins of true doctrines' (ibid., p. 234); a clear-cut criterion for judging the truth or falsehood of economic theories is available: 'There has been a troublesome search for hypotheses that are both *clear* and *in conformity with reality* ... Facts and hypotheses have then been used, and what could be deduced from them has been deduced. The theorems have also been checked on empirical reality' (ibid., p. 217).

acceptance or rejection can be established. *Analytic statements,* concerning abstract theoretical reasoning, are either tautological, i.e. logically implied in the assumptions, or self-contradictory, i.e. they contain logical inconsistencies; in the former case, the analytic statement is accepted, in the latter rejected. Similarly, *synthetic statements,* concerning the empirical world, are either confirmed or contradicted by evidence and hence accepted or rejected for objective reasons. All other statements for which no analogous criteria of acceptance or rejection can be found are termed *metaphysical* and are considered external to the field of science.

This view has come in for severe criticism, discussed in the following section. Nevertheless it remains the basis for the cumulative view of economic science, namely the idea that successive generations of economists contribute new analytic or synthetic propositions to the common treasure of economic science, which – as a science – is univocally defined as the set of 'true' propositions concerning economic matters. New knowledge is thus added to that already available, and in many cases – whenever some defect is identified in previously accepted accounts – is substituted for it. Hence, the study of economics must be conducted on the theoretical frontier, taking into consideration the most up-to-date version and not the theories of the past. However, the latter may deserve some attention: as Schumpeter (1954, p. 4) says, studying economists of the past is pedagogically helpful, may prompt new ideas and affords useful material on the methods of scientific research in such a complex and thought-provoking field as economics, on the borderline between natural and social sciences.

Among adherents of the cumulative view, Viner (1991, pp. 385 and 390) proposes a subtle defence of the history of economic thought, pointing to the importance of 'scholarship', defined as 'the pursuit of broad and exact knowledge of the history of the working of the human mind as revealed in written records'. Scholarship, although considered inferior to theoretical activity, contributes to the education of researchers, being 'a commitment to the pursuit of knowledge and understanding': 'once the taste for it has been aroused, it gives a sense of largeness even to one's small quests, and a sense of fullness even to the small answers ... a sense which can never in any other way be attained'. Education in research thus appears to be a prerequisite for informed application of analytical tools.[2] Thus, even if the history of economic thought is

---

[2] Schumpeter (1954, p. 4; italics in the original) says something similar when stating that the history of economic thought 'will prevent a sense of *lacking direction and meaning* from spreading among the students'.

considered to be of little use in learning modern economic theory, an important role is attributed to it in the education of the researcher.

1.2   The Competitive View

Over the past few decades a number of economists have referred to Kuhn's (1962) 'scientific revolutions' or Lakatos's (1978) 'scientific research programmes' in support of the idea that it is impossible to choose among competing theoretical approaches with the objective criteria indicated by logical positivism (logical consistency, correspondence of assumptions to empirical reality).

First of all, some criticisms concern the clear-cut dichotomy between analytic and synthetic statements. Analytic statements, if interpreted as purely logical propositions, are devoid of any reference to the real world; as a consequence, they are empty from the point of view of the interpretation of real-world phenomena. Synthetic statements, in turn, necessarily embody a large mass of theoretical elements in the very definition of the categories used for collecting the empirical data and in the methods by which these data are treated; as a consequence, the choice of accepting or rejecting any synthetic statement cannot be clear-cut but is conditioned by a long series of theoretical hypotheses that cannot, however, be subject to separate evaluation. Thus, there are no univocal objective criteria for evaluating analytic and synthetic statements.

Another important critique of the criterion for accepting or rejecting synthetic statements – their correspondence or non-correspondence to the real world – is developed by Popper (1934). No matter how many times a synthetic statement is corroborated by checking it against the real world, says Popper, we cannot exclude the possibility that a contrary case will eventually crop up. Thus, for instance, the statement that 'all swans are white' may be contradicted by the discovery of a single new species of black swans in Australia. The scientist cannot pretend to verify a theory, that is, to demonstrate it to be true once and for all. The scientist can only accept a theory provisionally, bearing in mind the possibility that it may be falsified, or in other words shown to be false by a newfound empirical event contradicting it. In a subsequent book (1969), Popper maintains that the best method for scientific research consists precisely in the formulation of a potentially never-ending series of 'conjectures and falsifications'. In other words, the scientist formulates hypotheses and then, rather than looking for empirical confirmation – which in any case could not be definitive – seeks out refutations. These, by stimulating and guiding the search for better hypotheses, contribute to the advancement of science.

The influence of some historians and philosophers of science, such as Kuhn, Lakatos and Feyerabend, then contributed, in the last decades of the twentieth century, to abandonment of the positivistic methodology in the field of economic theory.

According to Kuhn, the development of science is not linear but can be subdivided into stages, each with its own distinctive characteristics. In each period of 'normal science', a specific point of view (paradigm) is commonly accepted as the basis for scientific research. On such a basis, an ever more complex theoretical system is built, capable of explaining an increasing number of phenomena. This process of growth of normal science, however, is accompanied by the accumulation of anomalies, phenomena either that are unexplained or that require for explanation an increasingly heavy load of *ad hoc* assumptions. The result is a growing malaise prompting a 'scientific revolution', or in other words proposal of a new paradigm. This marks the beginning of a new stage of normal science, within which research proceeds without calling into question the underlying paradigm.

Kuhn does not consider the succession of different paradigms as a logical sequence characterised by a growing amount of knowledge. The different paradigms are considered as not commensurable among themselves; each of them constitutes a different key for interpreting reality, necessarily based on a specific set of simplifying assumptions, many of which remain implicit. No paradigm can encompass the whole universe in all its details. Strictly speaking, it is incorrect to say either that the earth goes round the sun or that the sun goes round the earth, since there is no fixed point within the universe. Each of the two hypotheses requires the choice of a fixed point as reference for the study of the universe or, better, concentrates on a part of the universe that is in continuous movement relatively to any other possible fixed point. Since both the earth and the sun move in space, those of Copernicus and Ptolemy are but two alternative theoretical approaches that explain in more or less simple terms a greater or smaller number of phenomena. We may also recall that a heliocentric view had already been proposed by Aristarchus of Samos in the third century BCE, nearly five centuries before Ptolemy: paradigms do not necessarily follow each other in a linear sequence but can reappear as dominant after even long periods of eclipse.

Kuhn's 'scientific revolutions' are intended more as description of the paths followed by the different sciences than as a normative model of behaviour for scientists. On the other hand, Lakatos adopts a normative attitude (1978) with his 'methodology of scientific research programmes', consisting in a set of working rules for both critique and construction of theories (negative and positive heuristic), organised around a 'hard core' of hypotheses concerning a specific set of issues and utilised as foundations for constructing a theoretical system. The hard core remains unchanged even when anomalies arise, thanks to a 'protective belt' of auxiliary hypotheses; it is abandoned only when the scientific research programme is clearly recognised as 'regressive', i.e. when going ahead with it appears a waste of time and effort. Thus Lakatos sees acceptance or rejection of a scientific research programme as a complex process, not an act of judgement based on well-defined, univocal, objective criteria.

Thus interpreted, Lakatos's view is not very different from – although less radical than – the approach proposed by Feyerabend (1975) with his 'anarchistic theory of knowledge'. Feyerabend stresses the need for open-mindedness towards the most disparate research approaches; at the same time, he guards against unqualified application of his own motto: 'Anything can go'. Critique of the idea that there exist absolute criteria of truth (or better of acceptance and rejection of theories) coexists with the idea that rational debate between different, even conflicting, points of view is practicable. Obviously, when debating the different viewpoints one should not use the criteria of judgement based on one's own worldview but rather try to understand and adopt the rival viewpoint and possibly to criticise it from inside. We are thus confronted with a procedure for scientific debate analogous to that commonly followed in legal proceedings, where prosecutor and defence each bring argumentations in support of their positions.

Feyerabend's views were brought into the economic debate by McCloskey (1985), albeit with some changes. McCloskey speaks of a 'rhetorical method of scientific debate' that rejects neat, mono-dimensional criteria for the evaluation of theories and stresses, in contrast, the role of their relative power of persuasion.[3] This does not mean denying any value to the theoretical debate: far from it, the main message is the need for tolerance in the face of different views of the world and hence of different theoretical approaches. We may also recall that, thus interpreted, the rhetorical method in economics can be traced back to Adam Smith's *History of Astronomy* (Smith, 1795).

---

[3] Within the field of the natural sciences, experiments performed in controlled conditions (that is, keeping *ceteris paribus*) as a rule constitute decisive proof of the superiority of one theory over other theories. In the field of the social sciences, however, such experiments are practically impossible. Hence the greater complexity in this latter field for comparison between different theories.

In the case of Kuhn, Lakatos and Feyerabend alike, economists are led to recognise the existence of alternative approaches, deduced from the succession of different paradigms or from the coexistence of different scientific research programmes. It is here that the history of economic thought comes into play. Those who accept a competitive view of the development of economic thought and participate in a debate between contending approaches are induced to investigate the history of such a debate, seeking out the points of strength and weakness that account for the dominance or decline of the different approaches.

In particular, those who support approaches competing with the dominant one may find HET very useful. First, analysis of the writings of economists in the past often helps in clarifying the basic character-istics of the approach proposed and the differences between it and the dominant one. Second, HET helps in evaluating theories based on different approaches, by bringing to light their worldviews, the concepts and hypotheses on which they are based. Often this helps in retrieving the notes of caution and the qualifications originally accompanying the analysis and subsequently forgotten. Third, recal-ling illustrious cultural roots sometimes serves a tactical purpose, namely to shake up the inertia that constitutes such a strong advantage for the prevailing mainstream.

The competitive view implies neither equivalence between competing approaches nor absence of scientific progress. What the competitive view specifically rejects is the idea of a mono-dimensional process of scientific advance. There can be progress both within each approach (where indeed it is the general rule, in terms of both greater internal consistency and higher explanatory power) and along the historical sequence of research paradigms or programmes. In the latter case, however, the idea of progress is more imprecise and greater caution is required. An undeni-able element of progress is provided by the increasing number of ever more sophisticated analytical tools made available by developments in other fields of research (new mathematical tools, better and more abundant statistical material, higher computing power with the new computers). But between successive research paradigms or programmes there are commonly crucial differences in the underlying worldview. Some aspects of reality are given greater prominence, others less, so that there are differences in the set of (explicit or implicit) assumptions on which theories are built and hence in the domain of applicability of the theories. Analytical variables or concepts (such as the market, competi-tion, natural price, profit, rent), although indicated by the same name, take on different meanings when used within different theories. We thus need to analyse the conceptual foundations of the different theories, and the changes in the meaning of the concepts when inserted in different theoretical frameworks, as part of theoretical research work.

1.3 The Stages of Economic Theorising: Conceptualisation and Model-building

Schumpeter (1954, pp. 41–2) stresses the importance of analysing the conceptual foundations by subdividing economic research into three stages. First, we have the 'pre-analytic cognitive act', or 'vision', which consists in locating the problem to be dealt with and suggesting some working hypotheses with which to start analysis, the aim being to arrive at, if not a tentative solution, then at least the way to tackle the problem. Second, we have the stage where the aim is 'to verbalize the vision or to conceptualize it in such a way that its elements take their places, with names attached to them that facilitate recognition, or manipulation, in a more or less orderly scheme or picture': what we can call the stage of conceptualisation. The abstract system of concepts thus obtained isolates the elements of reality that are considered relevant to the issue under consideration. Finally, the third stage concerns the construction of 'scientific models'.

As we saw in the preceding section, the debate between contending approaches is above all a matter of choosing the conceptual system to be used in representing economic reality. HET plays a decisive role in this respect. It is impossible to provide an exhaustive definition of a concept: the best way to analyse it is to study its evolution over time, examining the different shades of meaning it acquires in the writings of different authors and occasionally in the different writings of the same author. This is the common experience of all studies in the humanities, from philosophy to politics.

Furthermore, by utilising HET for analysis of a concept (and of a conceptual system) we can investigate two basic issues: first, whether it is possible to adapt the content of concepts to the continuous changes in the reality to be explained; second, how the mechanism of interaction between the conceptualisation stage and the stage of model-building operates. The first point – the interaction between economic history and economic theory – is a well-known issue. The second point is rarely considered but is crucial: the difficulties that arise in the stage of model-building and the analytical solutions to those difficulties often imply modifications in the conceptual foundations of the theories, and such modifications may imply a flight from reality into purely utopian worlds.

The systems of concepts underlying any theory are thus changing continuously, which makes it impossible to conceive evaluation of economic theories on a mono-dimensional scale. Theoretical advances may constitute scientific progress under certain aspects but not under others. Most importantly, the steps forward continuously made in the direction of a higher logical consistency and a growing use of more advanced analytical techniques do not necessarily imply a higher explanatory power: they may call for further restrictions to the meaning of the variables under consideration, excluding crucial aspects of reality from the field of applicability of the theory. When we are confronted with this problem HET, by focusing attention on the shifts in the meaning of the concepts used in the theory, can help in evaluating the multifaceted path followed by economic research.[4]

1.4   Economics and the History of Economic Thought

Economics is an investigation of society, with two main characteristics. First, it is a scientific investigation, which follows specific methodological rules (although not necessarily unchangeable or univocal). Second, it considers society in a particular, but fundamental, aspect: the mechanisms of survival and development of a society based on the division of labour. In such a society each worker is employed in a specific activity, collaborating in the production of a specific commodity, and has to obtain from other economic agents, in exchange for (part of) the product, the commodities required as means of production and subsistence. These mechanisms consist in institutions, habits, norms, knowledge and preferences, which constitute constraints and behavioural rules. Economists investigate the results, both individual and collective, of specific sets of constraints and behavioural rules.

As investigation of society, political economy is a social science, with a historical dimension. As a science, it implies adhesion to the methodological criteria prevailing in the economists' working environment. Hence we have a tension between the scientific rules of logical consistency and the nature of economics as a social science. HET helps to achieve a positive resolution of the previously mentioned tension, by bringing to the fore the historical dimension in economic enquiries and, simultaneously, by referring to both criteria – logical precision and empirical relevance – in selecting and evaluating the theories on which to focus attention and in locating a connecting line of development.

---

[4] For an illustration of the recent debate on the topic, cf. D'Ippoliti and Roncaglia 2016.

A fairly clear answer to the question we started from thus emerges. HET is useful not only and not simply on the didactic level or to provide a sense of direction to economic research or material for epistemologists. It is an essential ingredient both of the theoretical debate between contending approaches, since it helps to clarify the differences and modifications in their representations of the world, and of the theoretical work within each approach, since it contributes to developing the conceptual foundations and clarifying the changes intervening in them in response to theoretical difficulties and evolving realities.

HET also constitutes an education in democracy, in the sense indicated by Kula, quoted at the beginning of this chapter, by educating to the exchange of ideas, also thanks to the effort it involves in understanding the ideas of others, the perception it fosters of the complexities of the worldviews underlying the different theories and determining their potentialities and their limits and the links it reveals with other fields of human knowledge and action.

'There are more things in heaven and earth, Horatio, than are dreamt of in your philosophy': HET, with its own various research strategies, is of great help in keeping economists fully aware of the truth of Hamlet's observation. Not least for this reason, it is a field that every economist should explore.

2   The Prehistory of Political Economy

2.1   Why We Call It Prehistory

The naissance of political economy was a very complex process that took place over a long time horizon: at least from the classical Greek period to the sixteenth and seventeenth centuries.[1] Only in the nineteenth century, with the creation of the first economics chairs in universities, was the economist recognised as an autonomous professional figure.[2]

References to issues now commonly considered as belonging to economics already made their appearance in classical antiquity and the Middle Ages. Authors such as Diodorus Siculus, Xenophon or Plato, for instance, considered the economic aspects of the division of labour, maintaining among other things that it favours a better product quality. However, for a long time – at least up to the seventeenth century – the approach to economic issues was substantially different from present-day practice. Indeed, the very economic mechanisms regulating production and income distribution have since seen radical transformation. Suffice it to recall just how much sheer violence, authority and tradition weighed in the economic life of classical antiquity, based on slave labour, and of the feudal period, based on serf labour, in comparison with economic life in a market economy. Moreover, given the relatively primitive technology in use in those historical periods, human life was dominated by natural phenomena (such as natural calamities, epidemics) as well as wars and arbitrary exercise of political power. If we add to this a largely superstitious religious sensibility, we can understand how repetitive cycles of

---

[1] In that period the term *political economy* began to be used; the first to use it as a title for a book (the *Traité de l'économie politique*, 1615) was the Frenchman Antoine de Montchrétien (a. 1575–1621).

[2] To be precise, the first chair in political economy was established in Naples in 1754, for Antonio Genovesi; in 1769 Milan followed with Cesare Beccaria. Elsewhere (France, England) things moved more slowly. Alfred Marshall was still fighting for the institution of a degree course in economics in Cambridge and the professionalisation of economics between the end of the nineteenth and the beginning of the twentieth century.

work and life, day by day, year by year, were systematically preferred to innovation and change. We can also understand why the philosophers of classical antiquity and theologians of the Middle Ages considered it their task not so much to describe and interpret the way the economy works as, rather, to provide advice on morally acceptable behaviour in the field of economic relations.

Actually, political economy was born from the conjunction of two major issues. On the one hand, we have the moral issue: which rules of conduct should human beings respect in the domain of economic activities? On the other hand, we have the scientific issue: how does a society based on the division of labour function, where each person or group of persons produces a specific commodity or group of commodities and needs the products of others, both as subsistence and as means of production, to keep the production process going?

The two questions are connected, both with respect to the search for objective grounds for moral evaluation of human behaviour and for the idea (dominant in the Aristotelian tradition) that 'good' is what 'conforms to nature'. For a long time, authors writing on economic matters seemed not to distinguish clearly between the two issues, as shown by the ambiguities of the notion of 'natural law' itself: ambiguities still to be perceived in protagonists of the classical school such as Adam Smith and David Ricardo.

Political economy was thus born as a moral science and as a science of society. At this stage, distinction between the different aspects now included in the field of economics was in many instances more clear-cut than the dividing line between economics and the other social sciences. Thus, for instance, the distance between the study of economic institutions and that of political institutions was minimal. Much larger was the distance separating the study of institutions from that of the behaviour of the good *pater familias* with respect to consumption activities and supervision of the family budget: for instance, discussion on the economic tasks of the *pater familias* generally involved reflections on the upbringing of children.

An important factor in the progressive separation between the two fields of research, as we shall see in the next chapter, was a change in perspective prompted by discoveries taking place in the natural sciences: from Galileo's (1564–1642) contributions in the field of astronomy to the discovery of the circulation of blood announced by Harvey in 1616; from Newton's (1642–1727) physics up to the shift, with Lavoisier (1743–1794), from descriptive chemistry to chemistry based on quantitative relations. Such discoveries favoured gradual recognition of the existence of scientific issues, concerning our understanding of the physical world, to be tackled independently of moral issues, with methods of analysis other than those traditionally applied to the latter. Earlier on, Niccolò Machiavelli (1469–1527) had taken a turn in the same direction with his distinction between political science and moral philosophy, between analysis of the behaviour princes must adopt in pursuit of power and moral judgement on such behaviour.

The importance of the formative stage of political economy derives from the fact that it left as inheritance to successive stages a set of deeply embedded ideas and concepts. Around the seventeenth century, however, a change took place in the way economic issues were tackled, connected to the radical changes that had intervened in the organisation of economic and social life. In particular, we may take the role of exchanges as an example.

The market, interpreted as exchange of goods against money, was already in existence in Pericles' Athens and Caesar's Rome. However, exchanges then accounted for a relatively limited share of the total social production and took place under conditions of extreme irregularity, due to factors such as the incidence of meteorological factors on crops, difficulties of transportation and above all widespread insecurity about property rights arising not only from private criminality but also, and indeed mainly, from the arbitrary intervention of the political authorities, exercising a drastic and often unpredictable re-distributive function.

As far as the former aspect is concerned – the limited share of exchanges – we may recall that, for instance, in the feudal economy exchanges through the market mostly concerned the surplus product, namely that part of the product that is not necessary as a means of production or of subsistence for the continuance of productive activity. On the other hand, there was already a network of exchanges involving luxury products – spices, lace, precious metals – connecting geographical areas even over great distances; side by side with it, a web of financial relations gradually developed connecting major commercial centres, based mainly on letters of exchange. At this stage, self-production – i.e. production for direct consumption on the part of the producers themselves – characterised small rural communities. In these small communities some degree of productive specialisation and payments in money coexisted with exchanges in kind.

Self-production lost ground to production for the market only as private ownership extended over land and as artisan manufacturing production grew. A different system of social relations and a different technological structure were thus born. With this new system, neither in agriculture nor in manufacturing were the workers now owners of the means of production or the goods they produced, which, in any case, were usually different from the goods they themselves consumed. Moreover, artisan manufacturing – and later on industrial plants – were increasingly characterised by use of specialised means of production, produced by firms other than those utilising them.

As far as the second aspect is concerned – the irregularity of exchanges – suffice it to recall the multiplicity and continuous variability of the standards of measurement for commodities – standards of weight, of length, of volume – only gradually superseded.[3]

It is precisely the absence of regularity and uniformity in economic activity that may possibly account for the generic remarks by writers of this period about the conditions of demand and supply as determinants of market prices. In the presence of a marked variability in demand and supply and in the absence of clear indications on the factors determining them, such generic remarks cannot be considered as adding up to a fully fledged theory of prices, let alone anticipating the marginalist theories that take equilibrium prices to correspond to the point where demand and supply (defined as well-specified and stable functions of prices and incomes) of the given commodity meet.

Indeed, up to the end of the seventeenth century reflection on economic issues, when not addressing a technical aspect connected, for instance, with the origins of accountancy (up to the invention of double-entry bookkeeping, commonly attributed to the Italian Luca Pacioli, c. 1445–c. 1517), essentially formed part of the study of rules for the government of society: Plato's *Republic* or Aristotle's *Politics*, for example, were fundamental texts. The writings of the philosophers of classical antiquity or the Middle Ages held ideas or observations of interest for the development of political economy, but embedded in a context that failed to constitute systematic analysis of economic issues.

The acceleration in economic debate from the sixteenth century onwards was also catalysed by a more general technical factor, namely the invention of the printing press with moveable type, which led to a rapid and significant reduction in the cost of books.

---

[3] Standards of measurement were, for a long stretch of human history, the object of harsh social conflict regulated by local conventions, generally temporary and fairly flexible. The central authority of the new nation states succeeded in imposing legal standards of measurement only after great efforts, which came to fruition towards the end of the eighteenth century. This most interesting story is described in Kula 1970.

2.2   Classical Antiquity

We can find traces of discussion of economic issues going far back in time. The Babylonian code of Hammurabi (around 1750 BCE), engraved on a monolith conserved in the Louvre museum in Paris, provided, among other things, normative prescriptions for economic relations. The first written text of the Old Testament, which contains a wealth of considerations on different aspects of economic life, has been traced back to the twelfth to ninth century BCE. In India Kautilya's *Arthasastra*, dealing entirely with the functioning of the state in its economic aspects, belongs to the fourth century BCE and is full of references to previous texts. In China, *Guanzi* brought together writings dating from the fifth century BCE and the first century CE dealing with a variety of matters including economic issues.[4]

Among the many themes dealt with in the Bible, the most important from our viewpoint concerns the role of labour in human life. This is a complex issue, which we will have occasion to come back to more than once. In Genesis work was seen both as expiation for original sin and, with a decisively positive connotation, as an element intrinsic to the very nature of man and means for his fulfilment as part of a divine project. God himself 'works' and on the seventh day rests. Then, with original sin, work assumes a negative aspect. Work, however, represents not only a hard necessity for survival: it is also an essential aspect of good behaviour, conforming to divine law.[5]

The simultaneous presence of 'compulsory labour' and 'labour as self-fulfilment' constitutes a most important contribution of the biblical tradition to modern culture, and we may note that in this respect the biblical tradition proved stronger than Greek culture, which appears rather a typical expression of the dominant classes in a slave society: work (as distinct from the activity of organising and

---

[4] Cf. Kautilya 1967 and Rickett 1985–98 for the commented text of the *Guanzi*.
[5] 'Six days shalt thou labour, and do all thy work' (Bible: Exodus 20:9; cf. also Deuteronomy 5:13). A strong work ethic lay behind Paul's Epistles in particular. The idea of work as the source of dignity and a positive value in human life, as the road to self-fulfilment of man in the world resurfaced repeatedly in the course of the centuries, in particular among utopian thinkers and currents of the sixteenth and seventeenth centuries. Some such currents, and in particular those associated with the protestant reform, set as their objective liberation of the worker from the subjugation to the masters (and not the liberation of man from the 'serfdom of labour', which is truly utopian!). Among the authors of utopian writings, we may recall Thomas More (1478–1535; *Utopia* appears in Latin in 1516), Tommaso Campanella (1568–1639; the *Città del sole* is dated 1602 but was published, in Latin, only in 1623), and Francis Bacon (1561–1626; the *New Atlantis* is dated 1626).

supervising productive activities) was viewed with annoyance, if not indeed contempt.

In general, in Greek culture economic issues were dealt with either in the framework of discussion concerning sound management of the household (in the broad sense of a family group, slaves included) or in discussion of the political institutions. In the first field – household economics – we find the *Oikonomikos* by Xenophon (a.430–a.355 BCE), or the *Oikonomikos* that an old tradition attributed to Aristotle and which was probably written somewhere between the third century BCE and the first century CE. The very term 'economy' derives from *oikos*, 'house', and *nomos*, 'norm or law', thus designating the field of household management. In the second field, that of economic-political discussion, we find the *Republic* by Plato (a.427–a.347 BCE) or the *Politics* by Aristotle (384–322 BCE). However, the distinction cannot be considered clear-cut: there was no contrast between the viewpoint of the family administrator and the viewpoint of government of the *polis*. Efficient management of the means of production (including in particular the supervision of slave labour) was considered a decisive element for obtaining a good quality of product, while the possibility of technical improvements was on the whole overlooked.

In the *Oikonomikos* attributed to Aristotle we find the oft-quoted advice: 'no one, indeed, takes the same care of another's property as of his own; so that, as far as it is possible, each man ought to attend to his affairs in person. We may commend also a pair of sayings, one attributed to a Persian [... who] on being asked what best conditions a horse, replied "His master's eye".'[6] In this respect we find significant differences between the various authors, and in particular between Plato, who favoured collective ownership of the means of production and a collectivistic organisation of consumption activities, and Aristotle, who invoked a realistic view of human nature: 'Property that is common to the greatest number of owners receives the least attention; men care most for their private possessions, and for what they own in common less, or only so far as it falls to their own individual share.'[7]

There was a general convergence of ideas on the origins of social stratification, to be found in the differences in the innate abilities of different persons and the consequent subdivision of tasks. Such was the case of the division between peasants, soldiers and philosophers in Plato's *Republic*. Aristotle followed Plato in considering intrinsic to human nature the foundations of social stratification. This held first of all for the basic

[6] (Pseudo)Aristotle 1935, p. 341: *Oeconomica*, I, 6.3.
[7] Aristotle 1977, p. 77: *Politics*, II.3, 1261b.

difference in the roles of man, woman and slave. Up to this point, however, a distinction of roles within society rather than a distinction of working tasks was being discussed. In Aristotle's opinion, this second aspect concerned the slaves and not the masters.[8]

2.3   Patristic Thought

Patristic thought is represented by the most influential Christian thinkers, in the period spanning from the first century CE up to the eleventh century.

Originally the Christian religion was a minority sect, oppressed with persecution, spreading mainly among the lower strata of society. The search for margins of survival naturally led to acceptance of the existing social structure and economic system following Christ's teaching to 'render unto Caesar the things which be Caesar's'.[9] This obviously does not mean that the Church Fathers never considered practical issues. When considering these aspects, we should bear in mind a distinction crucial in the period between ideals valid for a small minority of believers and moral precepts applicable to the whole community of believers.

Thus, on the question of private property an opinion widely held among the Church Fathers was to see it as a creation of civil, not divine, law and that the moral ideal is constituted by some form of common property. John Chrysostom (a.345–407) maintained that God had assigned earthly goods as common property to all men; the same opinion was held by Ambrose (a.340–397), who saw the origin of private property in an act of usurpation, and by Jerome (a.347–a.419), who argued that a rich man is either an unjust person or heir to an unjust person. Augustine of Hippo (354–430) considered private property as a source of wars and social injustice. However, the advice to completely despoil oneself of all property – as centuries later Saint Francis of Assisi (1181/2–1226) would in fact do – was considered a 'counsel of perfection', not a precept applicable to all. The general norm concerning private property as indeed all the other aspects of social life consisted in respect of existing laws. As a matter of

---

[8] This thesis, quite different from Adam Smith's views and imbued with authoritarian connotations, prevailed for a long time. For instance Thomas Aquinas – and after him the Scholastic tradition – spoke of an equitable distribution of talents between men assigned by Providence and accepted as just a distribution of incomes and wealth based on the inequalities of rank, merit, capabilities, craft and condition of each individual.

[9] Bible: Matthew 22:21.

fact, the role attributed to laws on private property after the Fall, hence taking into account the limits of human nature, was that of setting limits to human greed and reducing conflict and social unrest to a minimum.

Slavery was recognised as a fact, part of the existing social system, and as such not condemned. The Fathers who discussed it – Augustine and Lactantius, for example – limited themselves to recalling that before God all men are equal, regardless of their place in society, and a slave may be more worthy of Paradise than a rich man. This represented a step forward from Plato and Aristotle: slavery was no longer considered a natural institution; insofar as it concerned the right to property, it fell within the field of human, rather than divine, laws.

The attitude of the Fathers towards labour was positive on the whole and, in any case, based on its recognition as a social duty, also useful for keeping men away from sin. The quest for luxury or wealth was condemned, especially as it diverted men from the pursuit of eternal salvation. Commerce was considered with distrust, as a likely source of moral risks, but was not the object of a direct condemnation: what was important was that it be conducted in an honest way, within a Christian life.

The theses of the Fathers illustrated above became the official doctrine of the Church in the following centuries, through the mediation of Thomas Aquinas (1225–1274). He argued that private property does not violate natural law and favours socially useful behaviour (a thesis already proposed by Aristotle), while common property constitutes an ideal of perfection suited only to the few (for instance, within monastic orders).[10] Similarly, Thomas considered the pursuit of mercantile profits legitimate in many instances. With Thomas Aquinas we come to the full bloom of Scholasticism.

2.4   The Scholastics

In the twelfth and thirteenth centuries a new cultural model gradually came in, based mainly on the intellectual life of the 'schools' – hence the name 'Scholastics' – and characterized by systematic reference to some philosophers from Antiquity (mainly to Boethius in the twelfth and to Aristotle in the thirteenth century).

---

[10] The standing of the Catholic Church subsequently changed. In the encyclical *Quod apostolici muneris*, 1878, and *Rerum novarum*, 1891, Pope Leo XIII proclaimed that the right to property conforms to natural law.

The primary objective, as in all Antiquity and the Middle Ages, was to find rules of moral conduct. The method, in keeping with the objective, was based to an extent for us now unacceptable on the principle of authority, namely on the deduction of rules of conduct from first principles that amounted to articles of faith. However, theological debate during the Middle Ages came up with a great many pointers for definition of the conceptual framework that constitutes the foundation for any abstract analysis of the economy.

Such was the case of certain eternal commonplaces, including the view of the social body as an autonomous subject. Thus the Church was seen as the *corpus mysticum* (mystic body), as *universitas* (universality) of the faithful, namely as a superior reality above the individual Christian or social bodies of secular origin. From here it was but a short step to the idea that the state is logically superior to the family and the individual: the so-called organic doctrine of the state, whose origins date back from Plato and Aristotle. The Scholastic writers adopted a more moderate version of the organic doctrine than Aristotle's original conception, only stressing that life in society is a natural state of affairs for human beings: an intermediate position in the face of the clear-cut dichotomy between methodological individualism and organicism commonly accepted in the twentieth century, especially by dint of the liberal reaction to totalitarian regimes.

A parallel with the debate between methodological individualism and organicism may be located, within medieval philosophy, in discussion of the problem of universals, as it came to be called, and more precisely in the counter-position between 'nominalism' and 'realism'.

According to the nominalists, universal terms – those that do not designate individual entities, for instance 'horse' or 'humanity' – are simply names used to designate a set or a class of individual objects: a mere *flatus vocis* (utterance), as Roscelin of Compiègne (a.1050–a.1120) apparently put it, while individuals alone were endowed with reality. On the other hand, realists such as William of Champeaux (a.1070–a.1121) associated the universal term with the existence of a property common to a set of objects, and hence with a 'real essence' present in identical form in individuals, distinguishable on the basis of a variety of incidental qualities. A pupil of both Roscelin and William of Champeaux, Pierre Abélard[11] took a position strongly

---

[11] One of the greatest medieval logicians, Pierre Abélard (a.1079–1142), professor at Paris for a number of years and then a monk, is also known for his tragic love entanglement with a pupil of his, Héloïse, and for the letters they exchanged following their forced separation.

critical of the more extreme versions of both nominalism and realism. According to Abélard, the universal term was born to designate (and communicate) an effective aspect of reality; hence it has a *causa communis* (common cause) and cannot be considered a simple *flatus vocis* devoid of objective foundations. At the same time, it does not designate in a precise, univocal way a specific element (be it an individual or a collective, such as a specific football team) but provides a shadowed image, focused on some elements while ignoring others (the generic term 'football team' cannot designate the names of the players nor the colours of the team). Abélard therefore, though critical of the realistic view, defended the validity of universal terms: an analytical validity, we might say. In terms of the modern dichotomy between methodological individualism and organicism, we might say that Abélard would have rejected the extreme versions of both and would have maintained the legitimacy of an analysis conducted on the basis of aggregate categories, which would avoid dispersing attention on the multiform variety of individual accidents, but without attributing to such categories the nature of essence, of something logically superior to the individuals, and in any case with all the caution due to the fact that the universal term offers a confused image, unlike the precise image we have with the 'singular name'.

2.5   Usury and Just Price

Let us now return to strictly economic themes. The dominant issues, between the twelfth and the sixteenth centuries, were the just price and usury, always considered from the standpoint of ethics.

Thomas Aquinas is commonly considered the most important philosopher and theologian of the late Middle Ages. A teacher in various cities (from Paris to Rome, from Anagni to Naples), his main work, the *Summa Theologiae*, written between 1265 and 1273, was to remain for centuries a central reference point for Catholic doctrine. Characteristic of this work was an original fusion between the Christian tradition and Aristotle's philosophy.

Aristotle himself considered as unnatural any wealth stemming from commerce and condemned commerce in money, i.e. loans with interest. In the Christian tradition we also find decided opposition to interest-bearing loans; in this respect a passage from the 'sermon on the mount' is often quoted, when Jesus says 'lend, hoping for nothing again'.[12] Thomas

---

[12] Bible: Luke 6:35; we find analogous expressions in the Gospels of Matthew and Mark. Cf. also Ezekiel 18:8 and 18:13.

Aquinas adopted a more moderate attitude: condemnation of interest in principle[13] was followed by a detailed casuistry, in which cases of loans at interest to be condemned are distinguished from cases in which it was justified (in particular, cases in which we can speak of a *damnum emergens* (supervenient damage) for the lender, so as to justify a positive but relatively moderate rate of interest, while justifications based on *lucrum cessans* (losing a gain) are rejected, since these would open the way to legitimising a competitive rate of interest – as in fact gradually happened in subsequent centuries).

The road followed by Thomas – casuistry, or analysis of specific cases, with different answers to the question of the legitimacy of the loan at interest according to the circumstances – was adopted in subsequent centuries in a long series of writings that reveal, among other things, how little respect was accorded to the prohibition of usury and how much inventiveness was shown by the financial operators of the time in finding new kinds of contracts to circumvent the prohibitions. In general the authors of the time, Thomas included, were aware of the role of money as means of exchange and standard of measurement but not as a reserve of value.

Ethical and legal debate often intersected.[14] The importance of this debate was such that some commentators consider the various answers given to the question of the legitimacy of usury as a central element in explaining the rate of transition to capitalism. Condemnation of usury was not accompanied by hostility towards commercial activity in general, as was the case with Aristotle. The Scholastics simply called for correct behaviour, condemning fraud or coercion but also taking advantage of a counterpart's weaker position in bargaining.

Transition towards the legalisation of interest was slow, though favoured by the Reform (Calvin, 1509–1564, condemns interest on consumption loans but not on commercial loans). At the end of the sixteenth century we still find strong opposition to usury, as in the severe *A discourse upon Usurye* by Thomas Wilson, published in 1572.

---

[13] In fact, interest constitutes payment for the use of a commodity, money, the value in exchange of which is already paid with the pledge to return an equal amount. A more radical but substantially analogous thesis was that interest is the payment for the time that goes between the loan and the return of the money lent: hence, it was condemned because time belongs to God.

[14] As far as canonical law is concerned, the Council of Nicaea (312) only prohibited clergy from involvement in loans at interest; gradually regulations became more severe, extending their field of application to all; then in the fourteenth century a move in the opposite direction began, with increasingly shrinking definitions of usury (condemnation of which in principle, however, was confirmed by Pope Benedict XIV in the encyclical *Vix pervenit* in 1745 and still applies).

Shortly before its publication, in England the Act of 1571 declared all loans for interest at a rate above 10 per cent devoid of legal value, while it did not prohibit loans at lower interest rates – without, however, providing any legal protection for them. This compromise opened the way to the view that not all loans at interest should be considered usury, but only those which, exploiting the borrower's need, applied 'excessive' interest.

Reaction to the regulation of loans at interest only arrived with the rise of liberalism – we may mention Turgot (1759) and especially Bentham's *Defence of usury* (1787) – while Adam Smith himself, in the *Wealth of Nations* (1776, p. 357), still judged legal limits to the interest rate opportune, maintaining that otherwise 'prodigals and projectors' ready to pay even very high interest rates would crowd 'sober people' out of the loan market. In England, the usury laws were only abolished in 1854.

Let us now turn to the just price, another theme that goes back at least to Aristotle. Voluntary exchanges were considered useful for both seller and buyer: exchange is a *fluxus et refluxus gratiarum*, namely a giving and receiving graces, as Albert the Great (1206–1280) nicely put it. Following the tradition of the Roman law doctrine and certain Church Fathers such as Ambrose and Augustine, Thomas identified the just price as the price prevailing in the markets in the absence of fraud or monopolistic practices. Reference to the market price, however, had a normative, not a descriptive, value, since at the time the competitive market was the exception, while the rule consisted in the possibility of exchange open to few parties. Among other things, in the twelfth to thirteenth centuries, at least in Italy, the political authorities (municipalities, corporations) actively intervened, setting compulsory prices, or maximum limits for prices, of many among the main commodities subject to exchange. Moreover, because of the close regulation of productive techniques characterising the arts and crafts corporations, reference to necessary costs of production did not imply competition that eliminates the less efficient producers, but reference to costs entailed by respect for the existing regulations.

References to cost of production and particularly to labour costs were numerous but decidedly outnumbered by references to utility and rarity. Moreover, the structure of labour costs was clearly determined by social stratification, assumed as a given datum: in substance, the Scholastic writers considered as 'just' that price that allowed producers to maintain a standard of living befitting their position in society.

In the wake of Aristotle, Thomas and others confirmed that the value of goods does not reflect the 'natural' hierarchy (inanimate objects – vegetal world – animal world – human beings) but the ability of goods to satisfy needs (*indigentia*). More precisely, as Peter of Johann Olivi (1247–1298) noted, we must refer to three sources of value: *virtuositas, complacibilitas and raritas*, namely ability to satisfy human needs, correspondence to the preferences of the person utilising the good and scarcity.

The problem of the just price should not be confused with that of the legitimate price: following the tradition of Roman law doctrine and of canonical law, any transaction agreed on by the participants free from compulsion was considered as legitimate: '*Tantum valet quantum vendi potest*', or, more precisely, '*Tantum valet quantum vendi potest, sed communiter*' ('A thing is worth as much as it can commonly be sold for').

2.6   Bullionists and Mercantilists

In the period of the formation and rise of the nation states, a new kind of thinking on economic phenomena arose alongside that of the theologians and philosophers with the 'counsellors of the prince'. In their writings, these authors adopted the viewpoint of the economic power of the prince as a complement to and necessary prerequisite of his military power. Significantly, a group of authors of this period was designed as *cameralists*, since they approached economic issues as members of the chamber of the counsellors to the sovereign. The notion of national wealth thus took on a central role in economic thinking.

We may distinguish two kinds of interpretations for the economic views prevailing in this period. On the one hand, the counsellors of the prince were accused (for instance by Adam Smith) of holding a basically erroneous notion of wealth: the so-called 'chrysoedonistic view', namely the simplistic identification of wealth with gold and precious metals in general. Hence the term *Bullionists*, utilised for authors such as Thomas Gresham and John Hales in sixteenth-century England. On the other hand, beginning with the German historical school and Schumpeter (1914), we see a revaluation of these authors, credited with a less simplistic view, for instance justifying their preoccupation with monetary issues by the fact that the stock of metallic money might be considered an index of national wealth in a period when there was virtually no statistical information on the yearly product of a country.

Defending the right of the Company to export precious metals to the East in exchange for local commodities often destined to be re-exported to other European countries, as influential an author as Thomas Mun (1571–1641), a managing director of the India Company, maintained that the export of money allowed the country to increase its wealth. In fact, through international trade, the commodities available to the country are increased, even more than through manufacturing and, at a still lower level, agriculture.

Mun's writings may be taken as the reference point for the transition from bullionism to mercantilism, characterised by a fully developed theory of the balance of trade, which viewed the balance of the foreign trade of a country as a whole rather than bilateral balances computed for each foreign country taken in isolation. Mercantilism is a rather generic label, to be utilized with caution: it embraces authors who were often quite heterogeneous and active over a long period of time, stretching from the sixteenth to the eighteenth century, up to the publication of Adam Smith's *Wealth of Nations*. In general, immediate practical interests dominated over theoretical work.

Another interpretation only partly justified by the writings of certain mercantilist authors concerns the explanation of the origins of profits as *profit upon alienation*, i.e. profit deriving from sale and hence born of the circulation process, or in other words commerce. According to this thesis, profits stem from buying cheap and selling dear. It was a thesis in consonance with the stage of mercantile capitalism, which, among other things, accounted for the privileged role attributed to foreign trade. In fact, the gains obtained by one party to the act of exchange correspond to the losses of the other party, so that when buyers and sellers belong to the same country the gains of some exactly offset the losses of the others. Therefore, trade may be the source of gains for the wealth of a country only when we consider exchanges with other countries.

This thesis underplays the role of production in generating a surplus, which was to be stressed by Classical authors; yet, behind it, we can detect crucial signs of the times: the importance of military power in international economic relations, the spread of the colonies and the monopolistic nature of the big trading companies. If we also include in foreign trade the transference of wealth enacted by force, the importance that this sector took on for what Marx called 'original accumulation' becomes clear, and the impression of unequal exchange that the theory of *profit upon alienation* conveys appears fully justified.

2.7   The Naissance of Economic Thought in Italy: Antonio Serra

The economic vitality of municipal Italy, the financial activity of Florentine bankers and the role of maritime republics – particularly

Venice – in international trade were accompanied by a flourishing of mercantile tracts and writings that incidentally touched on economic issues. However, there were few authors of any interest for a history of economics. A far more relevant contribution emerged from a different environment, characterised by economic decline.

On 10 July 1613, a prisoner in the Neapolitan prison of Vicaria, Doctor Antonio Serra from Cosenza, signed the dedication of his book, *Breve trattato delle cause che possono far abbondare li regni d'oro, e argento, dove non sono miniere. Con applicatione al Regno di Napoli.* The book offered economic policy advice aimed at improving the conditions of the Neapolitan kingdom, seen to be lagging far behind other parts of Italy in development.

Of Antonio Serra himself we know hardly anything, only that he was from Cosenza and that he was in prison in 1613. The reason for his imprisonment is uncertain; equally uncertain is his profession, and the dates of his birth and death are unknown. The *Breve trattato* was cited by Galiani (1751, pp. 339–40) but subsequently only rescued from total obscurity by Pietro Custodi, who proclaimed Serra 'the first writer of political economy' (Custodi 1803, p. xxvii) and assigned him the first place, violating the chronological order, in his famous collection of *Scrittori classici italiani di economia politica* (*Classical Italian Writers of Political Economy*, in fifty volumes, 1803–1816).

After the dedication and the preface, the *Breve Trattato* was divided into three parts. The first, and for us the most interesting, discussed 'the causes for which kingdoms may abound with gold and silver', as the title of chapter 1 went: that is, in substance, the causes of the economic prosperity of nations in the broadest sense of the term, also through comparison of conditions prevailing in the Kingdom of Naples with those prevailing in other parts of Italy, particularly Venice. The second part was essentially concerned with refuting the proposals advanced a few years earlier by Marco Antonio de Santis with the aim of reducing the exchange rate to attract money into the kingdom from outside. The third part presented systematic discussion of the different policy measures adopted or proposed 'in order to make gold and silver abundant within the Kingdom'.

The economic prosperity of a country, Serra explained, depends on 'own accidents', i.e. original characteristics specific to each country, and 'common accidents', or in other words more or less favourable circumstances that may be reproduced anywhere. Among the former, Serra mentioned the endowment of natural wealth, particularly fertile lands, and localisation. The 'common accidents' number four: 'quantity of manufactures, quality of people, large amount of trade and ability of those in power'. In other terms: manufacturing production, moral qualities and professional skills of the population, extent of trade (especially international transit trade), and the politico-institutional system, the latter being the most important of the four elements (Serra 1613, p. 21).

Serra noted that, as far as the 'own accidents' were concerned, the Kingdom of Naples was at an advantage (except for the site), particularly in comparison with Venice: if Naples was so much poorer than Venice (which explains why gold and silver flowed out of the Kingdom of Naples), this could only depend on 'common accidents'. In showing how this happened, Serra reconstructed the situation of the country's balance of trade, although without systematic treatment of this notion. He considered the unbalance in the currency market to stem from a negative balance of payments, inclusive of so-called invisible items, caused in turn by a feeble productive structure and the scant entrepreneurial spirit of the subjects of the Kingdom of Naples. There was, then, a decisive connection between scarcity of money in the kingdom and its feeble productive structure.

It is, in fact, a mistake to attribute to Serra the identification of wealth with money and precious metals on Bullionist lines. However, it is also difficult to consider Serra the founder of economic science, as suggested by Custodi. For such a status, the importance attributed to real phenomena, in particular to manufacturing production, is certainly not sufficient, in the absence of a sufficiently clear exposition of the notion of surplus, that constituted in the following two centuries the basis for the development of classical political economy, or of even the slightest trace of any theory of value and distribution. It is also clear that Serra can have had scant influence if any at all on the initial stages in the development of political economy, given the minimal circulation of his work before it was reprinted in Custodi's series. Serra was, however, an interesting author who put his finger – almost intuitively, we might say – on the relationship of interdependence between financial and real aspects of the economy and who found it natural to connect political, social and economic aspects. He was an author of a commendable mentality: 'favourable to activism, open to recognise the role of free will, idealistic'.[15] Serra, to sum up, well represented the potentialities

---

[15] Tagliacozzo (1937, p. xxxiv).

of the formative stage of economic science and that openness to a variety of possible lines of theoretical development; re-reading his *Breve trattato* helps us to recall that constructing well-defined conceptual and analytical structures may mean leaving aside elements potentially important in our understanding of reality.

3   William Petty and the Origins of Political Economy

3.1   Life and Writings

William Petty (1623–1687) had an eventful life.[1] The son of a clothier, he was a ship-boy on a merchant ship at the age of thirteen, but ten months later he was put ashore on the French coast with a broken leg. Here he succeeded in getting admission to the Jesuit college in Caen. After serving in the Royal Navy, when the civil war broke out he joined other refugees, in Holland first (1643) and then in Paris (1646), where he studied medicine and, with Hobbes, anatomy. When his father died, in 1646 he returned to Romsey, his birthplace, but soon we find him in London, where he tried to patent an invention of his own, a machine capable of producing duplicate copies of a written text simultaneously. Then in 1648 he was awarded the degree of doctor of medicine at Oxford University. Here he had an incredibly rapid career, favoured by political circumstances (the rise of Cromwell, which led to the old professors considered supporters of the king being set aside): in 1650 he became the professor of anatomy. But by the following year he had already moved to the chair of music at Gresham College, London.[2] In the same year he became chief medical officer of the English army sent to Ireland by Cromwell. After the victories over the Irish, Petty was entrusted with the task of conducting geographical survey of the Irish lands, as the first step for distributing them among the English soldiers, the state domain and the financiers of the military expeditions. Petty proved extraordinarily able in rapidly concluding the survey and emerged from it as a very rich man, with large estates in Ireland, thanks also to trade in debentures (representing rights to the lands to be distributed) sold by the soldiers.

---

[1] On the topic of this chapter, cf. Roncaglia 1977.
[2] At the time mathematical relations were an essential part in the study both of human anatomy and of the laws of harmony. On Petty's connection with the new English philosophical culture of the time, cf. McCormick 2009.

From then up to his death, Petty was busy with administration of his estates and with unending legal controversies over the titles to the Irish lands as well as over taxes and moved continuously between England and Ireland. Nevertheless, in 1660–1662 he took part in the founding of the Royal Society for the Improving of Natural Knowledge. In 1667 he married a widow, who gave him five children; but he also fathered at least one illegitimate daughter, who was to appear on the scene in London as a dancer.

Only a small part of Petty's manuscripts were published during his lifetime under his own name. With the exception of the *A Treatise of Taxes and Contributions* (1662), the main writings relating to economic matters were published after his death, when the 1688 revolution rendered the political climate more favourable to his ideas.

3.2   Political Arithmetic and the Method of Economic Science

William Petty is commonly remembered as the founder of political arithmetic, constituting an extension to the field of social sciences of the new ideas that were taking roots in the field of natural sciences. With it Petty aimed to introduce the quantitative method into the analysis of social phenomena, so as to allow for more rigorous treatment of them:

[Algebra] came out of Arabia by the Moores into Spaine and from thence hither, and W[illiam] P[etty] hath applyed it to other than purely mathematicall matters, viz.: to policy by the name of Political Arithmetick by reducing many termes of matter to termes of number, weight, and measure, in order to be handled Mathematically.[3]

This methodological innovation reflected what was happening at the time in the field of natural sciences: the new, quantitative approach to physics taking over from the old view of physics as description of the sensible qualities of physical objects; in all fields of scientific research, measurement of quantities becoming the central object of enquiry; the materialistic-mechanical view of man and the world, supported in particular by Thomas Hobbes (1588–1679), with whom Petty had studied in Paris (in Hobbes's view, the method of enquiry – the logic of quantities, *logica sive computatio*) – reflected the very nature of the object of enquiry); a radical critique of traditional culture dominated by Aristotelian thought.

---

[3] Petty 1927, vol. 2, p. 15: letter to Southwell of 3 November 1687.

In this direction Bacon (1561–1626) had set out before Hobbes: he was one of the few authors who Petty cited and whom he admired. In opposition to the syllogistic-deductive method of the Aristotelian tradition and to the Renaissance tradition of pure empiricism (technicians and alchemists), Bacon proposed the inductive method, a fusion of empiricism and rationalism:

the men of experiment are like the ant; they only collect and use: the reasoners resemble spiders, who make cobwebs out of their own substance. But the bee takes a middle course; it gathers its material from the flowers of the garden and of the field, but transforms and digests it by a power of its own. Not unlike this is the true business of philosophy; for it neither relies solely or chiefly on the powers of the mind, nor does it take the matter which it gathers from natural history and mechanical experiments and lay it up in the memory whole, as it finds it; but lays it up in the understanding altered and digested.[4]

This was the method followed by Petty, who described social phenomena in quantitative terms but also, and above all, attempted to give a rational explanation to the assembled data, often reconstructing the data required for an investigation on the basis of chains of deductive reasoning of an arithmetic-quantitative nature that permitted scarce available information to be exploited for a myriad of different purposes.

Furthermore, Petty (1690, p. 244) emphasised his decision to ground his own analysis on *objective* data:

The Method I take to do this, is not yet very usual; for instead of using only comparative and superlative words, and intellectual Arguments, I have taken the course (as a Specimen of the Political Arithmetick I have long aimed at) to express my self in Terms of *Number, Weight,* or *Measure*; to use only Arguments of Sense, and to consider only such Causes, as have visible Foundations in Nature; leaving those that depend upon the mutable Minds, Opinions, Appetites and Passions of particular Men, to the Consideration of others.

We have here a clear-cut opposition to the logical-deductive method of the Scholastics. However, for Petty it was not only a matter of *recording* and *describing* reality 'in terms of number, weight or measure', but rather a matter of expressing reality in such terms in order to *interpret* it by identifying its main characteristics considering 'only such causes, as have visible foundations in nature', that is, *objective*, rather than *subjective*, causes.

Inchoate in Bacon, but already developed by Hobbes and other scientists, was the tendency to direct research towards identification

---

[4] Bacon 1620, pp. 92–3: Book 1 of the Aphorisms, No. 95.

of precise quantitative relationships between the phenomena under study. The first who clearly expressed such a tendency was Galileo (1564–1642), according to whom 'this great book which is open in front of our eyes – I mean the Universe – ... is written in mathematical characters';[5] knowledge of the world therefore requires the construction of arithmetic or geometric models. Furthermore, a view of the world similar to that of Galileo and Hobbes was reflected in the formula 'number, weight or measure' that Petty repeatedly utilised.[6] Political arithmetic was considered as the most appropriate instrument not only for the description of reality but also for representing it, precisely because, according to the materialistic-mechanical conception supported by Galileo and Hobbes, a quantitative structure is embedded in reality itself.

Another essential feature of the new methodological approach adopted by Petty was the sharp separation between science and morals; the moral problem could not arise for science in itself, since it is simply a means, but only for the ends that humans propose to attain by means of the utilisation of its results. This position has retained dominance up to our own day, although with recurring crises, and has been of decisive importance for the development of human sciences.[7]

---

[5] Galilei 1623, p. 121. This was not a side issue: in the first stages of the theological controversy over Copernicus's and Galileo's thesis, that the earth moves around the sun, the Jesuit, then Cardinal, Roberto Bellarmino (1542–1621) had suggested that there would have been nothing wrong in proposing this as a useful hypothesis but not as a true statement about reality. Rejection of Cardinal Bellarmino's position, which at the time could appear as a subtle – typically Jesuitical – political compromise but which in fact pointed towards a modern epistemological view, was expressed by Newton with the well-known motto 'hypotheses non fingo' ('I frame no hypothesis').

[6] The formula derives from the Bible: 'You ordered all things by measure, number, weight', it is said in the Book of Wisdom, xi.20. Petty's followers – the 'political arithmeticians' Gregory King (1648–1712) and Charles Davenant (1654–1714) – interpreted it prevailingly in the limited meaning of description of quantitative phenomena. It is true that there is the so-called 'King's law', connecting increases in the price of corn to poorer crops. To Petty, political arithmetic meant something more: it aimed at discovering the quantitative relations that constitute the very basic structure of social reality – in analogy to what physical laws do according to Galileo – since it identified the elements essential to what had been selected as the object of investigation and abstracted from the elements that were considered useless or of minor importance: those that, as Ricardo was to put it a century and a half later, only 'modify' the analysis but do not change its substance.

[7] Within the latter, the crucial point of transition was represented by Niccolò Machiavelli (1469–1527; his main work, *Il principe*, is dated 1513), whose writings, significantly enough included in the index of forbidden books, enjoyed a very wide circulation in the sixteenth and seventeenth centuries. On the scientific and cultural background of the birth of political economy, cf. Maifreda 2012.

3.3 National State and the Economic System

Money, international trade and the fiscal system were already subjects of everyday debate in Petty's time. What differentiated Petty's treatment of these subjects from that of his contemporaries and predecessors, beyond differences in the positions he supported, was not only the method (political arithmetic) but also the object of analysis: the 'body politick', that is, the state, in the combined sense of political system and economic system: however, neither Petty nor his contemporaries felt the need to distinguish between the two aspects.

The birth of capitalism is generally associated with the birth of the nation state. A unified conception of the nation state, paying particular attention to the problem of the political unification of the city and the countryside, was developed by Machiavelli. He singled out of the complex network of social interdependences, as being of greatest importance, those among citizens of the same state, and between the sovereign and his subjects. Petty adopted a similar view with his notion of the 'body politick', whereby the web of relations of production and exchange are subjected to a univocally identified political authority. Neither Machiavelli nor Petty perceived the interrelations that exist between city and countryside, or between agriculture and industry, from the point of view of production. As we shall see in the next chapter, it was precisely the ability to go beyond this limit, and to discover the technological relations of production that link the various sectors of the economy, that constituted Quesnay's major contribution to the development of economic science.

Machiavelli's and Petty's writings reflected the still limited development of the productive structure of their period. The mining, manufacturing, agricultural, cattle breeding and fishing activities that Petty had launched on his Irish properties, for instance, were largely vertically integrated, with only very rough book-keeping distinctions among different stages of the productive processes and different sectors. In addition, changes in political institutions were necessary for the transition from feudalism to capitalism, for example in order to guarantee private property in the means of production and the possibility of buying and selling them, land in particular. Thus Petty supported the creation of a land registry and in general a standardisation of deeds for landed property. The still partial notion of economic system adopted by Petty seems to reflect a particular historical phase, that of the transition from feudalism to industrial capitalism.

The notion of the 'body politick' underlay Petty's specific views on money, foreign trade and taxes. We should recall that Petty's writings did not have the form of systematic treatises but were rather immediate interventions in the then current political debates, often brief working notes or memoranda aiming at demonstrating policy theses, such as the economic strength of England relatively to France and hence the possibility for a greater political autonomy for the English king. Let us take a look at some of these ideas.

As far as money is concerned, an important difference between Petty's views and those dominant at the time underlies his substitution of the traditional comparison between money and blood with another parallelism between political and human anatomy:

Money is but the Fat of the Body-politick, whereof too much doth as often hinder its Agility, as too little makes it sick. 'Tis true that as Fat lubricates the motion of the Muscles, feeds in want of Victuals, fills up uneven Cavities, and beautifies the Body, so doth Money in the State quicken its Action, feeds from abroad in the time of Dearth at Home; evens accounts by reason of its divisibility, and beautifies the whole, although more especially the particular persons that have it in plenty.[8]

According to Petty (1662, p. 28), 'the blood and nutritive juyces of the body politick' are constituted by the 'product of husbandry and manufacture'. This comparison points in the direction of the classical notion of the economic system based on the division of labour as functioning through a circular process of production, exchange, reconstitution of initial inventories of means of production and consumption goods, new production process. We should recall in this respect that the discovery of the circulation of blood, made by Harvey at the beginning of the seventeenth century,[9] had generated lively interest and that Petty (like Quesnay after him) was a physician.

Connected to his ideas on money are those concerning foreign trade. Petty, agreeing with his contemporaries, considered a surplus in the balance of trade desirable as a means to bring about an influx of precious metals into the country but subordinated this target to that of a high level of internal employment and production. Gold, silver and jewels are considered superior to other goods on account of their durability and their role as means of exchange and store of value.

As for taxation, Petty considered reform of the fiscal system the first step for ensuring uniformity of conditions within the country and

---

[8] Petty 1691b, p. 112. Another interesting definition of money was given by Petty in a brief glossary of economic terms: 'Money. Is the common measure of commodityes. A common bond of every man upon every other man. The equivalent of commodityes.' (Petty 1927, vol.1, p. 210).

[9] William Harvey (1578–1657) announced his discovery in 1616 but published it only in 1628.

certainty of rules: two prerequisites for the development of the economy. Most of *A Treatise of Taxes and Contributions* is concerned with the systematic examination of the various types of government income: an intricate labyrinth of often self-contradictory regulations, considered as one of the major 'impediments of England's Greatness' while at the same time insisting that these obstacles 'are but contingent and removable' (Petty 1690, p. 298), since they derived from the stratification caused by continuous additions to the initial system that, as a result, had lost its initial coherence. Thus, the burden of taxation was borne almost exclusively, and with a varying and unpredictable intensity, by the landowner. In addition, the cost of collection, subcontracted to private agents, was very high and brought further elements of injustice and uncertainty into the system.

Petty proposed proportional taxation, levied on consumption, since it alone constitutes 'actual' riches.[10] The proportionality criterion is 'just', leaving income distribution unaffected by taxation (and in Petty's opinion the differences in wealth and income are necessary to economic growth). Besides, taxes on consumption encourage parsimony, avoid double taxation and facilitate collection of statistics on the economic conditions of the nation, which are essential for good government. Fiscal regulations must be certain, simple, clear and evident (this also for avoiding controversies and legal proceedings, which constitute a social waste), impartial and with low collection costs.

3.4   Commodity and Market

Petty's contribution to economic science referred primarily to the formulation of a set of key concepts, such as commodity, market and price; we will illustrate them referring to the *Dialogue of Diamonds* (Petty 1899, pp. 624–30).

The dialogue has two protagonists: Mr A, representing Petty himself, and Mr B, an inexperienced buyer of a diamond. The latter sees the act of exchange as a chance occurrence, a direct encounter between buyer and seller, rather than a routine episode in an interconnected network of relationships. The problem is a difficult one because the specific individual goods included in a single category of marketable goods – diamonds in our case – differ from one another on account of a series of quantitative and qualitative elements, even leaving aside differing

---

[10] Cf. Petty 1662, pp. 91–2. In this Petty was preceded by Hobbes, and was to be followed by a long series of economists, up to Luigi Einaudi and Nicholas Kaldor in the twentieth century.

circumstances (of time and place) of each individual act of exchange. Thus, in the absence of a norm that might provide for definition of a single reference point for the price of diamonds, Mr B considers exchange a risky act, since it appears impossible for the buyer to avoid being cheated, in what is a unique event in his experience, by the merchant, who has a more extensive knowledge of the market.

In the absence of a web of regular exchanges, that is, of a market, the characteristics and circumstances of differentiation mentioned above operate in such a way as to make each act of exchange a unique episode, where the price essentially stems from the greater or lesser bargaining ability of seller and buyer. The existence of a market, on the contrary, allows transformation of a large part of the elements that distinguish each individual exchange from any other into sufficiently systematic differences in price relatively to an ideal type of diamond taken as reference. There is thus a relationship between the emergence of a regular market on the one hand and, on the other hand, the possibility of defining as a commodity a certain category of goods, abstracting from the multiplicity of effective exchange acts a theoretical price representative of them all.

Mr A, the expert, is in fact aware of the existence of precise quantitative relationships between the prices of different types of diamond determined by weight, dimension, colour and defects. Thus, for example, 'The general rule concerning weight is this that the price rises in duplicate proportion of the weight' (Petty 1899, p. 627). A similar rule applies to the dimension. The average of the prices obtained on the basis of these two rules determines the 'political price' (a notion to be considered later) as given by both weight and dimension. This will be the price for a diamond without defects and with good colour. Adjustment coefficients will then be applied to determine the price of diamonds exhibiting defects or less valued coloration, scales for such coefficients being provided by the market. Naturally, the blind application of these rules may lead on occasion to absurd results, correction of which will require adjustments determined by experience as well as simple common sense.

Petty's writings thus offer a representation of the process of abstraction leading to the concepts of market and commodity from the manifold particular exchanges that occur in the economy. Two qualifications are, however, necessary. First, a diamond is a commodity whose price is determined more by scarcity than by its cost of production; we have here a market isolated from other markets, at least as far as productive interrelations are concerned. Second, Petty only implicitly specified the analytical consequences of the fact that the market and the commodity are abstractions: not atoms of economic reality, clearly individualized (as the modern axiomatic theory of general economic equilibrium assumes), but corresponding to a certain level of aggregation, where the most opportune level of aggregation is determined by the extent of the interrelationships between the various acts of exchange. Thus, for instance, we may refer to apples, or to fruit, or to food in general, as a single commodity according to the level of aggregation thought to be most adequate, taking into account the relationships that come into play within the group of producers and within the group of buyers.

As for the notion of price, Petty distinguished between natural, political, current and actual price. The natural price depends on the state of technological knowledge and subsistence required for the workers. In addition to this, the political price takes into account social costs, such as labour input in excess of necessary labour: such costs are considered waste, indicative of the fact that actual production is lower than potential production. The current price is defined as the expression of the political price in terms of the commodity used as standard of measure, so that it, too, turns out to be a theoretical variable. Finally, we should distinguish between intrinsic causes determining the political price and extrinsic causes – those variable and contingent causes that combine with the former to determine the actual price.

Petty's 'natural price' thus has the meaning of an optimal price, corresponding to the best technology available and to the most efficient possible operation of the 'body politick'. For later classical economists, the 'natural price' has a different meaning, corresponding to that of Petty's 'political price', since it points to the price that regulates the behaviour of the market and depends on the actual conditions of production prevailing in the economic system. Petty's distinction between these two notions, in an historical period of far from fully developed capitalism, implies a stress on the higher costs attached to the then still backward level of social organisation.

3.5   Surplus, Distribution, Prices

Identification of the concept of the surplus is traditionally considered to have been one of Petty's most important contributions, although his surplus took the partial form of rent (and taxes) and, derivatively, that of rent on money capital (interest):

Suppose a man could with his own hands plant a certain scope of Land with Corn, that is, could Digg, or Plough, Harrow, Weed, Reap, Carry home, Thresh, and Winnow so much as the Husbandry of this Land requires; and had withal Seed wherewith to sowe the same. I say, that when this man hath subducted his seed out of the proceed of his Harvest, and also, what himself hath both eaten and given to others in exchange for Clothes, and other Natural necessaries; that the remainder of Corn is the natural and true Rent of the Land for the year; and the *medium* of seven years, or rather of so many years as makes up the Cycle, within which Dearths and Plenties make their revolution, doth give the ordinary Rent of the Land in Corn. (Petty 1662, p. 43)

Rent, which in Petty's example corresponds to the surplus, is expressed here in physical terms, as a given amount of corn. This is possible because the product is homogeneous, while heterogeneous means of production are all expressed in terms of the single produced good; this includes labour that is assumed to receive its means of subsistence, also expressed in terms of corn ('what himself hath both eaten and given to others in exchange for Clothes'). The problem of prices is circumvented, for it is implicitly assumed that exchange ratios between produced goods and means of production may be considered as given. The surplus can also be expressed in terms of the number of persons who can be maintained by a group of labourers who produce enough subsistence for themselves and for the others. Like production of luxury goods and services, unemployment thus appears as a way to employ the surplus.

The magnitude of the surplus depends on the number of productive labourers and the level of productivity per worker, as Adam Smith would maintain a century later. Petty then insisted on proposals aiming to provide employment for the greatest possible number of productive labourers, by reducing both unemployment and unproductive labour. Among the elements determining productivity per worker, Petty recalled those that may be called natural, such as ease of access to the sea, availability of harbours and natural avenues of communication or original fertility of land. Much greater importance was, however, attributed to technological and organisational factors, such as land improvements (drainage, irrigation and the like), investments in infrastructure (roads, navigable canals), technical progress embodied in new implements of production and above all developments in the division of labour.

Let us now come to the theory of relative prices, on which we have a number of different elements. The first interpretation, put forward by Marx, credits Petty with a labour theory of value. Petty considers hypothetical sub-systems of the economy within which all necessary means of production are produced and there is a surplus of a single commodity; the ratio between the quantities of labour utilized in two such sub-systems having as surplus two different commodities determines the relative price of these commodities.

We then have a theory of value based on labour and land:

All things ought to be valued by two natural denominations, which is land and labour; that is, we ought to say, a ship or garment is worth such a measure of land, with such another measure of labour; forasmuch as both ships and garments were the creatures of lands and mens labours thereupon. (Petty 1662, p. 44)

This passage (and the formula that Petty 1662, p. 68, uses to state his theory of value: 'labour is the father and active principle of wealth, as lands are the mother') should not be interpreted as a rudimentary statement of a theory of absolute value. These are traditional mottos, widely used for indicating the diverse roles of labour and land in production (the former playing the active, the latter the passive role: an idea that can be traced as far back as the writings of Aristotle); it is easy to see how such an idea might provide the basis for a theory of labour value grounded in the doctrines of 'natural law', conceiving labour as sacrifice. The price is, then, the 'just' reward for such sacrifice, precisely because it is proportional to the sacrifice endured. However, such a 'natural law' interpretation would be erroneous, since Petty considered labour as simply another production cost that is measured by its subsistence and ignored any possible moral implication of justice or injustice in his treatment of the problem of prices. Furthermore, in Petty's view, land and labour were to be placed on the same footing and the one could be expressed in terms of the other. In fact, 'the most important consideration in Political Oeconomies' was precisely 'how to make a par and equation between lands and labour, so as to express the value of any thing by either alone'.[11] For this problem Petty proposed a solution based on comparison between two sub-systems producing different quantities of food on the same quantity of land, but in one case using and in the other not using labour as a means of production: the difference between the two products corresponds to the wages of the labour employed in the first case.

Finally, we have an interpretation of Petty's theory of prices as based on physical costs of production. Petty repeatedly insisted on this idea, providing lists of the commodities required for some productive processes. In comparison, the reduction of costs to labour alone, or to labour and land, appears as a simplification. In any case, what is relevant here is the objective approach systematically followed by Petty by reducing prices to the difficulty of production: an approach

---

[11] Petty 1691a, p. 181; the same problem had already been raised also in *A Treatise of Taxes and Contributions* (Petty 1662, p. 44).

that, as we shall see, was to be taken up by later Classical economists and Sraffa, with greater consistency and analytical rigour.

Petty's contribution did not go much beyond simple formulation of the problem: heterogeneous goods cannot be summed together to make up costs of production unless they have been previously expressed in homogeneous units, that is, in terms of quantities of value obtained by multiplying the quantity of each commodity required in the process of production by its relative price. We are thus confronted with a circularity problem: the price of the product cannot be determined unless the prices of the means of production are known, but these are also produced by means of production that may include the first product. This difficulty may account for the attempts to reduce the heterogeneous components of the cost of production to primary factors alone, labour or labour and land; but such attempts also fail to solve the problem. The incompleteness of the conceptual scheme set out by Petty, and in particular the absence of a key concept such as the rate of profits, seems to have been decisive in preventing further advance to a correct solution of the problem, through construction of an analytical system that takes into account productive interrelations among the different sectors of the economy. But the path that leads to such a system is very long, as we shall see in the following chapters.

4   From Body Politic to Economic Tables

4.1   The Debates of the Time

In the century stretching between William Petty's writings and Adam Smith's, economic thinking proceeded in many directions: reflections on economic phenomena were part of general reflections on society and man, and the same authors would in the course of time range over a vast field of issues.

As we have seen, Petty was an inventor, doctor and professor of anatomy, responsible for the geographical survey of Ireland and a landowner engaged in the management of his estates. His reflections on economic, institutional and demographic issues constituted for him at the same time a civic and intellectual pursuit, a means to exercise political influence and an instrument for the defence of his own private interests. John Locke dealt with strictly economic issues in pursuit of his philosophical enquiries, as a few years later did David Hume. Locke wrote, among other things, about monetary issues in the course of a debate that also saw the famous physicist Isaac Newton (1642–1727) taking part; in 1699 Newton was appointed director of the Mint. Bernard de Mandeville was a doctor and philosopher, Richard Cantillon an international banker. François Quesnay, a physician at the court of King Louis XV, joined in the intellectual debate of the time in the hope that his ideas might contribute to social amelioration. Here we isolate the strictly economic contributions from their context, but we must not forget that excisions of the sort would have been considered arbitrary by the protagonists of that time.

One line in economic thinking (reference here must be brief) took a markedly different stance from Petty, insisting on a combination of analysis and ethics. In this ambit we find the representatives of the 'natural law' doctrine, such as the German jurist Samuel Pufendorf (1632–1694), important for putting ideas of natural rights and natural laws into circulation but, in terms of strictly economic issues, still engaged in 'just price' discussions. Within the same 'natural law' current we find the still numerous writings on monetary matters that, dealing in particular with determination of the rate of interest, were connected with the Scholastic debates on usury.

The numerous tracts designed to provide merchants with guidance in their activities display a curious analogy to this latter current. The most renowned among them is *Le parfait negociant* by Jacques Savary (*The Expert Merchant*, 1675). In Italy works of this kind were already flourishing in the fourteenth and fifteenth centuries; for England we may mention – although on the borderline between this current and economic analysis – Malachy Postlethwayt's *Universal Dictionary of Trade and Commerce* (1751–55), composed utilising a large number of plagiarised passages (including an almost complete version of Cantillon's *Essay on the Nature of Commerce in General*).[1]

We also have a long series of tracts *On Trade*, which generally dealt with monetary issues in connection with matters of international trade, in the wake of the mercantilist literature discussed previously. The most common arguments concerned the expediency of protecting national employment from foreign competition. However, we find also defenders of a liberal position, such as the merchant Dudley North (1641–1691) or Daniel Defoe (1660–1731), the well-known author of *Robinson Crusoe* (1719). The main argument in defence of free trade is a petition of principle, the idea that no obstacles should be opposed to the unfettered working of the 'natural laws'.

In France, the main champion of free trade in this period was Pierre le Pesant de Boisguilbert (1646–1714), whose motto was *laissez faire la nature et la liberté* (let nature and freedom do their course). Boisguilbert (1695) criticised Colbert's statism and policy favouring manufactures, blaming the depressed state of the French economy on stagnation in agriculture.

Finally, in the period between 1690 and the first decades of the eighteenth century, various authors propounded interesting ideas on economic development, such as the thesis that working class consumption had an influence on productivity and thus on growth.

4.2   John Locke

Among the writers concerned with monetary issues as part of more general reflections on society and human beings, let us recall the

---

[1] Within this current there is also a spate of publications considering issues of (elementary) financial mathematics. Cf. Poitras 2000.

English philosopher John Locke (1632–1704), author of a tract on *Some Considerations on the Consequences of the Lowering of Interest, and Raising the Value of Money* (1692; a preliminary version had been written in 1668): one of the first texts of the time (after Petty and before Cantillon) to utilize the notion of velocity of circulation of money.

Locke's essay was a contribution to the lively debate that arose in the last decade of the seventeenth century on the relationship between low interest rates and prosperity. Josiah Child (1630–1699), governor of the India Company and one of the richest men of his time, had maintained that the first element (low interest rates) is the cause of the second (prosperity) and on this ground had asked for legal constraints on interest rates (Child 1688). In criticising this thesis, Locke argued that it is prosperity that favours a moderate level of interest rates and that any attempt to reduce them by law is doomed to failure; besides, insofar as it may succeed, such an attempt may prove detrimental, slowing down accumulation.

In the *Two Treatises of Government* (1690), Locke presented his view of private property as a natural right of man. It opposed the ideas of Hobbes and others, who took private property to have been instituted through an agreement (or 'social contract') marking transition from the state of nature to organised society, and thus to be of a conventional nature.

Locke began his argument by recognising that land and all the lower creatures have been given to all men in common. However, he observed,

every man has a 'property' in his own 'person'. This nobody has any right to but himself. The 'labour' of his body and the 'work' of his hands, we may say, are properly his. Whatsoever, then, he removes out of the state that Nature hath provided and left it in, he hath mixed his labour with it, and joined to it something that is his own, and thereby makes it his property. (Locke 1690, p. 130: II.27)

Nevertheless, Locke attributed to the notions of labour and capital a broader connotation than usual. Labour included all kinds of productive activity – the entrepreneurs' as much as the wage labourer's – and therefore constituted the source of all wealth and the religious duty of every individual. Similarly, Locke (1690, p. 180: II.123) defined property as including not only private property in its common meaning but also man's fundamental rights: 'lives, liberties and estates, which I call by the general name – property'. We should thus view his argument not so much as a justification of an economic system based on private property but rather as a reaction to 'social contract' theses, particularly Hobbes's (1651), and the conclusions they lead to, favourable to political absolutism. Locke was a defender of the rights of the individual against government; this included a defence of private property against residual feudal elements, such as the fact that the political powers still played an important role as origin (and not simply guarantee) of property titles, with the arbitrariness that this implied for the distribution of wealth.

4.3   The Motivations and Consequences of Human Actions

Over the centuries, analysis of human behaviour and the functioning of society have been tackled starting from two key questions: what impulses drive human actions? What are the consequences for society of more or less radically selfish motivations, not directly finalised to the collective well-being?

The first question came under discussion as analysis turned from 'what should be' to 'what in fact is'. We have already recalled Machiavelli's contribution; a further prod in this direction came from the Protestant reform, since it recognised legitimacy for actions aiming at individual enrichment while denying opposition between individual and collective interests. Individual interests were considered as a force for constructive action while preserving a principle of moral judgement, thus allowing for discrimination between destructive and constructive actions. The multiplicity of motivations for human behaviour is thus recognized, avoiding the simplistic opposition between selfish and altruistic behaviour.

The motives for human action are summed up in two terms, 'passions and interests', each of which enclosed various elements: instinctual or customary – and in any case a-rational (although not necessarily irrational) – or implying reasoned choices, albeit not to be reduced to a mere matter of maximising wealth or income (Hirschman 1977). We should also bear in mind that in a time of profound uncertainties the room for rational behaviour was certainly not all-embracing, while the role of the passions remained important. In general, writers on economic issues tended to be rationalists, both in the sense of reasoning on the possible consequences of different kinds of behaviour, forming value judgements on them by evaluating their consequences and in the sense of attributing the same behavioural canon to the agents as objects of their analyses.

Let us now turn to the second question, concerning the outcomes of an individual behaviour motivated by individual passions and interests. A somewhat optimistic answer was provided: under certain conditions, when a constructive drive is generated from the interrelation between the different passions and interests, individual actions not directly aimed at the public good may have positive social consequences. The very social connections that developed between participants in a market economy played a civilising role, given a concept of civilisation connoting the ability to preserve some moral control over one's own passions and interests in the choice between alternative lines of behaviour. In the eighteenth century the idea of a civilising role for commerce – the idea of *doux commerce* – dominated over the pessimistic thesis of commerce having a destructive influence on social cohesion.[2]

In the eighteenth century a basically optimistic interpretation of the path followed by a society based on the division of labour and the market thus prevailed: an optimistic view intrinsic to the spirit of the time, and in particular to the Enlightenment culture and to its faith in the triumph of Reason. However, the idea of a progressive society did not stem, as effect from cause, from hope in the diffusion of individual behaviour guided ever more closely by reason, ever less by the passions. Rather, the cause and effect link worked in the opposite direction, from the economic and social progress achieved by a society driven by the spirit of commerce, and hence by individualistic motivations, to a growing cultural civilisation in which personal interest was not so much superseded as appropriately channelled towards collective progress.

4.4   Bernard de Mandeville

Born to a family of doctors, and subsequently himself a doctor, the Dutch Bernard de Mandeville (1670–1733) was christened in Rotterdam and attended the Erasmian school and then the University of Leyda, where he qualified as doctor in medicine in 1691. Shortly afterwards he moved to London, where he resided up to his death.

His best-known work is *The Fable of the Bees: Or, Private Vices, Publick Benefits*, published in 1714. This work had wide circulation and gave rise to heated debate; subsequent editions include Mandeville's defence against the charges of 'impiety' brought against him by the Grand Jury of Middlesex.

---

[2] The opposition between *Rival Interpretations of Market Society: Civilizing, Destructive, or Feeble?* is propounded by Hirschman 1982. What Hirschman defines as 'the self-destruction thesis' is exemplified by recalling Schumpeter and Hirsch in the twentieth century, Marx and Engels in the nineteenth century. 'Marx and Engels make much of the way in which capitalism corrodes all traditional values and institutions such as love, family, and patriotism. Everything was passing into commerce, all social bonds were dissolved through money. This perception is by no means original with Marx' (ibid., p. 1467).

Educated in a cultural environment among the most progressive of the time, in his work the Dutch doctor addressed some themes characteristic of libertine thinking of the seventeenth and eighteenth centuries, tackling what was seen as an irreconcilable clash between the criterion of rigour and the criterion of utility in choices concerning human behaviour. More specifically, Mandeville's polemic was directed against the idea of a universal harmony in which Good and Beauty coincided. In Mandeville's opinion, we should recognise that man is commonly driven by passions and interests that are centred on himself and not – or at least not directly – aimed at the good of society. However, the final outcome of a society in which selfish behaviour prevails may be the collective good: 'private vices' may turn into 'public virtues'.

The well-known formula 'private vices = public virtues' does not imply identity between the two elements. Selfish behaviour may, but not necessarily, lead to collective good. It all depends on the ability of those in power to play on the simultaneous presence of different passions at the root of human action, never denying them but channelling them in the right direction. 'Private vices by the dextrous management of a skilful politician may be turned into publick benefits.'[3] Thus Mandeville cannot be considered a supporter of 'vice' *tout court* (also considering that it was not understood as anti-social behaviour but simply as pursuit of individual motivations): he maintained that we should recognise the existence of vice as a matter of fact, for only thus will we be able to reap positive results.

Mandeville contrasted traditional society, typically on a small scale, where everyone could see what everyone else was up to, with mercantile society based on the division of labour and hence necessarily on a broader scale; moreover, since the division of labour favoured technical progress, the larger society grew, the richer it became. In Mandeville's opinion it was the former kind of society that was idealised by moralists taking a misleadingly optimistic view of society. The members of such a society, Mandeville (1714, vol. 1, pp. 183–4) asserted,

shall have no arts or sciences, or be quiet longer than their neighbours will let them; they must be poor, ignorant, and almost wholly destitute of what we call the comforts of life, and all the cardinal virtues together won't so much as procure a tolerable coat or a porridge-pot among them: For in this state of slothful ease and stupid innocence, as you need not fear great vices, so you must not expect any considerable virtues. Man never exerts himself but when he is rous'd by his desires.

---

[3] Mandeville 1714, vol. 1, p. 369.

It is the large mercantile society, in which the behaviour of men is driven by individualistic motivations, that favours the progress of wealth and with it the very enrichment of human personality, its civic growth. Obviously, this meant that there had to be pre-established rules of the game; together with laws, education and the very fact of being accustomed to community life were important, since through them the different passions may be directed towards the collective good.[4] In a sense, the interplay of well-balanced passions constituted a sort of 'invisible hand' that guaranteed the progress of society, even if this was not the immediate objective of individual actions. This invisible hand was not, however, a necessary result of individual actions: it was itself a conscious construction, through which the abilities of those responsible for governing society manifested themselves.

4.5   Richard Cantillon

For many economists the publication of Smith's *Wealth of Nations* marks the birthdate of economic science, while Marx went back still further, hailing Petty as the father of political economy. Jevons (1881) stopped midway; for him the founder of political economy was an international banker, Richard Cantillon. He appears to have been born in Ireland, lived most of his life in Paris, and was murdered in London in 1734 (though some mystery remained, with the hypothesis that Cantillon had staged his murder in order to escape to America). He was the author of an *Essay on the Nature of Commerce in General*, probably written between 1728 and 1734 and published posthumously in French only in 1755, after having been abundantly plagiarised in English by Postlethwayt (1751–55) and after a manuscript copy of the essay had remained for years in the hands of the Marquis of Mirabeau, who seems to have had every intention of using it in the same way.[5] Cantillon's influence on Quesnay and the physiocrats was indeed profound.

---

[4] Taking up another theme characteristic of the libertine thought, Mandeville noticed the variability of moral and sexual habits and of religious and political convictions (as were testified to by numerous accounts of travels in far-away lands, a literary genre widespread at the time). This implied negation of the idea of a moral conviction innate in men corresponding to dominant opinions (the *consensus gentium*). Hence, the notions of just and unjust are fruits of education and of associate life.

[5] *L'ami des hommes*, which Mirabeau published in 1756 and which had enormous success – more than forty editions in a few years and many translations – was in fact mainly a commentary on Cantillon's book, enriched with abundant doses of rhetoric. Subsequently various other authors including Beccaria drew on Cantillon, often without acknowledging their source.

The *Essay* has an admirable compactness and follows a rigorous logical scheme; it is composed of three parts: the internal organisation of the economy, money and internal monetary circulation, foreign trade and exchanges. The text was followed by a statistical appendix, subsequently lost, which probably contained exercises in political arithmetic on the lines of Petty.

Cantillon considered these arithmetical computations as approximate tools for describing reality and finding an interpretative key rather than (as Petty did) revealing underlying quantitative laws. He took a number of elements from Petty, such as the idea of a 'body politic' able to obtain a surplus produce over and above the requirements of means of production and subsistence. However, while in Petty the connection between the different parts of the 'body politic' resided mainly in the fact that they are subject to a single state power, Cantillon saw it as stemming from the process of circulation of commodities, explicitly connected to the production process. Thus Cantillon constitutes a crucial link on the road leading from Petty to Quesnay and Smith, contributing both to the specification of the basic concepts and to theoretical analysis.

For the first of these two elements, Cantillon associated the division into sectors (agriculture, artisan sector, commerce) with division into social classes (peasants, artisans, merchants and nobility) and the geographical organisation of society (countryside, villages, towns), namely the different viewpoints we may take on an economic system (those of the division into sectors, or social classes, or geographical areas. Yet the constraints imposed by direct correspondence between different classifications render Cantillon's categories inferior to the modern division into sectors (agriculture, manufacturing, services) and into social classes (workers, capitalists, landlords).

As for the theory of value, Cantillon (1755, p. 27) took up Petty's ideas: 'The price and intrinsic value of a thing in general is the measure of the land and labour which enter into its production.' However, with regard to the equation between labour and land, Cantillon abandoned Petty's criterion, based on the relative productivity of processes utilising alternatively labour or land, which implied either techniques with a single means of production or a circular reasoning. In fact, Cantillon (ibid., p. 35) reduced labour to its cost of production: 'the daily labour of the meanest slave corresponds in value to double the produce of the land required to maintain him'; effectively, apart from the subsistence of the worker we need to compute an equal cost for subsistence of two offspring, so as to ensure substitution of the worker at the end of his productive life, taking into account the mortality conditions of the time. Cantillon seemed to tend towards a pure land theory of value, since land remained the sole original non-reproducible factor of production creating value, thus providing the background for the physiocrats' thought, to be considered in the next section.

Cantillon attributed to upper-class luxury consumption the driving role of the economy: a thesis we may consider both an element of modernity, analogous to the role of autonomous demand items (particularly investments) in the Keynesian system, and a residuum of the feudal system, focusing attention on consumption by the proprietary classes while ignoring the dynamic role assumed by industrial investments within capitalism.[6] In any case, this idea constituted one of the main elements in Cantillon's influence on the physiocratic school.

However, the physiocrats were not to take up Cantillon's 'three rents' theory. The first rent was the part of the product that the farmer used to meet the costs of production, inclusive of the workers' subsistence; the second rent constituted the farmers' income, corresponding to what we would today call the profit of agricultural entrepreneurs; while the third rent was that going to the landlord for the use of his land. The profits of the agricultural entrepreneur (the dominant kind of capitalist, at the time) were considered jointly with rent proper. Profits, thus, were not yet related to capital advances in order to generate the idea of a uniform rate of return (rate of profits). This aspect, too, may better be understood if we recall the limited strength of competition in the conditions of the time, as can be seen among other things in certain passages in the *Essay* on the relationship between interest rates and real rates of return, where the widespread dispersion of returns in different activities and more generally in different circumstances emerges in full evidence.

Cantillon's ideas on money were much like Petty's: money is necessary for the circulation of commodities, but precious metals do not coincide with wealth; the quantity of money required for the sound functioning of the economy depends on the value of exchanges and the velocity of circulation of money itself. The interest rate depends on the ratio between demand for and supply of loanable funds and is therefore not directly related to the supply of money. The value of money (hence, inversely, the general level of prices) depends essentially on its cost of production, as in Petty, and unlike, for instance, the position taken by Locke, who focused on demand and supply. The evaluation of money made by the market may differ from its value; among other things, important here were the

---

[6] Berg (2005) shows how the development of luxury goods and their consumption by the middle classes in eighteenth-century England contributed to the formation of bourgeois culture and consciousness.

elements that influenced the velocity of circulation of money: financial institutions and customs – for instance the existence of clearing agreements – and commercial credit. Moreover, monetary phenomena influenced different goods in different ways. Cantillon appears to have been at his ease examining these relations given that they were connected to his activities as a banker, but he did not go into the details: his *Essay* was an economics treatise, not a treatise on banking and financial technique, though we cannot help noticing how much room monetary issues take up and how little – next to nothing, in fact – do fiscal issues, so important in the debates of the time. All the issues considered in the *Essay* were discussed with the utmost logical rigour, so that the discourse appears simple, at points obvious. It is clear that even in manuscript form this work had a profound impact on its readers.

4.6   François Quesnay and the Physiocrats

The *physiocrats* (or *les économistes*, as they used to call themselves) were a very compact and combative group of French economists grouped around François Quesnay (1694–1774), doctor to Madame de Pompadour at the court of Louis XV, author of the *Tableau économique* (1758–59). The physiocrats are the first school of economic thought to have equipped themselves with their own press organs in order to advocate definite points of policy. The span of time that saw them dominant was short – a quarter of a century or little more – but their influence on the development of political economy was significantly strong, thanks also to the central position Paris occupied in the cultural life of the time.

The physiocrats attributed a key role to the development of agriculture, which they considered the only sector capable of producing a surplus. Moreover, as the term they are now designated with shows (*physiocracy* originates from the Greek *fùsis* = 'nature', and *cratéin* = 'to dominate'), they shared with the Cartesian current of French Enlightenment the idea of a 'natural order', the logic and optimality of which – unchanging over time, since it is intrinsic to the very nature of things – should be evident to any person endowed with the light of reason, and which an enlightened prince should implement as 'positive order'. Private property also falls within this natural order, so the defence of property rights was considered one of the main tasks of the 'positive order'.

Victor Riqueti, marquis of Mirabeau (1715–1789), and various other physiocrats saw the capacity of agriculture to generate a surplus as being intrinsic to the fertility of the soil (which produces an ear of wheat from a grain) and hence as a gift of mother nature. This theory on the origin of the surplus may then be used to justify appropriation of the surplus by the nobility – not only the rightful owners of the lands but masters of the serfs living on them to boot. Quesnay, too, considered agriculture alone capable of yielding a surplus, although his explanation is somewhat different, taking account of the situation prevailing in France at the time: given the prices of agricultural products and manufactures on the world markets, with recourse to the best technologies French farmers could obtain a product whose value exceeded production costs, while manufacturers simply recovered their costs (including subsistence for manufacturing entrepreneurs). Quesnay thus stressed the potential a reformed agricultural system held for economic development – what he called *grande culture*, as compared with *petite culture*, the former characterised not only by larger concerns but also by technologies with higher capital intensity (such as the plough drawn by horses rather than oxen).

Thus, Quesnay stressed the potentialities of an agricultural revolution that had already begun but was proceeding too slowly: a thesis opposed to the mercantilist tradition and above all to Jean-Baptiste Colbert's (1619–1683) economic policy of supporting commerce and manufactures by liberalising the importation of raw materials and duties on manufacturing imports that hindered the development of agriculture, reducing its profitability while increasing that of manufactures. On the contrary, Quesnay argued, agricultural products should be given a *bon prix*: a price sufficient not only to cover production costs but also to favour the financing of investments by ensuring adequate returns.

Neither the *bon prix* nor the *prix fondamental* (which corresponded to mere costs of production) were prices spontaneously generated by the markets; according to Quesnay, market prices depended on supply and demand. Implementation of the *bon prix* was thus entrusted to a policy favouring the free exportation of agricultural products and consumption habits within the country such as would encourage the *luxe de subsistence* as compared with the *luxe de décoration*, or consumption of agricultural produce – but not of manufactures – in excess of the mere subsistence level.[7] Although the notion of a competitive rate of profits was still wanting (it would be outlined by Turgot a few years later and fully

---

[7] The physiocrats thus connected high prices with the idea of a flourishing, developing economy, in which high prices are the cause (or one of the causes) and economic abundance is the effect. This view was widely held during the whole of the mercantilist period, but far from unanimously, since in many cases high prices were seen as a symptom of dearth. On the contrary, Smith and the Classical economists held that moderate prices are associated with a situation of abundance, of which they are essentially the effect.

developed by Smith), Quesnay fully recognised the crucial role of capital accumulation for the productive process and above all in allowing improved technologies to be adopted. Quesnay distinguished between *avances foncières* (initial basic investments, required for cultivating a piece of land and increasing its productivity), *avances primitives* (production implements, cattle) and *avances annuelles* (circulating capital: seed, wages and the like). Quesnay thus focused attention on agriculture; at the same time, however, he made decided strides in the direction, subsequently followed by Turgot, Smith and the whole Classical tradition, of considering capital advances as a requirement for the production and accumulation of capital, hence a crucial element for economic development.

Quesnay and the physiocrats developed a theory admirable in its 'spirit of system' and consistency. In particular, Quesnay was the first economist to recognise and represent in an analytical scheme the productive interrelations linking the different sectors that, in an economic system based on the division of labour, stemmed from heterogeneity of means of production in each sector. This problem was tackled, with the *tableau économique*, by focusing on the exchanges required to ensure the continuous functioning of the economic system.

Let us see in broad outline Quesnay's model. Agriculture was considered the sole productive (i.e. capable of generating a surplus) sector in the economy; Quesnay assumed that the most advanced technology, the *grande culture*, was generally adopted in agriculture. Other activities were grouped under the 'sterile sector' heading, so called because these activities merely transformed into processed products a given set of raw materials (including means of subsistence for the workers of the sector); the value of the processed products proved equal to the value of the means of production and subsistence utilised to obtain them, so that there was no creation of new value. Subdivision of the economic system into sectors corresponded to the subdivision of society into social classes: the productive class composed of those active in agriculture (peasants and farmers), the sterile class composed of artisans (including manufacturing workers and

---

Obviously, at the logical level the two theses are not mutually exclusive, since they are based on consideration of different aspects of the process of development, hence on cause and effect relationships moving in opposite directions. On the one hand, relatively high prices stemming from high demand constitute a stimulus to production, while a low level of prices may signal difficulty in absorption of the products by the market and may thus constitute a disincentive for producers; on the other hand, increase in productivity accompanying economic development leads, under competitive conditions, to decrease in prices, while high prices signal bottlenecks on the supply side, namely the presence of obstacles to the growth of production.

merchants) and the aristocratic class, the landlords, to which the surplus obtained in the agricultural sector accrued, including together with the nobility the clergy. [1]

The *tableau économique*, or economic table, consists in a series of graphs, which outlined the series of exchanges of commodities against money between the different productive sectors and the different social classes necessary in order to allow for the survival and development of the economy through a circular process in which, year after year, the phases of production, exchange and consumption follow one upon the other. At the end of the productive cycle, the circulation process is set in motion by the nobility, utilising the money paid them as rent to acquire agricultural and manufactured products. A series of exchanges then follows: the sterile class utilises the money it has received to acquire food and raw materials from the productive class; the latter acquires manufactured products from the sterile class. At the end, the productive class has sold its surplus produce, thus obtaining the money with which to pay the rents to the landlords. A new cycle of production can thus begin. The surplus (what remains of the product, once the means of production and subsistence of the workers in the economy have been reproduced) corresponds to the consumption of the nobility and clergy, who do not produce anything and are able to buy agricultural and manufactured products year after year only because they receive their rents from the productive sector.

In the circular process described by Quesnay the different sectors and social classes are interconnected; the distribution of the product among the different social classes takes place simultaneously with the process of exchanges that allow each sector to reintegrate the initial endowments of means of production and of subsistence. Since the surplus accrues to the landlords, it is obvious that rents alone should bear the entire tax burden. Attempts to bring taxes to fall on other social classes were not only doomed to failure but were also costly for the economic system as a whole, given the disincentive to accumulation and technical change entailed by taxes on farmers, viewed by Quesnay and the physiocrats as the active agents for economic development.

4.7   The Political Economy of the Enlightenment; Turgot

The culture of the eighteenth century was dominated by the Enlightenment. The general characteristic was a faith in both material and civic progress, of society as of man, guided by reason. As we saw when considering the idea of the *doux commerce*, progress may involve human nature itself. Within these broad lines, while bearing in mind both the substantially international nature of the culture of the time and the dominant role played by Paris, we may distinguish various currents: the French, Scottish, Italian (Neapolitan, Milanese and Tuscan) and German Enlightenment.

Paris was at the time the centre of European cultural life. A number of leading intellectuals from other countries, such as the Scot David Hume or the Neapolitan Ferdinando Galiani, resided there as staff of their respective embassies; for Adam Smith a visit to France with a period of residence in Paris marked a crucial stage in the development of his ideas.

A deeply rooted characteristic of a great part of the French Enlightenment was represented by the heritage of Descartes[8] – an *esprit de système* and a rationalism raised to the level of an absolute methodology and ultimately to cult of the Goddess Reason. A systemic spirit is evident, for example, in physiocratic theory and its corollaries for economic policy. However, there were many and various positions: suffice it to recall the spirit of openness and tolerance of Voltaire (1694–1778). A manifestation of these manifold trends is to be seen in the economic entries in the monumental *Encyclopédie* edited by Diderot, which saw the collaboration of many protagonists of our history including Quesnay and Turgot.

One of the economic commitments of the Enlightenment was critique of the institution of guilds inherited from the Middle Ages, with their rigid regulation of production techniques, product quality, wages and the working conditions of apprentices. The Enlightenment also distinguished itself from mercantilism for its revaluation of agriculture in comparison with foreign trade and manufactures. In the wake of Petty and Cantillon, various authors based their analyses on the notions of surplus and value and took production, distribution and circulation (exchange) as connected processes. Often they were supporters of high wages and took into account the problems stemming from indigence and the difficulties of the poor (as in the debates on the creation of charitable institutions and hospitals and on public assistance for the sick and orphans) and more generally attributed importance to the connection between economic development and civic progress.

An eminent representative of French economic culture in this phase was Anne Robert Jacques Turgot (1727–1781), a man of letters, economist and high-ranking functionary, minister of finance from 1774 to 1776 and author of the *Réflexions sur la formation et la*

---

[8] René Descartes (1596–1650), French philosopher and mathematician, author of a *Discours de la méthode* (1637).

distribution des richesses (*Thoughts on the Formation and Distribution of Wealth*, 1766). Turgot belonged to the generation following after Quesnay and in various respects represented a bridge between the physiocrats and his contemporary, Adam Smith. In his theories he attributed an important role to capital and the capitalist-entrepreneurs; he also held decidedly liberal views, summed up with the motto *laissez-nous faire*.[9] *Laissez-faire* was also the hallmark of a number of policy measures adopted by Turgot, including liberalisation of the corn trade and abolition of the *jurandes*, or craft guilds. His policy measures constituted possibly the last attempt at rationalising the French economy before the revolution, but they clashed with vested interests, eventually leading to Turgot's downfall.

On the analytical level, Turgot outlined a theory of exchange value based on utility. All evaluations are subjective; buyer and seller accept the exchange because they have different evaluations (*valeurs estimatives*) of the commodity in question, constituting the lower and upper price limits. The actual price would, according to Turgot, come midway between these two limits, coinciding with the *valeur appréciative* given by the average of the *valeurs estimatives*.[10]

Other aspects of his analysis foreshadowed subsequent theories, for instance his theory of increasing returns focused on what was to be called the intensive margin, that is, utilisation of an increasing number of doses of capital and labour on a given plot of land. Some references to the interrelations linking elements in the economic field appear insufficient to hail Turgot as a forerunner of Walras and the theory of general economic equilibrium.

4.8 The Italian Enlightenment: the Abbé Galiani

In comparison with the French Enlightenment, the Scottish and Neapolitan brands showed greater readiness to recognise the imperfections of human nature and the impossibility of deducing directly

---

[9] Cf. Turgot 1759, p. 151. Turgot attributed to his friend Vincent de Gournay (1712–1759) this motto, together with the thesis that 'a man knows his own interest better than another man to whom that interest is wholly indifferent' (ibid., p. 131) – an expression recalling an observation by Smith in the *Theory of moral sentiments* (published in the same year as the *Éloge*): 'Every man is [...] fitter and abler to take care of himself than of any other person' (Smith 1759, p. 219), which may be traced back to the Greek tradition.

[10] This thesis, which Turgot enunciated but did not elaborate, possibly derived from the Scholastic debate on the just price, and in particular from the thesis that each participant should receive an equal advantage from the exchange.

from *a priori* reasoning interpretations of specific economic phenomena or clear-cut recipes for economic policy. An example of this approach is provided by the *Dialogues sur le commerce des blès* (*Dialogues on the Commerce of Corn*, 1770) by the Abbé Ferdinando Galiani (1728–1787), who had already written a celebrated treatise, *Della moneta* (*On Money*, 1751), at the age of twenty-three. His remarks on the physiocratic doctrines were based on direct criticism of the *esprit de système* and showed the importance of the specific circumstances of each real situation when reasoning on economic policy.[11] Galiani was a champion of theoretical minimalism. 'I am in favour of nothing. I am of the opinion that we should not talk nonsense,'[12] he declared, and all his writings show the validity of any idea at the level of theory or economic policy as relative in time and space. In this respect he stands as a major exponent of the sceptical current of the Enlightenment, even more extreme in this than Voltaire.

While we are still in Naples, let us recall Antonio Genovesi (1713–1769), the first holder (since 1754) of a chair in political economy, who stressed the close link between the economy and the civic issues of institutional organization and public morals in his writings. His major work in the economic field, *Delle lezioni di commercio* (*Lectures on Commerce*, 1765–67), was essentially didactic, aiming at uplifting the human spirit and enhancing the knowledge of the young within the perspective of the Enlightenment. The theses he supported were not new: a theory of economic development through stages, a position favourable to consumption (but not to high wages), a subjective theory of value including some reference to the cost of production side (possibly derived from Galiani 1751) and discussion of the factors favouring the wealth of nations, not unlike Serra's but less well-structured. The great success of Genovesi may well be due to his blending of philosophy and political economy, well befitting the spirit of the time.

The intellectuals writing about economic issues in Milan and in Tuscany were more interested in the immediate problems of reforms aiming at favouring economic and civic development. Cesare Beccaria (1738–1794) was the author of a treatise, *Elementi di economia pubblica*

---

[11] 'Nobody ever makes a mistake without a reason. Thus everybody wants to follow reason and experience, but if you follow an idea reasonable in itself and rely on an experience or a true and demonstrated fact but which does not fit in – is not applicable to the case at hand – you think you are doing well, and you are wrong' (Galiani 1770, p. 55). Or again: 'Nothing in politics can be pushed to the extreme. There is a point, a limit up to which good is greater than evil; if you pass beyond it, evil prevails over good. [... This point] only the sage knows how to find. People feel it by instinct. The man in power needs time to find it. The modern economist does not even suspect it' (ibid., p. 233).

[12] Galiani 1770, p. 61.

(*Elements of Public Economics*), published posthumously in 1804, but is above all known for his essay *Dei delitti e delle pene* (*On Crimes and Punishments*, 1764), a work that in all likelihood owed much to his friend Pietro Verri (1728–1797), where he condemned the then widespread recourse to the death penalty. Both Verri and Beccaria adopted a subjective theory of value based on comparison between scarcity and utility; in general, they conceived the market as the point where buyers and sellers meet (and this held true also for the rate of interest, determined by demand for and supply of loans). Moreover, both Verri and Beccaria took a wide interest in practical issues, from the fiscal and monetary situation to problems of customs duties and seasonal unemployment.

4.9   The Scottish Enlightenment: Francis Hutcheson and David Hume

The Enlightenment notion of a 'natural order' was adopted in Scotland purged of Cartesian rationalism and hence transformed into the view of a 'spontaneous order', considered the result of an adaptive process, in which a multiplicity of individual choices led to a result – a set of complex, sufficiently well-functioning, social structures – not assumed as the objective of a broad, rational design (thus taking some distance from the tradition of constructive rationalism that began with Descartes and ultimately led to attribution of a central role to the *deus ex machina* represented by a benevolent and enlightened legislator).

Smith was the most illustrious exponent of this current, although before him, and around him, other protagonists offered important contributions in various fields.

Francis Hutcheson (1694–1746), who taught Smith in Glasgow and wrote, among other things, a *System of Moral Philosophy* in three volumes, published posthumously in 1755, contributed to the utilitarian approach the thesis that the best moral action is that which ensures the maximum of happiness to the greatest number of persons. Hutcheson considered man as an essentially social animal, to the extent of rejecting any separation between ethics and politics. Benevolence towards others, together with utility, regulates human 'moral' actions; following this behavioural rule people can obtain their own good without this constituting the direct objective of their actions and thus without any contrast arising between utility and virtue.

Adam Ferguson (1723–1816) belonged to Smith's generation; his main work, *An Essay on the History of Civil Society* (1767), argues among other things an evolutionary view of the naissance of language.

Ferguson dealt at length with the division of labour, also stressing its negative aspects. For some of his theses he probably drew, without acknowledgement, on Smith's university lessons; thus Ferguson was credited with first publication (the *Wealth of Nations* came out ten years later than his book) but at the cost of some tension between himself and Smith.

A little older than Smith, James Steuart (1712–1780) was one of the major protagonists of Scottish politics and culture and the author of a massive work, *An Inquiry into the Principles of Political Oeconomy* published in 1767, nine years before Smith's *Wealth of Nations*, which would then overshadow it. However, Steuart is not to be seen as one of the protagonists of the Scottish Enlightenment but classed rather among the epigones of mercantilism given the role he attributed to active public intervention in the economy and the protection of manufactures with duties.

Twelve years older than Smith, who became a great friend of his, was the empiricist philosopher David Hume (1711–1776), author of the *Treatise of Human Nature* (1739–40). A spontaneous order in institutions as different as language and money gradually emerges as an unforeseen consequence of manifold individual actions guided by selfishness tempered with a sentiment of benevolence. As for human actions, it is habit rather than reason that guides them. Economists are best acquainted with his *Political Discourses* (1752). . In the essay 'Of the Balance of Trade' Hume illustrated the adjustment mechanism that – under the gold standard – brings the balance of trade of different countries into equilibrium. This mechanism was based on the quantity theory of money: in each country prices increase (decrease) when the quantity of money in circulation increases (decreases). Thus, whenever a country has a favourable balance of trade, and so sees an influx of gold, the supply of money within it increases, together with internal prices. This reduces the competitiveness of internally produced commodities and hence the country's exports. Exactly the opposite happens for countries with a balance of trade deficit.[13] . The protagonists of Scottish Enlightenment are important above all for their notion

---

[13] This theory, to which Hume did not attribute the importance attached to it by many subsequent scholars, is based on a sizeable set of implicit assumptions: that the quantity theory of money holds, that the ratio between gold base and quantity of money in circulation (including banking money) is sufficiently stable, that the balance of trade is the dominant component of the balance of payments and/or that the other components do not undergo significant variations, that the percentage increase of quantities exported and imported is superior to the percentage decrease (increase) of the level of prices for imported and exported goods. Finally, the gold standard must rule.

of man and society: notwithstanding some even important differences between the different authors, on the whole they displayed a moderate optimism with regard to the automatic, involuntary realisation of sound institutional organization for a society based on the pursuit of self-interest and a moderately positive evaluation of human nature while nevertheless recognising its many imperfections.

5   Adam Smith

5.1   Life and Writings

Adam Smith was born in the small town of Kirkaldy in Scotland in 1723. His father had died shortly before he was born, and Adam was raised by his mother with the help of relatives – a moderately well-to-do family of landowners – until 1737, when he moved to Glasgow in order to attend the local university.

At the time, fourteen was not an uncommon age to enter university, which was in fact a sort of upper secondary school. In the Scottish educational system the students paid their teachers course by course, and so the teachers' total salary depended on their students' assessment of their teaching. Smith deemed this system superior to that of the English universities such as Oxford, financed by public funds and private donations, where the professors, receiving a regular salary, had no incentive to put zeal into their profession.

It was in fact at Oxford that Smith continued his studies as from 1740, with an eleven-year scholarship awarded as preparation for an ecclesiastical career. Smith did not take to the celebrated English university, traditionalist and authoritarian as it was. For instance, the young Adam was punished when caught reading the *Treatise of Human Nature* (1739–40) by David Hume, an exponent of a vague theism and who would later become one of Smith's best friends. Thus, Smith dropped the idea of embracing an ecclesiastical career and in 1746 returned to Kirkaldy, where he spent two years studying on his own and writing some essays on literary and philosophical subjects. From 1748 to 1751, Smith held public lectures in Edinburgh on rhetoric and English literature, with some success in terms of audience and finance. In 1751 Smith became a professor at Glasgow University, first holding the chair of logic (but his lessons were essentially on rhetoric, like his Edinburgh lectures) and subsequently the moral philosophy chair, involving lectures on natural theology, ethics, jurisprudence, politics and political economy.

From those years we have the notes on a course of lessons on rhetoric, taken by a student in 1762–1763 (Smith 1983), and the notes of two courses on 'jurisprudence' (taken in 1762–1763 and in 1763–1764: Smith 1978). Already, evidently, before becoming acquainted with the French physiocrats, the author had the main themes that would weave together into the *Wealth of Nations* clear in his mind. In the same period Smith wrote and published *The Theory of Moral Sentiments* (1759), which met with wide success.

Among the readers of the book was the stepfather to the young Duke of Buccleuch, who invited Smith to act as tutor to the young nobleman, accompanying him on a tour on the continent in exchange for a nice life annuity. Smith accepted and resigned from his chair at Glasgow. Scotland had at the time a fair cultural life, but the real centre of intellectual life was Paris. Smith met Voltaire in Geneva, and in Paris he met D'Alembert, Quesnay and many others.

Back in his native Kirkaldy, between 1767 and 1773 Smith dedicated himself to composition of the *Wealth of Nations*. In 1773 he moved to London to follow the printing of his book, which arrived in the bookshops on 9 March 1776, meeting with a warm reception.

In 1778, consulted on the American situation, Smith wrote a memorandum in which he argued the case for adopting a uniform system of taxation for Great Britain, Ireland and the American colonies, accompanied by the election of representatives of these latter populations to Parliament (on the basis of the principle commonly summarised in the motto 'no taxation without representation'). Furthermore, Smith foresaw the loss of the American colonies (with the exception of Canada) and the gradual shift of the economic and political barycentre from England to America.[1] In the same year of 1778 Smith was appointed commissioner of customs for Scotland; he thus moved to Edinburgh, where he remained until his death on 17 July 1790. Complying with his instructions, the executors of his will destroyed sixteen volumes of manuscripts.

5.2   Method

In one of the *Essays on Philosophical Subjects*, the *History of Astronomy*, Smith proposed a flexible methodology with modern characteristics. In his view, our attitude towards scientific theories is explained by three

---

[1] Smith had long been a friend of Benjamin Franklin (1706–1790), one of the protagonists of the independence of the United States. Like other intellectuals of the time, Smith declared opposition to the slave trade.

'sentiments': 'Wonder, Surprise and Admiration'. Wonder is excited by 'what is new and singular', surprise by 'what is unexpected', admiration by 'what is great or beautiful'. The task of philosophy is 'to introduce order into this chaos of jarring and discordant appearances', 'by representing the invisible chains which bind together all these disjointed objects'. In this way philosophy 'render[s] the theatre of nature a more coherent, and therefore a more magnificent spectacle'. In accomplishing this task, 'philosophical systems' are built (such as the two different cosmological views, Ptolemaic and Copernican) that are 'mere inventions of the imagination, to connect together the otherwise disjointed and discordant phaenomena of nature'.[2]

In other words, the intellectual ('philosopher') who considers the world and tries to interpret its functioning has an active role, *creating* rather than *discovering* the theories. With this thesis, Smith opposed the Galilean idea that the task of the scientist consists in *revealing* (in the literal etymological meaning of taking away the veils that cover them) the laws of nature that constitute the skeleton of the real world. In this way we may also interpret Smith's declared mistrust towards Petty's political arithmetic: it was not only a matter of doubting the statistical data that political arithmeticians constructed with a notable effort of the imagination, in a situation where statistics collection was rudimental, but rather a question of denying the idea of a mathematical structure of reality, which Hobbes and then Condillac's sensism had already extended to the human body and which Petty and the political arithmeticians extended to the 'political body', namely society.

The 'philosophical systems', though 'inventions of the imagination', may help us to get our bearings in the chaos of real events. However, it is not possible to verify the theories by demonstrating their correspondence to supposed natural laws, since such laws do not have a real existence independent of the theories themselves but are a creation of our thought. As Feyerabend and McCloskey propose in our times, Smith himself, in the *Lectures on Rhetoric* (1983, p. 178), proposed the method of rhetoric, with particular reference to the model of legal proceedings, as the way to select the propositions to be accepted and those to be rejected. This idea should be understood bearing in mind (with a connection, typical of Smith, between ethics and theory of knowledge) the notion of the impartial spectator, discussed in the next section, to whom we may assign the role of the arbiter, in this case not of what is just and what unjust but of what is (provisionally, not absolutely) true and false.

---

[2] Smith 1795, pp. 33, 45, 46, 105.

Smith thus adopted a flexible methodology. Moreover, abandonment of the idea of a mathematical structure intrinsic to reality corresponds to attributing men with a complex set of motivations – the passions and the interests discussed above – the balance of which was the object of the *Theory of Moral Sentiments*. These elements – diffidence towards the idea of laws of nature hard and fast in their objective reality and systematic openness to recognising the complexity of the motivations of human action – were characteristic of the Scottish Enlightenment, the cultural environment in which Smith had grown up.

5.3   The Moral Principle of Sympathy

The broad context of Smith's work was the debate on the different motivations for human action. His contribution consisted in pointing out the complementarity between pursuing self-interest and attributing a central role to moral rules for the sound functioning of common life in society. This interpretation of Smith's contribution, which conforms largely to that of the editors of the critical edition of his works,[3] emerges from reading Smith's two main works, *The theory of Moral Sentiments* and *The Wealth of Nations*, as complementary rather than contradictory.[4]

In *The Theory of Moral Sentiments* Smith proposed the 'moral principle of sympathy'. 'The chief part of human happiness arises from the consciousness of being beloved'; sympathy, namely the ability to share the feelings of others, leads us to judge our actions on the basis of their effects on the others in addition to their effects on ourselves.

[3] The six volumes of the 'Glasgow Edition of the Works and Correspondence of Adam Smith' (edited by D.D. Raphael and A.S. Skinner, Oxford University Press, Oxford 1976–83; paperback anastatic reprint, Liberty Press, Indianapolis, 1981–85) include *The Theory of Moral Sentiments*, edited by A.L. Macfie and D.D. Raphael; *The Wealth of Nations*, edited by R.H. Campbell and A.S. Skinner; *Essays on Philosophical Subjects*, edited by W.P.D. Wightman, *Lectures on Rhetoric and Belles Lettres*, edited by J.C. Bryce; *Lectures on Jurisprudence*, edited by R.L. Meek, D.D. Raphael and P.G. Stein; *Correspondence*, edited by E.C. Mossner and I.S. Ross.

[4] According to one thesis, there is a contradiction between the two works, the free pursuit of self-interest corresponding to the mature position of the *Wealth of Nations* superseding reference to a sympathetic behaviour initially defended in *The Theory of Moral Sentiments*. This thesis appears untenable when we recall that *The Theory of Moral Sentiments* was repeatedly reprinted, on all occasions under the control of the author, even after the publication of *The Wealth of Nations;* moreover, in Smith's correspondence there is no hint that he himself or any of his correspondents saw even the slightest contradiction between the two works. The 'contradiction' thesis appeared in the stage (late nineteenth century) in which a mono-dimensional notion of man prevailed, while in the eighteenth century the simultaneous presence of even conflicting passions and interests as the foundation for human action was considered a matter of fact.

Thus man 'must . . . humble the arrogance of his self-love, and bring it down to something which other men can go along with. . . . In the race for wealth, and honours, and preferments, he may run as hard as he can, . . . in order to outstrip all his competitors. But if he should justle, or throw down any of them, the indulgence of the spectators is entirely at an end. It is a violation of fair play, which they cannot admit of.' This kind of moral attitude is a prerequisite for the very survival of human societies: 'Society . . . cannot subsist among those who are at all times ready to hurt and injure one another.'[5]

In other words, Smith's liberal views are based on a twofold assumption, namely that commonly each person knows better than anybody else her/his own interests and that among the interests of each there is the desire to be loved by the others and hence respect for the well-being of the others. The first assumption accounts for rejection of centralised management of the economy, even if by an enlightened prince; hence the preference for a market economy over a command economy. The second assumption constitutes a precondition to ensure that the pursuit of self-interest on the part of a multitude of economic agents in competition among themselves leads to the well-being of society.

Moreover, according to Smith, individuals evaluate their own actions by taking the viewpoint of an impartial spectator, endowed with the knowledge of all the elements they know.[6] Juridical institutions, the functioning of which is indispensable to guarantee the security of market exchange, find in this principle of moral behaviour the necessary concrete support. Thus the famous Smithian statement, observing that 'it is not from the benevolence of the butcher, the brewer, or the baker, that we expect our dinner, but from their regard to their own interest',[7] implies the assumption – vital for the functioning of a market economy – of a society grounded on the general acceptance of the moral principle of sympathy and endowed with the administrative and juridical institutions necessary to deal with the instances in which common morality is violated.

The distinction between private and public interest becomes opposition only if the private interest is interpreted in a restrictive way,

---

[5] Smith 1759, pp. 41, 83, 86.

[6] On the notion of the impartial spectator, and more generally on Smith's moral philosophy, cf. Raphael 2007.

[7] Smith 1776, pp. 26–7. This passage, or variants of it, also occurs in the *Lectures on Jurisprudence* and in the *Early Draft of Parts of 'The Wealth of Nations'* (now reprinted in Smith 1978, pp. 562–81). Smith's reference to benevolence is an implicit reference to Hutcheson, who attributed it an important role as a guide to human action.

as selfishness rather than self-interest, the latter implying attention to one's own interests moderated by the recognition of (or, better, 'sympathy' for) the interests of the others.[8] Thus, following in the tradition of the Scottish sociological school, Smith evoked a view of man and society differing both from the arbitrary absolutism that the social and political structure of his times inherited from feudalism, and which can be associated with the Aristotelian tradition, and from Hobbes's contractualism, in which a state, though enlightened and benevolent, dominates the life of its subjects. Smith (1759, p. 82) proposed the line of a greater confidence in the self-governing capacity of individuals: 'Every man is, no doubt, by nature, first and principally recommended to his own care; and as he is fitter to take care of himself than of any other person, it is fit and right that it should be so.' However, the free pursuit of personal interest comes up against two limits: one external to the individual (the administration of justice, one of the fundamental functions that Smith attributes to the state) and one internal to him, 'sympathy' for his fellow human beings. The simultaneous recourse to these two elements shows how Smith, faithful in this to the Aristotelian tradition of hostility to extreme positions, had a positive but not idealised vision of man (common, for instance, to Kant as well).

5.4 *The Wealth of Nations*

An Inquiry into the Nature and Causes of the Wealth of Nations (Smith 1776) is subdivided into five books: division of labour (and thus technological progress) together with theory of value and income distribution; money and accumulation; a brief excursus in the history of institutions and the economy since the fall of the Roman empire; a critical illustration of mercantile doctrines and physiocratic tenets; public expenses and receipts and, more generally, the role of the state in the economy.

Smith identified the 'wealth of nations' with what today we call per capita income, or in substance the standard of living of the citizens of the country under consideration,[9] thus abandoning the views of cameralist

---

[8] Smith's view of self-interest, not reducible to a mono-dimensional maximising behaviour, is evident for instance in the following passage: 'What can be added to the happiness of the man who is in health, who is out of debt, and has a clear conscience? To one in this situation, all accessions of fortune may properly be said to be superfluous; and if he is much elevated on account of them, it must be the effect of the most frivolous levity' (Smith 1759, p. 45).

[9] As a matter of fact, Smith's view is broader in scope: in a civilised society material wealth, liberty, individual dignity and shared rules (laws and moral norms) all matter. A flourishing economy is important both in itself and as a prerequisite for the development

and mercantilist writers, counsellors to the prince in the previous decades, who focused on maximisation of the total national income of a country as source of economic power and hence of military and political power (a view that would see Switzerland less 'wealthy' than India).

National income (Y) is equal to the quantity of product obtained on average by each worker (or labour productivity, π) multiplied by the number of workers employed in production (L):

$$Y = \pi L$$

If we divide national income by population (N), we obtain per capita income; as a consequence, per capita income proves equal to labour productivity multiplied by the share of active workers over total population:

$$Y/N = \pi L/N$$

More specifically, the standard of living of the population depends on two factors: the share of citizens employed in productive labour and the productivity of their labour.

Here the division of labour comes into play. In fact, according to Smith, labour productivity depends mainly on the stage reached by the division of labour. In turn, this depends on the size of the markets. Smith (1776, pp. 14–15) illustrated the first thesis – the positive effect of the division of labour on productivity – with the well-known example of the pin factory, taken from the item *Épingle* in the *Encyclopédie* edited by d'Alembert and Diderot. Three circumstances connect productivity to the division of labour: the improvement in the skills of the worker when he regularly accomplishes a specific task rather than a multiplicity of tasks, the saving of labour time usually lost when shifting from one task to another and technical progress made easier by the possibility of focusing attention on one specific work task.

Let us now consider the connection between growth of the market and development of the division of labour. When a firm expands to improve its division of labour, it will have to place on the market a product that has increased in quantity because of both the increase in the number of workers employed and the increase in their productivity. In Smith's example of the pin factory, a worker who does everything by himself produces around ten pins a day, while a small factory with ten workers

of letters and arts and because of the civilising function attributed to commerce. Smith's notion of the wealth of nations also leaves room for recognition of distributive conflicts (as, two centuries earlier, did the notion of the 'common weal': cf. Anonymous 1581 and, for a comment, Roncaglia 2015. On the 'science of wealth' in Smith and previously, cf. also Aspromourgos 2009.

produces about 50,000 pins a day. Production as a whole has increased five thousandfold, as a result of a tenfold increase in the number of workers and a five hundredfold increase in their productivity. Thus the market must also grow five thousandfold, in order to absorb the production of the small factory, compared with the size of the market sufficient for a single worker producing pins. Clearly, the size of the market constitutes the main constraint on the development of the division of labour. Hence Smith's economic liberalism: whatever is an obstacle to commerce also constitutes an obstacle to the development of the division of labour and so to increases in productivity and the welfare of the citizens, or in other words to the wealth of nations.

There are three connected but distinct aspects of the division of labour: the microeconomic division of labour, among the different workers within the same plant; the social division, among different jobs and professions; and the macroeconomic division, among firms and sectors producing different commodities or groups of commodities. It is therefore necessary to consider both the social stratification typical of such an economic system and the relations that set in between the different productive sectors.

The political arithmeticians King and Davenant had illustrated the economic situation of England utilising a partition of the national economy into geographical areas: a choice we can understand for a time when commerce was greatly hindered by the difficulty of transportation. Subsequently, instead, the criterion gained ground of dividing society into social classes and productive sectors. In the wake of Cantillon and Quesnay, Smith considered a society divided into three classes. His tripartition – workers, capitalists, landlords (with the three corresponding kinds of income: wages, profits and rents) – is different from that of his predecessors (agricultural workers and farmers, artisans, nobility and clergy). The latter classification reflects a society in transition from feudalism to capitalism, while Smith's classification reflects a capitalist society (though nowadays landlords have lost practically all their importance, while the middle classes have expanded). Thus, in this respect, too, Smith marks the rise of the conceptual scheme that characterised subsequent economic science.

Because of the differences in bargaining power between capitalists and workers, the latter receive a wage just sufficient to maintain themselves and their families. The incomes of capitalists and landlords, namely profits and rents, are thus equal in their total to the surplus obtained within the economy.

The surplus – a notion that Smith took over from Petty, Cantillon and Quesnay – is equal to that part of the product that exceeds what is necessary to reconstitute the initial inventories of means of production and means of subsistence for the workers employed in the productive process. Period after period, firms utilise the initial inventories of means of production (and the workers utilise the initial inventories of means of subsistence) in the course of the productive process, at the end of which they obtain a product that is used first of all to reconstitute the initial inventories so as to be able to repeat the productive cycle; what is left after this, namely the surplus, may be utilised to increase the inventories of means of production and subsistence, increasing the number of workers employed in the productive process and hence the product, or for 'unproductive' consumption (luxury consumption and the subsistence consumption of the unemployed or of those whose work does not give concrete results, that is, does not give rise to commodities that can be sold in the market).

Accumulation, or in other words the productive utilisation of the surplus, consists not only in investment in new means of production but also in the use of part of the surplus as means of subsistence for additional productive workers.

Here the problem arises of the distinction between productive and unproductive workers. In this respect, Smith appears to oscillate between three different definitions of productive labour: (i) labour that gives rise to physical goods: labour in agriculture and manufacture, that is, but not in the services sector; (ii) labour that recoups the funds employed in production and in addition generates a profit; and (iii) labour the wage for which is drawn from capital. On the other hand, when the wage is drawn from the income of the master, as in the case of servants, it is a matter of unproductive labour.[10]

These are not necessarily three alternative definitions. The last is useful for illustrative purposes, since it helps the reader to understand Smith's reasoning, but as a theory it would imply a logical vicious circle. The second and the first definition may coincide, if we assume that agriculture and manufacture correspond to the field of action of capitalistic enterprises. We may thus credit Smith with an able compromise between the tradition that identified productive labour with the production of durable goods (along a scale topped by precious metals and foreign trade, the latter being the means to obtain them) and the subsequent view, which will become dominant in Karl Marx's work, according to which productive labour is what comes within the capitalistic area of the economy.

---

[10] For the three definitions, cf. Smith 1776, respectively, pp. 330–1, 332, 332–3.

As for the theme of productive labour, again on the issue of the origin of the surplus Smith went beyond the traditional view of a hierarchy of productive sectors. In particular, he criticised the physiocratic idea that agriculture alone is capable of generating a surplus. The share of productive workers in the total population, L/N, depends on the stage reached by the process of accumulation, namely on the amount of means of production available to give work to new productive workers, on institutional elements and on customs, such as laws on primary public education for all or on child labour, or customs concerning women's attitudes towards working in a factory. In turn, such institutional factors and customs are influenced by the political choices of the public authorities.

The adoption of policies aiming at eliminating the obstacles to free trade and at favouring the expansion of the markets may set in motion a 'virtuous spiral': the expansion of the markets favours an increasing division of labour and with it an increase in productivity that in turn gives rise to an increase in per capita income and, consequently, a further expansion of the markets. These dynamic mechanisms, of a cumulative kind, constitute the essence of the Smithian theory of the wealth of nations.

5.5 Value and Prices

The distinction between value in use and value in exchange is perfectly clear in Adam Smith (1776, p. 82):

The word *value* ... has two different meanings, and sometimes expresses the utility of some particular object, and sometimes the power of purchasing other goods which the possession of that object conveys. The one may be called 'value in use'; the other, 'value in exchange'. The things which have the greatest value in use have frequently little or no value in exchange ... Nothing is more useful than water: but it will purchase scarce any thing; scarce any thing can be had in exchange for it. A diamond, on the contrary, has scarce any value in use; but a very great quantity of other goods may frequently be had in exchange for it.

Value in use is thus a prerequisite of value in exchange: a good that has no use, and which is not desired by anybody, cannot have a positive value in exchange. But once this condition is satisfied, the value in exchange of any commodity is determined on the basis of elements different from value in use: it depends on the conditions of reproduction of the economic system, not on the utility of the commodity under consideration. More precisely, the Classical economists do not consider the value in use of a commodity as a measurable quantity. At most, like Smith in the passage quoted above, we may speak of a greater or lesser value in use, but in a rather generic way that does not entail a complete ordering of the preferences of economic agents, and Smith explicitly rejected the idea that it is possible to explain the value in exchange of two commodities on the basis of their greater or lesser value in use.

When they referred to the value of a commodity, the Classical economists commonly meant value in exchange. However, the problem of value may assume different features, according to whether: (i) the aim is to go back to the first principle – the 'source' – of value; (ii) the focus is on the standard of value for inter-temporal comparisons or comparisons involving different countries; and (iii) the theoretical problem of determining exchange values is tackled.

Whatever specific problem came under consideration, economists initially focused on labour. Theories of labour-value were already common among the natural law philosophers; labour reappeared, side by side with land, among the elements that constitute the content in value of a commodity in the theories of Petty and Cantillon. However, labour-value theories assumed different meanings in the different authors. Natural law philosophers conceived labour-values as an index of the sacrifice made by people to obtain the desired commodity; Petty and Cantillon were nearer to a theory of physical production costs, devoid of the metaphysical features that characterise the idea of labour as sacrifice: labour-values are essentially no more than a simplified way of expressing the relative difficulty of production of the commodity under consideration in relation to that of other commodities.

In Smith both features were present; furthermore, the labour-value theory was proposed both as a theory of necessary labour (labour required for the production of the commodity: labour contained, in Marx's terminology) and as a theory of labour commanded. Let us consider this latter first:

Every man is rich or poor according to the degree in which he can afford to enjoy the necessaries, conveniences, and amusements of human life. But after the division of labour has once thoroughly taken place, it is but a very small part of these with which a man's own labour can supply him. The far greater part of them he must derive from the labour of other people, and he must be rich or poor according to the quantity of that labour which he can command, or which he can afford to purchase. The value of any commodity, therefore, to the person who possesses it, and who means not to use or consume it himself, but to exchange it for other commodities, is equal to the quantity of labour which it enables him to purchase or command. Labour, therefore, is the real measure of the exchangeable value of all commodities. (Smith 1776, p. 47)

In the passage quoted previously Smith did not intend to point out the factors that determine exchange values but simply to indicate the standard with which to measure them, and among other things he justified this choice by referring more generally to the central role of labour in the economy. Labour commanded, moreover, constitutes a standard particularly suited to comparison between different countries or different times within the same country and is thus appropriate for a dynamic theory of the wealth of nations like that proposed by Smith. It is also an appropriate measure for a society based on the division of labour, since exchange between the products of different sectors is in substance an exchange that connects the workers of the different sectors, bringing them together in a single society, within which each person depends on the labour of the others.

However, the problem of value in its usual sense remains open, namely that of identifying the factors that determine the value in exchange of the different commodities. We may obtain the quantity of labour commanded by a given commodity by dividing its price by the wage rate, although this clearly presupposes knowledge of both price and wage rate.

A solution to the value problem may be provided by the necessary labour theory, according to which the exchange ratios between two commodities are proportional to the quantities of labour necessary to produce them. Smith, however, considered this theory valid only in 'that early and rude state of society which precedes both the accumulation of stock and the appropriation of land'.[11] According to him, we can no longer utilise necessary labour to explain exchange values when we refer to a society in which workers are no longer the owners of the capital goods and land that they use in their work. In fact, necessary labour takes no account of the rents and profits that enter into the price of every commodity when capitalists and landlords constitute social classes distinct from the working class. In such a society, exchange values correspond to the 'natural prices', which Smith defined distinguishing them from 'market prices': 'When the price of any commodity is neither more nor less than what is sufficient to pay the rent of the land, the wages of the labour, and the profits of the stock employed in raising, preparing, and bringing it to market, according to their natural rates, the commodity is then sold for what may be called its natural price ...

---

[11] Smith 1776, p. 65. Smith did not refer to any real primitive society but to an ideal model of society in which economic agents (hunters and fishers) adopt the rational behaviour typical of a mercantile society, while the primitive character is given by the abstract hypothesis of absence of division into the social classes of workers, capitalists and landlords.

The actual price at which any commodity is commonly sold is called its market price.'[12] In other words, the market price is the price we see looking at the actual acts of exchange; the natural price, instead, is the theoretical price that expresses the conditions of reproduction of the productive process. In a society divided into social classes, the exchange values or 'natural prices' must cover production costs and guarantee, in addition, a return equal to that obtainable in other sectors for the capital invested in the productive activity.

Reference to costs of production is in itself insufficient to build a theory of prices, since it would imply circular logical reasoning: if we need steel in order to produce coal and coal in order to produce steel, we cannot determine the price of coal if we do not already know it. For this reason some economists, before and after Smith, had recourse to a first principle such as necessary labour (or labour-and-land, as in the case of Petty and Cantillon), which enabled them to explain prices without their having to be explained in turn. However, as we have seen, Smith did not agree, since he considered necessary labour as an explanatory principle acceptable only for an 'early and rude society'.

Exchange values remain an open issue in Smith's analysis. An attempt at solving it is seen by some exegetists in what has been called the 'adding-up-of-components-theory': namely, the idea that 'the price of every commodity finally resolves itself into some one or other, or all of those three parts', 'rent, labour, and profit' (Smith 1776, p. 68). In other words, the price of a commodity corresponds to wages, profits and rents plus the costs borne for the means of production other than labour and land; such costs are in turn decomposed into wages, profits, rents and costs for the means of production; we thus proceed backwards until the costs for the means of production have disappeared or become insignificant. The theory re-proposes a national accounting principle at the level of an individual commodity: the value of the national product corresponds to the value of national income, or in other words to the sum of the incomes of the different social classes, as Smith himself (1776, p. 69) stressed. However, it ignores the difficulties that arise at the level of the individual commodity because of the necessity to assume that the three distributive variables are independent the one from the other and of the fact that the residual of means of production cannot in general be reduced to zero. Thus it came under criticism from Ricardo, on account of its implicit idea that an increase in the wage rate causes an increase in the price while leaving unchanged the rate of profits. We can say, in conclusion, that Smith did not provide a fully adequate theory of exchange values; only

[12] Ibid., p. 72.

with Ricardo did the theory of value, in its modern meaning of theory of relative prices, come to centre stage.

5.6 Natural Prices and Market Prices

According to Smith, the market economy functions in a fairly satisfactory way: for each commodity, the flow of production coming out of the firms more or less corresponds to the flow of the demand coming from the buyers even if exchanges take place freely and the decisions on quantities to be produced, sold and acquired and on exchanges and prices are decentralised. It is the market that links up the productive units operating in the different sectors of the economy, in two distinct ways: through market exchanges each productive unit obtains from the others what it needs to continue its activity in exchange for its own product; through competition, a co-ordination of the myriad of decentralized decision centres is realized.

Smith considered two kinds of competition. The first is internal to the market for each commodity: each buyer seeks among the sellers the one that sells the desired commodity at the lowest possible price; the seller who asks too high a price risks being left with unsold merchandise. Similarly, each seller seeks among the buyers the one that is ready to pay the highest price; the buyers offering too low a price risk being left empty handed. Under ideal conditions, when competition among the sellers and among the buyers does not meet with obstacles, the price of each commodity is one and the same for all the buyers and all the sellers: the so-called 'law of one price'. The second kind of competition concerns the capitalists in search of the employment that offers the highest returns on their capital. When capitalists are free to move their capital from one sector to another in search of the most fruitful employment, it is not possible for a sector to offer capitalists a return higher than that obtainable in other sectors, since otherwise new capital would flow into it, with the consequence that production would increase, the market price would diminish, and with it also profits and the rate of return. In the same way, it is not possible for a sector to offer capitalists a return lower than that obtainable in other sectors, since otherwise there would be an outflow of capital from that sector, causing a fall in production, with an ensuing rise in the market price and hence in profits and in the sector's rate of return. Therefore, under free competition the return on capital – the rate of profits – tends to be equal in all sectors. In this way the 'competition of capitals' links up in a single capitalistic market the different sectors of the economy.

These two kinds of competition underlie the market adjustment mechanism based on the relationship between market and natural prices: when production of a commodity is in excess of the 'effectual' demand (i.e. the quantity that buyers are prepared to absorb at the natural price), then competition between sellers will drive the market price below the natural price: the producers will be unable to obtain the 'natural' profits, and an outflow of capitals from that sector will take place; production will decrease, and the excess supply will thus be absorbed.

It was in connection with this adjustment mechanism that Smith (1776, pp. 75, 77) used the famous 'gravitation' analogy:

> The natural price, therefore, is, as it were, the central price, to which the prices of all commodities are continually gravitating ... But though the market price of every particular commodity is in this manner continually gravitating, if one may say so, towards the natural price, yet sometimes particular accidents, sometimes natural causes, and sometimes particular regulations of police, may, in many commodities, keep up the market price, for a long time together, a good deal above the natural price.

Many authors interpreted the metaphor of gravitation as if it implied a theory of market price based on supply and demand. This idea is in fact totally alien to Smith's thinking: both because the market price, as we have seen, is not a theoretical variable for him but an empirical correlate and because the reference to gravitation itself, which seems to imply a precise theoretical structure, that of Newton's theory (in which the behaviour of the body that gravitates around another one is described by precise mathematical laws) is in fact quite vague, as testified among other things by the fact that in each of the two sentences in which the term 'gravitation' appears, it is accompanied by expressions ('as it were', 'if one may say so') that point to its use as an imprecise metaphor. In Smith's times, the terms 'demand' and 'supply' did not indicate stable and well-identified functional relations connecting price and quantity of a commodity but a set of fortuitous or contingent elements that cannot be reduced solely to technological (economies and diseconomies of scale) or psychological factors (consumers' preferences).

Smith only suggested that the market price will be above the natural price when for any reason supply proves lower than the 'effectual' demand and below it when the opposite holds true; moreover, deviation of the market from the natural price will provoke reactions on the part of buyers and producers that favour resolution of the disequilibrium situation. The concrete action of these general rules depends on circumstances, and it is not therefore possible to formulate precise reaction functions for the market prices to the disequilibria between demand and supply and of these two latter variables to the prices.

Thus, for Smith gravitation is no more than a metaphor used to evoke the role of competition as a force making for the stabilisation of the market. This is also the role of the 'invisible hand' metaphor, which, moreover, Smith uses only once in *The Wealth of Nations* and in a specific context (the capitalists' preference for investing in the most profitable sectors of the national industry rather than in foreign countries, although motivated by personal interest, has a positive effect for society since it tends to increase the national income, as 'led by an invisible hand').[13]

5.7   The Origin of the Division of Labour: Smith and Pownall

The origin of the division of labour was viewed differently by Smith, who attributed it to the human propensity for social life, and by Pownall,[14] who pointed instead to innate differences in capabilities. The two theses have profoundly different implications on issues such as the social contract theory, the view of social stratification as a fact of nature and indeed the positive or negative evaluation of labour itself. According to Smith (1776, p. 25),

This division of labour, from which so many advantages are derived, is not originally the effect of any human wisdom, which foresees and intends that general opulence to which it gives occasion. It is the necessary, though very slow and gradual consequence of a certain propensity in human nature ... to truck, barter, and exchange one thing for another. ... It is common to all men, and to be found in no other race of animals, which seem to know neither this nor any other species of contracts.

---

[13] Cf. Smith 1776, p. 456. The term 'invisible hand' is used only twice elsewhere by Smith, in different works and contexts (the *History of Astronomy*, III.2: Smith 1795, p. 49; and *The Theory of Moral Sentiments*, IV.1.10: Smith 1759, p. 184) and, moreover, at least on the first of these occasions, in ironical tones. The theme of the 'invisible hand' began to be propounded only after the development of the axiomatic general economic equilibrium theory and the two 'fundamental theorems' of welfare economics according to which perfect competition ensures an optimal equilibrium and any optimal equilibrium may be interpreted as the outcome of a perfectly competitive market. Attributing to Smith the idea of the market as an invisible hand that leads to optimal equilibria is instrumental to interpreting modern theory as crowning the Smithian cultural design. In reality, however, the two views are quite different. Cf. Roncaglia 2005b.

[14] Thomas Pownall (1722–1805) had been governor of Massachusetts in 1757–1759; from 1767 to 1780 he was a member of Parliament.

Smith's thesis, then, was that division of labour originates in the tendency of men to enter into relations of reciprocal exchange, or in other words – we might say – to human sociability. To this characteristic Smith also attributed the origin of language; moreover, it distinguishes men from animals. According to Pownall (1776, pp. 338–9), instead, the division of labour originates in the desire to exploit the innate differences of labour abilities of the different individuals:

> Before a man can have the propensity to barter, he must have acquired somewhat, which he does not want himself, and must feel, that there is something which he does want, that another person has in his way acquired . . . . Nature has so formed us, as that the labour of each must take one special direction, in preference to, and to the exclusion of some other equally necessary line of labour . . . This limitation, however, of [man's] capacities, and the extent of his wants, necessarily creates to each man an accumulation of some articles of supply, and a defect of others, and is the original principle of his nature, which creates, by a reciprocation of wants, the necessity of an intercommunion of mutual supplies; this is the forming cause, not only of the division of labour, but the efficient cause of that community, which is the basis and origin of civil government.

Pownall's position rests on two assumptions that appear extraneous to Smith's views. The first is that each individual knows his own abilities, what he wants and what the others can offer before getting in touch with them; such knowledge should be innate in order to constitute the origin of the division of labour and of exchanges. The second assumption is that there be original differences in abilities among the different individuals that, apart from constituting the spring that determines the division of labour, also constitute a 'natural' precondition of society's economic stratification.[15] As far as the first aspect is concerned, the view of the individual as a logical *prius* with respect to society is opposed to the Smithian idea, typical of the tradition of the Scottish Enlightenment, of the individual as an intrinsically social being. As for the second aspect, namely the existence of a natural basis for economic and social differentiations, it is explicitly rejected by Smith. In fact, he affirms that he considers the different

---

[15] The doctrine of the intrinsic differences of abilities was already present (and dominant) in the Greek tradition and then in the Scholastic period; around the middle of the eighteenth century, it was taken up, in the framework of a subjective theory of value, by Galiani (1751, p. 49): 'By providence men are born to various crafts, but in unequal proportions of rarity, corresponding with wonderous sagacity to human needs.' This passage also indicates a crucial difficulty of the traditional view: if we admit that the distribution of abilities among the individuals is innate, only the 'invisible hand' of Providence can guarantee that the availability of abilities corresponds to the requirements of society.

working abilities as mostly acquired as a consequence of the division of labour:

The difference of natural talents in different men is, in reality, much less than we are aware of; and the very different genius which appears to distinguish men of different professions, when grown up to maturity, is not upon many occasions so much the cause, as the effect of the division of labour. The difference between the most dissimilar characters, between a philosopher and a common street porter, for example, seems to arise not so much from nature, as from habit, custom, and education. (Smith 1776, pp. 28–29)

The contrast between the democratic content of the Smithian thesis and the conservative element in Pownall's thesis is worth stressing, both because it may help us in understanding the innovative and progressive nature of Smith's social philosophy and because the contrast between the two views repeatedly recurs in the course of time.

5.8 Economic and Political Liberalism: Smith's Fortunes

To say that Smith was the founder of the economic science would be wrong: before him there were authors such as Petty, Cantillon, Quesnay and many others. Perhaps, in comparison with previous authors, Smith's distinctive characteristic was that of being an academician, dedicating great care to precise definition and accurate presentation of his ideas, mediating between different views and theses while capturing the positive elements in each of them. This Smithian subtlety, the rejection of clear-cut theses without qualifications and specifications, is evident in some controversies over interpretation of his writings.

The first example concerns Smith's liberalism. Smith's was a progressive attitude to the major political themes of his time, such as the conflict over the independence of the American colonies. In pre- and post-revolutionary France *The Wealth of Nations* was viewed with favour by the progressive elements of the time, while Smith was seen as a dangerous subversive by the conservative intellectuals. All these thinkers, favourable or adverse to Smith's views, saw no difference in his thought between liberalism in the political field and economic liberalism, between the defence of political freedom and the defence of free trade.

The situation changed in the years immediately following, with a sharp negative reaction to the excesses of the French revolution (the Terror), which initially implied a growing diffidence towards Smithian liberalism. Thus in 1794 Smith's first biographer, Dugald Stewart (1753–1828), reinterpreted Smith's thought with the aim of making it more acceptable. To this end, he distinguished between economic and political liberalism. The latter, a politically progressive thesis bringing to the fore the need to fight concentrations of power of any kind, was transformed into economic liberalism, namely a conservative thesis – to leave maximum freedom of action to capitalists – which in the stage of industrialisation went so far as to serve to justify indifference on the part of the entrepreneurial class towards the heavy human costs of the new productive technologies and widespread indigence. This was a far cry from the sensitivity repeatedly shown by the Scottish economist for human sufferings, and from Smith's interest in the continuous improvement of living standards for the great mass of the population.

Another interpretative issue stems from the apparently contradictory position taken by Smith towards the division of labour. In the first book, the division of labour was extolled as the foundation for increases in productivity, hence for the well-being of population and for civic progress itself; in the fifth book, in an often quoted passage referred to as the precursor of the Marxian theory of alienation, Smith stressed the negative characteristics of fragmented labour, which can make a brute of man.[16] However, the contradiction is only apparent: the division of labour has both positive and negative effects, and Smith considered as dominant the positive effects. Thus, far from raising doubts about the expediency of pursuing continuous intensification of the division of labour, he advocated recourse to elementary education as a counter-weight.

There is in this respect an aspect that should be stressed, since it may well constitute the main point of difference between Smith's social philosophy and that of Marx. Both are fully conscious of the negative implications of the division of labour and of the need for work (or 'compulsory labour') that accompanies them. Marx, however, held

---

[16] In the progress of the division of labour, the employment of the far greater part of those who live by labour, that is, of the great body of the people, comes to be confined to a few very simple operations; frequently to one or two. But the understandings of the greater part of men are necessarily formed by their ordinary employments. The man whose whole life is spent in performing a few simple operations, of which the effects too are, perhaps, always the same, or very nearly the same, has no occasion to exert his understanding, or to exercise his invention in finding out expedients for removing difficulties which never occur. He naturally loses, therefore, the habit of such exertion, and generally becomes as stupid and ignorant as it is possible for a human creature to become. The torpor of his mind renders him, not only incapable of relishing or bearing a part in any rational conversation, but of conceiving any generous, noble, or tender sentiment, and consequently of forming any just judgement concerning many even of the ordinary duties of private life. Of the great and extensive interests of his country, he is altogether incapable of judging. (Smith 1776, pp. 781–2)

that the need for compulsory labour can be overcome in a communist society; the possibility of reaching full freedom from compulsory labour morally justifies, and renders politically acceptable, the costs in blood and tears of the proletarian revolution and of the subsequent dictatorship of the proletariat, as necessary stages (together with capitalistic accumulation) for development of productive forces, which constitutes the indispensable premise to achieve the final objective. Smith, on the contrary, considered overcoming the division of labour clearly impossible. Increases in productivity and growing economic welfare made possible by the intensification of the division of labour are the precondition for progress in human societies. This is, however, conceived as a continuous process, without any evident prospect of a 'way out' of the arrangement of market economies or a way to overcome their limits and defects, such as compulsory labour and the inequalities of social conditions. Progress in human societies is possible, but the perfect society remains a utopia.

6 Economic Science at the Time of the French Revolution

6.1 The Perfectibility of Human Societies: Between Utopias and Reforms

The English 'Glorious Revolution' of 1688 took place with practically no bloodshed and, albeit marking a radical change in the political order, producing no drastic break in continuity for the English institutions. On the contrary, the French Revolution of 1789, and especially the radicalisation it subsequently went through, once again, and in dramatic terms, found social scientists faced with two crucial issues. First, can a change in institutions lead to a better society? Second, if the change has a cost in terms of violence and bloodshed, do the advantages that may be reaped justify these costs?

In the eighteenth century the tradition of the Enlightenment gave a more or less positive answer to the first question: intervention guided by reason may favour social progress, which in any case remains the direction human history tends to move in. The second question, on the other hand, was commonly left aside.

We also have different answers to the first question: the conservatives held endeavours to foster social progress futile, opposing the revolutionaries, who held radical change a necessity, also for the political institutions, often referring to Utopian models of ideal societies, frequently characterised by forms of collectivism extending not only to control over means of production but also and above all to the customs of everyday life. As a literary genre Utopian writings had been circulating since the late sixteenth century, side by side with another stream of writings providing accounts of travels in faraway lands, often invented and in fact very often romanticised, in any case illustrating forms of social organization strikingly different from the European ones. The rationalistic spirit of the Enlightenment encouraged intellectuals to consider human intelligence able to design institutional systems surpassing those inherited from history; some went so far as to assert the right and indeed the duty to impose their implementation in the face of resistance by conservative rulers or ignorant masses.

The tradition of the Scottish sociological Enlightenment was also favourable to institutional changes: for instance, we may recall Smith's fight against the remnants of feudalism. However, this was not a matter of a priori designs for ideal institutions but rather indications on possible improvements to the existing institutions. Trust in reason is, moreover, tempered by two elements: the liberal idea, maintained by Smith in *The Theory of Moral Sentiments*, that each is the best judge of his own interests; and a non-idyllic, although basically optimistic, vision of human nature, open to a certain amount of scepticism extending to the true abilities and motivations of rulers. In turn, this implied diffidence, if not hostility, towards projects for revolutionary change inspired by theoretical models of ideal societies. This position was substantially shared by the exponents of Neapolitan Enlightenment, such as Galiani and Genovesi, as also by the Tuscan intellectuals, mainly concerned with agrarian reforms, and a Milanese circle including Verri and Beccaria, and some exponents of the French Enlightenment, such as Voltaire, Turgot or the marquis of Condorcet (1743–1794).

It is in fact in pre-Revolutionary France that we have an interesting example of confrontation between reformist and conservative theses in the clash that saw Necker versus Turgot and subsequently Condorcet versus Necker.

Turgot, the Minister of Finance from 1774 to 1776, tried to implement reforms aiming at abolishing feudal constraints (restrictions on free trade in agricultural produce, corporatist regulations on labour and productive processes) and improving social policies for the poor. Jacques Necker (1732–1804), a banker, political opponent of Turgot and the last Minister of Finance before the Revolution, by contrast, considered the indigence of the poor as a fact of nature resulting from the tendency of population growth to exceed the growth of production of means of subsistence.

Reacting to theses such as Necker's, Condorcet (who belonged to the circle of the Encyclopaedists and a mathematician renowned for his foundational studies on probability theory applied to social sciences) maintained that the problems of contemporary society stemmed not from the forces of nature but from human institutions: therefore, measures of institutional reform might influence economic and civil progress. Like Smith, Condorcet supported public interventions in favour of universal education; he also advocated schemes for collective insurance against accidents and to guarantee an income to the old. More generally, like Smith, he maintained that political liberty and social integration of the poor favoured economic development. Condorcet was among those progressive intellectuals who played leading roles in the early phases of the French Revolution only to fall prey to the Terror, whose exponents saw moderate reformism as an enemy possibly even worse than conservatism itself.

As a reaction to the radicalisation of the French Revolution, there was also radicalisation in the opposition to change. The reformist currents, squeezed between the extremism of revolutionary Terror and the conservative reaction, lost ground, to recover some of it only half a century later, with the cooperative movement in England and with John Stuart Mill, but once again to find themselves hemmed in between revolutionary radicalism (Marx and perhaps more importantly the Paris Commune) and conservative reaction.

6.2   Malthus and the Population Principle

In Great Britain, too, the sympathetic response that various intellectuals had shown to the storming of the Bastille gave way to conservative reaction against the Terror. Among the few who retained a position favourable to the Revolution we find William Godwin (1756–1836), author of a widely read *Enquiry Concerning Political Justice* (1793) and advocate of small-scale production and social decentralisation, together with a drastic redistribution of income in favour of the neediest strata of the population. Like Condorcet, Godwin was a strenuous upholder of the perfectibility of human beings: an end to be pursued by abolishing or modifying those institutions, both political and social, that obstructed economic development and the development of human reason alike.

Thomas Robert Malthus (1766–1834) took an entirely different view. A student at Cambridge, on graduating he was appointed a minister of the Anglican Church. He married in 1804 and had three children. In 1805 he became professor of history and political economy at the East India College; his teaching was based on Smith's *Wealth of Nations*.

His most famous work is the *Essay on Population* (1798), born out of discussions with his father, who was a follower of Godwin. The *Essay*, in fact, constituted the conservative answer to Godwin's views. The first edition was a lively, provocative political pamphlet; in subsequent editions it gradually swelled into a heavy, erudite volume, stuffed with empirical references and qualifications to the central thesis but somewhat indigestible. The *Essay* had a wide readership and a strong influence, stimulating lively, prolonged debate.

Malthus's thesis is often summed up in a famous formula: agricultural production tends to grow in arithmetical proportion, while population tends to grow in geometrical proportion and, more precisely, to double every twenty-five years. Actually, the point – illustrated by Malthus in various numerical examples – was not essential to the principle of population that consisted, quite simply, in the idea that population growth is necessarily limited by the availability of means of subsistence. As soon as these become available in excess of the strictly necessary, the population tends to grow more rapidly than agricultural production. This causes an increase in agricultural prices and a worsening of the living conditions of the poorest classes, thus forcing down the growth rate of the population as the mortality rate rises and the birth rate falls, both effects being determined by ever more widespread poverty and hardship.[1]

Alongside this automatic mechanism, Malthus pointed out two other possible routes to preserve equilibrium between population and means of subsistence: the path of 'virtue', namely chastity in celibacy and continence within marriage, or the path of 'vice', namely contraception. The latter solution was to be upheld by the so-called neo-Malthusians but had already been addressed approvingly before Malthus by authors such as Bentham or Condorcet.

Malthus's thesis was not new. We have already seen that it had emerged in France in the debate between Turgot and Necker, but as early as the sixteenth century an Italian, Giovanni Botero (1544–1617), contrasting *virtus generativa* with *virtus nutritiva*, had stressed the tension between the potential of population growth and the difficulties in increasing production of means of subsistence to keep up with it. Another Italian, Gianmaria Ortes (1713–1790), in the *Riflessioni sulla popolazione* (*Thoughts on Population*, 1790), had stressed the potentiality of population to grow in geometrical progression.

However, Malthus's pamphlet had a stronger impact, focussing attention not simply on the relation between growth of population and growth of the means of subsistence but also on the political implications (a change in institutions was useless) and the implications for the distribution of income. A number of economists of the time, including David Ricardo, referred to the Malthusian principle of population in support of the so-called iron law of wages, according to which the wage rate tends to oscillate around the subsistence level.[2]

---

[1] Charles Darwin (1809–1882) recalled the Malthusian thesis as a source of inspiration for his theory of evolution based on natural selection.

[2] The subsistence level was not to be interpreted in merely biological terms but in the social sense, as that level that allowed workers not only to survive within the country, hence excluding emigration, but also to form a family and raise children.

To sum up the argument in a few words, let us assume that the wage of the great mass of workers is above mere subsistence level. The population begins to grow, and agricultural production is unable to keep up; food prices consequently rise, and the real wage declines, returning to the subsistence minimum. If, on the contrary, we start from a wage rate lower than the subsistence level, then the population decreases (due to a rising mortality rate and falling birth rate but also due to increasing emigration); hence the demand for wage goods diminishes, their prices fall, and the real wage increases.

As we saw previously, Smith also held that there was a tendency to subsistence wages but attributed it to the different bargaining power of workers and capitalists. Smith's thesis appears more solid than the one based on the population principle. Suffice it to recall that, if the increase in population due to a wage rate above subsistence level is associated with an increase in the birth rate or decrease in the rate of infant mortality, then the downward pressure on wages can only be felt on the labour market after a lag of fourteen to sixteen years, necessary for a newborn baby to join the labour force. Moreover, the Malthusian population principle presupposes absence of technological progress in the primary sector; in actual fact, as historical experience shows, a decreasing share of population (from more than 70 per cent to less than 4 per cent in contemporary OECD countries) has succeeded in producing food more than sufficient for a growing population.

The main aim of Malthus's *Essay* was, however, to assert the uselessness of any attempt at improving the situation of the great mass of the workers. Even if these attempts were successful in the short run, Malthus said, improvement in the standard of living would nevertheless immediately be followed by a faster rate of population increase, which brings wages back to simple subsistence level. Hopes for improvement should not rely on institutional changes or social policies in favour of the poor: such hopes can only rely on preventive checks on population growth that the workers will only exercise with the spectre of poverty hanging over them, also acting as a stimulus to industriousness. Therefore all measures designed to eliminate indigence were useless; indeed, they were counterproductive.[3]

On the contrary, according to Smith, Condorcet, Godwin and the whole of the reformist tradition, it is the hope to improve one's conditions, and not the fear of poverty, that stimulates industriousness. Godwin, in his essay *On Population* (1820), maintained that preventive

---

[3] Malthus nevertheless supported free basic education and free medical support for the poor.

checks on population increase are prompted by improvement in the standards of living of the workers, not the spectre of poverty.

However, it was Malthus's theses that eventually dominated the field; their pessimism on the prospects of social progress led the public opinion of the time to identify political economy as the 'dismal science':[4] a construction of abstract theories that led to defeatism cloaked in scientific rigour. In a sense, political economy would represent the pessimism of science as opposed to the optimism of the will; however, it was a pessimism that, when confronted with the facts, proved substantially misleading, since it underrated the potentialities opening up with technological progress. There was thus a negative reaction against the cold abstract logic and pessimism of economic science, perceived to be based on unreal assumptions. Thus the whole of Classical political economy, and in particular Ricardo and his followers, met with growing diffidence on the part of public opinion, despite the fact that the Malthusian population principle was not an essential component of their analytic structure.

6.3   Say's Law

A few years after Malthus's *Essay*, the French economist Jean-Baptiste Say (1767–1832) enunciated what came to be known as 'Say's law'. In its simplest formulation, it said that 'supply creates its own demand'; it was then utilised by many Classical economists, with subtle but often substantive differences; in a strong version (as an *ex ante* identity between aggregate demand and supply), it became a distinctive characteristic commonly attributed to the 'Ricardian school'.

Originally, in his *Traité d'économie politique* of 1803,[5] Say propounded it in criticism of certain aspects of the physiocratic doctrine utilised by various economists of the time to oppose the central role Smith attributed to savings and accumulation as the foundation for growth of the wealth of nations and to refute his criticism of 'unproductive' consumption. Let us recall in this respect that Cantillon and the physiocrats had the landlords and nobility playing an active role in setting the circulation process into

---

[4] The expression was due to Thomas Carlyle (1795–1881), in an essay of 1849, *The Nigger Question* (in Carlyle 1888–89, vol. 7, p. 84.

[5] It was a successful book, also utilised as a university textbook in the USA and Britain (as well as France, where Say became the first professor of political economy in 1815). It included among other things a theory of value based on utility and, in opposition to Smith, the identification of productive labour with labour generating utility; this means that labour that produces services is also productive, and not only labour that produces commodities.

motion: at the end of the productive process they are in possession of the money and utilise it to acquire commodities from the 'sterile' and the 'productive' classes. However, if the landlords and nobility decide not to spend part of their income, and if for any reason their demand fails, the possibility arises of a situation of 'general over-production' or want of market outlets. Given the active role that it plays in the circulation process, the spending of the landlords and nobility regulates the rate of exchanges and the level of production.

In its original version, however, 'Say's law' was less clear-cut, the main aim being to reassert two theses already present in Smith: first, the possibility for technological progress to give rise to a long period development of production, with improvement in the living standards of the population accompanied by a parallel growth in demand; second, the idea that growth is favoured by savings (and by investments, which savings automatically turn into) more than by unproductive consumption. In upholding these two theses, which were the true objects of the current debate, Say (and subsequently James Mill)[6] also developed other arguments, such as the thesis that money is not in demand per se but only as a means to acquire goods, with the consequence that aggregate supply would necessarily equal aggregate demand and that no general over-production crisis would be possible. The latter thesis was later christened 'Say's identity' by historians of economic thought to distinguish it from what came to be known as 'Say's equality', according to which short period disequilibria between overall supply and demand for goods may exist but equilibrating mechanisms soon overcome them.[7]

---

[6] James Mill (1773–1836), father of John Stuart, follower and friend of Bentham, friend of Ricardo whom he helped in the writing of the *Principles*, was for years manager of the East India Company; he also authored a Ricardian textbook, *Elements of Political Economy* (1821).

[7] Baumol (1977, pp. 147–54) distinguishes different theses, for each of which it is possible to find some reference in Say's writings: 1. 'A commodity's purchasing *power* (effective demand) is limited by and is equal to its output, because production provides *the means* by which output can be purchased'; 2. 'Expenditure increases when output rises'; 3. 'A given investment expenditure is a far more effective stimulant to the wealth of an economy than an equal amount of consumption'; 4. 'Over the centuries the community will always find demands for increased outputs, even for increases that are enormous'; 5. 'Production of goods rather than the supply of money is the primary determinant of demand. Money facilitates commerce but does not determine the amounts of goods that are exchanged'; 6. 'Any glut in the market for a good must involve relative underproduction of some other commodity, or commodities, and the mobility of capital out of the area with excess supply and into industries whose products are insufficient to meet demand will tend rapidly to eliminate the overproduction'.

The less restrictive versions of Say's law had already been taken up by Smith, in support of the importance attributed to savings for accumulation and development; on the other hand, the stronger versions of the law were utilised in the Ricardian school to criticise the Smithian theory of the competition of capitals, according to which accumulation of capital

Criticising the most radical versions of Say's law, authors such as Sismondi, Malthus and Lauderdale argued not the existence of long period tendencies to stagnation but more simply the possibility of general over-production crises. Much the same line was followed by other Ricardian economists, such as Robert Torrens and, notably, John Stuart Mill (1844, second essay), who recognised the possibility of demand for money as a liquid inventory not to be spent immediately. This line was later adopted by Marx and especially by Keynes, who presented his theories as directly opposed to Say's law, interpreting it in the strong sense that it had acquired, much more than in the writings of Classical economists, within the marginalist tradition.

6.4 Under-consumption Theories: Malthus, Sismondi

In the first two decades of the nineteenth century, after Malthus had published the first edition of his *Essay* and Say the first edition of his *Traité* and before the Ricardian orthodoxy based, among other things, on Say's law had set in, a number of authors entered the arena arguing the possibility of general over-production crises.[8]

In his main work on economic theory, the *Principles* (1820), Malthus took from Smith the idea of labour commanded as a standard of value, which he contrasted with the Ricardian theory of labour embodied in a commodity. The role of demand was stressed in respect to the determination of both the prices of commodities and the global level of production and income. Confronted with the risk of inadequate demand, he stressed the role in support of income played by the 'unproductive consumption' of the landlords.

However, unlike others, Malthus did not derive the possibility of insufficient demand from the distinction between savings and investments, which may not coincide in a monetary economy. For Malthus, as for Ricardo, investments and savings automatically correspond to one another. Malthus's thesis concerned, rather, the possibility that the increase in productive capacity generated by investments exceeds the

would imply a gradual reduction of the profit rate, as a consequence of the progressive exhaustion of the most profitable employments of capital and the need to shift to ever less profitable uses. In the strong version, Say's law actually maintains that an increase in production by itself creates *ex novo* market outlets that guarantee the new employments of capital the same returns as the preceding uses.

[8] The fear of over-production must be distinguished from the 'fear of goods', namely a hostile attitude to economic growth, which has distant origins, being traceable in Classical Greek and Latin authors, and cyclically resurfaces in cultural debate. Cf. Perrotta 2004.

growth in demand; in fact, in the absence of unproductive consumption on the part of capitalists or landlords, the increase in wages due to the increase in employment associated with investments generates an additional demand, insufficient to keep pace with the increase in productive capacity. Here the Malthusian theory of value based on supply and demand entered the scene: in the situation we have illustrated, the increase in production will find an outlet, but at decreasing prices, and thus with a decrease in profits and in the profit rate. The result is a situation of generalised crisis.

All this, however, has nothing to do with Keynesian theory, based precisely on the distinction between savings and investments in a monetary production economy. The idea that Malthus was a precursor of Keynes (first suggested by Keynes himself, in the essay on Malthus in his *Essays in Biography*, 1933) seems, rather, to find support in Malthus's opposition to the quantity theory of money. In fact, Malthus (1800) maintained that the increase in prices is the cause, not the effect, of the increase in the quantity of money in circulation, which banks adjust to demand.

While Malthus may be considered a moderate conservative, Jean Charles Léonard Simonde de Sismondi (1773–1842) was undoubtedly a leftist, critical towards capitalism, upholding ideas of solidarity and social justice that in many instances anticipated theses characteristic of the socialist movement; he advocated public intervention to enforce a minimum limit to wages, a limit to working hours and public assistance for the sick, the old and the unemployed. At the same time, he was favourable to widespread private property and forms of worker participation in the profits of enterprises, with the objective of reducing inequalities in income distribution and favouring social mobility. His under-consumption theory was related to the thesis of the need to defend the purchasing power of the workers: wages were seen as a source of demand, while the growth of income required an expansion of demand that was not automatically ensured by increasing production. His main work was the *Nouveaux principes d'économie politique* (1819).

As these summary remarks suffice to show, the economists considered the major representatives of under-consumption theories were not lacking in interesting insights, even when they failed to detect one of the major weaknesses of the Classical tradition, namely identification between savings and investments. However, their insights were not incorporated into sufficiently solid analytical schemes; when confronted with Ricardo's architecture (illustrated in the next chapter) their positions must have appeared analytically inferior, although we should not underrate how well they reflected pre-analytical viewpoints and political ideas widespread at the time.

6.5   The Debate on the Poor Laws

One of the fields in which the Malthusian principle of population played a central role, at least since the first decades of the nineteenth century, was the debate on the poor laws, which involved a number of other themes such as the role of the government in the economy and the risks of public interference with individual responsibility. Once again we are confronted with a problem that is continually cropping up anew: the issue of 'what is to be done' about the poverty afflicting the lowest strata of the population.

Obviously, the problem of poverty takes on different forms. Let us simplify: on the one hand, we have the orphan and the foundling, the old and the invalid: all those who, for one reason or another, are unable to work and do not have a family to provide for their subsistence. On the other hand, we have those who could work but fail to find a job or have a job yielding an income insufficient for survival. Finally, a third group includes those who prefer a life of privation and poverty like that of beggars or a life fraught with risks like that of bandits rather than work. The importance attributed to this latter group is variable: it is attributed greater importance by conservative economists, hostile to extending public intervention in favour of the poor from the first to the second category; it is considered negligible (or included in the first two groups, for instance by considering social deviancy as a psychiatric illness) by progressive economists favourable to public intervention.

The problem of the poor is endemic, but it takes on particularly acute forms in periods of marked technological change, such as those characterising first the agricultural and then the industrial revolution and leading to impoverishment for masses of workers. In the sixteenth-century enclosures – delimiting the land reserved for stock raising – generated poverty-stricken masses, uprooted from lands their families had cultivated for generations. Thomas More (1516, pp. 65–7) ironically remarked in this respect that sheep, 'which are usually so tame and so cheaply fed, begin now ... to be so greedy and wild that they devour human beings themselves and devastate and depopulate fields, houses, and towns'. In the second half of the eighteenth and in the first half of the nineteenth century, in England as in the more advanced countries of continental Europe, manufacturing industries arose to squeeze out traditional artisan activities, giving rise once again to mass pauperism.

We shall consider later the debate on *compensation*, or in other words the thesis that jobs lost with the introduction of machinery are compensated for by the creation of new jobs, thanks to the new demand deriving from the improved standards of living generated by technical progress. In actual fact, however, pauperism was there, for all to see: the compensation was, at least, not immediate.

In Elizabethan England the poor laws contemplated not only systematic support for the first category of poor – the orphaned, old and invalid – but also more generally for all those unable to support themselves with their own work. The 1601 Statutes introduced on a nationwide scale a tax going to the support to the poor; however, collection of the tax and distribution of the revenue were administered locally, under the surveillance of elected supervisors, and local administrations were left free to follow the direction of *outdoor relief* (distribution of foodstuff, subsidies, public works) or *indoor relief* (the assisted poor obliged to reside and work in public workhouses) or a combination of the two.

The onus of intervention thus fell on the well-to-do classes of the local communities where the poor lived. This meant a tax burden differing from place to place, according to the proportion of poor in the local population; as a consequence, the communities were seeking to encourage their poor to emigrate to other areas of the country and to bar the poor from entering from other areas. Moreover, the tax provoked continual complaints about the incentive to idleness offered by a system of assistance considered too generous to people who did not work although able-bodied. (Among the advocates of this viewpoint in the eighteenth century we find Daniel Defoe and Bernard de Mandeville.)

This twofold series of problems eventually gave rise, in the eighteenth century and in particular with the new Poor Law of 1772, to a set of rules that in practice prohibited the migration of the poor from one parish to another and made the provision of food, as small as it was, dependent on living in a workhouse – and the workhouse thus became a sort of prison without bars. Despite these constraints, assistance to the poor grew to considerable dimensions, receiving a boost from, among other things, the so-called Speenhamland system (from the name of the place where the magistrates of Berkshire used to meet), which began to spread in 1795, providing for supplementation of the lowest wages to reach a minimum level determined on the basis of the number of dependants and indexed to food prices.

This was the background for the debate on the Poor Laws in England in the first half of the nineteenth century. As we saw previously, the Malthusian principle of population was utilised by many Classical economists, including Malthus and Ricardo, to argue that aid to the able-bodied poor was useless. Others, like Senior, maintained that aid to the able-bodied poor reduces the work incentives, thus weakening the workers' efficiency and, as a consequence, the scale of production and availability of resources to pay wages (the so-called 'wage fund').

The debate between the conservative and progressive theses concerned whether disincentives to work arose with assistance to the able-bodied poor not made conditional upon compulsory labour in the workhouses. Thus the debate revolved not so much about the desirability of aid to the poor in principle as the choice between outdoor and indoor relief. Problems of bad administration, of little interest from the point of view of theoretical economic debate, were mixed with issues including incentives for individuals to work, the role of public intervention and the idea that poverty was the inevitable lot of a great part of the population.

6.6   The Debate on the Colonies

The Malthusian principle of population, namely the idea that population growth exerts pressure on the means of subsistence, had every appearance of realism in England at the time of the Napoleonic wars, when the continental blockade obstructed imports from continental countries producing low-cost agricultural goods. In the years immediately following the 1815 Congress of Vienna, recollection of the war years could still account for the persistent and widespread acceptance of a theory already superseded by the realities of the time. One field where the population principle was already quite clearly wearing thin was the debate on the colonies, now largely ignored by historians of economic thought but a burning issue of the time.[9]

This debate, too, had begun well before the period we are considering here. On the relations between colonies and fatherland, for instance, Adam Smith wrote in the conclusion of his *magnum opus* itself, published in the same year as the Declaration of Independence of the American colonies. Smith (1776, pp. 761–71; 1977, pp. 377–85) not only appeared ready to recognise the rights of the colonies but went so far as to delineate a 'commonwealth', similar to that which took shape only much later on, grasping the potentialities of North America as

---

[9] The importance of the debate on colonies and on conflicts between colonising countries and colonies is illustrated by Reinert 2011.

future leader of the world economy. Even before Smith, we may recall Petty's participation in the American adventure of his friend Penn that led to the foundation of Pennsylvania[10] or the role played by Cantillon and, above all, by the Scottish banker-economist John Law in the financial vicissitudes involved in the colonisation of Mississippi.

But let us return to the golden period of Classical political economy. One of the main problems for countries across the oceans – both the recently independent United States and the new colonial frontier of Australia – lay in the extremely thin population. The land available for cultivation was vast, the number of immigrants scant, which meant enormous difficulties for the newborn manufacturing firms seeking wage-workers, thwarting the development of an integrated economic system with a manufacturing sector thriving on the division of labour.

These problems were dealt with by various authors. Torrens (1817) recalled the Malthusian principle of population, being one of the first authors to present the colonies as outlets for the emigration that was to improve the conditions of the workers of the Kingdom, and in particular the Irish. Others, like Senior, opposed colonization policies, arguing that the void left by emigration would soon be filled by an increase in population.

Edward Gibbon Wakefield (1796–1862) (1829, 1833) argued that land in the colonies should be sold to the settlers at a price that not all could afford in order to guarantee the availability of wage labour; were they to take possession of land to cultivate freely, the settlers would scatter over vast areas, and the division of labour would thus be rendered impracticable, with enormous loss in productivity and poverty looming for the new colonies.

Once he embraced Wakefield's ideas, Torrens (1835) defended them with his characteristic vigour, playing an active role in the colonisation of South Australia (where his name was given to a large lake). Population theory thus turned away from the old, pessimistic views on the possibility of progress of human societies to form the basis for theoretical rationalisation of the expansionist forces leading to the formation of the British Empire.

6.7   Bentham's Utilitarianism

Let us now turn to another important stream of thought, Bentham's utilitarianism, which took shape and rose in influence in the period

---

[10] Petty also repeatedly proposed a 'transplantation', or mass deportation of the Irish, so as to transform Ireland into an immense cattle raising ground, with a limited number of workers tending the cattle.

between Smith's *Wealth of Nations* (1776) and John Stuart Mill's *Principles* (1848). In some respects – as we shall see in Chapter 10 – it opens the way to Jevons's 'marginalist revolution'; in other respects, it may help us in understanding the transition – on many counts a big step backwards – from the Smithian notion of human beings as moved by a rich mixture of passions and interests to the Ricardian notion of economic man.

The 'utilitarian revolution' of Jeremy Bentham (1748–1832) fell within the field of ethics, where a centuries-long debate saw the confrontation of two views: the deontological and the consequentialist approach. Bentham gave a crucial contribution to the development of the latter.

In a few words, the deontological approach maintained that actions are 'good' or 'bad' in themselves; the consequentialist approach maintained instead that any action is to be judged by its consequences. Deontological theories in ethics were commonly based on the principle of authority and associated with religious commandments and were typical of societies oriented towards respect for traditions. Consequentialist theories of ethics, on the other hand, came to the fore with the new rationalistic orientation of the Age of Enlightenment.[11]

According to Bentham (1776, p. 393), 'it is the greatest happiness of the greatest number that is the measure of right and wrong'. This principle implied two elements ('greatest happiness' and 'greatest number') to be simultaneously maximised; however, Bentham's 'felicific calculus' – which consisted in quantitative evaluation and algebraic summation of pleasures and pains stemming from any action or set of actions (where pleasures obviously have a positive sign, pains a negative sign) – implied just one maximand, total social happiness. Good is whatever gives as its result an algebraically positive felicific magnitude and hence increases the amount of happiness within human societies; bad is whatever gives as its result a negative felicific magnitude and as a consequence decreases the amount of social happiness.

The felicific calculus was thus directed to evaluate the *social* impact of both individual actions and public policy choices; Bentham, however, concentrated attention on the latter.

---

[11] Such a clear-cut dichotomy between deontological and consequentialist approaches is simplistic and hides many a problem. As shown by Sen 1991, deontological theories in general are open to recognising, at least indirectly, the importance of the consequences of actions, while the consequentialist approaches commonly retain some elements of a priori judgements. On the whole, however, the distinction remains a most useful interpretative key.

Let us ponder this point. The private and the social impact of individual actions coincide if individuals, while pursuing their own personal interests, do not have an impact on the interests of others; in such a case selfish behaviour automatically also realises the common good and the so-called 'thesis of the natural identity of interests' holds. This was the thesis on which the most extreme ideas of *laissez faire* relied, holding that optimal social conditions are realised when individuals pursue their own personal preferences. This thesis was different from the position maintained, for instance, by Adam Smith, holding that individuals interact within society so that individual actions affect other individuals; consequently individual behaviour is to be guided by an adequate set of legal and moral norms upheld by public bodies – the police and the administration of justice. Smith's *laissez-faire* approach lay, rather, in the conviction that in an imperfect world we should abandon the dream of the 'enlightened prince', since each citizen can look after his own interests better than he can anybody else's. Bentham, instead, combined the idea of the 'enlightened prince' (to whom the central role of Legislator is attributed) and extreme *laissez-faire* views (implicit, for instance, in his defence of usury against Smith's proposal to set a ceiling on interest rates, Bentham 1787).

Bentham's guiding aim was in fact the construction of a legal code such as to achieve the supremacy of Reason within human societies. With the felicific calculus the Legislator could intervene with laws setting rewards and punishments so as to modify individual behaviour in the direction of the optimal situation corresponding to the greatest happiness principle. Of course, the greater or lesser quantities of happiness stemming from different courses of actions were computed for society as a whole and assessed by the Legislator himself. The felicific calculus implied two prerequisites: first, that the different pleasures and pains of each individual were reducible to quantitative measurement along a one-dimensional scale; second, that felicific magnitudes referring to different individuals could be algebraically added up (and all individuals were assumed to be identical in their ability to experience pleasures and pains).

Bentham was in many respects a true believer in the powers of Reason and in the applicability of the felicific calculus to homogeneous, one-dimensional human nature. However, in his impressive output of manuscripts no example is to be found, at least to my knowledge, of factual computations of this kind, with numerical estimations of pleasures and pains. Bentham systematically limited himself to illustrating the elements that influenced the 'quantity' of pleasures and pains (such as 'intensity, duration, certainty, propinquity, fecundity, purity and extent'). This was sufficient for his purposes, for instance to establish which criteria the laws (especially those relating to punishments, as in the debate on the death penalty) should follow. The felicific calculus was introduced by Bentham in this context (and more generally in the context of the debate on ethics) and not in the context of an analysis of consumers' behaviour. The notion of marginal utility and the postulate of decreasing marginal utility were unnecessary from the perspective of Bentham's Legislator; indeed, it is likely that Bentham – and even more so his followers, in particular John Stuart Mill – would have considered this line of argument as stretching application of the felicific calculus too far. There remains a very long stride ahead from this to the marginalist theory of prices, requiring assumptions such as closely defined demand and supply functions, without which it was impossible to utilise the tools of differential calculus.

7   David Ricardo

7.1   Life and Works

David Ricardo was born in London in 1772, the son of a well-to-do stockbroker and a Sephardic Jew. Following the family traditions, he studied in Amsterdam, an important financial centre that, in fact, the Ricardo family hailed from. Back in London at the age of fourteen, David began work in the Stock Exchange with his father. Soon, however, he was to become the protagonist of a romantic story: falling in love with a young Quaker girl, he married her against his family's will and was disowned. Thus compelled to launch out on his own, thanks to his ability he soon became an established member of the business community.

His work at the Stock Exchange spurred him to systematic consideration of the economic vicissitudes of the country. While on holiday, in 1799, Ricardo happened to read Smith's *Wealth of Nations*. He was not a scholarly type, but he had a logical mind and sharp intelligence. His analytic penchant thus germinated around three elements: the immediate economic events of his time, debate revolving around them and Smith's book.

His first economic writings entered upon the field of the monetary controversies of the time. However, his main contributions to political economy came after his departure from the Stock Exchange in 1815, when he was only forty-three years old but already a wealthy person, thanks in particular to successful speculations on the placing of public debt. Ricardo moved to the countryside, at Gatcomb, and there led the tranquil life of a rich gentleman. He also got involved in politics and in 1819 became a Member of Parliament representing Portarlington, a borough in Ireland with only twelve electors who, as was usual at the time, sold their vote to the highest bidder. He joined in the economic debates of the period but more through correspondence with friends and parliamentary speeches than with publications. Among the latter, his

Essay on the Influence of a Low Price of Corn on the Profits of Stock, published in 1815, met with positive response. His main work is titled *On the Principles of Political Economy, and Taxation*, published in 1817.[1]

In his publishing and parliamentary activity Ricardo dealt with monetary, fiscal and public debt issues, proposing recourse to wealth taxes in order to pay back over a few years' time the public debt that had piled up during the Napoleonic wars. In 1823 he proposed that the issue of bank notes be entrusted to a National Bank and that the Bank of England be limited to the activity of a commercial bank. Ricardo died in 1823. He left a large estate to his wife and his surviving children, with bequests to his friends Malthus and James Mill.

Although he was acclaimed as the leading figure, in the years immediately following his death his scientific heritage was already gradually being dissipated, with increasing distortion of his original thought. With the rise of the marginalist approach, after 1870, the idea gained ground of Ricardo as a genius but not worth reading; indeed, it was even suggested that with his extraordinary intelligence he had set political economy on a wrong track. It was only with the ten-volume edition of his works and correspondence edited by Sraffa (Ricardo 1951–55) that Ricardo and his scientific contribution were brought back to the attention of economists.

7.2 Ricardo's Dynamic Vision

Ricardo took over from Smith his vision of the economic system and upon it built an analytical construction admirable in its systematic and logically consistent character. Like Smith, Ricardo took into consideration a society based on the division of labour, with two broad sectors (agriculture and manufacturing) and three social classes (workers, capitalists and landowners) with three corresponding income categories (wages, profits and rents). Wages correspond to subsistence consumption and therefore constitute part of the necessary expenses of production; rent and profits correspond to the surplus, namely to that part of the product that remains at disposal once the initial inventories of means of production and means of subsistence for the workers employed in production have been reconstituted. While the landlords allot their rents to luxury consumptions, the capitalists are induced by competition to invest practically the whole of their profits. Therefore economic development stems from accumulation, realised by capitalists on the basis of their profits.

---

[1] The *Essay on corn* is reprinted in Ricardo 1951–55, vol. 4, and the *Principles* in vol. 1.

Ricardo departed from Adam Smith, however, in the method of analysis. Smith utilised a historical framework; within it, the economist focussed on the most important factors in play but with continual reference to the other elements left in the background. Ricardo had an analytical mind, with an innate need for logical rigour, which led him to build an analytical construction squared with an axe, excluding from analysis anything considered not directly relevant to the problem at hand. Furthermore, while Smith had illustrated the evolution of the economic system as a whole, connected to developments in the division of labour, Ricardo focussed on the distribution of the surplus between rents and profits and on its implications for the rhythm of capital accumulation and economic growth. This means taking technology and wage rate as given, while, as a consequence of his acceptance of 'Say's law', the level of production is, at any moment in time, the quantity that can be produced given the available production capacity being determined by the process of capital accumulation.[2]

As for the assumption of a given wage rate, Ricardo followed Malthus's theory of population and assumed the wage to be at subsistence level (to be interpreted, as suggested by Torrens, not in a purely biological sense but as a historical-social minimum standard of living acceptable for the workers). Thus the surplus turns out to be divided between rents – mainly utilised in luxury consumptions – and profits – mainly earmarked for investments.

The problem of rent was then solved with the differential rent theory: a theory often attributed to Ricardo but in fact proposed, during a short but lively debate on the duties on corn in 1815, by Malthus and (possibly) West before Ricardo, who was, however, ready to understand and use it. According to this theory, for any plot of land the rent is equal to the difference between unit costs of production on the less fertile among lands in cultivation and unit costs on the land being considered multiplied by the quantity of product obtainable on it. Rent on the less fertile of the lands under cultivation is nil and so does not enter into the cost of production. Profits thus turn out to be a residual magnitude, namely that part of the surplus that is not absorbed by rents.

Since economic growth stems from accumulation, and hence from profits, whatever reduces profits constitutes a hindrance to accumulation. For any given amount of the surplus, profits fall when rents on land increase. According to Ricardo, *ceteris paribus* this is a consequence of economic growth itself, since it is accompanied by an increase in food

---

[2] Ricardo was accused of under-valuing technical progress, pessimistic as he was about decreasing long-run economic trends up to the stationary state.

consumption, which in turn leads to expansion in cultivation. Let us assume that the lands brought under cultivation are more fertile than the ones left uncultivated. As new lands are brought under cultivation, the less fertile of the cultivated lands proves ever less fertile. Therefore, profits earned on the marginal land decrease, due to the increase in costs per unit of output. The rents increase on already cultivated lands, and as a consequence the profits of the farmers decrease. The decrease in profits is transmitted from agriculture to manufacturing through the increase in the price of agricultural products and hence in wages. All this hinders accumulation.

The policy implication is obvious. Imports of foreign corn are the best way to cope with increased demand for food rather than bringing under cultivation new, less fertile, lands. It is therefore opportune to eliminate all obstacles – such as custom duties – to the importation of agricultural products. The theory of comparative advantages, which we shall consider later, reinforces this policy conclusion: the international division of labour brings about increased availability of commodities for every country.

Ricardo thus expressed at the analytical level the clash of interests between the landlords, politically dominant at his time, and the manufacturing bourgeoisie: the confrontation over the expediency of duties on corn imports was one of the central episodes of this clash.[3] The construction of a sound analytical structure for classical political economy constitutes Ricardo's main contribution both to the progress of economic science and to the gradual victory of the political position he supported.

7.3   From the Corn Model to the Labour Theory of Value

We saw that Ricardo assigned profits a central role in the development of the economy. However, rather than the aggregate amount of profits, it is the rate of profits that is at the centre of his analytical edifice. This is due essentially to two reasons.

First, in a capitalistic society driven by competition, in which capitalists are free to move their capital from one investment to another, the return on the funds invested in the different sectors – the rate of profits – must be more or less equal. Hence, the rate of profits regulates

---

[3] Abolition of duties on corn imports in England went through only many years later, in 1846, after fierce political battles in which the Anti-Corn Law League, founded in Manchester in 1838 by Cobden, played a central role. Hence the term 'Manchesterism' designating, as from this period, free trade ideology.

the effort that society puts into the production of the different commodities, and it is this competitive mechanism based on the tendency to a uniform rate of profits to ensure that the quantities of different commodities produced more or less correspond to the quantities sold in the economy.

Second, the rate of profits is also – under the assumptions adopted by Ricardo – an indicator of the potential pace of growth of the economy. In fact, it is by definition equal to the ratio between profits and capital advanced; assuming that profits are wholly allotted to investments, the ratio proves equal to the ratio between investments and capital advanced, namely to the rate of accumulation. Furthermore, if we leave aside technical change and if – following Say's law – we assume available productive capacity to be fully utilised, we find that the rate of profits is equal to the rate of growth of national income.[4] To be sure, Ricardo did not explicitly illustrate these relations, but they do express in analytical form the substance of his thinking. For Ricardo, to explain if and why the rate of profits tends to decrease over time, and to locate the factors that may counter this tendency, meant explaining the pace of development of the economy.

For these two reasons – its role in regulating the competitive working of the capitalistic economy and its role in the process of economic development – determination of the rate of profits constitutes a central aspect in Ricardo's analytical edifice and more generally in the whole classical tradition. In this field, Ricardo made crucial analytical contributions, going farther than the Smithian idea of a normal rate of profits determined by the pressure of competition between the capitals available for investment.

According to the interpretation set out by Sraffa (1951), we can distinguish two successive stages in the development of Ricardo's thought. The first, Sraffa conjectured, started in 1814, with a note on the 'profits of capital' since lost, and ended with the 1815 *Essay*; the second stage began with Malthus's criticism of Ricardo's 'corn model', to conclude with the 1817 *Principles* (although Ricardo continued to ponder over the different aspects of the problem to the very last days of his life). Let us take a closer look at this issue.

The rate of profits is equal to the ratio between profits and capital advanced. In order to compute this ratio both must be expressed in

---

[4] Let us denote with Y income, with P profits, with I investments, with K invested capital, with r the rate of profits and with g the rate of accumulation (which, if the capital-income ratio is constant, corresponds to the rate of growth of the economy). By definition, $r = P/K$ and $g = I/K$. If we assume that investments correspond to profits, namely that $P = I$, we have $r = g$.

terms of homogeneous magnitudes. In the first stage of his research, Ricardo achieved this condition by interpreting profits and capital advanced in the agricultural sector as different quantities of the same commodity, 'corn': corn being the only commodity produced in the sector, and also the sole means of production, as seed, and the sole means of subsistence for the workers employed in cultivating the land. We saw that, according to the 'Ricardian' theory of the rent, on the less fertile among the lands under cultivation rent is nil, and all the surplus goes to profits. Let us assume, for instance, that on the marginal land 100 tons of corn are produced, utilising 30 tons as seed and 50 tons as subsistence for the workers; the surplus, that goes entirely to profits, is equal to 20 tons of corn (100 − 30 − 50 = 20), and the rate of profits amounts to 25 per cent (20/80 = 0.25).

In this way we can circumvent the problem of value: that is, the need to determine the relative prices of the goods that enter into the capital advanced and the surplus so as to be able to compute the value of profits and of capital advanced, and hence the rate of profits. Obviously, since under competition the rate of profits must be the same in the different employments of capital, a rate of profit equal to that computed on the marginal land will have to prevail not only in the whole agricultural sector but also in all manufacturing activities, while relative prices adjust in such a way as to ensure the uniformity of the rate of profits in all sectors of the economy.

In a letter of 5 August 1814, Malthus had objected to Ricardo that 'in no case of production, [therefore not even in the agricultural sector] is the produce exactly of the same nature as the capital advanced'.[5] In other words, Ricardo could not get round the problem of value by determining the rate of profits as a ratio between different physical quantities of the same commodity, since in any productive process means of production are used that are heterogeneous among themselves and with respect to the product.

After pondering at length over these criticisms, the validity of which he was ready to recognise, Ricardo came up with a new solution in the *Principles*, adopting the labour embodied theory of value to explain relative prices. According to this theory, the exchange ratio between two commodities corresponds to the ratio between the quantities of labour directly and indirectly required to produce each of them. Ricardo considered this new solution a step forward from the previous one, although he did not see it as perfect since it was based on drastically simplifying assumptions – as Torrens and Malthus

[5] Ricardo 1951–55, vol. 6, p. 117.

immediately reminded him. However, from the point of view of his political objectives – attack on rents – Ricardo thought that his reasoning was sufficiently valid and that the difficulties (the 'complications' that have to be introduced in order to deal with the problem of value) could be overcome.

Smith had already proposed this theory, also present in the Scholastic tradition, as holding in the 'early and rude state' that preceded separation between labour and the ownership of capital and land, and hence between wages, profits and rents. Ricardo extended application of the theory to cover capitalistic economies too, assuming that for each commodity the amount of profits and rents that have to be added to the cost of labour in order to arrive at the price is roughly proportional to the amount of labour employed in the productive process. Once again, this is clearly an unrealistic assumption, but this did not worry him too much. His main objective was, in fact, to work out not so much a theory of relative prices as, rather, a theory of income distribution and accumulation, which does not concern individual productive processes but the economic activities of a country as a whole.

Thanks to the labour theory of value, Ricardo was able to measure both the product and the means of production and subsistence in homogeneous terms, as the quantities of labour bestowed on their production. More precisely, the value of the yearly produce of an economic system is equal to the quantity of labour spent as a whole in the same period of time. Computed as the difference between the value of the product and the value of the means of production, the value of the surplus also emerges expressed as a certain quantity of labour. Once the problem of rent is settled and done with, profits too turn out to be determined. The rate of profits is then equal to the ratio between profits and capital advanced, both expressed as different physical quantities of one magnitude (labour time).[6]

---

[6] Let us denote with L the number of employed workers (hence the amount of labour, expressed in man-years, expended in a year). L thus corresponds to the value, in labour terms, of the yearly produce of the economy. Let us indicate with Lw the value, again in terms of labour embodied, of the commodities required for the subsistence of employed workers, which by assumption corresponds to the wages paid to them, and with Lc the value of means of production utilised overall within the year (under the assumption that only circulating capital is used). Let us disregard rents for the sake of simplicity. Let us assume that all productive processes last one year and that wages and circulating capital are advanced by capitalists at the beginning of the year. The value of capital advanced on the whole is then equal to $Lw + Lc$, while the value of profits P is equal to the difference between product and costs of production, namely $P = L - Lw - Lc$. The profit rate r is equal to the ratio between profits and capital advanced, namely $r = (L - Lw - Lc)/(Lw + Lc)$.

7.4   Absolute Value and Exchangeable Value: The Invariable Standard of Value

In the *Principles* Ricardo pointed out the limits of the labour theory of value. The relative prices determined as the ratio between the quantities of labour directly and indirectly required to produce the different commodities violate the condition of a uniform rate of profits in the different sectors of the economy for three reasons: different durability of productive processes, changing ratio between fixed and circulating capital, and different durability of fixed capital in the different sectors. The labour theory of value may therefore be considered at most an approximate theory of relative prices. For Ricardo, however, the problem was not so much that of establishing how wide the margin of approximation might be; rather, the problem revolved upon the possibility of finding rigorous anchorage, an 'invariable standard', for exchange values.

In the search of this anchorage, Ricardo utilised a traditional term of reference, namely the labour time required to obtain a certain quantity of product. The use of labour as a standard – that is, the choice to use as standard a commodity produced by a given and unchangeable quantity of labour – has the advantage that it provides precise answers when confronted with changes in technology; it also satisfies the dialectical need to oppose to the thesis of exchange values based on the notion, ever present in economic debate, of a mechanism based on demand and supply, a theory based on the difficulty of production. In Ricardo's thought, as already in Smith's, the interrelationship between supply and demand only concerns the adjustment of market prices to natural prices, not determination of the latter:

It is the cost of production which must ultimately regulate the price of commodities, and not, as has been often said, the proportion between supply and demand: the proportion between supply and demand may, indeed, for a time, affect the market value of a commodity, until it is supplied in greater or less abundance, according as the demand may have increased or diminished; but this effect will be only of temporary duration.[7]

However, the standard chosen by Ricardo proves inadequate when confronted with changes in the distribution of income between wages and profits. Indeed, when two commodities produced by the same quantity of labour are obtained over different periods of production or with a different proportion between fixed and circulating capital, their relative value changes when distribution changes, and our invariable

[7] Ricardo (1951–55, vol. 1, p. 382).

standard can give no indication of the origin of this variation in exchange value.

When we take these difficulties into account, the path Ricardo took appears a dead end. Let us try to see why. Like so many economists since Petty, Ricardo adopted a theory of exchange values based on the relative difficulty of production of the various commodities. The problem of value would then be solved, taking this approach, were it possible to find an exact measure of the difficulty of production. To address this task, the invariable standard of value should have a twofold characteristic, namely invariance both with respect to changes in technology and with respect to changes in the distribution of income. Labour embodied fulfils the first requisite, but as far as the second requisite is concerned, it contradicts the assumption – a crucial one for the whole of classical political economy – of a uniform rate of profits in the presence of competition.

Ricardo realised that his efforts in this direction were getting nowhere, but he remained convinced – at a pre-analytical level, we might say – that labour time must have something to do with such an invariable standard of value. This means that there was in Ricardo (as there would be, in still more acute form, in Marx) a metaphysical residuum: the purely analytical problem of a precise measure of value was mixed up with the purely metaphysical problem of finding the foundation, the ultimate origin (or, as Marx said, the 'substance') of value: and such an ultimate origin, in Ricardo's (or Marx's) mind, cannot be found but in labour. The search for an absolute measure of the difficulty of production corresponds to the desire to isolate a 'natural' aspect in interpreting the functioning of a society based on the division of labour. However, any such attempt is vitiated by a basic flaw: the division of labour is only possible in the presence of a web of exchanges linking the different sectors of the economy and the different economic agents; the mechanisms of exchange then express not only the relative difficulties of production of the various commodities but also the institutions, customs and social structure of the society under consideration that regulate the functioning of the web of exchanges and income distribution between social classes. In the case of a capitalistic economy, alongside technology (difficulty of production, in Ricardo's terminology) it is essential to take into account also such elements as the assumption of a uniform rate of profits, expressing at the analytical level an essential characteristic of a capitalistic society, namely the 'competition of capitals'. No society exists devoid of social institutions: the idea of an absolute value, grounded on exclusively natural foundations, is a chimera.

7.5 Money

The classical economists, Ricardo included, are generally attributed with the quantity theory of money. According to this theory, variations in the quantity of money in circulation – that are considered as exogenous, that is, independent of the other economic variables – determine variations in the general price level without influencing either the level of production (which, in accordance with Say's law, depends on available production capacity, hence on the accumulation of capital realised over time) or the velocity of circulation of money, which depends on institutional and customary factors such as frequency in the payments of wages, rents and taxes.

Various elements of this theory already had a long tradition in Ricardo's times. For instance, the notion of velocity of circulation of money dates back as early as authors such as Petty or Locke, who also considered it to be relatively stable. The idea that the quantity of money in circulation influences prices was common amongst writers of the sixteenth and seventeenth centuries, confronted with the inflationary phenomena stemming from the discovery of new gold and silver mines in the New World. In the eighteenth century David Hume considered the quantity theory of money as a well-established fact in his explanation of the automatic adjustment mechanisms of the trade balance.

The different elements that compose the quantity theory of money – from Say's law to the idea of a relatively stable velocity of circulation of money – were all present in Ricardo. However, he also considered other elements that contribute to complicate the picture. First, there was the idea that gold, or more generally precious metals, are produced commodities, so that it is possible to increase their quantity. The price of gold relative to other commodities was thus determined, according to the labour theory of value, by the ratio between the quantities of labour directly and indirectly necessary to produce gold and the other commodities. Second, there was the problem of the relationship between gold and the notes issued by the banks. This was the crux of Ricardo's theory of money. By money Ricardo meant the set of standardised financial activities commonly used as means of payment, such as the notes issued by the main banks. It was to this notion of money that Ricardo applied the central tenet of the quantity theory: the value of notes issued by the main bank changes in inverse relation to their quantity. In other words, the purchasing power of money (bank notes) relative to commodities in general must be decomposed into two distinct relations: the exchange ratio between money and gold, i.e. the value of money, and the exchange ratio between gold and other commodities. This latter relationship is but a particular case of the general theory of exchange value for produced and reproducible commodities, while the former relationship is dealt with by recourse to the quantity theory.

Ricardo (like other contemporaries of his and unlike the modern followers of the quantity theory) did not consider the problem of how to deduce the level of prices from the quantity of money, which is quite difficult to observe and extremely variable. Thus, in Ricardo's analysis the crucial variable for monetary policy was not the price level of the commodities but the value of money, that is its ratio of exchange with gold: when this ratio is stable, then the quantity of money, which remains unknown, is at its natural level. Furthermore, through the use of gold as the standard of money it is possible to determine, whenever the money price of a commodity changes, whether this happens for 'real' reasons, which can be traced to technology and income distribution, or for 'monetary' reasons, which can be traced to changes in the quantity of money: in the first case, it is the ratio of exchange between commodity and gold that varies, while in the second case it is the value of money that varies in terms of its standard, namely gold.

It was with this analytic structure that Ricardo tackled the monetary debates of his times, and in particular the Bullionist controversy, concerning the role of the central bank, and which saw all the major economists of the time involved. The main contribution to the debate was the *Enquiry into the Nature and Effects of the Paper Credit of Great Britain* (1802) by Henry Thornton (1760–1815), banker and member of Parliament. Preceding Ricardo in this, Thornton considered the link between prices and quantity of money to be indirect and hence not automatic; in his case, however, the intermediary element was represented by the discount rate. Also, preceding Wicksell, Thornton analysed the process of credit expansion, connecting it to the divergence between the bank rate of interest and the rate of profits. In this context, Thornton attributed an active role to the monetary policy choices of the central bank.[8]

---

[8] The debate on monetary problems took on new life a couple of decades later with confrontation between the *Currency School* (Robert Torrens, Lord Overstone and others) and the *Banking School* (Thomas Tooke, John Stuart Mill and others) over the way banks function and the rules that the issue of notes should be subjected (or not subjected) to, i.e. on the active or passive role attributed to banks in the process of creation of the circulating medium (or, in other terms, on the exogenous or endogenous nature – in response to variations in demand – of the money supply). Thomas Tooke (1774–1858) is known for the extensive *History of Prices, 1793–1856*, in six volumes (Tooke, 1838–57), and for the *Inquiry into the Currency Principle* (1844). A friend of Ricardo, Malthus and James Mill, he was among the founders of the Political Economy Club.

7.6   International Trade and the Theory of Comparative Costs

International trade was among the most keenly debated issues of the seventeenth century. However, the numerous *Tracts on Trade* represent a somewhat primitive stage; only with Antonio Serra and Thomas Mun, for instance, do we have a sufficiently precise notion of the balance of trade and the various items composing it. Overall, the idea of *absolute advantages* prevailed, according to which each country exports those commodities that it succeeds in producing at a lower cost than other countries.

In this respect Ricardo took a decisive step forward with his theory of *comparative costs*. According to this theory, each country specialises in the production of those commodities for which it enjoys a relative advantage in the cost of production. This means that there can be international trade between two countries even if, in terms of difficulty of production (expressed in terms of the hours of labour necessary for their production), all commodities have a higher cost in one country than in the other. For instance, if it takes 10 hours of labour to obtain one measure of cloth and 1 hour for a litre of wine in Portugal, while in England the same cloth and wine take 20 and 5 hours respectively, it will so happen that England will export cloth and import wine. In fact, international trade is advantageous when it allows a country to obtain a commodity from a foreign country at a cost – in terms of labour embodied in exported commodities – lower than that necessary to produce it internally. Both countries become richer thanks to foreign trade. This is the most important point in Ricardo's theory.[9]

Ricardo's theory of comparative costs was based on the existence of differences between the technological structures of the different countries. Nothing was said of the origin of such differences. It would be up to marginalist theory to connect such differences with the different endowments of the 'factors of production' capital, land and labour. Instead, it was on a critique of the assumption of given technologies in the two countries that the defence of protectionism was based, pointing out the difficulties faced by countries lagging behind in the

---

[9] The problem of how to distribute the gains from international trade between the various countries remained open. John Stuart Mill (1844) dealt with it, stressing the importance of the relative size of the demand coming from the two countries. Through this relatively secondary route demand appeared in the classical economists' analysis among the factors determining relative prices; as we shall see, it was precisely by establishing a link between the 'pure theory of foreign trade' and the 'pure theory of internal prices' that Marshall began building his analytical edifice aiming at a synthesis between classical and marginalist analysis.

industrialisation process. This thesis, known as the infant industry argument, was already being argued around the mid-nineteenth century by German and American economists; we may recall in particular Friedrich List (1789–1846) and his *Das nationale System der politischen Oekonomie* (1841). Other, more recent criticisms stressed the possibility that international trade, in the presence of increasing returns to scale, influences the technological differences between the different countries, compounding them and rendering them permanent. While constituting important qualifications to the free trade policies, however, these criticisms do not invalidate Ricardo's thesis on the immediate advantage that opening to foreign trade implies for the countries concerned – an advantage equivalent to an improvement in the technology in use.[10]

7.7   On Machinery: Technological Change and Employment

We have already discussed Say's law and its variants. In the variant adopted by Ricardo, Say's law states that supply and demand are equal for any level of income, hence for any level of employment. If this is true, technical progress cannot be a source of occupational difficulties: increase in per capita productivity translates into an increase in production, absorbed by a greater demand (corresponding to an improved standard of living), and not into a decrease in employed workers, production remaining unchanged.

According to what is known as the theory of compensation, accepted by Ricardo too, technological progress, when introduced in a given sector, generates unemployment in the sector itself; however, in a subsequent stage the jobs lost in the first sector are made up for by new jobs in other sectors, and the general standard of living improves. This is due to the fact that technical progress implies a reduction in costs in the sector where it is introduced and hence a decrease in the price of the product; this brings about a generalised increase in real incomes all over the economy, which then generates an increase in demand. In turn, this induces an increase in production and hence in employment, since in the other sectors the technology is by assumption unchanged. In other words, the decrease in employment in the sector in which

---

[10] In this respect Ricardo's theory is recalled nowadays in defence of globalisation. However, we should distinguish between commercial and financial globalisation; Ricardo's theory does not apply to the latter, which may be susceptible to Keynesian criticism.

technical progress takes place is compensated for by an increase in employment in other sectors.

The opposite thesis – technical progress generates unemployment – was illustrated by John Barton in a short pamphlet, *On the Conditions of the Labouring Classes* (1817). In the depressed conditions following the conclusion of the Napoleonic wars, Barton's argumentations – more at the level of applied economics than of a theoretical nature – had appeared sensible to many. However, Ricardo's authority in those years helped in no small measure to assert the compensation theory as an integral part of the body of classical political economy. But on the occasion of the third edition of the *Principles* (1821), a *coup de theatre* took place: in a new chapter 'On Machinery' Ricardo abandoned the theory of compensation and analytically developed the thesis that introduction of machinery in a sector may imply reduction of employment in the economy as a whole.

Ricardo's reasoning may be summarised thus. The capitalist introduces new machinery with a view to generating an increase in profits. The net product of the economy, identified with profits and rents, increases. However, the investment in machinery implies the decision to employ in the production of machinery a certain number of workers, previously employed in producing subsistence goods. We thus have a lower production of subsistence goods. As a consequence, the number of labourers that the economy can maintain necessarily decreases. Thus employment decreases, and this decrease, although destined to be reabsorbed by the higher rate of accumulation allowed for by the growth in net income, may be far from negligible in the immediate aftermath and may persist for a rather long span of time.

The provocative stance taken by Ricardo, a typical manifestation of his intellectual honesty and passion for logical rigour, stirred up heated debate. The theory of compensation had assumed a central role within the essentially optimistic view of economic development supported by the classical school within what had in fact become a canonical view. Thus, in the decades following his death Ricardo's argumentation was simply left aside, while the major protagonists of the economic debate restated in their writings a substantially unchanged theory of compensation.

8 The Ricardians and the Decline of Ricardianism

8.1 The Forces in the Field

Ricardo's theoretical construction, his policy tenets such as the abolition of corn duties and his dynamic vision, including the profits-accumulation link, constituted essential reference for anyone tackling economic issues after the publication of the *Principles*. However, even Ricardo's followers (including John Stuart Mill, author of the text – Mill 1848 – which Ricardianism had to thank for its lasting influence in the second half of the nineteenth century) abandoned this or that aspect of his analysis or introduced more or less important changes, thus opening the way to a change of paradigm. Moreover, among the economists of the time we find many exponents of an approach radically different from Ricardo's, which looked to supply and demand, scarcity and utility, rather than the relative difficulty of production, to determine exchange values.

The debate waxed lively even within the walls of the Political Economy Club, by and large a Ricardian institution, although the foundation, in 1821, and proceedings also saw the participation of Malthus, among others. Only a few years after Ricardo's death a question raised for debate at one of the meetings was just how much was still alive in his theories. Economic debate crossed with political debate, within the club as in the major cultural journals of the time: the *Edinburgh Review*, founded in 1802, showed a Whig leaning, favourable to reforms and supporting Ricardo's ideas; the *Quarterly Review*, founded in 1809, a Tory orientation; while the *Westminster Review*, founded in 1824 and close to Bentham's utilitarianism and the philosophical radicalism of his followers, was also favourable to Ricardo's ideas.

In the following sections we will summarise the debate as it progressed in the fifty years separating Ricardo from Jevons. The field saw many protagonists; a central position is naturally occupied by Ricardo's thought. Lined up by his side were his most faithful friends: James Mill and McCulloch. On the right wing, after his friend and rival Malthus came Bailey, Senior, Lloyd, Scrope and various others. On the left wing, the 'Ricardian socialists' can be separated into two currents: the relatively moderate supporters of cooperativism and the advocates of ethical interpretations of the theory of labour-value. On the inside right we can place Torrens and possibly De Quincey; the corresponding role on the inside left should go to John Stuart Mill (although precisely this fact shows just how schematic and reductive this linear representation of the positions in the field really is).

As we see, the debate took place largely in England: at least as far as political economy was concerned, the centre of European and world culture in the central decades of the nineteenth century was London, not Paris. There are various reasons for this: economic conditions (the leading role of England in the process of industrialisation), political conditions (a greater freedom of thought) and the presence of some exceptional personalities, such as Ricardo, and the influence that such personalities exerted in the development of a culture flourishing on direct contacts (as in the Political Economy Club).

8.2 Robert Torrens

Among the first critics of the Ricardian theory of labour value, Robert Torrens (1780–1864), a heroic officer of the Royal Marines and for some years a member of Parliament, was among the founders of the Political Economy Club and chaired its first meeting, in the presence of Ricardo, Malthus, James Mill and Tooke.

In 1808 Torrens published *The Economists Refuted*, criticising Spence's thesis that the continental blockade imposed by Napoleon, which hit English foreign trade, could not have damaged the nation, whose wealth sprang solely from its agriculture.[1] Returning to Smith's criticisms of physiocratic theory, Torrens pointed out that the manufacturing sector, too, and not only the agricultural one, contributes to production of the surplus and that both sectors produce means of subsistence and means of production necessary to productive activity. Finally, he stressed the advantages of trade in favouring the division of labour, formulating the fortunate expression 'territorial division of labour'. All such arguments were re-proposed at length in the *Essay on the Production of Wealth* (1821).

Torrens returned to the advantages of the territorial division of labour in 1815, with *An Essay on the External Corn Trade*. A few days before Torrens's essay came out, two pamphlets by Malthus and one by West

---

[1] William Spence (1783–1860), *Britain Independent of Commerce* (1807).

were published (respectively on 3, 10 and 13 February) and, on the same day as Torrens's (24 February), Ricardo's *Essay on Profits*. The near-simultaneity of these different publications gave rise to two problems of attribution, the first concerning the theory of rent, the second the theory of comparative costs. As far as rent is concerned, the issue was settled attributing priority of publication to Malthus; West and possibly Torrens were credited with independent formulation, while Ricardo for his part explicitly declared his debt to Malthus. As for the theory of comparative costs, Torrens's priority as well as Ricardo's found supporters; however, Torrens developed his analysis in terms of differences between the costs of producing the same commodity in the different countries and not in terms of differences between countries in the cost structure for different commodities, in contrast with Ricardo's – more correct – approach.

The following years saw Torrens engaging in the debate on the theory of labour value. Criticising it, Torrens pointed to the importance of exceptions, due to different proportions of labour, of fixed and circulating capital in different industries and different lengths of active life of fixed capital goods. Consequently the theory of labour value was to be rejected and substituted with a theory endowed with general validity: 'When capitalists and labourers become distinct, it is always the amount of capital, and never the amount of labour, expended on production, which determines the exchangeable value of commodities' (Torrens 1818, p. 207). He returned to this statement in his *Essay on the Production of Wealth*, proposing the thesis that products of equal capitals have equal exchange value. These are generic expressions, which Ricardo faulted for circular reasoning: 'I would ask what means you have of ascertaining the equal value of capitals? ... These capitals are not the same in kind ... and if they themselves are produced in unequal times they are subject to the same fluctuations as other commodities. Till you have fixed the criterion by which we are to ascertain value, you can say nothing of equal capitals.'[2] In other words, if we determine the relative prices of commodities on the basis of the values of capitals employed in producing them, how can we then explain the value of capital, made up of heterogeneous means of production? However, the arithmetical examples that Torrens used to illustrate his analysis contained precious pointers to go on beyond Ricardo's criticisms and develop a modern theory of prices of production.

---

[2] Letter by Ricardo to McCulloch, 21 August 1823 (in Ricardo 1951–55, vol. 9, pp. 359–60). Cf. also the essay on *Absolute Value and Exchangeable Value*, in Ricardo 1951–55, vol. 4, pp. 393–6.

The first examples in the *Essay* seem to confirm Ricardo's strictures: the commodities produced are different from the commodities utilised as means of production, the prices of the latter and the rate of profit being assigned in a wholly arbitrary way. As we go on, however, the examples become better fitted to the issue: in the chapter on agriculture a 'corn' model analogous to Ricardo's was utilised (corn was produced by means of corn and labour, and corn was also the means of subsistence) until finally, discussing the effects of a technological improvement in the manufacturing sector on the levels of production in the agricultural sector, Torrens was compelled to utilise a model with two basic commodities: the product of the agricultural sector and the product of the manufacturing sector. Given the wage rate (at the subsistence level), there remain to be determined the rate of profits and the relative price of one of the commodities in terms of the other.

In Torrens's example, determination of the unknowns was immediate thanks to the fact that the two commodities are produced in the same proportions in which they are employed. The rate of profits may then be determined as a physical ratio between the quantities (produced and utilised as means of production and subsistence) of the same composite commodity; the exchange ratio between the two commodities is also determined as a physical ratio between the capitals employed in their production. Translation in terms of a system of equations raises no great difficulties for today's readers. Torrens's example in fact displays substantive analogy with Sraffa's (1960, p. 7) first example of production with a surplus (wheat and iron produced by means of wheat and iron); indeed, the theory of prices of production formulated by Sraffa might look, at least at first glance, like full, rigorous expression of Torrens's vague intuitions, pointing as they do to the difficulty of production expressed in physical terms.

Two other problems remained: the different velocities of rotation of circulating capital and the existence of fixed capital goods. Torrens made only passing reference to the first issue: when for a given quantity of capital employed in production this velocity increases, there arises an advantage for society, but – he added – the details are rather complex. More interesting is the way Torrens addressed the second issue, the existence of fixed capital goods: fixed capital was considered a specific kind of joint product; machines used in production appear among the outputs of the same production process, side by side with outputs proper, and reappear among the means of production in the following period. This method was then adopted by Ricardo, Malthus and Marx and, more recently, von Neumann (1937) and Sraffa (1960, Ch. 10).

In the 1830s Torrens focussed mainly on colonial policy issues. In particular, he criticised the advocates of complete freedom in international trade, since by imposing customs duties a country is able to modify exchange ratios to its own advantage; therefore, he favoured a policy of reciprocity, with customs abolished (or lowered) only towards countries adopting a similar policy. Moreover, since such reciprocity is more easily obtained with the colonies, the combative colonel of the Royal Marines advocated the creation of an imperial free trade area.

In the 1840s Torrens spent his energies above all on monetary theory and policy, as leading exponent, together with Lord Overstone, of the currency school. Opposing Tooke's banking school, Torrens and his friends maintained that convertibility of paper money into gold was a necessary but not a sufficient condition to ensure the stability of the system. Therefore, they advocated rigorous limitations to issues of paper money and the division of the Bank of England into an issue department and a banking department, subsequently accomplished with the Peel Act of 1844.

8.3   Samuel Bailey

Torrens's criticisms of Ricardo's theory of value were in one important respect similar to, and in another different from, the criticisms advanced by a quiet provincial gentleman, Samuel Bailey (1791–1870), who was born, lived and died in Sheffield, joining in the economic debate of the time with some original ideas but remaining on the fringe of the circle associated with the Political Economy Club.

In a work dated 1825, *A Critical Dissertation on the Nature, Measure and Causes of Value*, Bailey – like Torrens – reacted against the metaphysical intimations of absolute value lurking behind Ricardo's recourse to labour contained in accounting for exchange values. Both Torrens and Bailey perceived behind the choice of labour contained, aside from the analytical obstacles it involves, a misrepresentation of the issue of exchange value, which in their opinion was purely a matter of relations between different commodities in the market and had nothing to do with the presence of a 'substance of value' within each commodity.

For the problem of exchange value itself, however, Bailey proposed a solution – albeit barely sketched out – drastically different from that based on the 'difficulty of production' common to Torrens and the whole classical tradition. Bailey referred instead to a subjective theory of value, maintaining that, in general, exchange value depended on the evaluation of the economic agents taking part in the act of exchange; the very definition of value was 'the esteem in which any object is held'

(Bailey 1825, p. 1). The causes of value concern the attitude of the human mind towards an object and cannot be studied by considering such an object in isolation (ibid., p. 16) but only considering the relationships between different objects (ibid., p. 15), so that we can speak of money-values, corn-values, etc., according to the commodity with which the comparison is made (ibid., pp. 38–9). This means that it is impossible to compare commodities belonging to different moments in time (ibid., pp. 71–2). Bailey then distinguished (ibid., p. 185) three classes of goods: those that are the object of a monopoly, those whose supply can be increased but only with an increase in costs and finally those whose supply can be increased at will, costs remaining constant. Thus he maintained that Ricardo's theory (with the qualifications that Ricardo himself introduced for the principle of labour-value and with a further note of caution in view of the heterogeneity of labour)[3] only held for the third category, which was far more limited than Ricardo's followers appeared to believe, while in the real world the second category was the most important. What mattered in this category was the relation between the buyers' evaluation and the (relative) scarcity of supply. Bailey thus anticipated the Marshallian tripartition of constant, increasing and decreasing costs, though skipping over the third category.

Bailey departed from the line followed by authors such as Senior and others, who against Ricardo re-proposed the viewpoint of scarcity and utility – a vision of society that survived from the times of the medieval fairs to modern marginalist theory. Bailey followed his own path, in virtue of which we may classify him among the progenitors of the subjective theory of value but above all of the 'Marshallian compromise'. At the time, however, the importance of his contribution was perceived as lying in his radical opposition to the metaphysical element that many economists, and not only the 'Ricardians', included in the notion of value. We find here an important element, namely Bailey's criticism of economists who 'attempt too much' when 'they wish to resolve all the causes of value into one and thus reduce the science to a simplicity of which it will not admit' (Bailey 1825, pp. 231–2): in other words, a warning against the pretence of *reductio ad unum* involved in metaphysical notions of value.

---

[3] It is precisely the heterogeneity of labour that makes it less suited than other commodities to act as a standard for the evaluation of other commodities. According to Bailey, the heterogeneity of labour should be placed on the same plane as the heterogeneity of land, which constituted the basis of the Ricardian theory of differential rent. An extension of the notion of rent to the case of superior personal qualifications was proposed a few years later by Senior and John Stuart Mill, who thus advanced on a road that was to lead to Marshall.

8.4   Thomas De Quincey and John Ramsay McCulloch

While Torrens and Bailey were considered as more or less radical critics of Ricardo's theories, other authors were considered 'Ricardians' (although it would be incorrect to speak of a Ricardian school in the strict sense of the term, i.e. with a cultural identity like that of the physiocrats during their short-lived splendour). Among them, side by side with Ricardo's friend and mentor, James Mill, and before his son John Stuart Mill (1806–1873), on whom I have more to say later, we find another Scottish economist transplanted in London, John Ramsay McCulloch (1789–1864), and a man of letters, Thomas De Quincey (1785–1859).

A prolific writer, McCulloch was one of the keenest advocates of Ricardo's ideas. Editor of *The Scotsman* from 1817 to 1821, journalist, professor of political economy at London University and Comptroller of the Stationery Office, in 1825 he published *The Principles of Political Economy*: a textbook that enjoyed great success, notably in the United States, where – together with Say's text – it proved the most widely read.

The first edition of his *Principles* is notable for a defence of the labour-contained theory of value so extreme as to appear a verbal trick: the idea that 'accumulated labour' included a 'wage' that remunerated for the time during which the labour remained locked up, between the moment it was performed and the moment when the product could be sold on the market. It was, however, a purely verbal solution: an artificial redefinition of the notion of labour contained, which deprived it of direct correspondence with the quantity of labour actually spent and transformed it into something like a 'real cost', given by wages paid plus profits accrued on wage advances. It was precisely this element of 'real cost' that gradually acquired importance, to the point of transforming the Ricardian theory of value, related to the difficulty of production, into John Stuart Mill's and then Marshall's theory of the cost of production.

McCulloch exerted an important influence on the economic debate of the time. He supported a policy of high wages and opposed the Combination Laws, which were against the workers' organisations. Besides, he was among the first professional scholars of the history of economic thought, publishing various reprints of rare texts and an important annotated bibliography, the *Literature of Political Economy* (1845).

De Quincey is best known for his 'Confessions of an English Opium Eater' (1821–22). In this autobiographical novel the author tells how he was stirred from his drug-induced torpor thanks to the intellectual stimulus of reading Ricardo's *Principles*. He then published a brilliant illustration and defence of Ricardo's theory of labour value, the 'Dialogues of Three Templars on Political Economy' (1824), in which he insisted in particular on the fact that the labour contained in a commodity is a measure of its 'real value', not of 'wealth'; the latter indicated the amount of commodities available and can increase when the productivity of labour increases, while its value remains unchanged if the quantity of labour employed remains unchanged. The distinction was already present in Ricardo's *Principles*,[4] but De Quincey brought the matter to life with a vivacity lacked by the master of the school and accompanied it with a defence of labour contained as 'real value' similar to McCulloch's.

De Quincey was the ideal representative of a stage of transition from the more intransigent Ricardianism to its gradual corruption and abandonment. His most important work in the economic field, *The Logic of Political Economy* (1844), constituted a step, even more decisive than that taken by John Stuart Mill, in the direction of a theory of prices based on demand and supply and a subjective theory of value. De Quincey emphasised – with a series of brilliant, lively examples repeatedly returned to in subsequent literature – the role of utility in determining the value of scarce and non-reproducible commodities; moreover, he interpreted market prices no longer as empirical variables explained at the theoretical level by natural prices but as theoretical variables in themselves, utilised in studying the process of gravitation towards/around natural prices based on supply and demand mechanisms.[5] This view, later taken up by John Stuart Mill in his *Principles*, together with Bailey's ideas discussed previously, opened the way to the Marshallian notion of different levels of analysis (very short, short, long period). These different levels of analysis are characterised by the simultaneous presence of demand and supply, utility and costs in the determination of prices. When the length of the period of time allowed for adjustment increases, the first of these elements decreases in importance and the second increases.

8.5 The Ricardian Socialists and Cooperativism

In the economic debate arising in England on publication of Ricardo's *Principles*, a group of authors subsequently labelled 'Ricardian socialists'

---

[4] Ricardo 1951–55, vol. 1, pp. 273–8.
[5] Cf. De Quincey 1844, pp. 206–7. Side by side with natural and market prices, De Quincey considered the category of 'actual prices' and criticised Ricardo for having left it out (ibid., pp. 203–7).

acquired some importance: William Thompson, Thomas Hodgskin, John Gray, John Bray. Some of these authors – Hodgskin in particular – utilised the Ricardian theory of labour value in support of the thesis that the equitable income for workers corresponds to the entire value of the product. More precisely, if commodities derive their value from the labour directly or indirectly necessary for their production, workers have a natural right to the whole product of their work, without deductions for profits or rents.

However, this picture is overly simplistic. These authors were part of a current of socialist literature (in the pre-Marxian sense of the term 'socialism') characterised by radical criticism of the institutional organization of market economies that guaranteed an income to the idle classes of landlords and capitalists in virtue not of their contribution to the productive process but of their social standing. The privileged tenet of this socialist literature was cooperativism, propounded in more or less Utopian or realistic forms, often associated with a drive for the moral regeneration of social life.

The leading figure – and as such recognised by his contemporaries – was Robert Owen (1771–1858), a textile manufacturer and supporter of cooperativism in practice and theory alike. His major writings (*A New View of Society*, 1813, and the *Report to the County of Lanark*, 1820) took his textile factory at New Lanark (and subsequently the community of New Harmony in Indiana, where he had in the meantime moved and which he himself described in his autobiography, Owen 1857–58) as an example to advocate a policy of active involvement of workers in plant management and, more generally, cooperative organisation of the social aggregation that had the productive plant as its core. Ricardo, and many others, took an interest in Owen's theses, up to the mid-nineteenth century and beyond.

Both aspects – cooperativism and 'natural law' use of the theory of labour value – were present in the writings of William Thompson (1775–1833), an Irish landowner who considered profits and rents as deductions from the value of the product of labour within the framework of an extensive discussion of the institutional forms in which distribution of the social product may take place. Cooperativism emerges as a solution to potential conflict between productive efficiency and distributive justice (in the sense of social equality) (Thompson 1824). Thompson enjoyed great prestige at the time.

A 'socialist political arithmetic' current tried to evaluate the labour time necessary to society net of the waste corresponding to subsistence of otiose classes or, more generally, deriving from a social system based on the distinction between workers, capitalists and landlords. Patrick

Colquhoun (1745–1820), in his *Treatise on the Wealth, Power and Resources of the British Empire* (1814), proposed a statistical table meant to illustrate the distribution of income among the different social classes. This analysis prompted John Gray (1799–1883) to maintain, in *A Lecture on Human Happiness* (1825), that the 'productive' workers receive only one-fifth of the social product. After an initial cooperativist phase, in the second part of his life Gray went on to uphold theses closer to the Marxist tenets of central planning for production.

Thomas Hodgskin (1787–1869) played a leading role in the movement for education in political economy for the working classes, centred on the Mechanical Institutes; in *Labour Defended against the Claims of Capital* (1825) he proposed a distinction between 'natural price' and 'social price', the former corresponding to what the capitalists paid the workers, the latter to what the capitalists received from the sale of their products, thus also including the rents and profits through which the property-owning classes appropriated the surplus. More than on cooperativism, Hodgskin focussed on the role that workers' associations (which constituted the early buds of the modern trade unions) could have in combating expropriation of part of the product of labour in the form of profits and rents. He also recalled the Smithian distinction between 'human institutions' (which may as such be modified) and 'the natural order of things'.

This literature offered a wealth of thought-provoking ideas, unfortunately lost sight of when it was, misleadingly, reduced to a pre-Marxian current. Together with cooperativism we may recall analyses connecting the distribution of social income with the productive organisation of society and illustrating the waste intrinsic to an institutional system that left a great deal of room for forms of income corresponding to no productive contribution. Proceeding in this direction, some exponents of this socialist literature (in particular Gray) went so far as to propose a society in which necessary labour was equitably shared among all, reducing the sacrifice each had to make in labour to a few hours a day. These ideas were taken up by Marxists such as Paul Lafargue (1880) and by radical reformists such as Ernesto Rossi (1946) but had already been appearing in Utopian literature since Thomas More (1516) and Tommaso Campanella (1602).

8.6 Nassau William Senior and the Anti-Ricardian Reaction

The conservatives of the time were wary of Ricardo's ideas, while a view alternative to Ricardo's and Smith's held on, playing an important role in the debate of the time. At the political level, it was argued that the landlords played a positive role in the economic process; at the analytical level, a theory of value based on scarcity and utility was proposed.

The best-known author in this tradition is Nassau William Senior (1790–1864), professor of political economy at Oxford. In a series of writings (1827, 1836) Senior proposed a subjective theory of value based on scarcity and utility (considered a subjective judgement that differs from one person to another) and touched upon the principle of decreasing marginal utility. His own definition of wealth included all goods and services that were useful and scarce; the objective of each person was 'to obtain, with as little sacrifice as possible, as much as possible of the articles of wealth' (1827, p. 30). Senior interpreted distributive variables as determined by the same mechanism as prices, locating behind the profit rate a cost (negative utility) borne by the capitalist, namely *abstinence*. This element, later embodied in Mill's *Principles*, constituted a decisive step for transformation of the classical approach (where the 'difficulty of production' pointed to an objective element, technology) into the Marshallian 'real cost' approach, which, as we shall see, combined objective and subjective elements alike. Abstinence was in fact the capitalists' contribution to the productive process; as wages were the reward for the workers' toil, so profits were the reward for a specific sacrifice, the negative utility borne by capitalists in abstaining from consumption. Senior, however, stressed that if abstinence meant the right to a reward for those who bore it, this right did not extend to their heirs.

Senior is also remembered for the part he took in the debate on the Poor Laws and for his contribution to the reforms these laws underwent in 1834, attempting to limit their scope of application. He opposed legal recognition of the workers' associations but was quite favourable to social legislation ranging from housing and health to state-funded education, free elementary education for all and constraints on child labour (a terrible plague at the time).

Marx's criticism focussed not only on the theory of abstinence but also on the decidedly captious argumentation Senior lined up (in the *Letters on the Factory Act*, 1837) against the reduction of working hours by law (to 'only' ten hours a day!). Senior maintained that the whole profit – necessary for capitalists to be induced to bring productive activity under way – stemmed from the 'eleventh hour'. The thesis was not, however, set out as a theory of profit but as empirical reasoning based on numerical examples assembled for the purpose, and here Marx's irony appears fully justified.[6]

In the wake of Senior, similar positions on the subject of value and distribution were upheld by his successors to the Oxford chair, Richard Whately (1787–1863; his *Introductory Lectures on Political Economy* are dated 1831) and William Forster Lloyd (1794–1852; his *Lecture on the Notion of Value*, dated 1833, is included in Lloyd 1837). Lloyd, in particular, clearly distinguished between what we now call total and marginal utility and connected his subjective theory of value with a principle of decreasing (marginal) utility.

Once raised to the archbishopric of Dublin, Whately founded there a school of political economy faithful to the subjective view of value. The chair in political economy named after him at Trinity College, Dublin, had as its first holder Mountifort Longfield (1802–1884). Those who entertain the illusion of a 'marginalist revolution', born in the space of just a few years, between 1870 and 1874, already adult and armed like Athena from the mind of Jupiter (in our case, from the mind of the trio Jevons-Menger-Walras), are advised to meditate on Longfield's *Lectures on Political Economy* (1834), where the essential elements of the marginalist theory of value were already all present, including the idea of wages regulated by the (marginal) productivity of labour. Moreover, in a work dated 1835, *Lectures on Commerce*, Longfield developed the Ricardian theory of international trade along the lines later adopted by Ohlin and Samuelson, taking endowments of

---

[6] Senior (1837) assumed that the weekly wage remains constant, hence that the hourly wage and, given the productivity per hour of work, the cost of labour per unit of product increase in proportion to the decrease in the hours worked; he also forgot about the circulating capital and hence the fact that costs relating to it fall with the decrease in working hours. For criticism, cf. Marx (1867–94, vol. 1, pp. 222–8: Ch. 7 Section 3). If the wage per hour of work remains constant (hence, assuming that the productivity per hour of work remains unchanged, if the cost of labour per unit of product remains unchanged), with fixed technical coefficients for circulating capital goods, and if the wear and tear of fixed capital goods depend on the quantity produced and not on the passage of time, the reduction in working hours leaves the profit per unit of product unchanged, while total profits decrease in proportion to the reduction in working time and the rate of profits falls more slowly (at a pace that depends on the proportion between fixed and circulating capital). If the reduction in working hours is accompanied not only by an unchanged hourly wage but also by a compensative increase in the number of workers employed and reorganisation of shifts such as to leave the degree of utilisation of the plant unchanged, neither total profits nor the rate of profits need change. As a matter of fact, the secular increase in the hours worked in a year has been accommodated by technical progress, with part of the increase in productivity making room for the reduction of working hours with no need for a reduction in workers' income (and another part making room for an increase in real wages).

labour and land as elements determining the international specialisation of labour.

8.7   Charles Babbage

Charles Babbage (1791–1871), an English engineer among Newton's successors to the Lucasian chair of mathematics at Cambridge, is considered a precursor of Taylorism and computer science. His best-known work is *The Economics of Machinery and Manufactures* (1832), where he combined close analysis of various productive processes and attention to technological change based on the introduction of machinery with general reflections on the causes and consequences of the division of labour. With respect to the latter, his contribution was twofold.

First of all, Babbage considered the division of labour a key element in reducing wage costs. Breaking a complex labour process down into simple operations allows for the utilisation of less qualified workers who receive less pay, since each worker need have only part of the qualifications necessary for completion of the whole set of working operations going into any given labour process.

This thesis suggests a theory of proletarisation much like Marx's, although Babbage then went in a completely different direction. His idea was that developing the division of labour, precisely because it means breaking down each operation into its elementary constituent elements, favours the invention of machinery able to perform these elementary activities,[7] thereby generating a process of continuous substitution of workers with machinery. Thus the more noble and complex activities involved in organising the work process and research and development of new technologies are reserved for human beings, while the duller, more repetitive activities disappear from the scene. This was, after all, the same idea that lay behind the quest of his whole life – a 'numerical computing machine', the distant progenitor of mechanical calculating machines that were, in turn, the forerunners of modern computers – based on the principle of breaking down any computation into its elementary components.

---

[7] Decomposition of the working process into its elementary operations, to be then recomposed in such a way as to optimise the productive process, was brought to the level of scientific exactness by Frederick Winslow Taylor (1856–1915), an American engineer, with his *scientific management* (or Taylorism, from his name). Taylorism favoured the spread of assembly lines, the first examples of which date from around 1860 (in the Chicago slaughterhouses and in the production of the Colt revolver); the triumph of the assembly line came in 1912 when the famous Model T Ford went into production.

Division of labour and mechanisation thus interact in the process of development, bringing about not a tendency, as Marx foresaw, to the progressive impoverishment of increasing masses of the population but rather progressive growth in the wealth of nations, which also allows, albeit in alternate stages, for the progressive enhancement of the role played by the workers in the productive process (thus at least in part compensating for what Smith himself considered a crucial negative aspect of the division of labour, namely the fragmentation of work tasks).

8.8 John Stuart Mill and Philosophical Radicalism

Important as he was as an economist – an exponent of the mature Ricardianism and author of an authoritative overview of the economic doctrine of the time – John Stuart Mill (1806–1873) was the leading light of the political current of 'philosophical radicalism', a line of thought originating from Bentham. In the history of political culture, Mill is the main reference for a progressive view of liberalism – an advocate of a democracy where the minorities are not overwhelmed by the majority (*On Liberty*, 1859), a staunch believer in the emancipation of women, open to suggestions of socialist cooperatives and a leader of the anti-slavery and anti-racist movement; with his intellectual honesty and open-mindedness he was a key figure whose influence reached well beyond his own times.

The son of James Mill – the friend who helped Ricardo in writing the *Principles* – and a pupil of Bentham, the young John Stuart grew up in an environment rich in cultural stimuli. Subjected by his father to a formidable educational *tour de force* (when three years old he began studying Greek and arithmetic), intelligent and cultivated, but also sensitive to the stimuli of poetry, after a period of psychological crisis at the age of twenty-five Mill fell in love with Harriet Taylor, two years younger but already married and mother to two children. John Stuart and Harriet married only twenty years later, in 1851, after the death of her husband; but Harriet had by then long been, and would remain until her death in 1858, an important source of inspiration for John Stuart. Like his father James before him, he worked for the Company of the Indies, with positions of increasing responsibility, from 1823 up to his retirement when, in 1858, the Company was wound up and the administration of India came under the direct responsibility of the British government.

We will consider here in outline two main aspects of his many contributions, regarding utilitarianism and (in the next section) political economy (thus disregarding his important contributions on logic and on liberty and democracy). With regard to utilitarianism, we shall focus on the substantial differences between his view and Bentham's. We shall also see that Mill's utilitarianism has nothing to do with the subjective theory of value developed by newborn marginalism, constituting rather a critique of it well ahead of his time.

Bentham's felicific calculus consisted in evaluating the pleasures and pains (considered as positive and negative quantities in a one-dimensional space) deriving from any given action. This provides the 'consequentialist' solution to the problem of ethics: an algebraically positive result for the felicific calculus indicates a good action, a negative result a bad action. Obviously, the calculus of pleasures and pains concerned the implications of the action under consideration for the whole of society. In his famous pamphlet on 'Utilitarianism' (1861), Mill defended consequentialism as opposed to deontological morals. At the same time, however, he criticised the idea that human feelings could be reduced to different quantities of a one-dimensional magnitude, pleasure (or, in the negative, pain).

Abandoning the sensistic view of human nature underlying Bentham's theories, Mill made a clear-cut distinction between utilitarianism as a moral criterion and utilitarianism as interpretation of individuals' behaviour. Habit, rather than conscious felicific calculus, accounted for a large part of human actions; moreover, when we wish to pass moral judgement, the utilitarian criterion was to be applied not to some immediate sensistic 'pleasure' but to a more complex mixture of feelings and reason, situated at a higher level.

This idea of a complex mixture of feelings and reason was connected to Mill's recognition that there are qualitative differences between different kinds of pleasures (and pains), which cannot be reduced to quantitative differences. Mill stressed, at times even scathingly, Bentham's failure to recognise this aspect (for instance recalling Bentham's declared indifference towards poetry). Mill thus rejected the image of an all-embracing, univocal felicific calculus that individuals could safely apply as a criterion for moral judgement without different evaluations and controversies continually arising. As a consequence of the multi-dimensional nature of men, conflict is inevitable and may even rise to the intensity of the conflicts underlying Greek tragedies. By the way, recognition of this fact – namely, the legitimacy of profound differences of opinion – played a crucial role in Mill's theory of politics, centred on the notion of liberty (to which he dedicated a famous essay, *On Liberty*, published in 1859).

Mill's 'modified utilitarianism', in short, did not reject consequentialist ethics, as opposed to the deontological a priori principles. However, it was even remoter than Bentham's position from Jevons's subjective theory of value, based as we shall see on a one-dimensional notion of utility, in terms of which individual preferences were expressed; these were, moreover, assumed to be independent of one another and sufficiently stable as to allow for their use in analysis of economic agents' behaviour. Even in Bentham consequentialist ethics did not imply the notion of rational economic agents maximising a one-dimensional utility; in Mill, the cautions and qualifications with which the felicific calculus was surrounded sharply differentiated the classical notion of 'economic man' from the Jevonian conception, the former being nearer to the Latin idea of the good *pater familias* than to the sensistic idea of an automaton maximising happiness conceived as a one-dimensional magnitude.

Mill's view linked back with Adam Smith's and, more generally, that of the Scottish Enlightenment, in at least two important respects: the idea of the 'impartial spectator' propounded by Smith (1759) and taken up again by Mill (1861, p. 288) in his formulation of the maximum happiness principle and the view, common to Smith (and the Scottish Enlightenment as a whole) and to Mill, of human beings as 'social animals', thus able to perceive the existence of common interests and to go beyond mere selfishness, pursuing, rather, an enlightened self-interest.

We may thus conclude that the classical economists, from Smith to John Stuart Mill, focussed attention on a complex individual, simultaneously guided by personal interest and social rules. The classical economists' analyses certainly assumed that the economic agent behaved in a rational way, but this did not imply accepting a one-dimensional view of human nature. In their analysis of consumption, individual choices were considered as the outcome of habits and customs, continuously modified by the appearance of new goods, so that producers were in fact considered the *primum movens* in determining consumption structures. All this appears confirmed by Mill's definition of political economy, as limited to a specific aspect of human nature, namely the desire to possess wealth.

8.9   Mill on Political Economy

Mill's first writings in the economic field, the *Essays on Some Unsettled Questions of Political Economy*, were written in 1829–30 but only published in 1844. Here (p. 112) Mill defined political economy as 'the science which treats of the production and distribution of wealth, so far as they depend upon the laws of human nature'. The *Essays* also contained a crucial contribution to the theory of international trade, namely the theory of reciprocal demand utilised to determine the exchange ratios between imports and exports. Furthermore, in these essays Mill developed an important critical evaluation of Say's law, by assigning to the economic agents' state of confidence a leading role in accounting for economic vicissitudes.

After a deservedly famous treatise on logic (Mill 1843), Mill produced what was for more than forty years (up to the publication of Marshall's *Principles of Economics* in 1890) to remain the standard text for the study of political economy, at least in the Anglo-Saxon world, namely the *Principles of Political Economy* (1848). This was essentially an exposition of Ricardian thought, but it also incorporated some ideas developed by anti-Ricardian economists, such as Senior's theory of abstinence, and Mill's own version of the positivism expounded by Auguste Comte (1798–1857; the *Cours de philosophie positive*, in six volumes, is dated 1830–42), who advocated a 'general science of society' able to capture the interdependences linking up all social phenomena. Mill tackled the problem of interpreting human societies from different vantage points by utilising a substantially inductive discipline (Comte's sociology) together with a substantially deductive discipline, political economy, and with a science still to be formed, namely ethology, or the science of national character. A supporter of cooperativism, Mill – foreshadowing in this modern environmental thinking – considered the stationary state not as a menace but as a state of affairs leaving room for moral and cultural progress of society.

The *Principles* were divided into five books: production, distribution, exchange, economic development and the role of the government. The theory of value made its appearance only in book three, dealing with exchange; this choice marks the distance between Mill and the subsequent marginalist theories, the latter considering income distribution as an instance of the problem of value. The distinction between production and distribution is also to be noted: the former is considered the field of natural laws, independent of the institutions, which by contrast are held to be relevant for the latter, subject to historically relative laws. The theory of production builds on the Smithian analysis of the division of labour; Mill proposed the thesis of a tendency to industrial concentration, pointing out the issue of natural monopolies (the remedy for which is nationalisation), while in the case of agriculture small-scale peasant farming is favoured.

Book two, on distribution, opens with a chapter on property and a balanced discussion of the pros and cons of different institutional frameworks. The judgement on private property depends on whether it is organised in such a way as to avoid excessive and arbitrary inequalities; Mill was also favourable to progressive inheritance taxation and to safeguards against the abuse of property rights. Communism, identified with realisation of generalised equality, is considered inferior to socialism, which allows for individual differences according to merit. Cooperatives and profit-sharing, discussed in detail in book four, represent Mill's favoured solution.

As for income distribution itself, profits are identified with abstinence, following Senior, and are thus determined by society's evaluation of the present compared to the future. Malthus's population principle looms large in the discussion of wages: Mill insists on the need to contain population growth as priority for improving the conditions of the working classes. Elements of a wage fund theory are also present but not in the rigid form sometimes attributed to the whole of classical political economy. The theory of the wage fund stated that the wage rate is determined by the ratio between two magnitudes: the amount of capital available for the maintenance of the workers and the number of workers employed; in its rudimentary form, but not in Mill's treatment, the numerator is taken as a given datum of the problem, while it is clear that the amount of capital available for the maintenance of the workers (the wage fund) not only varies in the course of time as a consequence of accumulation but can also vary at a given moment in time if the maintenance of productive workers involves making use of goods previously utilised for other purposes, such as luxury consumption (or, we can add nowadays, if additional production is provided by previously unemployed workers).

Together with acceptance of Senior's theory of abstinence, Mill's theory of value, particularly with the transformation of the notion of market prices into a theoretical variable determined by supply and demand, represents a transitional stage from the classical to the Marshallian approach, although Mill kept his feet firmly in the classical field, rejecting any idea of bringing to the centre of the theory of value those elements – scarcity and utility – upon which the subjective approach relied.

9   Karl Marx

9.1   Life and Writings

Karl Marx (1818–1883) was born in Trier in Prussia, where he attended the gymnasium; he attended university first in Bonn (1835) and then in Berlin (1836–41), finally graduating in Jena in 1841. In 1843 he married Jenny von Westphalen, the daughter of a high-ranking Prussian civil servant.

During the university years Marx was influenced by the Hegelian left (Ludwig Feuerbach and Otto Bauer). In May 1842 he became editor of the *Rheinische Zeitung*, a liberal newspaper of Cologne that was, however, soon closed by the Prussian authorities. Marx then emigrated to Paris, where he met Friedrich Engels (1820–1895), his great friend and lifetime collaborator. Some notebooks, posthumously published as *Economic and Philosophical Manuscripts*, date from this period; they are important for his theory of alienation.

In 1845 Marx was expelled from Paris and moved to Brussels. From this period we have some mainly philosophical writings (*The German Ideology*, 1845–46, and the *Theses on Feuerbach*, 1845, both written with Engels; *Misery of Philosophy*, 1847). Entrusted with the task by the League of the Communists, formed in 1847, Marx and Engels wrote its programme, the *Communist Party Manifesto* (1848), one of the most influential writings of all times. The revolutionary project that Marx and Engels would remain faithful to for the rest of their lives was set out there in incisive terms.[1] Thus, for instance, their formulation of historical materialism was expressed in a single sentence: 'The history of all hitherto existing society is the history of class struggles.'[2] The *Manifesto* foresaw

---

[1] Let us recall, for instance, the opening and closing sentences of the *Manifesto*: 'A spectre is haunting Europe – the spectre of communism'; 'Let the ruling classes tremble at a communistic revolution. The proletarians have nothing to lose but their chains. They have a world to win. Workingmen of all countries, unite!' (Marx and Engels 1848, pp. 48 and 82).

[2] Ibid., p. 48.

private ownership of the means of production overcome through expropriation, to be transferred under direct control of the state (which would no longer be the political expression of the bourgeoisie but of the proletariat).

The year 1848 was one of revolutions, all over Europe. Marx returned to Cologne. The revolutionary fever soon died down, and Marx, expelled from Prussia, moved to London. Here he spent the rest of his days, leading a life of study although taking part in the activities of the First International (more precisely, the International Working Men's Association, founded in 1864).[3] In those years he wrote his main works.

In the *Critique of Political Economy* (1859) Marx illustrated the materialistic conception of history: the continuous change of technology ('the powers of production') generates increasing tensions within the static element represented by 'production relations', namely the set of institutions and habits within which economic activity takes place, in turn connected to the cultural 'superstructure'. The dynamic element – productive forces – is destined to overturn the system of production relations and the superstructure in a revolutionary stage. We then have the transition to a new 'mode of production': from feudalism to capitalism and then to socialism and subsequently to communism, with corresponding upheaval of the superstructure. Historical materialism did not indicate a mechanical dependence of ideological superstructures on the economic structure but a complex interrelation in which the causal link going from structure to superstructure is far stronger than the link running in the opposite direction. The path of development of human societies was conceived as a dialectical process in which stages of normal development inevitably lead to revolutionary stages.[4]

---

[3] The First International was dissolved in 1867, following increasing friction in the internal political debate between Bakunin, Lassalle and Marx. The Second International was born in 1889 as an alliance of the European socialist parties and was dissolved when, on the outbreak of the First World War, nationalist feelings prevailed even within the socialist parties. The Third International or Komintern (1919–43), born in Moscow and dominated by the Soviet Union, was followed after the Second World War by the Kominform (1947–89). There still exists a Fourth International, founded by Trotsky in 1931 in Paris. The Socialist International (or Fifth International), founded in Zurich in 1947, groups together the social-democratic parties. Mikhail Bakunin (1814–1876) supported anarchist ideas. Ferdinand Lassalle (1825–1864), supporter of universal suffrage as means for the emancipation of the workers, also advocated cooperatives and was the founder of the General Association of German Workers, which led to the SPD, the German social-democratic party.

[4] Marx (1859, p. 84). According to Marx's critics, this implies underestimating the role of nationalistic and religious feelings in determining the history of peoples and countries. Cf. for instance Huntington (1996).

Years of work were invested in the fundamental work, *Capital*. The first volume was published in 1867, the second and third volumes coming out posthumously, edited by Engels, in 1885 and 1894 respectively. What Marx probably intended to be a fourth volume of *Capital*, the *Theories of Surplus Value*, a survey of the history of economic thought, was edited by Kautsky and published in 1905–10.

Marx died in 1883: the same year in which Keynes and Schumpeter were born.

9.2   The Critique of the Division of Labour: Alienation and Commodity Fetishism

The notion of alienation (from the Latin *alius*, 'the other') is developed in the *Economic and Philosophical Manuscripts* of 1844. The workers are alienated for three main reasons: because they do not own their means of production nor the product of their activity, which belong to the capitalists, and because they do not control organisation of the productive process, where they play only a limited, specific role. Thus tools, product and labour process appear to the workers as extraneous entities; as a consequence, work proves for the workers the means to one particular end – to earn the means of subsistence – rather than self-fulfilment within society. All this also implies the estrangement of the human being from other human beings.

The notion of alienation gave way to the concept of 'commodity fetishism' in *Capital*. Any society based on the division of labour, Marx recalled following Adam Smith's lead, is based on cooperation between producers. Each worker performs a specific task the results of which are in general utilised by others, while the worker needs the product of the work of others for subsistence and means of production. With the notion of commodity fetishism, Marx connected his critique of the division of labour to the specific form it assumes in capitalistic economies. Here not only do the flows of exchanges connecting different productive units go through the market, but the workers themselves are compelled to sell their labour on the market and buy their means of subsistence there. In this way the social relations of production – cooperation between workers active in different economic sectors and different productive units – is obscured by the fact that what is exchanged is not the labour time of one worker for that of another but different commodities. The market, while constituting the common ground for the necessary connection between separate workers, operates in such a way that commodities become fetishes, coming to be considered the ultimate end of production and exchange activity and not simply as necessary condition (both as means of production and as means of subsistence) for the survival and reproduction of individuals, as indeed of the economic system as a whole. Only closer critical scrutiny reveals what is hidden at first sight, namely that the exchange of commodities in the market constitutes the means for collaboration between workers, each performing a specific activity. However, this social collaboration is obscured by commodity fetishism.

9.3 The Critique of Capitalism and Exploitation

The main aspect of Marx's critique of capitalism lies in the thesis that capitalist societies are based on the exploitation of the workers by the capitalists. In order to demonstrate this thesis Marx introduced the distinction between *labour*, the exercise in real practice of some productive activity, and *labour power*, the worker as a person, incorporating the potential to exercise a productive activity. The distinction between labour and labour power may be compared to the difference between heat and a specific source of heat, for instance coal. Coal is the commodity bought and sold on the market, at a price such as to cover its costs of production. The buyer then utilises coal to get heat but could utilise it for other purposes, for instance writing on a wall or in any other way: once bought, the commodity belongs to the buyer and can be utilised as s/he likes. Something of the sort happens in the relationship between worker and capitalist. The commodity sold by the worker is labour power, or work capacity; the capitalist pays for it at its value, or in other words s/he pays enough to cover the costs for its production, corresponding to the means of subsistence required to keep the worker alive (together with the worker's family, so as to ensure substitution of the worker when s/he retires or dies). Thus the value of labour power corresponds to a minimum subsistence wage. On paying for it, the capitalist acquires the right to utilise the worker in the productive process, to get from her/him a given number of daily (or weekly) hours of labour that as a rule is greater than the value of the labour power, or the number of hours of labour 'contained' in the worker's daily means of subsistence. The total amount of labour performed in our economic system may then be divided into two parts: the *necessary labour*, required to produce the means of subsistence for all the workers employed within the economy, and the *surplus labour*, all the rest of the labour performed, equal to the difference between total social labour and necessary labour.

This representation of an economic system presupposes separation of the workers from ownership of the product and of their means of production. Capital, understood as the capacity to control means of production and labour power itself, is in Marx's opinion above all a *social relation of production*, expressing the subordination of the workers to the capitalists. The origin of capital in this sense of the term coincides with the formation of a class of workers dispossessed of their means of production and is the result of a long social process that Marx called 'primary accumulation' and which marks the transition from feudalism to capitalism.

Marx took up the labour theory of value from Ricardo. The annual national product has, then, a value equal to the quantity of labour employed during the year, L. With a wage rate equal to the subsistence minimum, the total wage of all workers in the economy has a value equal to necessary labour, LN. The surplus has a value equal to the labour time exceeding necessary labour, or surplus labour PL $(= L - LN)$, going to the capitalists in the form of profits P (and to landlords in the form of rent, but for the sake of simplicity here we will disregard this element, as well as financial capital and interests, which Marx and the classical economists considered part of the profits). Thus, even if the workers receive the full value of the commodity they sell (namely their labour power, the value of which as we saw is equal to its cost of production), or in other words even if what Marx considered the criterion of economic justice under capitalism – exchange of equal values – does indeed hold, the surplus value going to the capitalists corresponds to unpaid labour, and hence to exploitation of the workers by the capitalists.

Marx defined the *rate of exploitation s* as ratio of 'unpaid labour' or surplus labour to 'paid labour' or value of labour power; hence $s = PL/LN$. The rate of exploitation therefore depends on both the length of the working day and the share of it corresponding to necessary labour, and so to the value of labour power. Marx distinguished in this respect between *absolute surplus value*, due to a lengthened working day, and *relative surplus value*, resulting from a reduction in the value of labour power.

The rate of exploitation is equal to the rate of profits (given by the ratio between profits and capital advanced) only when the capital advanced consists solely of wages, or in other words when the workers do not utilise means of production (raw materials, tools and machinery). However, such an assumption contradicts the very nature of the capitalistic system, where the capitalists' role precisely derives from their control over the means of production. Thus, in general the capital advanced also includes means of production other than labour, and the rate of profits will be lower than the rate of exploitation. Therefore the rate of profits gives a reductive idea of the exploitation of the workers by the capitalists.

With his theory of exploitation Marx showed how the surplus emerges from the productive process and not from the circulation of commodities. The latter thesis is described as *profit upon alienation*, the idea being that profits accrue from buying at low prices and selling at high prices. Marx attributed this thesis to the mercantilists and attacked it vehemently. According to Marx, in the sphere of circulation 'liberty, equality, property and Jeremy Bentham are supreme': liberty, since everybody enters freely into exchange agreements; equality, because 'the buyer and the seller . . . exchange equivalent for equivalent'; property, 'because each of them disposes exclusively of his own'; Bentham (that is, utilitarianism) since 'the power . . . which makes them enter into relation one with another, is self-interest, and nothing more'.[5]

Marx aimed this criticism not only at mercantilist thought but also at the various socialist currents that condemned profits as unjust deduction from the fruits of labour, a group including both the Ricardian socialists and anti-capitalistic writers such as Proudhon (known for his motto: 'property is theft').[6] Marx stressed that his was a 'scientific socialism', which recognised that the equitable criterion of exchange of equals was honoured in the capitalist system.

The *profit upon alienation* thesis can be represented by the scheme $M - C - M'$, where M indicates money and C commodities: money M buys commodities C that are then sold again for a greater sum of money, M'. This scheme violates the rule of exchange of equals: if C is equivalent to M in the first step, it cannot be equivalent to M' in the second step. Marx proposed, instead, a scheme that represented the process of circulation and the process of production simultaneously,

$$M - C(LP \text{ and } MP) \ldots C' - M'$$

where exchanges are represented by hyphens and the productive process by a series of dots: money M buys commodities, and more precisely labour power LP and means of production MP; through the productive process we get a different set of commodities, C', which is exchanged for a sum of money, M', greater than the initial sum. The value of the means of production other than labour is transmitted unchanged in the value of the product; the profit P $(= M' - M)$ originates from the fact that labour power transmits to the value of the product not only its own value

---

[5] Marx (1867–94, book 1, pp. 164).

[6] Pierre-Joseph Proudhon (1809–1865), French typesetter and proof-reader, self-defined anarchist, supporter of projects for monetary reform and advocate of associationism, followed the 'Ricardian socialists' in deducing from the labour theory of value the thesis that profits, interests and rents are 'unearned income'. His main work, *What Is Property?*, was published in 1840.

(equal to the value of its means of subsistence) but also the surplus labour or unpaid labour.

Exploitation can be overcome, Marx held, with transition to still more advanced modes of production, socialism first, and then communism. Socialism is characterised by collective property of the means of production. Marx considered transition from capitalism to socialism a necessary consequence of certain 'laws of movement of capitalism': the growing bi-polarisation of society between an increasingly vast, ever poorer proletariat (the 'law of increasing misery') and an increasingly strong but numerically small bourgeoisie (the 'law of capitalistic concentration'); such bi-polarisation must of necessity end in revolution.

The theory of exploitation relies on the labour contained theory of value to express in homogeneous terms the different magnitudes (product, means of subsistence, surplus). Like Ricardo, Marx too was conscious of the fact that exchange values determined on the basis of the labour theory of value do not correspond to the prices at which commodities are exchanged in competitive markets, where the rate of profits is uniform throughout all sectors of the economy. The labour theory of value can at best be utilised as an initial approximation, provided that it can then be shown, as a second step, not to have led to irremediable errors. As we shall see later, Marx set out to tackle this crucial weak point in his theory in Book 3 of *Capital*, but the solution he proposed – the so-called transformation of labour values into prices of production – also proved insufficient, with the consequence that a number of crucial elements of the Marxian theoretical castle must be called into question, including the theory of exploitation itself.

9.4   Accumulation and Expanded Reproduction

In Book 2 of *Capital*, Marx illustrated two analytical schemes respectively dealing with simple reproduction and expanded reproduction, or accumulation. Both schemes incorporate the *reproducibility condition*: for each commodity, the quantity produced must be equal to or greater than the quantity utilised in the productive process as means of production or necessary subsistence.

In the case of *simple reproduction*, period after period the levels of production remain unchanged. If there is a surplus, it goes into luxury consumption or subsistence for the unemployed or unproductive workers. In the case of *expanded reproduction*, at least part of the surplus is accumulated – added, that is, to the previous amounts of means of production and subsistence. In this way, period after period the number of workers employed in the productive process can increase. Without any change in technology, a progressive widening of the economy takes place. Over and above this process, there is technical progress generally taking the form of an increasing use of machinery, according to a representation of economic development common to both Marx and classical economists.

Marx distinguished two sectors of the economy, one producing means of consumption, the other means of production. The relative activity levels of the two sectors are in equilibrium when the entire production of the two sectors can be absorbed by the economy. In the case of simple reproduction, this happens when the quantity of means of production that are produced equals the quantity employed in the productive processes in the two sectors, while the quantity of consumption goods produced equals the requirements of means of subsistence for the workers employed in the economy plus the quantity utilised for luxury or unproductive consumption. In this case, the entire surplus consists of consumption goods.

In the case of expanded reproduction, the surplus must consist of both means of production and consumption goods. Furthermore, the ratio between consumption goods and means of production within the surplus must be equal to or higher than the corresponding ratio between means of subsistence and means of production available at the beginning of the production process. This is due to the fact that the surplus means of production can only be used for accumulation, while surplus consumption goods can be partly used for luxury or unproductive consumption. The maximum rate of growth of the economy obtains when the proportion between the two groups of goods in the surplus is equal to their proportion at the beginning of the production process, so that no waste of consumption goods occurs, all going to 'necessary' consumption, for the maintenance of productive workers.[7]

---

[7] Applying a labour theory of value, Marx calls v the variable capital, i.e. the value of subsistence goods utilised in the productive process; c the constant capital, i.e. the value of means of production (labour excluded); s the value of the surplus. Let us call the sector producing means of production 1 and the sector producing consumption goods 2; C stands for the value of production in sector 1 and V for the value of production in sector 2. We may then express Marx's reproduction schemes as follows:

$$c_1 + v_1 + s_1 = C$$
$$c_2 + v_2 + s_2 = V$$

In the case of simple reproduction, the equilibrium production levels of the two sectors are:

$$C = c_1 + c_2$$
$$V = v_1 + v_2 + s_1 + s_2$$

In other terms, the level of production of sector 1 corresponds to the quantity of means of production utilised in both sectors; the level of production of sector 2 corresponds to the means of subsistence required for all the employed workers plus the consumption goods that capitalists buy with their profits, the latter being equal to the entire surplus of

With the reproduction schemes Marx showed that given a certain set of conditions the system may grow endlessly, without any need for problems of realisation of the product to arise. This result contradicts the under-consumption theories proposed by Malthus, Sismondi or Rodbertus. It did not, however, imply for Marx adhesion to Say's law, according to which any level of production can be absorbed by the market. Firstly, *crises of disproportion* may occur whenever equilibrium proportions do not hold between the two sectors (and growth in equilibrium, Marx said, can only come about by chance). Secondly, and more importantly, Marx did not rule out the possibility of *general over-production crises* in a system based on decentralised investment decisions distinct from decisions to save. Marx attributed an important role to fluctuations in production levels and built one of the first theories of the trade cycle.

Marx's theory of the trade cycle was based on the fluctuations in the *industrial reserve army* (a term by which Marx designated not only unem-ployed workers but also artisans and workers employed in agriculture but ready to change to employment in manufacturing). In the recovery phase, income grows and unemployment falls, as does the industrial reserve army. As a consequence, the bargaining power of the working class increases, while the competition between entrepreneurs in search of workers grows tougher: the real wage rate rises.[8] The increased cost of labour gives rise to a reduction in profits per unit of output. Firms then react to the increase in wages by trying to save on the labour utilised in

---

the economy. We can reduce these two equations to one equilibrium condition for the exchanges between the two sectors: the value of capital goods sold by sector 1 to sector 2 is equal to the value of means of subsistence sold by sector 2 to sector 1. Algebraically:

$$c_2 = v_1 + s_1$$

In the case of enlarged reproduction, a share of the surplus, q, goes to accumulation of new capital goods; correspondingly, a share equal to $(1 - q)$ of the surplus thus consists of consumption goods. Algebraically:

$$C = c_1 + c_2 + q(s_1 + s_2)$$

$$V = v_1 + v_2 + (1 - q)(s_1 + s_2)$$

As we saw above, capital goods and means of subsistence serving to increase the number of employed workers must grow in the same proportion. Besides, the surplus may include a residuum of consumption goods to serve for luxury goods or the consumption of the unproductive workers; the rate of growth is at a maximum when this residuum is nil and the entire surplus goes into accumulation.

[8] This inverse relation between wages and unemployment anticipates the so-called Phillips curve, namely the inverse relationship between rate of change of money wages and level of unemployment empirically estimated for the United Kingdom between 1861 and 1957 by the New Zealand economist A.W. Phillips (1914–1975), in a much cited article published in 1958. Furthermore, Marx's analysis of income distribution was based on the relative bargaining power of workers and capitalists, as in Smith, and in contrast to the supporters of the 'iron law of wages' based on the Malthusian principle of population.

the productive processes. To this end they mechanise production. This favours technical progress, which forms the basis for economic development.

The process of mechanisation allows firms to reduce the number of employed workers. The industrial reserve army thus grows, and this puts a brake on wage increases. Thanks also to the productivity increases obtained with mechanisation, the cost of labour per unit of output decreases with a consequent rise in profits. Firms again expand and hire new workers, the increase in profits constituting both an incentive to increase production levels and a source of finance for investments to expand productive capacity. The industrial reserve army again shrinks. We thus have a stage of expansion, marking the beginning of a new cycle.

This theory dealt at the same time with the trade cycle, economic development and the evolution over time of employment and distributive shares. In twentieth-century theoretical analyses, instead, the tendency set in to analyse economic growth and the cycle separately.

9.5   The Laws of Movement of Capitalism

The link between the division of labour and social structure underlies the major attempts to single out the basic trends in human society, or in other words to understand 'where we are going'. The most celebrated of such attempts is that of Marx. In his opinion, capitalism is not the final stage in the history of human societies, but only an intermediate stage: it was preceded by other forms of organisation of society (serfdom, feudalism) and will give way to new forms of social organisation (socialism first, then communism). By studying the laws of motion underlying capitalism, we understand how it came into being, how it has changed in the course of its evolution and the reasons why it will have to give way to a new form of social organisation, namely socialism.

In this respect Marx noted the tendency of capitalistic societies towards increasing economic and social polarisation: on the one hand we have the growing misery of an increasing proportion of population, in other words *proletarisation*, i.e. the formation of ever vaster masses of common workers; on the other hand we have the tendency to increasing *concentration* of manufacturing production in a few big firms, entailing ever greater economic and political power concentrating in a few hands, while small entrepreneurs and independent artisans end up joining the ranks of dependent workers. Hence the thesis of inevitable collapse facing the capitalistic mode of production, when the proletariat – by then the overwhelming majority of the population – expropriate the capitalist class, economically dominant but numerically weak. The way is thus opened to socialism.

Another thesis developed by Marx, the *law of the falling rate of profits* illustrated in Book 3 of *Capital*, takes much the same course.[9] The process of increasing mechanisation entails progressive increase in the organic composition of capital, or in other words of the ratio between constant capital c (the value of means of production utilised in the productive process other than labour power) and variable capital v (the value of labour power employed in production), both expressed in terms of labour contained. Therefore, if the organic composition of capital increases and the rate of exploitation does not increase *pari passu*, the rate of profits necessarily decreases.[10]

The reasoning is flawed, though, by confusion between variables expressed in terms of labour values and underlying quantities of the various commodities. In fact, mechanisation does not necessarily imply an increase in the organic composition of capital. This is not the case, for instance, if a growing number of machines, thanks to technical progress, require the same or a smaller quantity of labour for their production, so that the organic composition of capital remains constant or decreases. Furthermore, technical progress itself, by reducing the quantity of labour required for the production of subsistence goods, causes an increase in the rate of exploitation for a constant real wage.

9.6   The Transformation of Labour Values into Prices of Production

As we saw, in *Capital* Marx adopted the labour theory of value. However, just like Ricardo, he too realised that such a theory was inconsistent with the assumption of a uniform rate of profits expressing in analytic terms a central feature of the capitalistic mode of production, namely competition. Marx tackled the problem, in Book 3 of *Capital*, through the so-called transformation of labour values into prices of production.[11] Marx's idea was to show that this transformation did not modify the substance of

---

[9] Marx 1867–94, vol. 3, pp. 317–75.

[10] The rate of profit $s/c + v$ may be expressed (dividing numerator and denominator by v) as $(s/v)/(c/v + 1)$, with the numerator being the rate of exploitation and the denominator the organic composition of capital plus 1. If the denominator grows while the numerator remains unchanged, the ratio, i.e. the rate of profits, must decrease.

[11] Section 2 of Book 3 of *Capital* is devoted to the subject: Marx (1867–94, vol. 3, pp. 245–316). Book 3 was published posthumously, edited by Engels on the basis of notes left by Marx; thus we have no certainty about just how convinced Marx himself was of the solution he worked out.

the results reached on the basis of the labour theory of value, in particular insofar as the thesis of exploitation was concerned.

Let us recall that Marx called v the variable capital (the value of labour power employed in the productive process), c constant capital (the value of means of production employed in the productive process), s the surplus value, corresponding to surplus labour, or in other words the labour employed in excess of the requirements to reconstitute the means of subsistence. The *rate of exploitation* is equal to the ratio between surplus labour s and necessary labour v. If we assume that competition in the labour market brings out uniform working conditions in the different sectors of the economy, and in particular an equal length of working day, and that the subsistence wage is the same for all workers, then the rate of exploitation corresponds to the ratio between surplus value and variable capital, s/v, and is the same for each individual worker, for each sector and for the economic system as a whole.

However, the condition of a uniform rate of exploitation in all sectors of the economy is inconsistent with the assumption of a uniform rate of profits. Let us indicate the different sectors with $1, 2, \ldots, n$. The condition of equal rates of exploitation is expressed by:

$$s_1/v_1 = s_2/v_2 = \ldots = s_n/v_n \tag{1}$$

The assumption of uniform rate of profits (computed for each sector as the ratio between profits and value of capital advanced, which includes both constant and variable capital, or wages) is expressed by:[12]

$$s_1/(c_1 + v_1) = s_2/(c_2 + v_2) = \ldots = s_n/(c_n + v_n) \tag{2}$$

Let us divide both numerator and denominator of the different terms of this series of equalities respectively by $v_1, v_2, \ldots, v_n$. We get:

$$(s_1/v_1)/(c_1/v_1 + 1) = (s_2/v_2)/(c_2/v_2 + 1)$$
$$= \ldots = (s_n/v_n)/(c_n/v_n + 1) \tag{3}$$

At the denominator we thus have the ratio between constant and variable capital, c/v, which Marx called the organic composition of capital, plus 1. At the numerator we have the rates of exploitation of the different sectors, by assumption all equal. As a consequence, the series of equalities (3) – which we have just deduced from the assumption of uniform profit rates – hold if, and only if, the denominators, too, are all equal. Uniformity of profit rates hence requires that the organic compositions of capital in the different sectors also be all equal:

---

[12] Here we disregard the complications that might arise from the presence of fixed capital goods.

$$c_1/v_1 = c_2/v_2 = \ldots = c_n/v_n \tag{4}$$

However, there is no reason for this to happen. In fact, each sector adopts a technology specific to it. Thus, the assumption of a uniform rate of profits contradicts the assumption that the quantities of labour contained are a correct measure of the exchange values of commodities produced and of means of production.

Marx recognised this difficulty and proposed transformation of the magnitudes expressed in terms of labour values that do not comply with the condition of a uniform rate of profits into magnitudes expressed in terms of prices of production. In order to do this, he added to the production costs of each sector (given by the sum of constant and variable capital) the profits for that sector, computed by applying the average rate of profit calculated for the system as a whole, expressed by $s/(c + v)$, to the capital advanced for the sector. Let us consider a two-sector economy; we then have

$$(c_1 + v_1) + r(c_1 + v_1) = A\, p_1$$

$$(c_2 + v_2) + r(c_2 + v_2) = B\, p_2$$

where A and B represent the quantities of product obtained in the first and second sector respectively, expressed in terms of labour values (that is, $A = c_1 + v_1 + s_1$ and $B = c_2 + v_2 + s_2$), while p_1 and p_2 represent the prices of production of the two commodities and constitute the two unknown variables determined by the two equations, the rate of profits being known (since, let us recall, $r = (s_1 + s_2)/(v_1 + v_2 + c_1 + c_2)$).

However, the solution cannot be considered satisfactory: costs and advanced capital are expressed in terms of labour contained, while it is obvious that capitalists compute their profit rate as ratio of profits and capital advanced *measured in terms of prices, not of labour values.*[13]

---

[13] Marx (cf. 1867–94, vol. 3, pp. 261–72) recognised the existence of this difficulty but put it aside, considering it as practically irrelevant when referring to aggregate magnitudes representing the economic system as a whole. In sum, Marx imposed a double constraint: (i) equality between total surplus value created in the economy and total value of profits and (ii) equality between the total value of the product of the various sectors in terms of labour contained and its value in terms of prices of production. However, the two constraints are simultaneously satisfied only in very rare circumstances.

Objections to Marx's solution were raised on many sides, in particular by Böhm-Bawerk (1896). Ladislaus von Bortkiewicz (1868–1931) tried to formulate a corrected version of Marx's proposal (Bortkiewicz, 1906–7, 1907) by adopting as unit of measurement for each of the two commodities a and b the quantity of that commodity corresponding to a unit of labour contained. In this way the prices of production p_1 and p_2 can be interpreted as those multiplicative coefficients that allow us to move on from magnitudes measured in terms of labour contained to corresponding magnitudes

9.7   A Critical Assessment

Marx's economic and political construction has given rise to debate on a vast scale. Here we will only briefly consider a few aspects.

On the subject of the *laws of movement* of capitalism, Marx was right in stressing the process of industrial concentration, stimulated by large-scale production economies: although the last few decades may have seen a relative growth in importance of small and medium-size firms, especially in the more technologically advanced sectors, the fact remains that in a span of over a century as from the publication of *Capital* the size of firms grew enormously, with the development of large financial groups and big multinationals.[14] However, all this has not led to bipolarisation between an ever smaller capitalist class and an ever vaster proletariat: other factors were at work in the meantime, leading to the formation of large and growing *middle classes*, which eventually outweighed the proletariat represented by unskilled workers.[15] The growth of the middle classes was associated with a decreasing proportion of workers directly employed in the production of commodities, and an increasing proportion engaged in producing services, or only indirectly employed in the production of commodities (administrative employees, technicians and such like).

The new political and economic strength enjoyed by employed workers favoured re-distribution of income in the direction of wages and salaries, even if recent trends went once again towards a greater concentration of incomes and wealth. Thanks to broader-based shareholding, and above all thanks to the notable weight of the public sector in the economy,

---

measured in such a way to comply with the condition of a uniform rate of profits. Therefore, not only the quantities of the two commodities, A and B, but also the quantities of constant and variable capital (that is, of capital goods and subsistence means) utilised in the two sectors, are to be multiplied by such coefficients. Thus we get:

$$(c_1 p_1 + v_1 p_2)\,(1 + r) = A\,p_1$$

$$(c_2 p_1 + v_2 p_2)\,(1 + r) = B\,p_2$$

that is, two equations in which, considering c_1, c_2, v_1, v_2, A, B as given, we have three unknowns: p_1, p_2 and r, which can easily be reduced to two: the relative price p_1/p_2 and the profit rate r. The solution is formally correct, but with it labour contained is reduced to a simple standard of measure for the commodities utilized as means of production; substituting it with physical units of measure, as was done for the quantities produced A and B, labour contained exits the scene.

[14] On Marx's lead, the thesis of an increasing concentration of financial capital was developed by Rudolf Hilferding (1877–1941; his book, *Das Finanzkapital*, was published in 1910). Non-Marxian economists as well, such as Schumpeter and John Kenneth Galbraith (1908–2006), took the tendency to industrial and financial concentration as a central aspect in their analyses of capitalism.

[15] Cf. Sylos Labini 1974.

the process of industrial concentration did not – contrary to Marx's prediction – entail parallel concentration in a few hands of the totality or near totality of wealth and economic power.

This fact sees the thesis of inevitable revolution looming up in the evolution of the capitalistic system deprived of one of its main pillars, and with it also the thesis of the progressively increasing misery of the proletariat is undermined. Another pillar – the thesis of the tendency of the rate of profits to fall – also turns out to have shaky foundations (as we saw in Section 9.5). As for the theory of labour value, it turns out to be nothing but a complicated and substantially useless way of measuring the quantities of the means of production to determine production prices: Sraffa's contribution, as we shall see, will show that relative prices and the rate of profits can be determined, given the real wage rate, through a system of equations in which means of production are measured as physical quantities and any reference to quantities measured in terms of embodied labour disappears.

Let us now consider the issue of communism. On the evidence of the *Critique of the Gotha Programme*, it is clear that Marx and Engels had in mind not the absolute disappearance of the division of labour but the possibility of superseding compulsory labour. Until then, even with the crucial transition from capitalism to socialism, compulsory labour retains the nature of a necessity imposed on the individual worker.

We may compare Marx's attitude to Smith's. According to the Scottish philosopher, the division of labour is a source of economic and civic progress, but also of social problems; the former aspect may be held to outweigh the latter, and the division of labour thus deemed desirable, but steps must also be taken against the negative aspects, to offset them as far as possible. Marx, by contrast, seemed to consider the liberation of men from the serfdom of compulsory labour a real possibility, which implied a more drastically negative judgement of the transitional stages before the target was reached and readiness to bear the costs necessary to reach it, including the 'dictatorship of the proletariat' in the socialist stage preceding the ultimate construction of communist society. Now, not only have the theoretical elements invoked by Marx in support of the thesis of the inevitable transition from capitalism to socialism (social polarisation, tendency of the profit rate to fall) proved faulty, but above all, the socialist mode of production has proved a fragile form of social organisation as compared with the market economies on the crucial evidence of historical reality, precisely with respect to what Marx considered the decisive element, namely the development of productive forces. The apparently more modest Smithian perspective – a path of progress but with no definite point of arrival – seems preferable then, both as an interpretation of the evolution of human societies and as a guide to action, to the more radical – in fact, substantially utopian – perspective within which Marx created his theoretical architecture.

9.8 Marxism after Marx

Marx's influence has been enormous, until recent times. His thought inspired communist movements in industrialised Western countries, and political regimes in the major developing countries, from the Soviet Union after the 1917 revolution to China after the Second World War.

Marx's immediate successors – his friend Friedrich Engels and his pupil Karl Kautsky (1854–1938) – edited some major works by their master published posthumously: Books 2 and 3 of *Capital* by Engels and the *Theories of Surplus Value* (Marx 1905–10) by Kautsky. In his political activity Kautsky was also one of the first 'revisionists', stressing the importance of the market for political and social progress, showing a preference for a long phase of transition from capitalism to socialism rather than the abrupt revolutionary leap.

The same line was followed by Eduard Bernstein (1850–1932); his best known work is *The Prerequisites of Socialism and the Tasks of Social-Democracy* (1899). In contrast with Marxian theories on the necessity of dictatorship of the proletariat in the socialist stage of transition towards communism, he stressed the central role of democratic institutions for political and social progress. A similar line of thinking was followed by the socialists belonging to the Fabian Society, founded in 1884 by a group of British intellectuals that included George Bernard Shaw (1856–1950) and economic historians Sidney Webb (1859–1947) and his wife Beatrice (1858–1943).[16]

Other currents that were placed under the heading of 'Marxist orthodoxy', essentially on account of their political success, can also be considered heterodox when we compare them with Marx's original thought. The first name to be recalled here is that of Vladimir Ilyich Ulyanov (1870–1924), also known as Lenin, author among other writings of *Imperialism, the Final Stage of Capitalism* (1916), a brief essay that began

---

[16] The Webbs supported, among other things, social security schemes to be financed through taxes rather than through compulsory contributions, as was the case with the system adopted by Bismark and the system that was established in Great Britain after the Second World War. They also founded the London School of Economics, in 1895, designed to favour the development of a progressive economic culture well-rooted in empirical research and not conditioned by the conservative ideology prevailing in the traditional universities.

by recognising an element that contradicted Marx's analysis, namely the fact that the workers and socialist parties in the different countries had identified with their respective national interests during the war. Lenin took up a thesis propounded by British economist John Hobson (1858–1940) in an essay on *Imperialism* published in 1902, which saw in colonial developments the quest for outlets for the population and capital that remained unused in the industrialised countries. Lenin combined this thesis with an interpretation of monopoly capitalism fusing the Marxian law of industrial concentration with the theory of integration of financial and industrial capital propounded by Hilferding (1910). As far as the post-revolutionary Soviet Union was concerned, Lenin's writings pointed in the direction of the NEP, the New Economic Policy based on recognition of a certain role to the market, above all for determination of the crucial exchange ratio between agricultural products and manufactures, within a centralised economy characterised by state ownership of the means of production.

A leading supporter of NEP was Nikolai Bukharin (1888–1938), who argued the expediency of leaving greater leeway to market mechanisms, albeit guided by the state authorities through control over the nerve centres of the economy. Subsequently, Bukharin was converted to the Stalinist views on state agriculture and forced accumulation, but this did not save him from the Stalinist purges of the late 1930s, which also hit Yevgeni Preobrazhensky (1886–1937), critical of the NEP and advocating a primitive accumulation that could be achieved in Russia only with systematic state extortion of the surplus produced by the agricultural sector.

The theme of disequilibrium in the process of accumulation had already been subjected to analyses by Tugan-Baranovsky (1865–1919) and Rosa Luxemburg (1871–1919). Both utilised Marx's simple and enlarged reproduction schemes. Tugan-Baranovsky (1905) thus showed both the error of under-consumption theories holding crisis from deficiency of aggregate demand to be inevitable, and just how difficult it is to follow a growth path so as to maintain equilibrium between the propensity to save and investment opportunities. Rosa Luxemburg (1913) focused on the relationship between accumulation and growth of demand in the presence of a continuous drive towards technological change. Her book is a mine of ideas – albeit not always fully developed – which prompted a profusion of interpretative studies. Among other things, Rosa Luxemburg stressed the monopolistic nature of capitalism, the role of political elements (and military violence) in the functioning of the economy, imperialistic tendencies and the internationalisation of capitalism.

After the end of Stalinism, a number of exponents of the 'Warsaw school' including Oskar Lange (1904–1965) supported the thesis of a socialist market. The leading light of this school was Michal Kalecki (1899–1970), on whom more follows.

Among Western Marxist economists we may mention Paul Baran (1910–1964) and Paul Sweezy (1910–2004). Baran (1957) authored an analysis of the processes of capitalistic development based on the notion of 'potential surplus' and singling out the reasons standing in the way of full use of productive capacities in different countries and epochs. Sweezy, a pupil of Schumpeter, authored *The Theory of Capitalist Development* (1942) – still the best illustration of Marx's economic theory – but also, together with historian Leo Huberman, founded the *Monthly Review* in 1949. In 1966 Baran and Sweezy together published *Monopoly Capital*, a book that, together with the writings of philosopher Herbert Marcuse (in particular *One-Dimensional Man*, published in 1956), became one of the main reference points in the student unrest that spread from California to Paris in 1967–68, to then sweep the whole world over.

10 The Marginalist Revolution: The Subjective Theory of Value

10.1 The Marginalist Revolution: An Overview

The term 'marginalist revolution' is commonly utilised to indicate the abandonment of the classical approach and the shift to a new approach based on a subjective theory of value and the analytical notion of marginal utility. The years between 1871 and 1874 saw publication of the major writings of the leaders of the Austrian marginalist school, Carl Menger (1840–1921); of the British school, William Stanley Jevons (1835–1882); and of the French (Lausanne) school, Léon Walras (1834–1910).

The marginalist revolution, however, had had important precursors. Moreover, the differences between the Austrian imputation approach, the French general economic equilibrium and Marshallian partial equilibriums were by no means negligible, as we shall see. Among the English economists, then, Alfred Marshall (1842–1924) followed a path differing from the radically subjective line taken by Jevons. There are, however, some basic elements common to these different lines of research, differentiating them from the classical approach illustrated in the previous chapters.

Sraffa (1960, p. 93) summed up the contrast with two images: the classical approach consists in the 'picture of the system of production and consumption as a circular process', while the marginalist approach aligns the perspective along 'a one-way avenue that leads from "Factors of production" to "Consumption goods"'. The differences concern definition of the economic problem, the notion of value, the concept of equilibrium, the role of prices and the theory of distribution.

First of all, within the classical approach the economic problem was conceived as analysis of those conditions that guarantee the continuous functioning of an economic system based on the division of labour, and hence analysis of production, distribution, accumulation and circulation of the product. In the case of the marginalist approach, by contrast, the economic problem concerned the optimal utilisation of scarce available resources to satisfy the needs and desires of economic agents.

Secondly, the classical economists' objective view of value, based on the difficulty of production, contrasts with the subjective view of the marginalist approach, based on evaluation of utility of commodities on the part of the consumers (and possibly on the disutility of labour or of abstinence from consumption on the part of producers).

Thirdly, as a consequence of these differences, the notion of equilibrium took on a central role in the marginalist approach: equilibrium corresponded to optimal utilisation of scarce available resources and was therefore identified by a set of values for all economic variables, prices and quantities simultaneously. The classical approach held the problem of relative prices distinct from the problem of decisions concerning accumulation and production levels; at the most, one might speak of equilibrium with reference to the levelling of sector profit rates stemming from the competition of capitals, while the term 'balancing', which did not imply a precise equality, was preferred when speaking of demand and supply (as in the expression 'the balance between supply and demand').

Fourthly, prices acquired the meaning of indicators of relative difficulty of production for the classical approach and of indicators of scarcity (relative to consumers' preferences) within the marginalist approach.[1]

Fifthly, income distribution was a specific case of price theory in the context of the marginalist approach (where it concerned the prices of the 'factors of production'), while within the classical approach it concerned the role of different social classes and their power relations.[2]

With the marginalist approach, such common characteristics took on different forms in authors belonging to different currents within the marginalist approach. For instance, the French current of general economic equilibrium founded by Walras was based on the assumption

---

[1] The difficulty of production, though, did play a role within the marginalist approach, as mediation between original productive resources on the one hand and final goods and services on the other; scarcity, too, played a role within the classical approach, through constraints concerning technology – as in differential rent – or levels of production, through the stage reached by the process of accumulation.

[2] Also within this approach, however, the determination of prices and of distributive variables were connected, as was to become evident in Sraffa's analysis. With some imprecision (within the general economic equilibrium approach, all variables are simultaneously determined), Walras 1874, p. 45, stated that, in opposition to the classical approach ('the school of Ricardo and Mill'), in the new theory 'the prices of productive services are determined by the prices of their products and not the other way round'.

of initial endowments of resources (different kinds of working abilities, lands, capital goods) considered as given in physical terms and matched with economic agents' preferences. The English current of Jevons and Marshall, by contrast, tended to consider the quantities available of the different resources also as variables to be determined within the theory, utilising as exogenous data utility and disutility maps of the various economic agents. In particular, the balance between the utility of goods obtainable through productive activity and the worker's toil and trouble, or in other words the disutility of work, determined the amount of work done and hence, given the production function, the amount of product. Finally the theorists of the Austrian school adopted a radically subjective viewpoint according to which the value of each good or service was deduced from its utility for the final consumer, directly in the case of consumption goods and indirectly in the case of production goods (by imputing to the means of production a share of the utility of the consumption good proportional to their contribution to the productive process, hence the expression 'imputation theory').

10.2   The Precursors: Equilibrium between Scarcity and Demand

Side by side with the classical view of the economic system based on the idea of the circular flow of production and consumption, we thus have a different view involving the idea of scarcity of available resources with respect to potential demand. The latter view was not born with the marginalist revolution in the years between 1871 and 1874 but has accompanied economic science from its very beginnings.

Even in the pre-history of political economy we find discussion of the just price attributing an important role to the play between demand and supply. Here we also find conceptualisation, primitive though it may be, of the issue of prices in relation to the medieval markets, conceived as place and time for encounter and comparison between supply and demand. Moreover, as early as the Scholastic writers we find the thesis that utility is the true source or cause of value; in other words, the comparison between supply and demand was considered to reflect the comparison between scarcity and utility. This view survived and developed over time, side by side with the idea that the value of commodities lay essentially in the difficulty of production, and particularly in labour requirements. While in the seventeenth, eighteenth and nineteenth centuries this latter view found its way into the classical approach of Petty, Smith and Ricardo, various authors took on and developed the alternative view, connecting prices with the comparison between scarcity and buyers' evaluation and coming close, in some cases, to establishing a link between value in use and value in exchange based on the notion of marginal utility. The subjective approach to the theory of value had important roots in England as in Italy, in France as in Germany, in the eighteenth and nineteenth centuries. In Italy, the Neapolitan Abbé Ferdinando Galiani (1751) dedicated some pages to the role of scarcity and utility in determining the value of commodities. Various French economists supported a subjective theory of value: together with Jean-Baptiste Say we may recall Condillac and Dupuit. In Germany, Hermann Heinrich Gossen (1810–1858), in a book that immediately fell into oblivion (Gossen 1854), developed a marginalist theory of consumer equilibrium; Johann Heinrich von Thünen (1783–1850) produced a work in two parts (*The Isolated State*, first part, 1826; second part, 1850), in which he developed a theory of rent connected to the distance from the place of consumption and proposed an analysis of substitution between land and labour, based on equality between marginal productivity and price for each of these productive factors. In England, the subjective approach to value was confined to a secondary plane; worth recalling, however, are Samuel Bailey, Senior, Whately, Longfield and above all William Forster Lloyd (1794–1852).

In the development of a subjective analytical construction, a central role was played by consumers' choices, and hence demand: exchange value is explained on the basis of use values. Within the classical approach, the distinction between value in use and value in exchange was explicit: value in use – the fact of being useful to some purpose – was considered an indispensable characteristic (a prerequisite) for goods to have a positive exchange value; not a measurable characteristic, however, and hence not an element to rely on when explaining exchange values.[3]

The key element of marginalist theory was the idea that value in use (assumed as capable of measurement) decreases when the quantity

---

[3] The classical economists also spoke of large or small value in use, but in very generic terms. This happened, for instance, with the well-known paradox of water and diamonds, already recalled previously: the former, it was said, has a large value in use but a small value in exchange, while diamonds have a modest value in use but a considerable value in exchange. The paradox is easily solved recalling that the most useful good may also be the most abundant one, while it is scarcity vis-à-vis the demand from potential buyers that determines the price. Within the classical approach, where attention focuses on reproducible commodities, scarcity can be overcome through production of additional units of the commodity; as a consequence, exchange value is brought back to the relative difficulty of production. Scarcity concurs in determining the price only when the available quantity of the commodity is given.

consumed of each commodity increases. Value in use thus became a decreasing function of the quantity consumed of each commodity, and value in exchange could be derived from the value in use of the last dose consumed of the good under consideration. The subjective theory of value derived the value in exchange of commodities from the consumer's subjective evaluation, thus requiring the notion of marginal utility, a notion which some of the subjective theorists foreshadowed as forerunners of marginalism.

10.3   William Stanley Jevons

What characterised Jevons in his break with the classical tradition were his views on the psychology of the human being and his aim to mathematise economic theory. Moreover, Jevons was representative of the professionalisation of economics typical of his times: personal success coincided with publication of new theories and their acceptance on the part of university colleagues, while for Petty or Cantillon, Quesnay or Smith, Ricardo or John Stuart Mill success was manifested in the wider circle of men of culture or in acceptance of their ideas in the political arena.

Jevons was born in Liverpool in 1835. He studied natural sciences, chemistry and mathematics at University College, London. As a chemist he was hired by the Australian mint, and at the age of nineteen he moved to Sydney, where he resided from 1854 to 1859, and soon decided to make the 'study of Man' his mission in life. To this end, he returned to London and graduated from the University College in 1862. He worked as a journalist and began the academic career as tutor in Manchester. After a few uneventful publications, fame was reaped with a book published in 1865, *The Coal Question*, in which Jevons maintained the thesis of the impending exhaustion of coal reserves, hence the existence of a constraint to the development of British manufactures, similar to the Malthusian thesis of constraints stemming from the scarcity of fertile lands. Malthus's dire predictions had not come true, according to Jevons, because of the abolition of the Corn Laws, and hence of duties on corn imports. As a matter of fact, both Jevons and Malthus erred in their pessimistic forecasts of thwarted development because of undervaluation of technological change.

The fame thus conquered brought him nomination to a professorship in Manchester in 1866. Finally, after publication of the *Theory of Political Economy* in 1871 and the treatise on the *Principles of Science* in 1874, in 1876 he became professor of political economy at University College, London. In 1880 Jevons decided to resign in order to work full time on his research, but in 1882 he drowned while swimming during a seaside holiday.

Jevons's personal itinerary helps us to understand the background to his subjective revolution: a view of political economy no longer as a moral science, much like history or politics, but as a hard science such as physics or mathematics, pointing in the direction of necessary quantitative connections ('laws') also in the field of the social and human sciences. Jevons was convinced – in this respect following a tradition going at least from Petty to Condorcet – that numbers are capable of expressing everything.

10.4   The Jevonian Revolution

Jevons did not pursue an axiomatic method, in which what matters is the logical construction of the theory and not its realism: had he not embraced a sensistic view of man, he would not have found himself at ease in developing a subjective theory of value.

In developing this theory Jevons modified the meaning of some key concepts, thus breaking with the earlier tradition. Such modifications, essential to build the marginalist analytical edifice, mainly concerned the notion of utility inherited from Bentham, which Jevons oriented in the opposite direction to that suggested by John Stuart Mill. Firstly, Jevons reduced to two, intensity and duration, the elements that determine the quantity of pleasure or pain connected to a given action and considered the quantity of pleasure as determined by their product, thus obtaining a quantitative, mono-dimensional expression of value in use. Time, hence duration, was treated as a continuous variable and, symmetrically, so was intensity. In this way the quantity of pleasure, or in other words utility, turned out to be itself a continuous variable, thus allowing for the applicability of differential calculus for defining the 'final degree of utility', nowadays commonly known as marginal utility.

Secondly, Jevons stressed that utility is an abstract relationship between object and person, not a property intrinsic to the object. Any object may, in fact, have a different utility for different persons or in different moments of time. What matters is not so much total utility, but rather the increment of utility when the quantity available of the commodity increases, i.e. the final degree of utility. Each individual signals such a magnitude with readiness to pay for the commodity itself. This allows us to compare through the market the valuations of a given individual for different goods, but also – through the amount of money each of them is willing to pay – those of different individuals for the same good; however, this fact is not in itself sufficient to ensure the possibility of a social felicific calculus, since nothing guarantees that every individual will attribute the same utility to any given quantity of money – and Jevons emphatically denied the possibility of interpersonal comparisons. Consequentialist ethics, requiring interpersonal comparisons, was thus made to disappear, leaving room for an economic science reduced to a theory of rational choice, under the postulate that each individual is able to compute in a mono-dimensional space all the consequences of her/his action, at least in the economic sphere.

Jevons's definition of economics also differed from Mill's, focussed on the desire to possess wealth. In fact, Jevons limited economics to a specific subset of feelings, 'the lowest rank of feelings': 'The calculus of utility aims at supplying the ordinary wants of man at the least cost of labour'.[4] Such a definition was essential for his crucial aim, the formulation of economics as a mathematical science: 'It is clear that economics, if it is to be a science at all, must be a mathematical science ... *our theory must be mathematical simply because it deals with quantities*.'[5] It was this crucial aim which led Jevons to assume human feelings as a one-dimensional quantitative variable: a point which was stressed again and again.

The core of the theory consisted of the analysis of individual choices between different pleasures (consumption) and pains (labour); the feelings (preferences) of each individual had to be assumed as an independent datum of the problem, not influenced by the choices of others. Only under these conditions could the summation of individual behaviours constitute a theory of the whole economy. In other words, methodological individualism[6] was a necessary requisite for the subjective theory of value but was in no way justified by Jevons: it was simply postulated, as implicit in the very structure of his theory. Jevons viewed economics as a problem concerning the maximum satisfaction obtainable from the allocation of a given amount of resources. In Jevons's own words (1871, p. 254; italics in the original): 'The problem of economics may ... be stated thus: *Given,*

---

[4] Jevons 1871, pp. 92–3. This definition is only apparently obvious and unproblematic. For instance, it would relegate my demand for Bach recordings to the lowest rank of feelings, exactly on the same level as my demand for chocolate (both, recordings and chocolate, being part of my ordinary wants and having effects on my budget); were it not so, economics would take into account only part of the consumer's expenditure decisions, and it would be impossible to define a budget constraint univocally.

[5] Ibid., p. 78; italics in the original. As a matter of fact the last sentence should be inverted: 'our theory must deal with quantities – namely with variables defined in such a way as to be liable to be treated as one-dimensional quantities – because only in this way are we able to work it out in mathematical terms'.

[6] There are a number of definitions of methodological individualism. Here we mean by it the assumption that society is nothing but a sum of individuals and that the preferences of every individual are independent of those of any other individual, so that the behaviour of the economy is explained starting from individual choices.

a certain population, with various needs and powers of production, in possession of certain hands and other sources of material: required, the mode of employing their labour which will maximize the utility of the produce.'
Jevons's decision to formulate economics as a mathematical science compelled him to redefine as measurable magnitudes the motivations of human actions: we abandon the difficult path of a social science that endeavours to take into account the complex nature of human beings and human societies, forking off along the path of 'economics' built on the model of physical sciences – at the price of substituting the real world with a fictitious one-dimensional picture.

10.5   Real Cost and Opportunity Cost

Jevons, as we saw previously, developed the notion of the 'final degree of utility (or disutility)', which corresponds to marginal utility (or disutility). The exchange value of each good was thus equal on the one hand to its marginal utility and on the other hand to the marginal disutility of the labour necessary to obtain it (even indirectly, i.e. through exchange with a good directly produced by the economic agent under consideration). In this way, for each good the quantity produced and/or consumed was determined simultaneously with its exchange value.

Under the simplifying assumption that production of each good required only labour, at first sight this approach gave a result analogous to the classical theory of labour value. In fact, each individual attributes the same disutility to the last dose of labour employed in the production of each commodity; as a consequence, the exchange ratio between different commodities is equal to the ratio between the quantities of labour necessary to produce each of them. We should recall, however, that each economic subject was seen as an island: 'labour differs infinitely', Jevons (1871, p. 187) said, between one economic agent and another, in terms of quality and efficiency; furthermore, different individuals may have different evaluations of the pain intrinsic to the same dose of labour. For these reasons, labour cannot be the cause or the origin of value: the 'real cost' that concurs in explaining the value of the commodity is understood as disutility rather than as labour time.

Also when introducing the notion of capital, Jevons was inclined to reject links with labour. According to Jevons, in fact, capital is not accumulated labour, as the classical economists considered it. The source of capital is the duration of its employment in production and the intention of its owner, while its value depends on a prospective evaluation of what can be obtained through its employment. In other words, Jevons determined the value of capital starting from the value of the product, with a procedure opposite to that of the classical economists. Thus, his notion of capital was defined in such a way that it could be referred to the isolated individual as well as to society as a whole. According to Jevons (ibid., p. 229), indeed, division of labour and exchanges were 'irrelevant complications', which could not substantially modify his theory of value, based on individual choices.

Philip Henry Wicksteed (1844–1927), in his book on *The Common Sense of Political Economy* (1910), took to its logical consequence the subjective approach, conceiving the theory of value as one of individual choices by connecting value to the *opportunity cost* of each good: in the presence of scarce resources, to obtain utility along a certain road (by producing and consuming a given good) implies foregoing the possibility to obtain utility in some other way (producing and consuming some other good).

Francis Ysidro Edgeworth's (1845–1926) main theoretical contribution concerned the contract curve, illustrated for the case of two individuals and two commodities available in given quantities and defined as the set of allocations of the two commodities between the two individuals that could not be modified without worsening the conditions of at least one of the two individuals. Edgeworth (1881, 1925) thus anticipated the notion of Pareto optimality; furthermore, in building the contract curve he utilised contour lines of utility maps to represent preferences, christening them with the name that has since become familiar of indifference curves. With respect to these curves, we also owe to Edgeworth explicit introduction of the assumption of convexity towards the origin of the Cartesian axes (and demonstration that this assumption, while stemming from the postulate of decreasing marginal utility, is not necessarily implicit in it). In his analysis, Edgeworth – like Menger – began with the case of bilateral monopoly to go on to competition and demonstrated that the indeterminacy of equilibrium in the case of two participants in the exchange recedes when the number of economic agents participating in the exchange increases.

As holder of the Drummond chair at Oxford from 1891 to 1922 and as editor and then co-editor (with Keynes) of the *Economic Journal* from its foundation in 1891 up to his death, Edgeworth played an important role in the professionalisation of economics and the rise to dominance of the new theories of value and distribution. However, given the extremely convoluted style of his writings, together with his proverbial reservedness, he remained in the shadow of Alfred Marshall, the great academic leader of England in those times, whom we will discuss later.

11 The Austrian School and Its Neighbourhood

11.1 Carl Menger

The founder of the Austrian school was born in Poland, then part of the Austro-Hungarian Empire, in 1840. He attended university in Vienna and Prague and went on to take his doctorate in Krakow. His first job was as a journalist, and by 1871, when he published the *Principles of Political Economy*, he had become a civil servant. Thanks to this book he had a rapid academic career: by 1873 he was professor; in 1876–78 he was made tutor to Crown Prince Rudolf of Austria, and from 1878 to 1903 he held the chair of political economy at the University of Vienna.

The *Principles of Political Economy* are hardly what a modern reader would expect of a key text for the marginalist approach. Menger had studied law, which, in the continental European tradition, implied an approach with a strong emphasis on history and illustration of concepts, often prolix. Menger appeared distant from the project – shared by Jevons and Walras – to construct economic theory as a quantitative science to be developed in mathematical terms. His text was devoid of mathematical formulas, and on various occasions Menger made no secret of his profound scepticism regarding the use of mathematical tools. His aim was, rather, to construct a theory transcending simple description of economic phenomena while retaining strong links with empirical reality. Moreover, Menger's subjectivism in the field of value theory, unlike Jevons's, owed little or nothing to utilitarian concepts.

A subjective approach to a theory of value based on comparison between supply and demand, value in use and scarcity was very much the rule in the tradition of Austro-German universities. This tradition had its roots in medieval Scholastic doctrines and implied systematic rejection of Ricardian labour-value theory but not of the theory of differential rent or the Smithian theory of the growth of the wealth of nations associated with the division of labour.

Menger's *Principles* thus followed the structure of the great German textbooks: extensive discussion of goods and needs led up to the theory of value, exchange and price, after which attention turned to distribution, development and money. The objective of economic theory was, Menger asserted, to analyse the causal relations between goods and human values; significantly, while Jevons stated his concern for a specific aspect of human activity, relating to the satisfaction of needs of the lowest level, Menger defined economic activity as a search for knowledge and power.

This was in fact one of the most innovative aspects of Menger's text. Another significant element was his interest in the interrelations between the different goods within the economic system, which saw Menger advancing beyond the traditional tendency (again dating back to Scholastic thought) to consider the formation of value, or price, of each good in isolation.

Menger's subjectivism was indeed radical, his analysis starting from the evaluation that each individual makes of his own situation – hence also his methodological individualism. Thus, value is given by the way human beings assess the varying importance of the various needs and the suitability of the different goods to satisfy such needs.[1] More precisely, the different needs were classified in order of importance, and it was assumed that the intensity of each progressively decreased when it was satisfied; a certain degree of satisfaction had to be reached for the most pressing need before tackling the immediately successive one in order of importance.[2] The determination of value then required that, along with the value in use of the goods, their scarcity be taken into account; their evaluation therefore concerned not the absolute importance of each need but its importance 'at the margin'. This evaluation was made directly in the case of consumption goods (goods of the first order) and indirectly in the case of production goods (goods of the second, third, etc. order). In the latter case, the means of production was imputed with part of the value that the good produced held for the consumer, this portion being computed in proportion to the contribution made by the good or service to the productive process (hence the name *imputation theory*). The role of

---

[1] Let us recall that according to Menger value had to do with the essence, and price with the phenomenic manifestation, of economic activity: a distinction that had some affinity with Marx's and was conversely absent from Walras's French approach or the Anglo-Saxon line followed by Jevons or Marshall.

[2] In contrast to the canonical marginalist theory of the consumer, where substitutability among goods plays a central role, Menger did not admit substitutability among needs (that is, the possibility that a lower degree of satisfaction of a need be compensated by a higher degree of satisfaction of some other need, leaving the situation of the consumer unchanged).

primum movens of the economic system is thus attributed to the consumer. The idea of the consumer as sovereign had at the same time a normative and a descriptive content, thus implying a justification for economic liberalism, in the sense of 'leaving it to the market'.

The subjective view of value in use proposed by Menger departed from the dominant line followed by German economists of the time, seeking objective foundations for the measurement of use values. To use Bernardine of Siena's (1380–1444) terminology, we might say that Menger focused on the goods' *complacibilitas* (that is, on their correspondence to the individual users' preferences), while the German tradition of the time looked to their *virtuositas* (capacity to satisfy human needs). Finally, we should stress that, possibly in order to mark his distancing from utilitarianism, Menger avoided the term 'utility', preferring to speak of the 'importance of satisfactions'.

In his analysis of exchange value Menger started from the case of two goods and two parties to the exchange, or bilateral monopoly.[3] In this case there is a range of values compatible with realisation of the act of exchange coming between the two extremes at which one of the two parties loses interest in the exchange. In general, then, Menger saw the exchange as a matter of unequal values implying an advantage for both participants.

Menger outlined, but did not fully develop, generalisation of this analysis to cases of more than two goods and two parties to the exchange: as a consequence of his refusal to apply mathematical tools his analysis fell short of the analyses produced by other authors of the time, or even of earlier times. His original contribution is to be found elsewhere, in the attempt to delineate a conceptual framework such as would allow the theoretician to keep account of crucial aspects of the real world, such as the limits of human knowledge and the uncertainty surrounding the decisions of economic agents. Moreover, Menger stressed the role of the market in favouring the diffusion of information. However, it proved difficult to relate these data to mathematical analyses of value within the subjective approach; as a consequence, they were tacitly disregarded in the canonical version of the marginalist theory.

Unlike Jevons or Walras, Menger did not assume utility functions to be maximised under budget constraints; value depended on the subjective evaluations people made of their needs and the way to satisfy them, and

---

[3] The role Menger attributed to the monopolistic market form in his analysis contrasts with the dominance of perfect competition in the analyses by his pupils, Wieser and Böhm-Bawerk, who came closer in this respect to the approaches of the French and Anglo-Saxon marginalist theoreticians.

such evaluations could change in unexpected ways. Menger appeared interested in dynamic aspects, such as the study of how goods *tout court* become economic goods, the issue of the original development of private property and the active way economic agents set out to increase their knowledge and consequently modify their preferences. In this context, Menger stressed the elements of inequality, irreversibility and gains from exchange. The notion of equilibrium was applied to the choices of the individual economic agent, but much less to the economic system as a whole, due to the difficulty of coordinating such choices (limited knowledge, importance of learning).

Similarly, Menger stressed the existence of transaction costs and thus the theoretical and not only practical importance of elements such as knowledge and distance. Hence the role attributed to the intermediaries, who help the economic agents towards fuller knowledge and better organisation of the market and the role attributed to money. This brings us to Menger's conception of the process of civilisation itself, identified with the reduction of ignorance and development of institutions that help human beings get to grips with an uncertain future. Institutions such as money, the market and the division of labour were explained – in accordance with methodological individualism – as unintentional effects of individual uncoordinated choices, modified in the course of time as a consequence of learning processes in response to the experience gradually acquired. On the whole, Menger had an optimistic view of economic progress, decidedly closer to Smith than to Malthus's *Essay on Population*; as in Smith, progress was related to improvements in the division of labour and to capital accumulation.

11.2   The 'Methodenstreit'

Historicism is commonly seen as rebellion against the rationalism of the Enlightenment, connected to the then newborn nationalistic spirit particularly strong in Germany. Indeed, by extolling the specific nature of each concrete historical situation, historicism opposed universalism, or the claim that it is possible to derive, from a few general principles, rules endowed with validity at all times and in all places.

The *old German historical school* flourished in the decade of 1843–1853, when the major contributions by Wilhelm Roscher (1817–1894), Bruno Hildebrand (1812–1878) and Karl Knies (1821–1898) were published. Supporters of statistical enquiry, they considered the 'economic laws' deduced from empirical enquiry to be historically relative.

As pointed out above, Menger saw no opposition between his theoretical contribution and the approach of the old German historical

school. The *new historical school* led by Gustav von Schmoller
(1838–1917), however, was characterised by a more decided opposition to abstract theoretical deductions and denial of the possibility of
distinction between political economy and politics, laws, institutions
and customs. A priori assumptions and deductive reasoning were to be
rejected, until a degree of knowledge was reached sufficient to constitute a solid basis for the generalisations through which the abstract
assumptions were obtained to constitute the necessary starting point
for economic theory. The deductive techniques of economic theory
were not rejected a priori; however, in the concrete situation of the time
abstract theory had insufficient foundations. The aim of the historical
school was precisely to provide such foundations, through systematic
analysis based on empirical investigations. To this end, in 1873 the
Verein für Sozialpolitik was founded, and work promptly began on the
systematic collection of data on the most diverse aspects of economic
reality. Moreover, the Verein generated a movement towards social
reform policies that was christened *socialism of the chair* favourable to
social reforms, the first experiment of a 'welfare state'.[4]

Two works by Menger (1883, 1884) marked the beginning of
a harsh ideological clash between rival academic schools, exacerbated
by the struggle for baronial power within universities. This implied
stretching the opponent's views while illustrating them, searching out
the weak points rather than addressing and assimilating the points
of strength of the rival approach. Thus, the defeat of the historical
school obscured the importance of an approach that tied in theoretical
work with historical research, which Menger himself had endeavoured to
practise.

Menger distinguished three components of political economy: the
historical-statistical aspect, theory and economic policy. Theory was
given a special role, and Menger proposed a causal-genetic approach,
which consisted of starting from the simplest elements to arrive at enquiry
into the composite laws. Thus political economy arrived at exact laws, but
they only concerned a subset of human actions; Menger insisted that the
notion of economic man was a fictitious construction. He too, however,
stressed the importance of a close connection between theory and reality,
guaranteed by the fact that the assumptions at the basis of the theory were

---

[4] External to the Verein but within the same cultural environment, Ernst Engel
(1821–1896), director of Prussia's statistical office, researched the differences in the
structure of consumption corresponding to different levels of income. (What is known
as Engel's Law, one of the best statistical regularities, stated that the share of food
consumption in the total expenditure of a family decreases with increase in income.)

considered data known from direct experience and hence true with no need for empirical verification: for Menger the intuitionist it was indeed the very essence of economic reality that manifested itself directly in the economists' reflections. The view of the economic system thus proposed by Menger was not that of a static equilibrium between supply and demand, but that of the development of an organic order as a process of discovery and accumulation of new knowledge through imitation, motivated by economic interest: an intrinsically dynamic view, imbued with historicism.

It is indeed this methodological approach that helps us to evaluate the results reached by the Austrian school. In principle we cannot but agree with Menger's position on method and hence the essential, central role of analytic reasoning in economic theory; perplexities arise over the compatibility between a dynamic-evolutionary approach and the marginalist analytic structure based on the notion of equilibrium between demand and supply. The same problem of tension between the stage of the formation of concepts and the stage of model-building arose, as we shall see, in the case of Marshall.

11.3   Max Weber

The debate on method also serves to prompt a few remarks on some developments now, but not at the time, considered external to the field of economics. Max Weber, who stands today as the most famous of the sociologists, was in fact the holder of a chair in political economy and was by many accounts closer to the economists of the Austrian school than to those of the historical school.

Max Weber (1864–1920) was professor of political economy, first at Freiburg and then at Heidelberg. His main work remains *Economy and Society*, published posthumously in 1922, while his *Protestant Ethics and the Spirit of Capitalism* (1904–5) is also widely known. The common theme of these writings is enquiry into the factors that determine the origin and rise to dominance of certain economic behavioural patterns, thus navigating between sociology and political economy in an area now commonly attributed to the field of economic sociology.

Weber is considered 'the Marx of the bourgeoisie': like Marx, he focused on interpretation of the capitalistic mode of production and its process of evolution, but unlike Marx, he held that in the historical process of development the main causal link did not go from the material conditions of economic reproduction to the sphere of institutions and culture, but rather in the opposite direction. Weber saw in the evolution of capitalism a gigantic process of rationalisation concerning not only economic activity but society as a whole, on this basis developing his forecast of a progressive bureaucratisation of the state organisation and the productive process, with the growth of middle ranks of clerks and technicians – a forecast that attributed crucial importance to the middle classes, thus contrasting with the process of proletarisation heralded by Marx. On the origins of capitalism, Weber also took a different path from Marx, maintaining that a crucial role was to be attributed to the assertion, with Protestantism, of a specific culture favourable to concrete engagement in society, against the ascetic attitudes of the medieval Catholic church and the Counter-Reformation.

Weber's method – influenced by the German historical-juridical tradition – was based on the definition of *ideal types*, or categories abstracted from concrete historical evolution. Conceptualisation was the dominant phase in this approach, while construction of abstract models based on these categories was conducted without recourse to mathematical tools, in opposition to the trend then coming to dominate the various currents of the marginalist approach (although less markedly than elsewhere within the Austrian school – the school with which Weber was in closest contact).

11.4   Eugen von Böhm-Bawerk

Among the most direct followers of Menger we find Friedrich von Wieser (1851–1926) and Eugen von Böhm-Bawerk (1851–1914), who went on from being fellow students to become brothers-in-law. A subsequent generation included Ludwig von Mises (1881–1973), originator of the theory of 'forced saving' and significant debate on the sustainability of a planned economy, and Joseph Schumpeter and Friedrich von Hayek (1899–1992), to be discussed later.

Böhm-Bawerk was professor of political economy at Innsbruck and Vienna and, thrice, minister of finances. In *The Positive Theory of Capital* (1889) he developed an original theory of interest, bringing the issue of accumulation within the Austrian theory of value.

The key notion was that of the average period of production, which draws on ideas already long present in the theoretical debate, such as Senior's notion of abstinence and Marshall's 'waiting'. Böhm-Bawerk considered the rate of interest as the price that compensated for the waiting intrinsic to recourse to more indirect but more fruitful methods of production. In other words, there is a longer interval of time between the moment the work is performed and the moment when the final product is obtained, but production is thereby increased.[5] In order to measure the capitalistic intensity of production processes, Böhm-Bawerk proposed reference to the average period of production, or in other words an average of all the intervals of time during which the hours of labour expended to obtain a certain product are immobilised, considering both the hours of labour directly employed and those indirectly employed for the production of the required means of production. The result was a series of dated quantities of labour, which was then reduced to a single magnitude, a weighted average of the different intervals of time, with weights proportional to the hours of labour immobilised during the different intervals of time. When confronted with an increase in the wage rate (that is, in the price of labour), firms tend to reduce the quantity of labour utilised; correspondingly, when the rate of interest (that is, the price of 'capital') decreases, firms tend to utilise a greater amount of time-capital, lengthening the duration of the productive processes. Applying the postulate of decreasing marginal productivity, when confronted with a reduction in the rate of interest, the average period of production is lengthened up to the point at which the marginal productivity of a further lengthening has come down to the new, lower level of the interest rate.

This theory was less of an approximation than the simple theory of labour value, which completely ignored the magnitude of the intervals of time during which the quantities of labour expended remain immobilised, but it was still an approximation. It failed to take the phenomenon of compound interest into account: the cumulated interest on an hour of labour performed ten years ago is far greater than the interest on ten hours of labour one year ago; nor is it possible to redefine the weights in order to take account of compound interest, since the average period of production would thus prove no longer independent of income distribution, and it would no longer be possible to utilise it to determine the value of a distributive variable such as the rate of interest.

Böhm-Bawerk's theory was taken up again in the Austrian school by Hayek and earlier on, at the very beginnings of the Swedish school, by Wicksell, while it was criticised by Schumpeter; Wicksell himself, in the

---

[5] We thus have two elements that, according to Böhm-Bawerk's theory, concur in determining the rate of interest: on the one hand, a psychological element, namely the tendency of human beings to over-estimate the utility of present goods compared to that of goods available in the future (and the disutility of a present cost compared to a future one); on the other hand, a technological element, namely the higher productivity of indirect methods of production.

course of his investigations, appeared increasingly dissatisfied with it. The definitive criticism of this approach would come with Sraffa's 1960 book.

11.5 Knut Wicksell and the Swedish School

Swedish Knut Wicksell was born in 1851 like Böhm-Bawerk. However his career as an economist followed a stage of lively activity as a neo-Malthusian polemist, freelance lecturer and journalist. His fame among his contemporaries derived from his radical opposition to the prevailing moral beliefs on family, religion, motherland and state authority. His provocative attitudes hindered his academic career, aroused widespread hostility and even landed him in prison – at the ripe age of fifty – on charges of offence against the state religion.[6]

His interest in economic issues concentrated for a long time on the population problem. His studies in economic theory were at first collateral to this interest and were seriously tackled only when, in 1887, the thirty-six-year-old Wicksell gained a scholarship abroad. He was thus able to study in London, Strasbourg and Vienna. In 1890 he also began an academic career, but only in 1905 did he become full professor. He died in Stockholm in 1926.

His main works in economic theory were *Value, Capital and Rent* (1893), *Interest and Prices* (1898), *Marginal Productivity as the Basis for Distribution in Economics* (1900) and the two volumes of *Lectures on Political Economy* (1901–6). In the 1893 essay Wicksell developed a marginalist theory of income distribution between capital, labour and land based on their respective marginal productivities, which came out a few years before Wicksteed's. In this work, and in the first volume of the *Lectures*, Wicksell utilised Böhm-Bawerk's theory of the average period of production; however, he eventually set out to develop it in such a way as to take into account the heterogeneity of the means of production. Thus, in essence, Wicksell wavered between an aggregate notion of capital and a disaggregated notion, which he adopted when identifying capital with the entire temporal structure of the direct and indirect labour flows necessary to obtain a given product.

---

[6] See the fascinating biography by Gårdlund 1956. Wicksell constitutes striking proof of the erroneousness of the thesis, typical of the Marxian tradition, of an opposition between a politically progressive classical approach and a politically conservative marginalist approach. Wicksell is no isolated exception in this respect: suffice it to recall, for instance, Walras's social reformism, with his support for land nationalisation, or the British Fabians.

Wicksell also developed a distinction between the money interest rate and the natural interest rate. The latter was determined by the real variables that concur to determine equilibrium for the economic system; more precisely, it corresponded to the marginal productivity of capital, as indicated by the marginalist theory of income distribution. The money rate of interest, on the other hand, was determined on the money markets, with some degree of autonomy with respect to the natural rate. The relationship between money and natural rate of interest was then utilised to explain the cyclical oscillations of the economy and the inflationary or deflationary pressures on the general level of prices. Whenever the money rate of interest is lower than the natural one, entrepreneurs find it advantageous to take out loans and invest, thus giving rise to inflationary pressure; conversely, whenever the money rate of interest is higher than the natural rate, investments are discouraged and deflationary pressure is generated.[7]

This theory takes its place in a current of monetary explanations of the cycle and inflation that tried to have it both ways, on the one hand safeguarding the marginalist theory of value and distribution, in terms of which to determine the equilibrium values for prices and distributive variables, and on the other hand recognising a fact obvious to any empirical economist, namely the existence of disequilibria and of a certain influence monetary vicissitudes have on real variables.

As from the late 1920s, the "Swedish school" (Erik Lindahl, 1891–1960; Gunnar Myrdal, 1898–1987, Nobel prize in 1974; Bertil Ohlin, 1899–1979) developed various aspects of Wicksell's theory and in contrast with Keynes's analysis re-proposed the tool of sequential analysis (already present in the Austrian tradition and later re-embraced by Hicks).

11.6   Friedrich von Hayek

Friedrich von Hayek (1899–1992, Nobel prize in 1974) is possibly better known for his extreme economic liberalism than for his theoretical contributions to economics. However, in the 1930s he appeared to many as the champion of the continental school, a point of reference of great theoretical strength to set against the Cambridge school for those who did not share the political implications of Keynesian theory.

---

[7] In his theory on inflationary and deflationary cumulative processes Wicksell assumed that no changes took place in production techniques; as a consequence, neither income distribution nor production levels or relative prices can change, and the disequilibria can only translate into changes in the monetary variables, namely the price level.

A pupil of Wieser and Mises at the University of Vienna after the First World War, in 1927 Hayek was made the first director of the newborn Austrian institute for study of the trade cycle.[8] In 1931 he moved to the London School of Economics. After the Second World War, he moved on to Chicago in 1950 and returned to Europe (at first Freiburg, in Germany, and then Salzburg, in Austria) in 1962.[9]

Let us consider four aspects of his thought: an individualistic methodology; a conceptual approach that took up and developed that of the Austrian school, in particular the elements of uncertainty and learning; a theoretical approach based on Böhm-Bawerk's theory of capital and Wicksell's theory of money; and contributions to the political and social theory of economic liberalism, opposing the collectivistic propensities that, many held, characterised not only Soviet planning but also Roosevelt's New Deal and Keynesian interventionism.

Methodological individualism, i.e. the idea that the functioning of an economic system must be explained starting from the choices of the individuals, constituted a dominant tradition within the different currents of the marginalist approach. For Hayek, as for many others, this was not only a rule of method but also a political dogma, given the connection between holism (namely the idea that social aggregates should be studied independently of the behaviour of the individuals making them up) and political organicism (the State, the community, is 'more' than the individuals making it up) that is at the basis of dictatorial regimes such as Nazism or Stalinist communism.[10]

The behaviour of individuals expresses itself through actions that stem from rationally selected plans of action. Methodological individualism thus dictated that the theory of the behaviour of the economic system be

---

[8] The Österreichische Konjunkturforschungsinstitut was founded on von Mises's initiative, in order to propose, in study of the trade cycle, an approach based on integration between theory and empirical analysis against the purely empiricist approach of the National Bureau of Economic Research at New York, focussing on the search for regularities in the behaviour of the economy.

[9] Hayek was an economist with an exceptional cultural background and a refined scholar of the history of economic thought. The Vienna of the 1920s was in this respect a unique melting pot: Konrad Lorenz the ethologist was a playmate in infancy, the philosopher Ludwig Wittgenstein was a relative and comrade-in-arms in the last year of the First World War, the physicist Erwin Schrödinger a family friend, and we might go on. Cf. Hayek's autobiography, Hayek 1994, and Caldwell's 2004 intellectual biography.

[10] A political critique of holism, from Plato and Aristotle to Marx, was provided by Hayek's friend, Karl Popper, in *The Open Society and Its Enemies*, 1945. However, as pointed out by Schumpeter, we can fully share Popper's critique of totalitarianism and its cultural roots without necessarily accepting the identification between political individualism, i.e. defence of individual freedom in the political sphere, and methodological individualism.

based on consideration of plans of action of all the agents in the system. Hence the central role of the notion of equilibrium, which identifies within the set of such plans of actions those that are compatible among themselves and with the given conditions in which economic activity takes place (technology, each agent's endowments of resources).[11] Given the limits to the knowledge of economic agents, it is realistically impossible for *ex ante* planning to ensure the coordination of individual plans of action. Coordination is entrusted to the market, which operates as an adjustment mechanism ensuring equilibrium.

A typical feature of Hayek's view, as of Menger's, is that subjective knowledge was included among the variables undergoing such adjustment processes, along with prices and quantities produced and exchanged. As he became aware of the unsolved problems in the theory of value and distribution he had adopted, Hayek gradually attributed growing importance to the role of the market as an instrument of diffusion of information and adjustment of individual knowledge. These are stimulating ideas; however, they do not find a counterpart in an adequate theory of equilibrium (or, in other terms, a theory of value, distribution, employment and choice of techniques) such as to prove the equilibrating efficacy of market mechanisms.

Hayek tried to develop such a theory in the first decades of his long activity, taking up from Böhm-Bawerk the idea of capital as a flow of dated labour quantities. Investment and production decisions thus have effect in a period subsequent to the period of adoption, and problems of intertemporal coordination of decisions arise. The subject of Hayek's analysis was thus the emergence of a spontaneous order from the decisions of economic agents coordinated, in a market economy, by the invisible hand of competition. Hayek considered the different obstacles preventing this spontaneous order from emerging, particularly scarcity of knowledge, but maintained that a market economy is superior to a planned economy precisely because the information needed in a market economy is far, far less than the information necessary to a planned economy.[12]

---

[11] The notion of equilibrium proposed by Hayek differed from the traditional marginalist concept based on equality between supply and demand. This was an important conceptual shift, which has failed to attract the attention it deserves.

[12] The controversy on the vitality of a planned economy, the possibility of which had been shown by Enrico Barone (1908) in the framework of a general economic equilibrium theory, was revived by Ludwig von Mises (1920), who appeared not to have taken account of the answer already provided by Barone. Hayek, instead, insisted on the impossibility of obtaining the necessary information in practice. Oskar Lange (1904–1965) in a famous article of 1936–37 proposed a trial and error approach to the planning process, which embodies elements of a 'socialist market'. Maurice Dobb (1900–1976) instead maintained (for instance in Dobb, 1955) the superiority of planned economies in terms of the ex-ante coordination of investments.

Hayek's political writings, too, stressed these aspects, also criticising active state intervention in economic life, as in Roosevelt's New Deal. Thanks to these writings, and especially the fortunate *The Road to Serfdom* (1944), Hayek achieved status as one of the most famous political scientists of the twentieth century. In these writings Hayek retained the main elements of the Austrian tradition (uncertainty, economic activity as quest for power deriving from knowledge, the analytical notion of equilibrium fused with the notion of spontaneous order, a complex characterisation of the economic agent). However, in the political writings the idea of the spontaneous order emerging from the functioning of the market was no longer an analytical result but a simple assumption or postulate, which his theoretical research failed to demonstrate adequately. In fact, in the field of economic theory Hayek's contributions had practically petered out by the beginning of the 1940s when Kaldor's (1942) scathing attack reaffirmed Sraffa's criticisms, to be discussed later.

In *Prices and Production* (1931), Hayek combined the marginalist theory of value with a theory of the trade cycle, drawing on Böhm-Bawerk's notion of the average period of production and grafting onto it the Wicksellian mechanism of the relationship between natural and money interest rate, together with the theory of forced saving proposed by Mises in 1912 and also utilised by Schumpeter (1912).

In short, the mechanism described by Hayek went thus: when the natural rate of interest is higher than the money rate, entrepreneurs are induced to ask for bank loans in order to implement investment expenditures above the equilibrium level. Since the starting situation is – by the very definition of equilibrium – characterised by the full utilisation of resources, the additional investments can only be made through the increase in prices brought about by the excess demand financed by bank loans; inflation deprives consumers of purchasing power, while entrepreneurs find advantage in it given the time lag between acquisition of the means of production and sale of the product. Furthermore, the additional demand for investment goods generates an increase in their relative prices as compared with consumption goods; this in turn corresponds to an increase in the real wage rate, which enhances the advantage of lengthening the average period of production. These elements constitute the ascending stage of the trade cycle. However, the increased incomes of the productive factors are transformed into greater demand for consumption goods; the relative prices of these goods increase, and the real wage rate decreases. Thus it becomes more advantageous to shorten the average period of production, and the capital goods characterised by higher duration lose in value. Hence the descending phase of the trade cycle, in which – given the mechanisms originating it – support to consumption as proposed by Keynes is counterproductive. In this stage the capital accumulated in the ascending stage of the trade cycle is economically destroyed, so that the economic system returns to its original equilibrium.

Hayek's theory took into account changes in technique, income distribution and relative prices, thus overcoming the dichotomy between real and monetary factors present in Wicksell. Thus it appeared the most solid alternative to the Keynesian research programme. Hence Sraffa's (1932) reaction (probably prompted by Keynes himself), criticising the foundations of the analytical edifice built by Hayek (and, before him, by Wicksell) by showing the inexistence of a natural rate of interest: in a world in which the structure of relative prices changes over time, there are as many natural rates of interest as there are commodities (and, for each commodity, as many intervals of time are considered). According to Sraffa, Hayek had not fully understood the difference between a monetary and a barter economy, so that the monetary factors proved superimposed on the real ones, and any assumption of an influence exerted by the latter over the former clashed with the marginalist theory of value.

Hayek's response (1932) was feeble. As a matter of fact, the impact of Sraffa's criticism was more general: the influence of monetary factors over real variables is incompatible with acceptance of a marginalist theory of value. As for the elements of Hayek's thought that aroused the greatest interest in contemporary debate – such as the role attributed to economic agents' learning when confronted with the market's responses to their actions – incorporating them in a coherent body of economic theory constitutes a challenge to be tackled on new foundations rather than an analytical result left as heritage by the Austrian economist.

12 General Economic Equilibrium

12.1 The Invisible Hand of the Market

Many economists identify general economic equilibrium theory with theory *tout court*, compared to which any other theory can be considered a particular case. This theory, it is said, shows that the 'invisible hand of the market' ensures a systematic tendency towards an equilibrium with perfect equality between supply and demand for each commodity (market clearing), even in the presence of many commodities and many economic agents. As a matter of fact, this is not true.

General equilibrium theory was originally developed by the Lausanne school, founded by Léon Walras. Its main constitutive elements are the general interdependence among all the parts that compose an economic system, the idea of the market as an equilibrating mechanism between supply and demand, the view of the economic problem as a problem of optimal allocation of scarce resources and the notion of a perfectly rational and perfectly selfish economic agent (the *homo oeconomicus*).

The idea of interrelations among the different parts that compose an economic system was already at the centre of Quesnay's analysis, with his *tableau économique*; subsequently, we have the simple and expanded reproduction schemes developed by Marx and more recently Leontief's input-output tables. None of these analytical contributions, however, included a price and quantity adjustment mechanism based on the reactions of agents in the market to disequilibria between supply and demand. Furthermore, these contributions all focussed attention on interdependencies among sectors in production, while interdependence (substitutability) in consumption choices was not considered, or at any rate remained in the background.

The role of demand and supply in determining the price of a good was conversely at the centre of a widespread tradition of economic thinking, which in representing the working of the market took as ideal reference points first the medieval fairs and then the stock exchanges, both considered institutions that ensure a meeting place, in time and space, for buyers and sellers. However, the idea of a general interrelation among the various parts of the economic system generally remained in the background. Jevons's utilitarian approach focused on analysis of individual behaviour, with comparison between disutility (labour) and utility (consumption), while interrelations among different economic agents in the market constituted a superstructure in many respects only outlined. Somewhat later Marshall, albeit keeping account of Walras's work, indicated – as we shall better see in the next chapter – his preference for 'short causal chains', hence the method of analysis of partial equilibrium, as compared with general economic equilibrium analysis, considered too abstract.

The grounds to represent the classical economists as precursors of general economic equilibrium theory are even more questionable. There are three aspects to which reference is usually made in doing so: the notions of the invisible hand of the market, of competition and of the convergence of market prices towards natural prices. Briefly returning to the points mentioned previously, it is worth stressing that none of these elements implies a subjective view of value or choice of the medieval fair (or of the stock exchange) as paradigm for representing the working of the economy. In particular, the idea of the convergence of market prices towards natural prices did not imply, for classical economists such as Smith or Ricardo, the idea of market prices as theoretical variables univocally *determined* by an apparatus of demand and supply curves (nor the idea that it be possible to define sufficiently precise and stable relations connecting quantities demanded and supplied to prices nor indeed the idea that such relations can be deduced as representing the behaviour of rational economic agents). Finally, the notion of the invisible hand was originally used by Smith in different contexts, *not* to uphold the idea of the optimality of a competitive market based on the demand and supply mechanism.

In conclusion, we must recognise that the idea of an economic system driven by the tendency of all its parts towards equilibrium between supply and demand is simply a specific viewpoint developed by Walras and his followers – one among the various viewpoints that have appeared in the history of economic thought. As we shall see, consolidation of the foundations and extension of the basic model of general equilibrium theory leads not only to dropping the initial idea of an invisible hand of the market but also to pointing out its limitations as an interpretative tool applicable to the real world.

12.2   Léon Walras

The general economic equilibrium approach, insofar as it implied including the supply and demand mechanism in a context of general interdependencies in production as in consumption, arose with Walras, who
drew particular inspiration from the field of physics, and specifically
mechanics, with its theory of static equilibrium.

Marie Esprit Léon Walras, one of the best-known and least widely
read economists of all times, was born in 1834 at Evreux in France, and
died in 1910 at Clarens in Switzerland; he studied at the École des mines
but soon abandoned engineering to dedicate himself to literature and
journalism. He published a novel, worked on the *Journal des Économistes*
and *La Presse* and was a clerk with the railways, co-editor with Léon
Say of a cooperativist review, *Le Travail* (1866–68), administrator of
a cooperative bank (which went bankrupt in 1868) and a paid lecturer.
Finally, after many abortive attempts in France, in 1870 he obtained
a position as a teacher at Lausanne in Switzerland and the following year
the chair of political economy. Married in 1869 after a long period of
cohabitation from which two daughters were born, Walras had to
undertake various additional jobs (collaboration with journals and ency-
clopaedias, consultancy with an insurance firm) in order to supplement
his meagre salary as professor; but only in 1892, thanks to the inheritance received from his mother, was he able to pay back the debts
contracted to finance publication of his writings. It was then that he
resigned from his chair, wishing to concentrate on research; he favoured
nomination of Pareto as his successor.

Walras's main work was the *Éléments d'économie politique pure*
(1874; second part, 1877; fourth edition, 1900; the edition commonly used today is Jaffé's 1954 English translation of the 'definitive'
French edition of 1926, which on many important accounts is quite
different from the first). The French economist's original research
programme entailed two other volumes to follow this work dealing
with pure theory: one concerning applied economics, the other social
economy. In their place, we have two collections of essays: the *Études
d'économie sociale* (1896) and the *Études d'économie politique appliquée*
(1898).

The original work plan derived from a distinction, in the field of
economic phenomena, between (a) the laws of exchange, assimilated to
natural laws like the laws studied in physics, the object of pure economics;
(b) the production of wealth (division of labour, industrial organisation),
the object of applied economics; and (c) problems of distribution,
involving also ethical issues, the object of social economics. The three

fields imply three different kinds of analytical work, with different levels of abstraction and different connections with other fields of research: greater proximity to natural sciences and particularly to physics for pure economics, to social sciences for applied economics and to philosophy for social economics. Parallel to this tri-partition, among other things, was the distinction between the theoretical assumption of absolute free competition, the competitive conditions of real markets and, finally, the 'principle' of free competition (understood not only as theoretical optimality of perfect competition but also of its equity).

In the 'definitive' edition, the *Eléments* were divided into three parts. After an introductory part on the definition of political economy and social economy, we have a step-by-step sequence: part two concerns the theory of exchange between two commodities, part three extends analysis to a greater number of commodities; subsequently we find production (part four), accumulation and credit (part five), money (part six), growth and critique of previous theories (in particular, the 'English' theory – that is, Ricardo's and John Stuart Mill's: part seven), and monopoly and taxes (part eight).

Underlying this construct was a stylised representation of the market economy, which assumed the Paris Bourse as archetype (already studied in Walras 1867, 1880, where he stressed the absence of exchanges at non-equilibrium prices). Continental stock exchanges in the past differed from the Anglo-Saxon ones, being based on the role of an auctioneer, who was to call out in succession the various stocks, proposing a price for each of them and ascertaining the corresponding demand and supply. The price was then adjusted, raising it when demand was higher than supply and reducing it in the opposite case. This adjustment process continued until an equilibrium was reached between supply and demand; actual exchanges only took place when this situation was arrived at.[1] The working of the stock exchange was taken as the archetype of the freely competitive market, which according to Walras constituted at one and the same time an analytical

---

[1] Anglo-Saxon stock exchanges, on the other hand, are based on *continuous trading*, a mode of operation subsequently adopted by continental stock exchanges as well and which constituted the term of reference for Marshall's theory as well as Hicks's. In any case, it is worth stressing that in Walras's theory exchanges only take place once the prices that ensure equilibrium between demand and supply simultaneously on all markets are reached; since demand functions depend on the prices of all goods simultaneously, we cannot consider the equilibrium price of a commodity to have been reached simply because equality between demand and supply for that commodity has been established, if equilibrium has not been established for all other commodities as well.

assumption and a normative ideal, the optimality of which was to be demonstrated.[2]

Here we will attempt a broad outline of Walras's analysis; faithfulness to Walras's text is in some respects sacrificed for the sake of simplicity.

As far as the *model of pure exchange* is concerned, the data of the problem consist in the number of commodities and of economic agents, their preferences and the endowments of each commodity for each agent. Preferences are expressed by individual demand functions for the different goods, which Walras derived from utility functions. For each individual we then have a budget constraint, which ensures equality between the value of goods demanded by her/him and the resources s/he commands. The equilibrium solution for the relative prices and the quantities of the different commodities acquired and sold by each individual is defined as a solution to a system of equations. Walras also provided illustration of an adjustment process (*tâtonnement*) proposed as an idealised representation of what takes place in reality under competitive conditions: the system begins with an initial price *crié au hazard* (given at random by the auctioneer); then the corresponding levels of demand and supply are compared, and the 'cried out' price is changed until an equilibrium is reached; only then does trading take place.

The analytical model is simple. For each individual we have as many demand functions as there are commodities; each function expresses the demand of that individual for that commodity as a function of the price of the commodity itself and of all other prices – which are unknowns to be determined – in addition to the initial endowments of the different commodities that the individual commands (and which, multiplied by their prices, determine the individual's disposable income). These functions are by assumption independent and remain unchanged in the course of the process of adjustment to equilibrium; moreover, the quantity demanded decreases when the price of the commodity under consideration increases, all other variables remaining unchanged. For each commodity, the demand functions of the different individuals are added up; we thus arrive at defining aggregate demand functions, one for each commodity. Corresponding to the individuals' budget constraints there is a system of equations expressing the aggregate equilibrium conditions: that is, for each commodity the quantity demanded is set equal to the quantity supplied. We thus have two groups of

---

[2] On the political plane, Walras was a progressive thinker who proposed cooperativism rather than class struggle and pursued ideals of social justice, for example with the proposal to nationalise land and attribute rent to the State.

equations: the demand functions and the conditions of equilibrium; in each of the two groups, the number of equations is equal to the number of commodities. 'Walras's law' then reminds us that one of these equations can be deduced from the others (namely that if $n - 1$ markets are in equilibrium, the same necessarily holds true for the n-th market). Hence, if there are n commodities, the independent equations are $2 n - 1$. We then have a number of independent equations equal to the number of unknowns to be determined (the $n - 1$ relative prices, that is the prices of the various commodities in terms of one of them chosen as standard of measure, and the n quantities of the different commodities demanded in the system as a whole). Once prices are determined, the quantities of each commodity acquired or sold by each individual are also determined on the basis of the individual demand functions. The result, analogous to that published three years earlier by Menger and Jevons, is that the prices of the various commodities are proportional to their *raretés*, or marginal utilities.

Walras was aware of the fact that simple equality between number of equations and number of unknowns alone did not ensure economically meaningful solutions for the variables to be determined; this essential function was implicitly attributed to the illustration of the *tâtonnement* process, which purported to ensure the stability of equilibrium. In the case of pure exchange, as in the following steps in which exchange and production, accumulation and money were considered step by step, the analysis of stability was an integral part of Walrasian theory: in Walras's opinion, as for all the other founders of the marginalist approach, an unstable equilibrium did not constitute an acceptable solution to the problem of representing the working of the markets. In each case, then, the analysis of equilibrium and of its stability was followed by comparative statics analysis, aiming at ascertaining what happens when some data of the problem – the initial endowment of some commodity, or consumers' preferences – change.[3]

In the case of the *model of production and exchange*, each individual has at her/his disposal given endowments of what we may broadly call capital goods: land, capital goods in the specific sense, personal capital goods (skills). Moreover the production functions are known, which express the quantities produced of the different commodities as increasing functions of the quantities used of the services of the various productive factors. Initially, for the sake of simplicity, such functions are based on the

---

[3] As Schumpeter (1908, pp. 360–1) would point out, in the absence of stability, static comparative analysis – which he considers the main contribution of marginalist economics, the notion of equilibrium being tautological – loses any value.

assumption of fixed technical coefficients, which implies absence of substitutability among different factors of production and constant returns to scale. Side by side with the markets for commodities we now have the markets for services of productive factors, which are 'hired' by their owners to entrepreneurs. The role of the latter is to acquire such services, organise the productive process and sell the commodities produced. Competition ensures that entrepreneurs do not obtain any profit, apart from a wage for management, which is included in the costs of production.

We thus have a new group of equations, as many as there are commodities, which ensures for each consumption good equality between its cost of production and product value. Moreover, we have a group of demand functions for the services of capital goods, as many as there are capital goods; the demand for each service corresponds to the quantity of it employed in the productive processes on the whole and is therefore expressed as a function of technology (more precisely, of technical coefficients of production) and of levels of production of different consumption goods. Another group of equations (once again as many as there are capital goods) expresses the equilibrium condition for the markets for the services of capital goods as equality between quantity demanded and quantity available for each service.[4] The additional equations correspond in number to the additional unknowns: the prices of the services of capital goods, in terms of the commodity chosen as standard of measure, the quantities demanded for each service and the quantities produced of the different consumption goods. The process of adjustment to equilibrium, or *tâtonnement*, is in this case much more complex than in the case of the model of pure exchange. Walras tried to define with precision the different aspects of this process, and in subsequent editions of the *Éléments* his analysis underwent major changes but beyond our scope in this broad outline.

Walras then tackled the third model, with *accumulation and credit*, namely the case in which capital goods are produced. In this stage, before money was taken into account, the problem of credit was introduced: we are thus confronted with demand and supply of credit in real terms, i.e. in terms of the commodity chosen as standard of measure. In order to deal with this problem, Walras introduced a commodity E (*épargne*, i.e. savings), which has the characteristic of

---

[4] In the model of production and exchange there is no production of new capital goods, which are assumed to last forever and to have an efficiency independent of their age. Moreover, in Walrasian terminology capital goods include both capital goods in the strict sense and land and personal capital goods (working abilities).

yielding an annual perpetuity equal to a unit of the commodity chosen as standard and which thus has a price equal to the inverse of the rate of interest. This commodity is demanded by those who desire to invest in the purchase of new capital goods (the entrepreneurs) and is supplied by those who decide to save (the capitalists). Demand and supply of this commodity thus depend, on the one hand, on the preferences of economic agents for current consumption over future consumption and, on the other, on the return on investment in new capital goods. The condition of equality between demand and supply of the commodity E constitutes an additional equation, which corresponds to the additional unknown represented by the price of the commodity E (or by its inverse, the rate of interest).

In equilibrium, the supply price of the capital goods that are produced (which is given by their cost of production) must be equal to their demand price, which corresponds to their net return, discounted on the basis of the rate of interest implicit in the price of the commodity E. Alternatively, it is possible to define, for each capital good, a rate of return, which is given by the net income (equal to gross income, consisting of the price of the service of the capital good under consideration less the costs for amortization and insurance) divided by the price of the capital good. Investment in different capital goods must yield the same rate of return, in turn equal to the rate of interest that brings to equilibrium demand and supply of the commodity E, savings. Furthermore, for each capital good in equilibrium demand must equal supply. If in the initial situation a capital good yields a higher rate of return than that of other capital goods, it proves profitable to increase production, and thus supply, of the good. This brings about a reduction in its price, up to the point at which its rate of return has decreased to the same level as the rates of return of other capital goods. Conversely, those capital goods for which the demand price turns out to be lower than the supply price will not be produced, and their price will be equal to the present value of the rents expected from sale of their services.

Money was introduced in a fourth stage of analysis as a bridge required by economic agents to cross the time intervals between outlays and takings. Money was thus considered one of the two kinds of circulating capital, side by side with non-durable means of production. Net demand for money balances depended on the level of the interest rate that represented their opportunity cost. At this stage in the development of his theory, too, Walras stuck to the assumption of absence of uncertainty in equilibrium states. As a consequence, his monetary theory did not lend itself to analysing the trade cycle as a sequence of disequilibria with its origin in the monetary phenomena; a contradiction arises between the static nature of Walrasian general economic equilibrium analysis and any notion of money as something different and far more than a simple standard of measure.

Despite many years' work, crucial analytical issues remained open: demonstration of the existence, uniqueness and stability of the solutions. Walras built the conceptual and analytical foundations of general economic equilibrium theory but did not succeed in even provisionally bringing his analysis to a close. This task was then attempted by successive generations of scholars. However, as we shall see, the results were to be a long way from the hopes that had inspired Walras's efforts: neither the stability nor the uniqueness of general economic equilibrium, even for the simplest model of pure exchange, can be proved under sufficiently general conditions. Given the objectives he had set himself, if Walras had known this outcome, he would have had to reckon that he had lost his wager in starting the new research stream centred on general economic equilibrium.

12.3   Vilfredo Pareto and the Lausanne School

When he gave up the Lausanne chair in 1892, Walras made sure that a forty-four-year-old engineer, Vilfredo Pareto, would be appointed in his place. Born in Paris in 1848, the son of a Genoan marquis in exile as a follower of Mazzini, Pareto studied engineering at Turin University, where he graduated in 1870. Subsequently he worked as a railway engineer and then as assistant director and general director of the Ferriere Italiane in Florence. Compelled to resign in 1890 when the company was hit by crisis, he began taking an interest in economics, reading the *Principi di economia pura* by Pantaloni and then Walras's writings; only in 1892 did he publish his first articles in the *Giornale degli economisti*. Activity as a full-time scholar only began with the Lausanne appointment. His lectures were collected in the *Cours d'économie politique* (1896–97). His main work in our field is the *Manuale di economia politica* (1906), and in particular the mathematical appendix to the 1909 French edition. The other best-known writings concern sociology: *Les systèmes socialistes* dated 1901–2 and the two volumes of the *Trattato di sociologia generale* dated 1916. Benefiting from an inheritance and then deserted by his wife, Pareto moved to Céligny, near Lausanne, and in 1907 resigned from his chair, living in isolation up to his death in 1923.

His contributions to economic theory essentially, but not exclusively, consisted of the application of mathematical tools to the general economic equilibrium approach developed by Walras. Intermediate between economics and sociology was the widely known Pareto law (Pareto 1896) concerning personal income distribution:

$$log N = log A - \alpha \, log \, x$$

where N is the number of families with an income at least equal to x, A is a parameter indicating the size of the population, and α is an estimated parameter, generally equal to 1.5. The apparent applicability of this formula to different populations and different epochs seems to indicate independence of income distribution from historical and social vicissitudes. A moral lesson seems implicit in this, analogous to that drawn from the Malthusian population law: policies aimed at improving the living conditions of the poor classes are useless, since they cannot modify an income distribution that is a law of nature, depending as it does – according to Pareto – on innate differences of personal abilities, distributed haphazardly among the population.[5]

Pareto's main analytical contributions are the abandonment of the cardinal notion of utility in favour of an ordinal notion and the notion of the Pareto optimum. Actually there were precursors for both notions: Irving Fisher for the ordinal notion of utility and Francis Ysidro Edgeworth, with his contract curve, for the notion of the Pareto optimum; Pareto returned the favour by christening with the name of 'Edgeworth box' an analytical tool developed by himself, which Edgeworth had never used.

In the *Cours* (1896–97) Pareto proposed the term 'science of ophelimity' (derived from the Greek and indicating the ability of a good to satisfy needs) to designate the subjective theory of value. In this way he meant to stress – possibly in the wake of Menger – that his theory did not deal with a value in use considered as an intrinsic property of the economic good but rather with a subjective evaluation. Then, in the 1906 *Manuale*, we find a systematic illustration of general economic equilibrium theory, on the lines of a rational mechanics textbook. Taking on the notion of indifference curves, introduced by Edgeworth in 1881, Pareto went on with construction of a general equilibrium system, in particular by outlining the so-called fundamental theorems of welfare economics, aiming to prove the optimality of the market economy in conditions of perfect competition.

---

[5] Pareto's law can in fact be obtained as the result of stochastic processes (Markovian chains) in which, period after period (or generation after generation), each individual has an income equal to that of the previous period plus or minus a normally distributed casual deviation.

The notion of *Pareto optimum* designates a situation such that it cannot be modified in order to improve the position of some economic agent without bringing out a worsening of at least one other economic agent. Pareto demonstrated that competitive equilibrium corresponds to an optimum in this sense. Naturally, given a multiplicity of competitive equilibriums, hence a multiplicity of Pareto optimums, a criterion would be necessary for inter-personal comparisons in order to locate an absolute optimum. Moreover, like Walras, also Pareto failed to complete the crucial steps with respect to the issues of the existence, uniqueness and stability of general economic equilibrium. Perhaps it was this outcome, his increasing awareness of the limits of pure economic theory – limits that grew the more evident the more rigorous the theory became – that decisively shifted Pareto's interests towards sociology

12.4 Irving Fisher

Among the first American economists of international fame, we find Irving Fisher (1867–1947). He had a mathematical background; gradually his interests moved towards economics and the general equilibrium approach. His first works concerned application of mathematics to the economic theory of value.[6] Gradually, his passion for social and political issues grew, and Fisher became an ardent supporter of monetary stability (developing in this context his theory of index numbers) and of many other causes, from Esperanto to defence of the environment. In 1930 he became the first president of the Econometric Society

In the theoretical field, Fisher contributed on different fronts. First of all, he developed an analysis based on the distinction between stocks and flows and proposed a definition of income connected to the flows of services that excluded savings. This led him to support the thesis (which dates back to William Petty and which in Italy was to find a supporter in Luigi Einaudi) of a taxation system focussed on expenditure. Secondly, Fisher anticipated Pareto in proposing a theory of consumer equilibrium based on the ordinal notion of utility, remarking that what matters in locating the equilibrium position is only the shape of the indifference curves (and he was probably the first to use the graph with convex indifference curves intersected by a budget line). Thirdly, he developed a theory of the rate of interest, deducing it from comparison between the

---

[6] Fisher (1892) opposed the then dominant orientation of American economists towards historicism and institutionalism, characterising, for instance, the birth of the American Economic Association in 1885.

rate of intertemporal preference of economic agents and the marginal rate of temporal substitution on the production side. In this framework, Fisher proposed the idea of a system of interest rates, as many as there are commodities, connected among themselves and to the monetary interest rate by expected changes in relative prices: a view later developed by Sraffa (1932) and by Keynes in chapter 17 of the *General Theory* but that at the same time foreshadowed the models of intertemporal general equilibrium of the Arrow-Debreu type.

Finally, the best known of Fisher's contributions is the so-called equation of exchanges, or Fisher equation, which constituted the foundation of the modern quantity theory of money: $MV = PQ$, where M is the supply of money and V the velocity of circulation (that is, the number of times in which money changes hands within a unit interval of time) while PQ designates the value (equal to price P multiplied by quantity Q) of the commodities exchanged during the same unit interval of time. Written in terms of flows of transactions, this equation is an identity that says that money flows going from one hand to another have the same value as the flows of goods and services that move in the opposite direction. In order to transform this identity into a theoretical relation connecting the price level to the money supply, three assumptions are then necessary: independence of the velocity of circulation and of the volume of exchanges from the amount of money in circulation and dependence of this latter on the decisions of monetary authorities.

The American economist thus worked on the frontier in various areas of research; thanks to his training as a mathematician he was able to formulate with a rigour, precision and completeness unusual at the time a number of elements of the theoretical construction now prevailing in university textbooks all over the world.

12.5   The Debate on the Existence, Uniqueness and Stability of Equilibrium

Walras, as we saw, attributed great importance to stability, considered an essential part of the very analysis of equilibrium, since in the absence of stability comparative static analysis would prove meaningless. However, simple equality between number of independent equations and number of unknowns alone is not sufficient to guarantee the existence of economically meaningful solutions (that is, non-negative solutions, for prices as well as for quantities), let alone their uniqueness and stability. Generations of mathematical economists tackled these themes.

The debate reached a climax in the early 1930s in Vienna, around the seminar organised by Karl Menger (1902–1985), a mathematician and son of the economist Carl who had founded the Austrian school. Remak (1929) recalled that in economics only non-negative solutions can be accepted as meaningful; insufficiency of the mere equality between number of equations and number of unknowns was stressed by Hans Neisser (1932), Friedrich Zeuthen (1933) and Heinrich von Stackelberg (1933). An initial solution to the problem of the existence of equilibrium was offered by Abraham Wald (1936). All these works used the distinction between free goods (that is, goods available in a quantity superior to that demanded at any non-negative price), the price of which is zero, and economical goods, for which equality between demand and supply is reached in correspondence with a positive price. The trick was in replacing the equalities of the Walrasian equations with feeble inequalities, so as to determine endogenously which goods are free and which are not free, which goods are produced and which are not produced. Wald (1936) demonstrated the existence and uniqueness (but not the stability) of equilibrium; however, this result was obtained through recourse to the restrictive assumption, which cannot be justified at the level of economic interpretation, that the so-called feeble axiom of revealed preferences, concerning the non-contradictory nature of individual choices, holds for the economy as a whole.

John von Neumann (1903–1957), a pupil of the mathematician David Hilbert (1862–1943), favoured the acquisition of the language of topology in economic theory, and in particular Brouwer's (or fixed point) theorem. In 1937, in an essay originally presented at Princeton in 1932, von Neumann presented a model of balanced growth, formulated in terms of inequalities: for each good, the quantity supplied must be greater than or equal to the quantity demanded; moreover, the price must be lower than or equal to production costs. As a consequence, some goods may prove free, that is, available in quantities superior to demand for any positive price: their price will be zero, and their production will be nil. By the same token, production of each commodity whose price proves lower than production costs will be nil. In other words, the solution to the system of equations, which include equalities and inequalities, defines a nucleus of goods for which both prices and produced quantities are positive. The model also established a strict relationship between rate of growth and rate of interest: the rate of growth emerged from the solution to the problem of quantities considered as a problem of maximisation under constraint, while the rate of interest emerged from the solution to the problem of prices considered as a problem of minimisation under constraint. In Chapter 17 we shall discuss his main contribution to economic theory (von Neumann and Morgenstern 1944).

Even before Austria's annexation to Germany, Karl Menger's seminar broke up with the rise of fascism and Nazism, which induced many of its protagonists (and all the leading Austrian economists) to choose the path of exile. Thus, after the conclusion of the Second World War, the centre of discussion on these topics shifted to the USA, while Europeans (such as von Neumann) still played a central role.

13 Alfred Marshall

13.1 Life and Writings

Alfred Marshall (1842–1924) did not figure among the protagonists of the 1871–74 marginalist revolution: his main contribution (*Principles of Economics*, 1890) was published nearly two decades after the works of Jevons, Menger and Walras. Marshall himself was averse to considering the new road taken by economic analysis a revolution, a clear-cut break with the past: his personal contribution, in his own opinion, consisted in a synthesis between the great tradition inherited from the past and the new yeast of the subjective approach. Indeed, Marshall contributed more than anyone else to redirecting economic science towards the approach that came to be called neoclassical, rather than marginalist or subjectivist, so as to stress the element of continuity with the past.

Marshall was born in London in 1842 to a modest family of the small-clerk bourgeoisie. Alfred studied at a school in the outskirts of London and then went on with mathematics at Cambridge, with brilliant results. Possibly as a consequence of a journey to America (1875), his interests shifted towards political economy. Participating in a scheme to promote the admission of women to university, he taught political economy to Newnham Hall's female students. There he met Mary Paley, whom he married in 1877.

Marshall's first important contribution was a volume of two essays on *The Pure Theory of Foreign Trade* and *The Pure Theory of Domestic Values* (1879b). In the same year he published, together with his wife, a didactic text offering an evolutionary view of the economy, *The Economics of Industry* (Marshall 1879a), which had good sales.

Following his marriage, Marshall was compelled to move out of Cambridge, returning there only when elected professor of political economy in 1884. In the meantime the Marshalls spent some difficult years in Bristol, and then – after a year's leave with a long stay in Palermo where the writing of the *Principles* might have begun – they moved to Oxford. The Cambridge appointment, which came unexpectedly, marked a turning point in his life. Marshall held the political economy chair up to retirement in 1908 but remained in Cambridge up to his death in 1924 and retained a strong interest in the vicissitudes of the economics curriculum created on his initiative in 1903.

From Cambridge, Marshall exercised significant influence over the teaching of economics in the rest of England. In 1890, with his active intervention, the British Economic Association was founded and the *Economic Journal* was launched. His *Principles of Economics* (eight editions, from 1890 to 1920) soon became the reference text for generations of economists. Among the students, the small guide he published in 1892, *Elements of the Economics of Industry*, was widely studied. His influence was exerted through his pupils, selected as presidents of the British Economic Association, as editors of the *Economic Journal* or as economics professors in the major English universities; in Cambridge he had Arthur Cecil Pigou appointed as his successor.

Side by side with the oral tradition of his lectures and the vast correspondence with interlocutors worldwide (Marshall 1996a), his *Official Papers* are also important, mostly testimonials to parliamentary commissions (Marshall 1926, 1996b), and a group of articles collected by Pigou after his death (Marshall 1925). Of less importance are the two volumes he published in the final years of his life: *Industry and Trade* (1919), and *Money, Credit and Commerce* (1923). Marshall died at eighty-two in 1924.

13.2   The Background

Marshall's thought is difficult to interpret: through a multiplicity of qualifications and shades of meaning (and significant changes in subsequent editions of the *Principles*) Marshall brought together different, even contradictory, elements, such as an evolutionary perspective and static equilibrium analysis.

Marshall maintained that he had autonomously developed his approach towards the end of the 1860s (hence before publication of Jevons's 1871 book) by translating John Stuart Mill's theories into mathematical terms. Indeed, when Jevons's book appeared, Marshall was ready (as attested by his review of the book, 1872) to understand its elements of novelty and to evaluate them in the light of an already sufficiently developed view of his own. This is not to deny Jevons's priority of publication, as regards the main innovative elements of the marginalist revolution, in particular the derivation of demand curves and the determination of prices connected to marginal utility. This fact impressed on Marshall the need to distinguish his ideas clearly from those of the founding father of English marginalism by stressing the one-sidedness of a purely subjective theory of value and countering it with the equally one-sided objective theory of the classical economists, based on cost of production, and then in presenting his own contribution as a synthesis that included what was valid in each of the two opposing approaches. This necessarily implied a somewhat misleading reinterpretation of the classical approach, as if it were based, like the marginalist one, on the pillar of the static notion of equilibrium between supply and demand.

Marshall's first book (1879b) began with analysis of equilibrium in foreign trade and as a logical development then arrived at a theory of internal prices. He started from the fact that, while the labour-value theory adopted by Ricardo and his immediate followers provided a univocal – though unsatisfactory – answer to the problem of determining relative prices, the theory of comparative costs proposed by Ricardo in order to explain the flows of foreign trade left the exchange ratios between imported and exported commodities indeterminate (though within an interval whose extremes are determined for each pair of imported and exported commodities by the ratios between their costs of production in the countries of origin and destination of the flows of exchange). John Stuart Mill (1844) had proposed a solution to this problem, based on recourse to the role of demand. In the simplified case of two countries and two commodities, we may thus reach conclusions such as 'the advantage of small dimensions', by which the smallest country obtains better terms of exchange, thanks to the reduced dimension of its demand for the imported commodity relative to the demand for the exported commodity coming from the larger country, or, to take another example, the forecast of a worsening of the terms of trade for that country in which demand for the imported commodity increases.

Marshall developed this line of research determining equilibrium terms of trade on the basis of a comparison between the demand curves for imports of the two countries. Thus the notion of equilibrium between demand and supply is utilised in determining values in exchange; Marshall also devotes extensive and closely argued discussion to the themes of multiplicity and the possible instability of equilibrium.

The same method, the same notion of equilibrium and the same themes concerning multiplicity and possible instability of equilibrium were then developed in *The Pure Theory of Domestic Values*. Here we also find the problem of increasing returns to scale, which so preoccupied Marshall in his *Principles*. Finally, we also find systematic use of temporal specification of the notion of equilibrium, with the distinction between very short-, short-, long- and very long-period equilibriums, connected to the assumption of given supply (very short or market period), variable supply but on the basis of a given productive capacity (short period), variable supply and productive capacity but on the basis of a given technology (long period) and general variability, including technology, consumer incomes and tastes (very long period).

The same year, 1879, saw publication of the work Marshall wrote with his wife Mary Paley, *Economics of Industry*, based on his university lectures. The theoretical essays on external and internal trade reflected Marshall's mathematical formulation and pointed in the direction of a neoclassical view based on static equilibrium between supply and demand; *Economics of Industry* more strongly reflected Marshall's studies in the social sciences and, whilst not seeking to build a rigorous analytical structure, was more receptive to aspects of historical evolution, aiming to represent a complex and constantly changing economic reality. The influence of Darwin's (1859, 1871) evolutionism was not explicitly recognised, but it was clearly visible.

Marshall's evolutionism expressed both a gradualist view summarised in the motto premised to the *Principles*, 'Natura non facit saltum', and a complex view of economic progress that laid stress on the quality of life more than per capita income. The idea of time as an irreversible flow was also repeatedly stressed. Finally, there is the shift from the classical notion of 'natural' prices to that of 'normal' values (including quantities produced and exchanged together with prices) reflecting with some delay the diffusion of normal (or Gaussian) curves in statistics and the connected idea that such curves represent laws of distribution for the phenomena of society just as they do for those of the natural world. In substance, deviation from the 'norm' was considered, at least within limits, quite a common event that did not constitute a violation of the norm itself, which emerged as a statistical average from a large number of cases observed, thus losing the element of 'corresponding to a law which is intrinsic to the nature of things'. Furthermore, the presence of technological change accentuated the indicative character of normal value as defined by the theory and thus the margin of imprecision with which the theoretical law could be applied to the real world.[1]

---

[1] Carl Friedrick Gauss (1777–1855) used the normal curve to represent the likely distribution of error in the theory of measure. Subsequently, Adolphe Quetelet (1796–1874) used the same curve to represent biological or social phenomena, interpreting the results as manifestations of natural or social laws, whose average (or median: in the normal distribution the two coincide) represents in synthesis the property of a population of cases, and the 'law' thus represented is not violated by individual cases differing from the average. We may consider as 'anomalous' only the cases that differ from the average by more than a pre-set quantity (bearing in mind that in the case of a Gaussian distribution, a difference higher than twice the mean square deviation has a probability of about

We thus have, as from Marshall's earliest publications, a twofold line of research: on the one hand, the attempt to build a rigorous theoretical system, based on a static notion of equilibrium between supply and demand; on the other, the attempt to work out a system of concepts such as to represent economic reality in a way that allowed for historical developments and evolution. Rather than the problem of a synthesis between the subjective marginalist approach and the objective approach of classical economists, it is the continuous overlapping of these two lines of research and the impossible conciliation between them which is the true key to interpreting Marshall's path, his contributions to economic science and the limits of his economics construct.

13.3   The *Principles*

When, in 1890, the first edition of the *Principles of Economics* appeared, the ground had already been prepared to ensure the book had a major impact on the economic culture of the time. Marshall was then settled in the Cambridge chair, and his pupils occupied important positions in the English academic world (the same year saw the birth of the Royal Economic Society and the *Economic Journal*). The influence of the classical tradition was still strong, together with that of the historical school, while the marginalist heterodoxy attracted some brilliant minds but was still a minority view. In such a situation, Marshall offered a set of elements designed to attract the convergent interest of the different streams of economic culture existing at the time: insistent reference to the classical tradition, from the Smithian theory of the division of labour to the Ricardian theory of rent; acceptance of the basic elements of the marginalist revolution, such as the notion of marginal utility, with attribution of a central role to demand, and hence to economic agents' preferences, within a theory of value in which prices were determined by the mechanism of equilibrium between supply and demand, already adopted by a string of post-Ricardian authors;[2] insertion of this analytical structure in the context of extended discussions on the meaning of the concepts

---

5 per cent). The idea of human sciences as concerning arguments to be deduced from 'human nature' was replaced by that of statistical laws about what is 'normal'. In this sense, the view of economic science as a theory of the behaviour of the rational agent (or *homo oeconomicus*) falls within the old view of human sciences; by substituting the term 'natural' with the term 'normal', Marshall was trying to escape such a view.

2   More precisely, for each commodity the normal price is determined by the point where two curves meet, graphically representing the demand and supply functions. These respectively connect the supply price (cost plus normal profit) and the demand price (the maximum price which the purchaser is ready to pay) to the quantity of the commodity under consideration.

used in the analysis and on the historical evolution of society; references to Darwinian evolutionism, which conferred an element of scientific modernity on the work and provided a flexible, open response to historical evolution as compared to the reference to physics prevailing in the theories of authors such as Jevons or Walras, which had not met with a warm reception.

From the first (1890) to the eighth (1920) edition, the *Principles* remained at the centre of Marshall's theoretical work, undergoing substantive revisions; this is especially true for the fifth edition (1907), the last before his resignation from the Cambridge chair. On the evidence of the voluminous *variorum editio* (1961), promoted by the Royal Economic Society, we can reconstruct this path. The importance of Marshall's revisions testifies to the difficulties he met in his work of synthesis between different approaches and in his attempt to build a theory of value that was to include simultaneously the objective (cost of production) and the subjective (utility) element and that was to be at the same time rigorous, realistic and open to historical evolution. Before discussing the difficulties Marshall came up against, it may be useful to run over the main aspects of his approach: method, the notions of equilibrium and competition, the concepts of the firm and the industry. We will then consider the problem of increasing returns and the two solutions suggested by Marshall, the representative firm and external-internal economies.

Marshall's methodological standpoint was simple: to recognise the extreme complexity of the real world. Theory cannot but be abstract but must keep its feet on the ground. Hence his tenet, which underlay his partial equilibrium method, that short causal chains should be favoured. At each step, theory proceeds by isolating a logical nexus of cause and effect held to be the main one and thus leaves aside other effects held to be secondary, though not non-existent. This is licit, indeed necessary, for construction of each individual analytical piece. However, when we put together many logical nexus and give rise to long causal chains – as happens for instance in general economic equilibrium theory – the secondary effects left aside may have repercussions that amplify step by step, and this may cause the conclusions drawn from the theoretical analysis to be misleading. Hence Marshall relegated to a mathematical note, in an appendix to his *Principles*, his illustration of general economic equilibrium (one of the most rigorous of the time). In the text, on the other hand, he preferred to focus on short causal chains, and in particular on the method of partial equilibriums. The latter consisted of considering demand and supply of each good as independent of what simultaneously happens on other markets for the other goods.

The same awareness of the complexities of the real world may also be perceived in the attention Marshall paid to the construction of the system of concepts by which to represent reality. In the first books of the *Principles*, step by step the concepts introduced are discussed, illustrating for each the shades of meaning that rendered their contours imprecise. This is true in particular for the key notions of equilibrium and competition to which, in the intertwining of affirmations and qualifications, it is very difficult to attribute a univocal meaning. Marshall's position oscillated between two terms of reference: on the one hand, the notions subsequently transmitted through the textbooks, the so-called Marshallian *vulgata*; on the other, the esoteric notions, disseminated among the circle of pupils, connected to an evolutionary view that drew more on Lamarck than on Darwin.[3] In the first case – the Marshallian *vulgata* – the notion of equilibrium corresponded to the static notion of equality between demand and supply and the notion of perfect competition to the presence of a large number of firms in each industry, so large as to render the size of each firm irrelevant to the dimensions of the industry as a whole and the choices of each individual firm irrelevant for the industry as a whole. In the second case – the evolutionary view – the notion of equilibrium took on dynamic features in the attempt to take account of the irreversibility characterising the actual movements of the firm and the industry along demand and supply curves;[4] the notion of competition was softened by attributing to each firm some room for manoeuvre that included, among other things, the possibility of violating the so-called law of the one price. Theoretical analysis – construction of well-structured models – inevitably led to refer to clear-cut concepts of the first kind, while in the case of the evolutionary view, as we shall see below, he remained in the realm of metaphors, which are evocative but certainly not rigorous. In other words, in the oscillation from the first to the second pole of the Marshallian construct, what was gained in terms of realism was lost in terms of analytical rigour.

The very notions of industry and firm constituted a bridge between the complexity of the real world and the simplicity requirement of abstract

---

[3] Jean-Baptiste de Lamarck's (1744–1829) thesis, rejected by Darwin, was the heredity of the characteristics acquired in life by an organism as response-adaptation to the environment in which it lives. Darwin's thesis was, of course, that the characteristics best adapted to existence (and above all to reproduction) in the end prevail because of a process of natural selection. Lamark's theses had been re-proposed, confounded with Darwin's evolutionism, as a tool for the analysis of society by the sociologist Herbert Spencer (1820–1903), very influential at the time.

[4] Marshall derived the 'evolutionary' notion of equilibrium from the theory of population, which can tend to a stationary age structure of the population through constancy over time of birth and death rates, even in the presence of a growing or declining population size.

theory. Marshall thus distanced himself from the extreme methodological individualism of the first marginalist theoreticians, favouring a classical feature, by which each commodity ('good', in the subjectivist terminology, which thus lays stress on their utility to the consumer) corresponds to a category that includes objects not identical amongst themselves but sufficiently similar to warrant unitary treatment, and in parallel each industry includes the firms (complex productive units) that operate in one of such commodity categories. Quite naturally, various problems arise when the categories thus defined are related to the real world: from the case of joint production to the problem of differences in the technologies adopted by different firms belonging to the same industry and on to the problem of greater or lesser similarity between the products of different firms belonging to the same industry. The latter aspect in particular renders less clear-cut, more flexible, the Marshallian notion of competition, and the notion was accordingly bent so as to allow for some degree of independence between the markets of the different firms belonging to an industry, hence some degree of autonomy in the price choices of the different firms.

Within this conceptual framework Marshall's analytical structure was based on (short- or long-period) equilibrium between demand and supply. The demand function for each commodity is assumed to be derived from individual preferences;[5] however, Marshall tended to skate over the relationship between utility maps and demand functions; for the purpose of determining equilibrium, it is sufficient to assume as given (and decreasing, on the basis of the decreasing marginal utility postulate) the demand functions for the different goods.[6] Attention was, rather, focused on supply functions: it was in this field that Marshall tried to provide an innovative contribution in comparison to the theories proposed by the first protagonists of the marginalist revolution, and in particular by Jevons. The latter had recourse to a principle symmetrical to that of decreasing utility, the principle of the increasing sacrifice or painfulness of labour; this allowed him to obtain increasing supply curves. Such an approach, however, cannot easily be extended from study of the behaviour of individuals to analysis of industries and firms in competitive markets, and it is even harder if we stick to the method of partial analysis: each firm or industry considered in isolation can easily obtain additional hours of labour by subtracting them from other firms

---

[5] In the context of partial analysis, the marginal utility of money was assumed to be constant.

[6] Recalling John Stuart Mill, in this respect Marshall stressed the need to develop a new science, ethology or the study of human habits and customs and their gradual changes in the course of time.

or industries without changing the marginal disutility of labour for the individual worker.[7]

Marshall thus proposed the road of partial equilibrium for supply side analysis and hence to construct supply curves referring to individual firms and industries. To this end he took two elements of the classical tradition and reworked them in a context different from the original one. The first was the Smithian theory of the connection between enlargement of the market and division of labour and consequently productivity increases. The second was the Ricardian theory of differential rent. Newly christened as *laws of returns to scale*, these two theories were simultaneously used to explain the variations of costs in response to changes in the quantity produced, respectively identified with the case of increasing returns to scale and with the case of decreasing returns. Clearly this is an artificial construct, which puts together quite different things. Furthermore, even if considered one at a time, the transposition of the Smithian and Ricardian ideas into the ambit of the theory of the firm and the industry gave rise to difficulties that Marshall saw or perceived but to which he did not attribute the importance they deserve.

Let us consider decreasing returns. Ricardo used them in the theory of rent with reference to the productivity of a means of production of a particular kind, such as land, taken to be available in a given quantity and with distinctive features for each unit of land. The Ricardian theory of differential rent did not revolve around the different productivities of the lands in the country, and so around decreasing returns for individual firms or industries, but around the problem of the distribution of national income among the social classes of workers, landlords and capitalists and in particular around the problem of determining the rent accruing to the landlords. In Marshall's modified form, on the other hand, the theory of decreasing returns concerned the means of production utilised by specific industries. The case in which an industry is the sole subject to use a given means of production is however a very peculiar one. Once again, outside this case, the *ceteris paribus* clause (hence the method of partial analysis) should be abandoned.

---

[7] On the other hand – we may now add on the basis of Sraffa's 1925 remarks – if we were also to take account of infinitesimal changes in the painfulness of labour, stemming from changes in production levels of a single firm or industry, such changes would equally affect all industries and firms in the economy. As a consequence, it would not be possible to use the *ceteris paribus* clause which is the basis of partial analysis; in particular, when faced with generalised changes in prices it would not be possible to assume as given the demand curve for the individual industry.

In his earliest writings, moreover, Marshall was considering a further problem: the existence – and importance – of increasing returns to scale, which are seen as the source of economic development in the Smithian theory. The theory of the equilibrium of the firm falls apart if the assumption of decreasing returns is abandoned in favour of that, decidedly more realistic, of increasing returns to scale. A stable equilibrium is possible in this case only if the demand curve decreases more rapidly than the supply curve; but this cannot hold in the case of competition, where the price is by assumption independent of the quantity produced by the individual firm. In other words, the assumption of perfect competition is incompatible with the case of increasing returns to scale.

As already stated, Marshall had already recognised the existence of this dilemma in his essays published in 1879; much of his analytical effort in the *Principles* and in subsequent revisions of the book was devoted to solving the dilemma, but the suggested solutions went in different directions.

First, we have the solution later developed by Pigou and Viner, and then adopted in most textbooks, based on the assumption of U-shaped average and marginal cost curves: initially, when production increases, cost curves are decreasing because increasing returns prevail; from a certain point onward, decreasing returns take the lead, and costs start increasing. Under competition and in the long run, the equilibrium point for the firm corresponds to the minimum of the average cost curve. The development of the industry then depends on the economies of scale internal to the industry itself (since the demand curve is decreasing for the industry, so that an equilibrium is possible even if the supply curve is also decreasing, provided that the speed of decrease is lower than that of demand) but external to the individual firms that compose the industry (so as to retain for them the possibility of a competitive equilibrium that needs cost to increase with the quantity produced, from a certain point onwards). Such a construct may thus be criticised both for its lack of realism and for its connection to a static notion of equilibrium.

Marshall, while hinting at the line of reasoning outlined previously, suggested, rather, a second path, consisting in the theory of the representative firm and recourse to biological metaphors. The core of the argument is this: the industry is made up of many firms which, like trees in a forest, are at different points of their life cycle: some, the young ones, enjoy increasing returns and develop although in a competitive environment; others, the mature ones, have already reached dimensions at which the elements of growth and decay balance out; yet others are decaying. In a world composed of individual firms distributed among the different stages of development, the *representative firm*, of average dimensions, turns out to be midway in its development process and can thus be identified with a firm experiencing increasing returns, even if overall the population of firms is stationary.

The weakness in this construct is not simply the difficulty of translating it into a well-structured analytical model; rather, it lies in the difficulty of accepting the assumption of the life cycle of firms. Marshall referred to the sequence of three generations in control of the firm: the founder, endowed with above-normal organisational and innovative ability; his immediate heirs, brought up in the hard school of the founder and used at least to rigorous management of the family business; and then the third generation, brought up in prosperous conditions and less ready to make the sacrifices that are often necessary in a competitive environment characterised by continuous technological change and hence by the need to save and invest.[8] Such an assumption refers to a world of small firms managed by their proprietor but does not apply to public companies. In the last editions of the *Principles*, Marshall appeared aware of these difficulties. Various among his followers nonetheless remained faithful to the construct of the representative firm, including Robertson, who re-proposed it in 1930, provoking Sraffa's (1930) sarcastic reaction.

On this count at least, the *Principles* constituted a failure. However, various other elements of Marshall's edifice are fully entitled to remain part of modern economic theory; we may recall, for instance, the notion of elasticity. And it should be added that Marshall's greatness as an economist lies also (and perhaps mainly) in his awareness of the limits of his analytical constructs, which have however been accepted without critical scrutiny by many of his followers.

13.4   Economics Becomes a Profession

When Marshall began his professional career, two general curricula could be distinguished in university studies: human sciences and natural sciences. Within the first curriculum, philosophy, history and morals coexisted. Political economy had a smaller role; the economics lectures that Marshall gave the female students of Newnham College were on many accounts lessons in civic education. In this sense we should

---

[8] In that period (eleven years after the first edition of Marshall's *Principles* but six years before the fifth edition, in which the idea of the representative firm reached full development) the idea of the life cycle of firms found literary expression in the famous novel by Thomas Mann, *Buddenbrooks* (1901).

interpret the support the young Marshall gave the movement for admission of women to university studies: support that was subsequently to become heated opposition, with a change of attitude that may have been due to Marshall's impression that the connection originally perceived between university instruction and civic and moral education (a connection consistent with the role he attributed to women as enlightened vestals of the family and society) had turned into a link between getting a university degree and starting a professional career, increasingly blurring the distinction between men and women. Marshall in fact appears a traditionalist Victorian, favourable to cultural enhancement as instrumental to moral enhancement in the case of women as in that of workers but poles apart compared to the pro-women position manifested, for instance, by John Stuart Mill some decades earlier or the contemporary supporters of women's accession to university, like his old friend Henry Sidgwick.

Establishment of professional education in the economics field required that economics be made to emerge from the wider field of study of the moral sciences. Marshall made a decisive contribution in this direction, with the foundation in 1890 of the British Economic Association (subsequently the Royal Economic Society) and of *Economic Journal* and with the long struggle for the institution of a specialised curriculum of studies at the University of Cambridge. Economics (no longer 'political economy') was conceived as a science whose development was entrusted to specialists, on the model of natural sciences, and no longer as a branch of knowledge entrusted in part to those who could ponder on their own practical experiences (from Cantillon the banker to Ricardo the stockbroker) and in part to persons endowed with good general culture and a political interest in understanding economic and social events (from the physicians Petty, Mandeville and Quesnay to a professional revolutionary such as Marx).

The professionalization of economics had both positive and negative effects. Among the positive effects, there was the diffusion of more refined techniques of analysis, which called for greater rigour and greater control of the logical consistency of arguments. The development of mathematical economics, but especially the collection and systematic analysis of statistical information, were aspects of this process. As for the negative elements, research activity lost its nature of participating in cultural and political life and became an instrument of academic careers. The importance attributed to originality and priority of publication of their own ideas, on the part of Marshall as well as of Jevons or Walras, can thus be better understood. However, at this point the theoretical debate acquired a dangerous autonomy with respect to the constant confrontation with the real world: showing scientific ability, essentially through use of refined analytical tools, gradually became more important than a good practical understanding of the real issues.

13.5 Monetary Theory: From the Old to the New Cambridge School

In the *Principles* Marshall did not deal with money; when, by then eighty years old, he succeeded in publishing *Money, Credit and Commerce* (1923), his analytical vigour had disappeared. His contributions are rather to be found in his participation in some commissions of enquiry into the subject (Marshall 1926, 1996b) and in the oral tradition stemming from his teaching. Here we find two contributions: transformation of Irving Fisher's quantity equation, $MV = PQ$, into the so-called Cambridge equation, $k\,Y = M;$[9] the role of monetary disturbances in explaining the cyclical oscillations of the economy around the long period equilibrium determined by the real factors considered within the neoclassical theory of value.

The first aspect might seem a simple change in symbols: Cambridge's k formally corresponds to the inverse of the velocity of circulation of money V in Fisher's equation. However, behind this formal change a different notion of the demand for money shone through, connected not so much to financing requirements for exchange as to economic agents' choices on the share of their income (or, in a different formulation, later to be developed by Keynes, on the share of their wealth) that they desire to keep in the form of money. In this way precautionary demand for money (and later, with Keynes, speculative demand) was made to appear explicitly side by side with demand for money for transaction purposes. The formal change in the equation of exchanges thus pointed to a new potentially revolutionary perspective, as was to be seen when his pupil Keynes accomplished decisive steps forward.

With respect to the role of money in the determination of the real variables of the economy, Marshall advanced further interesting ideas, admitting the influence of liquidity conditions on income and employment as well, together with its influence on money prices. However, in this case, too, the decisive step forward was accomplished

---

[9] M indicates the quantity of money in circulation in the economy, V its velocity of circulation, P the price level, Q an index of quantity produced, Y national income in money terms (so that $PQ = Y$) and k the share of income that economic agents desire to keep in money.

later, by Keynes. Marshall limited the non-neutrality of money to the short period, as after him so many economists were to do.

13.6   Marshallian Developments in Italy and the United States

Maffeo Pantaleoni (1857–1924), among other important achievements, contributed to the founding of what came to be known as the Italian school of public finance.[10] His most influential textbook, *Principii di economia pura* (1889, translated into English in 1898 as *Principles of Economics*), which preceded Marshall's *Principles* by a year, shared a substantially similar orientation, with the search for a synthesis between Jevons's and Menger's subjective approach and the classical tradition. Many ideas, including his analysis of predatory and parasitic phenomena, indicate an inclination towards an evolutionary approach similar to the one we may find in Marshall's *Principles*. Pantaleoni remained perplexed by the rarefied abstract nature of general economic equilibrium theory and showed little patience with the classificatory manias to which the Marshallian *vulgata* had given rise, with the distinction between increasing, constant and decreasing returns industries. However, his influence led to the rise of a Marshallian stream within Italian universities.

In the United States, the Marshallian approach was taken up and developed by, among others, John Bates Clark (1847–1938) and Jacob Viner (1892–1970).

Clark was one of the promoters of the American Economic Association in 1885 and professor at Columbia University in New York. His main work, *The Distribution of Wealth* (1899), offered an organic illustration of the neoclassical theory of value and distribution based on the aggregate notion of capital. Clark considered an economic system with only two factors of production, labour and capital, in which the quantity of product obtained depends on the quantity utilised of the two factors of production and their combination; rate of interest and wage rate correspond, in equilibrium, to the marginal productivity of capital and labour.[11]

---

[10] Among the economists who contributed to the development of an Italian school of public finance we should recall at least Antonio de Viti de Marco (1858–1943), one of the very few Italian holders of a chair who refused the oath of loyalty to fascism. This school originated the stream of public choice theory later revived by the 1986 Nobel prize winner James Buchanan (1919–2013).

[11] Clark (and Wicksteed, 1894, before him) left open the issue of the conditions under which the distributive rule based on the marginal productivities of the factors of production totally exhaust the whole value of the product. However, Flux (1894) had already stressed the need to assume constant returns to scale.

Clark rejected as irrelevant the attempts to develop a disaggregated theory of capital. Moreover, he proposed a 'universal measure of value' based on a combination of utility and labour. On the conceptual plane, his main contribution to the subjectivist approach consisted of the distinction between statics and dynamics; at the analytical level, in the demonstration of the erroneousness of considering the share of income going to capital or to land as a surplus, because of the symmetry between the determination of the wage rate and that of the interest rate, which correspond to the marginal product of the two factors of production, labour and capital.

In the generation following Clark's, Jacob Viner taught at the University of Chicago and later at Princeton. His main fields of research were the theory of international trade and the history of economic thought (Viner, 1937, 1991). His most influential contribution, however, was an article on 'Cost Curves and Supply Curves' (1931), in which he offered systematic treatment in four graphs of the determination of short-run and long-run equilibriums of the firm and the industry based on pairs of U-shaped curves representing average and marginal costs as functions of quantity produced. This systematic treatment was taken on substantially unchanged in economics textbooks of the subsequent half-century and beyond. In particular it was accepted – together with Clark's aggregate neoclassical version of the theory of value and distribution – as the central core of the famous textbook *Economics* (1948) by Paul Samuelson (1912–2009, Nobel prize in 1970), the best-selling textbook of recent decades and a model for various other authors.

13.7   Thorstein Veblen and Institutionalism

Thorstein Veblen (1857–1929), the son of Norwegian immigrants, born in a farming community and a student of John Bates Clark, often felt out of place in university life due to his unconventional lifestyle and his religious skepticism at a time when most American colleges and universities were church-affiliated. A prolific writer, the first managing editor of the *Journal of Political Economy*, in 1899 he published a provocative and successful book on *The Theory of the Leisure Class*, in which he discussed the influence of economic values on customs and fashion with heavy irony and showed how the business mentality came to dominate even within the institutions of learning, with a retrogression of cultural values.

According to Veblen, modern capitalism is characterised by persistence of old modes of thought, such as ancient predatory instincts and resort to conspicuous consumption to assert social superiority. In *The Theory of Business Enterprise* (1904), Veblen contrasted the men of industry (inventors, engineers, technical experts) with businessmen becoming salesmen or focusing on financial management rather than production. As an implication of this, in later writings he foresaw the separation between ownership and management of firms and the growth of giant corporations, foreshadowing Berle and Means's (1932) managerial capitalism, Galbraith's (1967) 'technostructure' and Minsky's (1993) notion of 'money managers capitalism' (notions we shall return to in Chapter 17). Two central aspects of Veblen's institutional approach, namely the idea that human nature should not be taken as given but as an endogenous variable in economic analysis and the idea of a decisive role played by cultural and institutional change in the process of economic development, disappeared from American economic culture with the rise to dominance of marginalism. Veblen also focused on the tensions stemming from the lag in cultural adaptation to the changing economic environment.

Veblen was too much of an outsider to belong to any 'school', but the important institutionalist current in the United States can be seen as largely inspired by his writings and teaching.

13.8   Welfare Economics and Imperfect Competition

Among Marshall's pupils, two emerged above the others: John Maynard Keynes, to whom the next chapter is devoted, and Arthur Cecil Pigou (1877–1959). Six years older than Keynes, Pigou was chosen by Marshall in 1908 as his successor to the economics chair in Cambridge. He supported an orthodox version of the Marshallian theory and was known for the stimulus given to welfare economics through recourse to the notion of external economies and diseconomies illustrated by Marshall in the *Principles*.[12]

Let us recall that we have external economies (or diseconomies) whenever an economic activity – be it production or consumption – generates indirect effects on third parties, from which they reap

---

[12] Pigou was also known for his defence, against Keynes's criticisms, of the idea of a tendency to full employment equilibrium under perfect competition, through the *Pigou effect*, later embodied in Modigliani's (1944, 1963) neoclassical synthesis discussed later. This adjustment mechanism is set in motion by the positive impact that the price reduction caused by increasing unemployment via the fall in money wages has on the real value of money balances held by families. Thus, the increase in the real value of the wealth of families brings out an increase in consumption and hence in aggregate demand, leading to a fall in unemployment. Cf. Pigou 1933, 1950.

a benefit (or suffer a loss), without having participated in the decision of the economic agent directly concerned. When the (assumedly rational, actually selfish) economic agent decides how much to produce and consume, s/he considers the effects of her/his action that directly concern her/him but not the effects on others; this implies that too little is consumed and produced of what generates external economies and too much of what generates external diseconomies. Hence the desirability of public intervention in the economic field, aiming at stimulating with subsidies the former kind and deterring with taxes the latter kind of activity. Welfare economics is precisely the field of analysis that studies the nature and measure of such interventions, designed to drive the economy towards optimal situations for the community as a whole. Pigou (1912) used the analytical tool of *consumer's surplus*, designating the gain of total utility obtained by the buyer from exchange thanks to the fact that, while for the last (infinitesimal) dose purchased the price paid corresponds to the additional utility obtained (marginal utility), the utility of the preceding doses was greater than the price paid. The difference between these two magnitudes (measured in terms of money, under the assumption of constant marginal utility of money), added up for all units purchased, gives the consumer's surplus. The choice between different situations is derived by comparing the consumer's surplus realised within the economy in different cases: this is in fact the road taken by welfare economics.[13]

In comparison to the traditional marginalist notion of perfect competition, in which the firm is too small to be able to influence with its behaviour the determination of the price, Marshall appeared to assume a margin of freedom of firms in determining their behaviour. This idea was developed in Joan Robinson's (1933) theory of imperfect competition, according to which the consumers do not consider as identical the products of different firms; as a consequence each firm faces a decreasing, and not a horizontal, demand curve, so that within a certain range it is able to increase the price of its own product without losing all its clientele. In a situation of this kind, the equilibrium of the firm is possible even under conditions of constant or slowly decreasing costs when the quantity produced increases.

---

[13] Because of the assumption of constant marginal utility of money and of the assumption that the demand curve does not shift when the quantity produced or consumed changes, the notion of consumer's surplus is exclusively applicable in the context of partial analysis (in which it had been originally formulated by Marshall). Another dubious aspect of welfare economics concerned the issue of interpersonal comparability of utilities, which was essential for determining the compensation to be offered to render a change acceptable to the agents who bear a loss while others obtain an advantage.

Joan Robinson's book remained within the traditional Marshallian framework, relying on the notions of the firm and the industry. The work by Edward Chamberlin (1899–1967) on monopolistic competition, published in the same year (1933), in stressing the margins of freedom enjoyed by each firm because of the widespread presence of market imperfections, remarked that in this way the very notion of industry loses meaning, since its boundaries had been established artificially on the basis of the assumption of homogeneity of the product of firms included in the same industry. In the place of group of firms (the industry) producing an identical commodity, we now have a continuum of qualitative variations among products of different firms. In this respect, Chamberlin's contribution represented a shift in the direction of the modern axiomatic theory of general economic equilibrium, in which each economic agent represents a case in itself.

14   John Maynard Keynes

14.1   Life and Writings[1]

John Maynard Keynes was born in Cambridge, England, in 1883. His father, John Neville Keynes (1852–1949), was a pupil of Marshall, a scholar of logic and economics and author of *The Scope and Method of Political Economy* (1891) but had preferred an administrative career to prospects of a professorship, reaching the top of Cambridge University administration; his mother, Florence Brown, was one of the first female graduates of that university and the first woman to be elected mayor of Cambridge.

Maynard's curriculum was in keeping with the highest standards of the bourgeoisie: secondary school at Eton, university at King's College, Cambridge. There he studied mathematics and classical humanities; he was also elected into the elitist secret society of the Apostles, devoted to 'the pursuit of truth'. By a few years older than Keynes, another Apostle, the philosopher George Edward Moore (1873–1958), had rejected the utilitarian identification between 'to be good' and 'to do good', proposing an ethics of inner self-searching for truth and personal coherence. In the climate of cultural renewal characterising the Edwardian period, to Keynes and his friends this meant a radical reappraisal of Victorian culture and ethics, manifested also in their personal conduct, marked by extreme intellectualism and the pursuit of aesthetic pleasures, while, departing from Moore, they rejected the idea of general rules of conduct, substituted by confidence in the ability of the 'elect' to evaluate case by case what the right behaviour would be.

This society enlisted among others Lytton Strachey, Bertrand Russell and Alfred Whitehead. In the following decades, some of the Apostles, in

---

[1] The main biographies are those by Skidelsky (1983, 1992, 2000; 2010 for a synthesis) and Moggridge (1992); now outdated is the biography by Harrod (1951). The *Collected Writings of John Maynard Keynes*, in thirty volumes, were published on the initiative of the Royal Economic Society between 1971 and 1989 (Macmillan, London).

particular Strachey, with other leading protagonists of English literature such as Virginia Woolf and Vanessa Bell, formed the Bloomsbury circle (from the name of the residential area of London where the protagonists of the circle lived). Keynes maintained close relations with this group, at least up to his marriage.

After graduating in mathematics, in 1906 Keynes took the civil service entrance examinations but, coming in second, had to content himself with a job at the India Office (while the top of the list traditionally went to the Treasury). There was little work to be done, and Keynes had the time to write a treatise on the Indian monetary system (1913) and a long essay on the theory of probability. Thanks to this essay, after a first unsuccessful attempt, in 1909 he obtained a fellowship at King's College, Cambridge, of which he was an active member up to the end of his life. In 1908 he resigned from the India office to became lecturer in economics at Cambridge; his modest salary was paid by Pigou out of his own pocket, thus continuing a tradition started by Marshall, whom Pigou had succeeded in the economics chair. As from 1911, with Marshall's support, Keynes took over editorship of the *Economic Journal*; two years later he also became secretary of the Royal Economic Society. He was to hold these two appointments for more than three decades, a period in which the *Economic Journal* rose to become the most prestigious economic journal of the time.

During the First World War, Keynes declared himself a conscientious objector, although working at the Treasury on issues connected with financing the war effort. In 1919 he was a member of the British delegation at the peace conference in Versailles but opposed the reparations imposed on Germany, considering them an unsustainable burden on the German economy and society: thus he resigned and, once back in Cambridge, addressed the subject in his highly successful *The Economic Consequences of the Peace* (1919).[2]

By now a widely recognised writer, Keynes contributed on the main issues of economic policy with a series of articles; he also published some books, among which the *Treatise on Probability* in 1921 (a revised version of his 1909 fellowship dissertation, to which Keynes dedicated more years

---

[2] Keynes's criticisms were not based on the internal sustainability of reparations, i.e. on the fiscal burden they implied, but on their external sustainability, i.e. the chances of realising a surplus in other items of the balance of payments sufficiently large to offset unilateral transfers for reparations. Keynes's attention focused on the impossibility of generating a sufficient surplus in the balance of trade and thus sparked off wide-ranging debate centred on export and import elasticities to the exchange rate and to income. As a matter of fact, Germany actually showed a substantial capital inflow, thanks also to loans from the United States.

of work and more care than to any other of his publications) and the *Tract on Monetary Reform* in 1923.[3] To his various academic responsibilities he then added that of chairman of an insurance company and, in partnership, launched into speculation on the exchange markets on his own account and on behalf of relatives and friends (although the results were not always happy). In 1925, having spent a great part of his life cultivating male friendships, Maynard married a famous Russian dancer, Lydia Lopokova.

In 1930 and 1936, respectively, he published the two works – the *Treatise on Money* and the *General Theory on Employment, Interest and Money* – to which he principally owes his fame as a theoretical economist. Other important contributions were the lively and provocative essays collected in the *Essays in Persuasion* (1931) and the well-documented and incisive biographies collected in the *Essays in Biography* (1933). In the same year that saw the *General Theory* published, in Cambridge Keynes inaugurated the Arts Theatre, built almost entirely on his own private funds; his wife Lydia was prima ballerina in the inaugural performance. In the following year he had a heart attack and was obliged to scale down his workload.

In 1940 he was appointed advisor to the Treasury and plunged once again into problems of war finance, negotiating loans from the United States. In July 1944 he played a leading role in the Bretton Woods conference. Suffering a further heart attack, he died on 21 April 1946.

There is an immense literature on Keynes's thought. Many concur that the conditions of high and persistent unemployment in the 1930s favoured the spread of Keynesian ideas. Some commentators stress the distinctly British viewpoint taken by Keynes, who saw his country losing positions to the United States. As for the international monetary system, Keynes outlined schemes that took into account the interests of the less strong currencies, as the British pound was likely to be in a world dominated by the US dollar. Keynes intended to contribute to a reformed system of capitalism, able to guarantee increasing fairness together with freedom and efficiency, in opposition to totalitarian systems, fascism and Nazism in Italy and Germany and Stalinism in the Soviet Union. He

---

[3] In this work Keynes distinguished between internal and external stabilisation of the value of money and declared a preference for stabilisation of internal prices rather than of the external value of the national currency; he was therefore critical of the idea of the pound returning to the gold standard – decided, however, a few months later, on 28 April 1925. Moreover, by the decision of the then Chancellor of the Exchequer Winston Churchill, return to the gold standard took place at the pre-war parity; this implied an overvaluation of the pound and a loss of competitiveness for English manufacturers. Keynes criticised the decision scathingly in a brilliant pamphlet, *The Economic Consequences of Mr. Churchill* (1925).

recognized the end of the ideology of *laissez-faire* in its most extreme form: hence his critique of the then dominant theory, showing how insufficient were the equilibrating mechanisms of the free market and his theorisation of an activist economic policy.

14.2   Probability and Uncertainty

The *Treatise on Probability* must be interpreted in the light of the culture of Cambridge at the time: the tradition of John Stuart Mill's logical inductivism (upheld also by Maynard's father, who in his 1891 book attempted an eclectic synthesis between it and German historicism). In the same years that saw Keynes at work on probability theory, Bertrand Russell (1872–1970) and Alfred Whitehead (1861–1947) went ahead on the project of deducing mathematics from purely logical premises, publishing the *Principia mathematica* (1910–13).

Keynes's ambition was to build a general theory of knowledge and rational behaviour, with respect to which the cases of perfect certainty and total ignorance are the extremes. For this reason Keynes rejected the frequentist interpretation of probability, applicable only to that class of phenomena for which we can assume the possibility of an infinite series of repetitions under unchanged conditions. He proposed, instead, a rationalist approach, centred on the degree of confidence that it is reasonable to have about a certain event, given the state of knowledge. To economists, the importance of this view lies in the fact that it deals with the problem of rational behaviour in a context in which the subject is devoid of certainties. Rational behaviour is then connected to subjective evaluations based on experience and personal intuitions; probability calculus is the technique by which these evaluations are screened.

Keynes distinguished between the proposition that expresses the probability of a given event and the confidence that one can have in such an evaluation, named 'weight of the argument'. When relevant empirical evidence – understood as the set of information directly or indirectly useful for our assessment of the event – increases, then the weight of the argument increases, while the probability attributed to the event may increase or diminish or remain unchanged. Moreover Keynes rejected the idea that it was always possible to attribute a numerical value to the probability of events: in some instances we can do it (for instance, in the game of dice or mortality tables: in general, in all cases of actuarial risk); in other instances we can express non-quantitative opinions on partial ranking of events; in yet other instances the knowledge basis is insufficient for us to formulate even relative judgments of this kind. When confronted with events belonging to the second or third class, it may be rational to rely on conventional forms of behaviour, conforming to or possibly anticipating the behaviour of the majority.[4]

14.3 The *Treatise on Money*

Various writings on the relationship between monetary phenomena and short-period production levels within the framework of the Marshallian approach were already available in the six years during which Keynes wrote his *Treatise on Money* (1930).[5] On many counts, the *Treatise*, too, belonged to this tradition; on other counts, it showed innovative elements constituting a bridge to the radical novelties of the *General Theory*.

Keynes avoided head-on criticism of the theoretical nucleus of the marginalist tradition, consisting of the idea of a long run equilibrium characterised by full employment of resources, labour included, and by the neutrality of money (that is, by the idea that the quantity of money in circulation affects the level of prices but not the 'real' variables of the system, such as production and employment levels). This view of the long period thus remained in the background. As far as the monetary and financial sector was concerned, the *Treatise* took up and developed the Marshallian critique of the quantity theory of money, focussing attention on the demand for liquid stocks rather than the velocity of circulation. The most interesting novelties of the *Treatise* concerned the connections between monetary-financial and real aspects: following the Marshallian method of short causal chains, Keynes set out to locate, link by link, the cause-and-effect connections in the interrelations between changes in prices and in produced quantities within a monetary economy in perennial movement.

In his analysis of the real side of the economy Keynes utilised a two-sector scheme: one sector produces investment goods, the other consumption goods. Keynes showed that it is not possible to attribute analytical rigour to the notion of a general level óf prices: a diffidence towards aggregate notions typical of the Marshallian tradition, which should be borne in mind when confronted with interpretations of

---

[4] Thus, Keynes's approach should be kept distinct from the subjective one developed a few years later by Ramsey (1931), De Finetti (1930, 1931, 1937) and Savage (1954), who saw probabilities in terms of subjective evaluations expressed through bets and thus generally quantifiable. Moreover, the Keynesian notion of uncertainty, which played a crucial role in his theory of money, income and employment, has rather more substance than both the distinction drawn by Knight (1921) between probabilistic risk and uncertainty and Menger's treatment (1871) of the limits of economic agents' knowledge. Cf. Roncaglia, 2009a.

[5] Let us recall here the books by Dennis Robertson (1890–1963), *A Study of Industrial Fluctuations* (1915) and *Banking Policy and the Price Level* (1926); by Ralph Hawtrey (1879–1975), *Currency and Credit* (1919); and by Pigou, *Industrial Fluctuations* (1927).

Keynes's theory based on the opposition between his (assumed) aggregate 'macro' analysis and a disaggregated 'micro' one, which would remain the foundation of economic theory.

The fundamental equations of the *Treatise* express the relations between prices and demand and supply levels in the two sectors, pointing to the elements that may cause prices to diverge from their equilibrium levels. Keynes considered a sequential scheme that connects production levels and realised profits, utilising notions of income, profits and savings at variance with those normally utilised in modern national accounting and with those that he himself was to utilise in the *General Theory*. At the centre of the analysis – as in the *General Theory* – there was the distinction between investments and savings. Insofar as they are an effect of the decisions of two different groups of economic agents (entrepreneurs and families), investments and savings may differ; their difference determines disequilibria between demand and supply in the two sectors, with price changes that generate unforeseen profits or losses,[6] to which entrepreneurs react with changes in production and employment levels. Savings are assumed to be connected to wealth, hence to be relatively stable in the face of short period changes in income. Cyclical dynamics thus depends on the variability of investments. Given the scant influence of investments in inventories, Keynes focussed attention on investments in fixed capital, mainly dependent on long-run interest rates.

The *Treatise* illustrated the different channels of liquidity creation, decisions on holding financial assets and international monetary relations. Keynes stressed the desirability of an international monetary standard and in the place of gold proposed a currency issued by an international central bank constrained by the obligation to keep its value stable in terms of a basket of internationally tradable goods. In this context, characterised by fixed exchange rates, national monetary policies lose any autonomy; thus it becomes necessary to resort to fiscal policies, and in particular to public works, to support employment – another theme taken up in the *General Theory*.

14.4   From the *Treatise* to the *General Theory*

The process of transition from the *Treatise* to the *General Theory* began when the *Treatise* was about to appear. Keynes succeeded in viewing his

---

[6] In the *Treatise* terminology, profits corresponded exclusively to such unforeseen gains or losses and were not included in the definition of income. However, interest on capital advanced, usually included in the category of entrepreneurial income, was considered as part of production costs and included in income.

own ideas with critical detachment as soon as he had put them forward, and even while correcting the proofs of the *Treatise* he arrived at the conclusion that a different analytical structure would have been better fitted to support his main ideas on the governance of the market economy. The key moment in the transition was from analysis of disequilibria to analysis of underemployment equilibrium. While the causal nexuses going from interest rate to investments and from these to income remained, the possibility – indeed, the likelihood – was recognised that the marginal propensity to consume might take on values lower than one, which opened the way to attributing investments with a crucial role in determination of the equilibrium level of income. Moreover, a theory of interest rates was required. As for the theory of value, Keynes settled for the more familiar confines of short-period analysis that, thanks to the diffusion of Marshallism in England, could more readily be grasped by his readers. Among other things, he was driven in this direction by Richard Kahn, his pupil and closest collaborator.

Between the *Treatise* and the *General Theory* there are thus certain crucial differences in analytical structure. The key idea, however, remained unchanged: that in a monetary economy entrepreneurial decisions on production levels do not lead automatically to full utilisation of available resources. In the *Treatise* we find an analysis of disequilibria; the idea of long-run equilibrium remained in the background. In the *General Theory*, the main thesis concerns the persistence of equilibriums characterised by unemployment. Hence the importance of active management of the economy – primarily with the monetary-financial lever in the *Treatise* and with both it and the fiscal lever (public expenditure in particular) in the *General Theory* – in support of demand in the long run and not only as an anti-cyclical device.

The influence of a group of Keynes's students and friends (including Richard Kahn, Joan Robinson, James Meade and Piero Sraffa) called 'the Circus', and in particular of Richard Kahn, appears important for the development of the analytical structure of the *General Theory*. Kahn's contribution consisted not only in the multiplier mechanism (Kahn 1931), although it constituted one of the three analytic pillars of the *General Theory*, together with the notion of effective demand and the theory of the rate of interest based on the speculative demand for money, but also in suggesting reliance on the Marshallian short-period equilibrium. As developed by Kahn 1929, this notion focussed on firms endowed with some margins of strategic autonomy and some decision-making power, not necessarily characterised by decreasing returns but constrained in their growth by difficulty in finding market outlets for their products. Thus we have market imperfections, outside of the Marshallian *vulgata* of perfectly competitive equilibriums that implied a passive role for entrepreneurs, while in Keynes's framework they had an active role with respect to decisions both on production levels and on investments in new productive capacity.

Within the Circus a variety of positions were represented. At one extreme we find (with Meade and Austin Robinson) a more traditional view, closer to the neoclassical tradition. At the other extreme we have, with Sraffa, frontal opposition to it. At the centre, with Kahn and Joan Robinson, we have views more directly influenced by Marshall's teachings, which eventually prevailed and indeed determined the analytical framework adopted by Keynes. The compromise suggested by Kahn (but also by Keynes's Marshallian background), despite its immediate success, subsequently showed significant limitations, in comparison both to the neoclassical synthesis foreshadowed by Meade and Austin Robinson and to a reinterpretation of Keynes's contributions internal to the classical framework revived by Sraffa.

14.5   The *General Theory*

The *General Theory of Employment, Interest and Money* appeared in February 1936. It immediately found a wide readership, although not repeating the success of *The Economic Consequences of the Peace*. However, it did have a more solid influence, concentrated in the field of professional economists: many young scholars soon adopted it as a basic reference point in their own research work and teaching.

The *General Theory* is not an easy book, and many 'Keynesian' economists did not read it. Only this fact could have rendered possible philologically untenable interpretations, like the idea that Keynesian theory was based on the downward rigidity of wages and prices (when chapter 19 of the book explicitly rejected this idea).[7]

First of all, let us recall Keynes's aims and his views on the economy. Defence of a liberal political system based, among other things, on freedom of individual initiative in the economic arena required, according to him, that the limits of the pure *laissez-faire* system be recognised; hence the need for active intervention of the state in the economy, in the interests not only of fairness but also of overall efficiency. Economic agents take their decisions under conditions of uncertainty, as defined in the *Treatise on Probability*. At the methodological level, this led to

---

[7] The assumption of downward rigidity of wages and prices may be utilised to get 'Keynesian' results in a different analytical framework, as was the case with the so-called neoclassical synthesis, but not to interpret 'what Keynes really meant'.

preference for open models, specifically designed for the problem under consideration, to be built with caution, and pondering the conditions under which individual causal relations hold. Various other aspects of Keynes's theory also derived from uncertainty, such as the role of financial markets, which not only acted as intermediary between agents with active and passive financial positions but also, and above all, provided flexibility for inter-temporal choices and allowed entrepreneurs to take decisions on production levels and investments concerning the future. It is in this context that we find the distinction between short- and long-run expectations, the former concerning choices on current production, such that they can be promptly adjusted to results, the latter concerning decisions on investment in fixed capital; for these the impact of uncertainty is indeed strong.

The analytical structure of the *General Theory* rested on three pillars: the notion of effective demand, the multiplier mechanism and the theory of interest. All these are well-known aspects, but they occasionally suffer some distortion – the first and third in particular – when illustrated in university textbooks, so let us take a brief look at them here.

Chapter 3 of the *General Theory* is devoted to the *principle of effective demand*. The *point of effective demand* is defined as the point of encounter of two curves: an aggregate supply function and an aggregate demand function, conceptually different from traditional supply and demand curves, since they relate the entrepreneurs' evaluations regarding costs on the one hand and receipts on the other to the number of employed workers. More precisely, the aggregate supply function Z indicates the minimum expected proceeds necessary to persuade entrepreneurs to employ N workers, while the aggregate demand function D indicates how much entrepreneurs expect to earn by selling on the market the product they hope to obtain through the employment of N workers. Both curves thus express the point of view – the evaluations – of the same category of economic agents, the entrepreneurs, not of two distinct and opposed groups of buyers and sellers (consumers and producers).

Both expected costs and expected proceeds increase with the number of employed workers. Thus both functions are increasing ones. However, Z increases ever more rapidly (its second derivative is positive), while D increases ever more slowly (its second derivative is negative). D is in fact made up of two components, consumption and investment; according to Keynes, because of a psychological law consumption increases less than income, and hence than employment, while investments depend on the entrepreneurs' long-run expectations, so that they may be considered as given in the context of determination of the point of effective demand.

As far as Z is concerned, in the Marshallian context of Keynes's theory it was natural to assume that when the number of employed workers increased (while, in the short-period context, it was assumed that the productive equipment remained unchanged), the marginal cost turned out to be increasing.[8]

The *point of effective demand* is the one at which $D = Z$. It thus tells us the expected level of employment, and hence of production, given the entrepreneurs' short-run expectations regarding costs and proceeds.[9]

Decisions concerning consumption and investment are taken by different categories of economic agents (respectively, families and firms) and thus follow two completely different logics. Consumption (and savings, defined as their complement to income) essentially depend on income. Investments depend on the entrepreneurs' decisions (hence on their expectations) and are independent from income. As a consequence, it is investment decisions that determine the equilibrium level of income, while savings adapt. More precisely, equilibrium income has to be such as to generate an amount of savings corresponding (in the simplified system without taxes and public expenditure and with no relations with foreign countries) to the amount of investments generated by entrepreneurs' decisions. It thus depends both on the level of investments I and on the propensity to save s ($s = S/Y$, where S are savings and Y is income); more precisely, on the equilibrium condition $I = S$ (equality between inflows and outflows in the circular income flow) and on the definition of the propensity to save we get $Y = I/s$: the multiplier, namely that multiplicative coefficient which, when applied to the level of investment, gives equilibrium income, is equal to the inverse of the propensity to save. When identifying the multiplier as the second of the three pillars of the *General Theory*, we are referring not simply to this equation but to the active role attributed to investments and the passive role attributed to consumption and savings in determination of income.

[8] This implied an inverse relation between real wage and employment analogous to the one postulated by Marshall and all versions of marginalist theory in support of the thesis of an automatic tendency to full employment. In Keynes's theory, which rejected this adjustment mechanism, the inverse relation was not essential; in fact, Keynes was ready to abandon it when confronted with Dunlop's 1938 and Tarshis's 1939 empirical criticisms and a sizeable mass of empirical evidence on the pro-cyclical nature of real wage movements. Indeed, as is obvious, abandonment of that assumption reinforces the Keynesian critique of the thesis of an automatic tendency towards full employment equilibrium.

[9] Therefore, it should not be interpreted as a point of equilibrium between two opposite forces of demand and supply, let alone as a stable equilibrium, as macroeconomics manuals have long done. Keynes's viewpoint and the textbook one only coincide under the assumption that the entrepreneurs' short-period expectations are always fulfilled, so that expectations and uncertainty exit the scene, while Keynes's thesis that supply (production) adapts to demand remains.

For the theory of investment, as for that of effective demand, Keynes adopted the entrepreneur's point of view. The latter decides whether to invest by evaluating expected returns on investment and comparing them with the monetary rate of interest indicating return on financial investments, which constitute an alternative employment of available funds. As pointed out previously, expectations relevant to investment decisions concern the 'long period', since they cover the whole foreseen life of the productive equipment acquisition of which is under consideration, and decisions taken on their basis may be revised within such a time interval only at high costs, while the expectations relevant for decisions on current production levels and employment concern the 'short period', open to ready revision with relatively low if not zero costs. Long-period expectations are not stable; on the contrary, precisely because they concern so long an interval of time as to elude sufficiently precise and reliable evaluation, they are far less stable than short-period expectations.

The third pillar of Keynes's *General Theory* was represented by the theory of monetary and financial markets, with the rate of interest conceived as premium for foregoing liquidity. This theory has two main aspects, often misinterpreted in macroeconomic textbooks. Firstly, behind the mass of large and small savers deciding what form to keep their financial assets in loom the financial institutions, the true protagonists of the decision-making process described by Keynes. Secondly, the decision-making process itself does not concern flows, on which traditional theory focussed, but the allocation of stocks; thus the speculative demand for money dominates the transaction demand for money. On well-developed financial markets transaction costs are very low, and it is possible to revise daily, or even from one hour to the next, decisions on the allocation of financial holdings between the various possible assets.

Simplifying the issue, Keynes considered two kinds of assets: money, extremely liquid since commonly accepted for all kinds of transactions but not yielding income, and bonds yielding a predetermined yearly coupon. As we know, the market price of pre-existing bonds increases when the rate of interest decreases, and vice versa. As a consequence, those who expect a fall in interest rates by the same token also expect an increase in bond prices and will be buyers on the bond market, while those expecting an increase in the rate of interest operate in the opposite direction, offering bonds in exchange for money. In the presence of different opinions on the prospects facing the monetary and financial markets, the rate of interest is set at each instant at that level which corresponds to equilibrium between the two opposite ranks, the 'bulls' and the 'bears'.

Thus, everything depends on the expectations of the financial operators. If for a moment we assume that these remain fixed, it is clear that when the rate of interest decreases, the number of operators who expect a subsequent increase (and thus offer bonds in exchange for money) rises: the demand for money thus turns out to be an inverse function of the interest rate. However, this relationship has very thin foundations, since expectations regarding financial events are extremely volatile. It is quite possible, for instance, for a reduction in the interest rate to induce many operators to revise their expectations and foresee further interest rate reductions, preferring bonds to money even more than before: a direct, rather than inverse, relationship would then hold between changes in the rate of interest and changes in the demand for money.

Within Keynes's analytical framework, the theory of speculative demand for money distanced interest rate determination from the traditional mechanism of comparison between savings and investments, respectively understood as supply of and demand for loanable funds. According to Keynes, decisions to save are logically distinct from those concerning the kind of financial asset (money or bonds) in which to invest the savings. Contrary to the interpretation advanced by many commentators, the main point was not that the amount of savings depended more on income than on the rate of interest – a point also acknowledged by a theoretician like Pigou, chosen by Keynes as paradigm of the traditional theory he was attacking. The point was the separation between the two kinds of decisions concerning, respectively, the amount of savings and the financial asset to invest the savings in; it was this latter decision that concurred together with the monetary policy followed by monetary authorities in determining the current level of the interest rate.

Also Hicks' idea, embodied in his famous IS-LL model (Hicks 1937), to set transaction demand and the speculative demand for money side by side, as if they were on the same plane, lost sight of the difference in nature between the two kinds of decisions. Speculative choices concern the allocation of the stocks of savings cumulated over time and thus dominate over the transaction demand for money, namely the liquidity requirements to finance the flow of current exchanges. This is all the more evident when the stocks of savings to be allocated between bonds and money are confronted not with yearly income and exchanges but, as is in the nature of continually revised financial choices, with daily flows. We thus have a hierarchy of influences: financial expectations dominate the allocation of the stock of savings, and hence the determination of interest rates, relegating to a secondary level all other factors, including the transaction demand for money. It is, then, the interest rates thus brought about, together with long-run expectations, that determine the level of investments, while the latter in turn, through the multiplier mechanism, determines income and employment.

This scheme of hierarchical relations was in sharp contrast to general economic equilibrium schemes, in which each variable depends on all other variables and on all the parameters of the system. It is precisely in this aspect that Keynes's theory, following through with the short causal chains methodology, fully revealed its Marshallian foundations, emphasised by the pragmatism characterising all Keynes's work. And, indeed, it is this aspect that has been submerged in the interpretations of Keynes's thought dominating successive generations of macroeconomics textbooks.

14.6 The Asymmetries of Economic Policy in an Open Economy and International Institutions

The *General Theory* analysed the case of a closed economic system – a world-economy, useful both as a theoretical simplification and to establish some principles holding for the industrialised countries as a whole.[10] However, at the level of economic policy, results arrived at for a closed economy cannot automatically be extended to an open economy, where for instance a reduction in real wages can have a positive effect on employment, by enhancing the competitiveness of national over foreign products. In this way the inverse relationship between wages and employment could be re-established; a country can favour its own development by subtracting market outlets from other countries with the so-called beggar-thy-neighbour policies – a zero-sum game, with advantages for one country corresponding to losses for some other country, which was played by a number of countries in the years of the Great Crisis and which Germany now wants to impose on the whole of the euro area.

As the Second World War drew to a close, in July 1944 Keynes took part in the conference held in Bretton Woods: an attempt to outline rules for the international economic game favouring cooperation among countries, which, however, saw his ideas watered down by American conservatism. His central idea was that the unemployment problem is recurrently raised by technical progress, making it possible to obtain the

---

[10] While still assuming a closed system, Keynes developed the notion of *inflationary gap*, proposed in *How to Pay for the War* (1940) in order to account for the inflationary pressures arising when aggregate demand overshoots aggregate supply, as happens in a country in a period of war with conspicuous military expenditures.

same quantity of product with an ever-decreasing number of workers. Waxing acute, the problem can become socially explosive in the absence of adequate policies to manage the economy. Moreover, on the strength of the thought experiment of the closed economy adopted in the *General Theory* Keynes was able to maintain that beggar-thy-neighbour policies involve a simple redistribution of the costs of a world crisis without offering any contribution to its solution.

According to Keynes, the international economic system should be organised not only in such a way as to facilitate the development of commerce (hence in a context of free trade, currency convertibility and stable exchange rates) but also to support world production levels. To this end, the rules of the international game should avoid any asymmetry in stimulating corrective action on the part of countries with a positive balance of trade or with a negative one. The latter are driven by dwindling currency reserves to adopt deflationary measures in order to reduce imports and favour exports or restrictive monetary policies in order to stimulate capital imports but with negative effects on growth. Conversely, the countries with an active balance of trade could look on calmly as currency reserves accumulated or might limit themselves to low interest rate policies to favour capital outflows. Keynes thought that a balanced international monetary system should govern international liquidity (through the issue, on the part of a super-national organisation, of an international currency, the Bancor) by lightening the pressure for adoption of deflationary policies on countries with a negative balance of trade; conversely, countries with an active balance of trade should be stimulated by the rules of the international game (for instance, regulations on foreign currency reserves) to adopt reflationary policies.

14.7   Michal Kalecki

Michal Kalecki (1899–1970) may be considered a precursor of Keynes's ideas, with some articles published in Polish immediately before publication of the *General Theory*, influenced by the growth schemes of Marx's *Capital*, taken up by Tugan-Baranowskji (1905) and in Rosa Luxemburg's (1913) under-consumption theories, thus external to the traditional marginalist analysis based on the notion of equilibrium between supply and demand and the thesis of an automatic tendency towards full employment. The set of relations between income, consumption, savings and investments that Kalecki proposed is similar to Keynes's, both in considering full employment as a borderline case rather than the general one and in attributing the driving role to autonomous expenditure and in particular to investment decisions. The differences were, however, significant. Uncertainty and expectations, crucial in Keynes, were virtually absent in Kalecki's work, where a fully worked-out theory of financial markets was also lacking.[11] Conversely Kalecki, despite showing signs – especially in his early writings – of a Marshallian influence, embodied in his analysis mechanisms such as the full cost principle,[12] which allow for links with modern theories of non-competitive markets. Moreover, Kalecki extended his formal structure to deal with problems of trade cycle and development and connected such theories with analysis of income distribution among the social classes.[13]

Many of Kalecki's main contributions concerned the planned and mixed economy.[14] In Warsaw a moving spirit of the liveliest economics research and teaching centre of Eastern European countries, Kalecki spent the last years of his life marginalized by the political authorities of his country. Comparison with Keynes shows just how much importance nationality, conditions of birth and political vicissitudes may have in determining the impact of an economist's ideas and analysis.

14.8 The New Cambridge School

Naturally enough, the impact of Keynes's *General Theory* was particularly strong in Cambridge. The role of Keynes's direct pupils, like Kahn and

---

[11] Kalecki proposed a *principle of increasing risk* to account for the limits to the possibilities of financing investments on the part of each individual firm. This theme was taken up and developed by Kalecki's collaborator, the Austrian Josef Steindl (1912–1993), in his theory of the firm: cf. Steindl 1945 and the writings collected in Steindl 1990, pp. 1–73. Steindl also developed Kaleckian themes in his best-known work, *Maturity and Stagnation in American Capitalism* (1952; II ed. 1976), where he maintained the thesis of a tendency to stagnation in capitalistic economies due to the gradual emergence of oligopolistic market forms. A similar thesis was also maintained by the American Alvin Hansen (1887–1975; cf. Hansen 1938), who also played an important role in circulation of Keynesian ideas in the United States, and subsequently by Sylos Labini (1956), who explained how transmission of the effects of technical progress generates development in a competitive system but not in a system of oligopolies.

[12] Cf. for instance Kalecki 1943. The full cost principle is a pricing criterion frequently adopted by firms enjoying some market power, hence especially in oligopolistic sectors, and consists in setting product prices by adding to variable costs a proportional margin destined to cover fixed costs and general expenses and to guarantee the margin of profit usual within the sector. Studied by Philip Andrews (1914–1971; see the writings collected in Andrews 1993), the full cost principle was then integrated within oligopoly theory by Sylos Labini 1956.

[13] Particularly interesting is his theory of the political cycle (Kalecki 1971, pp. 138–45).

[14] A selection of Kalecki's major writings, edited by the author himself but published posthumously, is divided between two slim volumes, one on capitalistic economies (Kalecki 1971, which includes the three articles of 1933, 1934 and 1935 originally published in Polish which anticipated important aspects of Keynesian theory) and one on socialist and mixed economies (Kalecki 1972).

Joan Robinson, was reinforced by others, such as Nicholas Kaldor who arrived from the London School of Economics where, in an early phase, he had followed Hayek's star. The odd one out there was Piero Sraffa who, though closer to Keynes than many commentators recognise, followed an autonomous research path. All these protagonists and many others, from the British Marxist Maurice Dobb (1900–1976) to the American Richard Goodwin (1913–1996),[15] constituted the new Cambridge school (thus dubbed to distinguish it from the old Cambridge school, of Marshall and his pupils), a particularly lively intellectual centre, particularly in the 1950s and 1960s.

Keynes's closest collaborator, his pupil and subsequently literary executor, was Richard Kahn (1905–1989). A student and then teacher in Cambridge, in the early 1930s Kahn was the moving spirit of the Circus that, as we saw previously, stimulated Keynes's transition from the *Treatise on Money* to the *General Theory*. He also contributed a crucial element to Keynes's analytical apparatus with his theory of the multiplier (Kahn 1931), which connected changes in employment to changes in autonomous expenditure (investments, public expenditure, exports): a relationship that presupposed the existence of unemployed workers. This was, for all the economists of those times, a fact of life that contradicted a central tenet of the dominant theory, namely the automatic tendency towards full employment. Kahn had begun a gradual departure from this theory through his research on 'the economics of the short period' (the title of his 1929 fellowship dissertation, which was to remain unpublished for more than fifty years, where he had taken up the theme of market imperfections). Kahn also made important contributions on monetary theory, in part through his influence on the famous *Radcliffe Report* (1959), which developed a Keynesian view of the working of financial markets and the role of monetary policy tools.[16]

Joan Violet Maurice Robinson (1903–1983; her husband was Austin Robinson, 1897–1993, a Keynesian as well and economics professor in Cambridge but more interested in applied policy issues) was the standard-bearer of Keynesianism: a lively and prolific writer,

---

[15] Dobb, a Marxist, was the author of important writings on theory, economic history and history of economic thought, including a volume on the Soviet Union (1928 and subsequent editions); a volume of *Studies in the Development of Capitalism* (1946) in which, among other things, the issue of the transition from feudalism to capitalism was discussed; and a volume of history of economic thought (Dobb 1973). By Goodwin we may recall the works on the multiplier and the cycle; in particular, Goodwin (1967) presented a model of economic cycle based on the prey-predator evolutionary scheme originally studied by the mathematician Vito Volterra (1860–1940).

[16] His main contributions are collected in Kahn 1972.

passionate and brilliant orator and vigorous polemist, she left her mark in universities all over the world. Among her contributions, together with various writings of divulgation of Keynesian theory, we may recall *The Economics of Imperfect Competition* (1933) and the attempt to extend Keynes's analysis to the long period, with *The Accumulation of Capital* (1956), where she offered a taxonomy of growth models and an analysis of the interrelation between effective demand and productive capacity, already taken up as a central element in Harrod's famous model (1939).

Nicholas Kaldor (1908–1986), born in Budapest and subsequently a British citizen, was an expert on the UN Commission for Europe in the immediate post-war period, consultant to many developing countries and to the British Labour government. He contributed to the theoretical *corpus* of the Cambridge school a theory of income distribution, in which distribution between wages and profits depended on the capitalists' propensity to save and the growth rate of the economy.[17] This theory was then flanked with theories of accumulation based on Keynesian and classical (Ricardian) ideas in successive versions of a growth model (Kaldor 1957, 1961) where he set out to represent the main 'stylised facts' of developed capitalistic economies.

---

[17] Kaldor 1956; this theory was taken up and developed by Pasinetti 1962; Kaldor (1966) then connected this theory to the financial choices of the firm and hence to the new stream of researches on managerial capitalism.

15   Joseph Schumpeter

15.1   Life and Writings

Joseph Alois Schumpeter (1883–1950) is best known for his idea that the process of economic development is generated by a succession of innovations achieved by entrepreneurs with the purchasing power supplied to them by bankers. The attractiveness of this idea stems, at least in part, from its twofold political implications: it brings to the fore entrepreneurs and bankers, the leading actors of the development process; it opposes Keynesian-type policy activism and considers crises a necessary evil, needed to stimulate the very vitality of capitalism. Moreover, the view of a dynamic process endogenous to the economy and society and of the decay of capitalism seems to align Schumpeter with Marx against the traditional theorising of economic equilibrium.

Schumpeter was born in Moravia (then part of the Austro-Hungarian empire) in 1883. His father, a small entrepreneur in the textile sector, died when Joseph was only four years old. His mother found herself a widow when twenty-six years old; she married again in 1893 to a high-ranking officer in the Austrian army, already retired and much older than her, who sent the young Joseph to study in the Theresianum in Vienna, the school of the young aristocrats. There he received a humanistic education. He then attended the Faculty of Jurisprudence at Vienna University. Böhm-Bawerk was one of his professors; at his seminars Schumpeter came into heated debate with Otto Bauer and Rudolf Hilferding, two future leaders of Austrian socialism, and one of the champions of liberalism, Ludwig von Mises.

After a brief stay in England, in 1907 Schumpeter moved to Cairo, earning his living as a lawyer and writing the first of his books, *The Essence and the Principles of Theoretical Economy*, published (in German) in 1908. In 1909 he went back to Austria, to be appointed to a professorship at Czernowitz and then at Graz universities, where he remained up to 1921. In the years before the war he published (in German) *The Theory of*

Economic Development in 1912, the *Epochs in the History of Doctrines and Methods* in 1914; in 1913–14 he gave lecture courses and seminars at Columbia University at New York.

Decidedly a non-conformist, during the war Schumpeter displayed pacifist and pro-Western views; in 1918–19, notwithstanding his own conservative views, he took part in a committee chaired by Kautsky and instituted by the Austrian socialist government to organise the nationalisation of private firms. In 1919 he became Minister of Finance in the Austrian government led by Renner, a socialist, and supported by an alliance between socialists and conservatives, charged with the impossible task of solving the problem of the public debt inherited from the war (according to Shumpeter's ideas, through an extraordinary wealth tax, incentives to the influx of foreign capitals and inflation with the aim of reducing the real value of the public debt). His experience as minister lasted only a few months, due also to his opposition to the nationalisation programme adopted by the government; the socialists accused him of having favoured acquisition of the biggest Austrian iron firm, the Alpine Montan-Gesellschaft, by foreign (Italian) interests and secured his resignation.

Schumpeter went back to the university, but by 1921 he had already resigned in order to become chairman of a small private bank, the Biedermann Bank, and headed it until bankruptcy struck in 1924. Many of its clients were hit by heavy losses; Schumpeter lost all his estate and something more, over the following years part of his income being used to pay back debts incurred in the bankruptcy.

Thus Schumpeter went back to university teaching, first at Bonn and then at Harvard. In the Bonn years he worked on a lengthy treatise on money; however, it remained incomplete and was published posthumously only in 1970. Schumpeter put it aside when, in 1930, Keynes's *Treatise on Money* appeared – a contribution setting out a line of thinking completely different from his own. Most likely, Schumpeter believed that without further intensive research his work would pale in comparison with Keynes's. After his move to the United States, the monumental work on *Business Cycles* appeared in 1939, followed by the provocative and successful *Capitalism, Socialism, and Democracy* in 1942, while at his death the great *History of Economic Analysis* was still incomplete.

Along with his impressive research activity, Schumpeter was quite influential as a teacher. Among his students we find many of the greatest economists of the twentieth century, from Leontiev to Samuelson, from Sweezy and Goodwin to Minsky, from Tsuru to Sylos Labini. He died in 1950.

15.2   Method

In his 1908 volume Schumpeter was already taking a position that he would maintain in his mature works, a methodological liberalism: in Schumpeter's own words (1908, p. 156, italics added), it is 'advantageous not to set the methodological assumptions once and for all our purposes, but to adapt them to each objective and, once such specific assumptions appear adequate to the purpose, *to be as liberal as possible*'.

Schumpeter (1908, p. 3) started from the statement that 'all sciences are nothing but . . . forms of representation' of reality, and criticised the idea that 'the formulation of exact 'laws' is possible' (ibid., p. 12). This methodological position was not very different from Smith's and Keynes's, which conceived of theories as tools for orientation within reality, and radically different from the position holding that mathematical laws expressed the intrinsic essence of things and the theoretician's task was to 'uncover' such laws from the accidental phenomena enshrouding them: a view still widespread at the time.

It was from the viewpoint of his methodological liberalism that Schumpeter criticised as sterile the debate on method still under way in those years between those who (like Menger) considered economics an abstract science and those who (like Schmoller, the leader of the historical school) saw it as closer to the historical-social sciences: 'the historical school and the abstract one are not in contrast and . . . the only difference between them is their interest in different issues' (ibid., p. 22) or, perhaps better, in different aspects of the same reality – an extremely complex reality that cannot be reduced exclusively to one problem or another. Schumpeter re-proposed this methodological position in various writings, stressing again and again that economic life has so many different aspects that it may usefully be analysed from a multiplicity of viewpoints.

A corollary of Schumpeter's methodological liberalism was his cautious attitude towards methodological individualism, in the sense of the method of analysis that starts from the individual – from his or her preferences and endowments – and that was at the root of neo-classical economic theory. Schumpeter (1908, p. 83) stressed the distinction between individualism in science and political individualism (liberalism), stating that 'there is no particularly close relationship between individualistic economic science and political individualism' and that 'from theory in itself we can draw arguments neither in favour nor against political individualism'. In this he followed the separation, strongly advocated by Weber as well, between theoretical propositions that fall within the field of science and value judgements that fall within the field of politics.[1]

15.3   From Statics to Dynamics: The Cycle

In the 1908 book, Schumpeter followed the marginalist tradition, according to which the value of economic goods is expressed by demand for them relative to their scarcity. However, he rejected Jevons's utilitarianism, based on the identification of value with the (subjective) measure of the ability of goods to satisfy such needs. In fact, 'psychological deduction is simply a tautology. If we say that somebody is prepared to pay something more than somebody else because he values it more, with this we do not give an explanation, since it is precisely from his evaluation that we infer the fact that he offers to pay a higher price' (ibid., p. 64). As a consequence, the so-called principle of decreasing marginal utility according to Schumpeter 'in economics ... is not a law ... but a basic assumption for the generalisation of given scientific facts. As such this assumption is in principle arbitrary' (ibid., p. 71). Similarly, 'the *homo oeconomicus* – the hedonistic computer – ... is a construction the hypothetical character of which is now known' (ibid., pp. 80–81).

Schumpeter considered the theory of prices to be 'the core of pure economics' (ibid., p. 106). His illustration of this theory was not without defects and did not offer novel analytical contributions. What is interesting, rather, is the interpretation he gave of this theory. In his opinion, the point of arrival of the theory of economic equilibrium is what he called 'the method of variations'. In fact, 'we can never explain an *actual* state of equilibrium of the economy' (ibid., p. 361) but only what consequences change in one of the data has on equilibrium: 'This is the only reason for which such laws have been constructed' (ibid., p. 360). Such a method – what is nowadays called comparative statics analysis – may be used only in a very limited ambit, with respect to infinitesimal changes: 'rigorously speaking, our system excludes any change whatsoever' (ibid., p. 375). However, the economic equilibrium approach is useful because with it light can be shed on a particular aspect of economic realities subject to

---

[1] This is also the background on the distinction between economic liberalism and political liberalism. The former is identified with 'the theory that the best way of promoting economic development and general welfare is to remove fetters from the private-enterprise economy and to leave it alone', while political liberalism is identified with 'sponsorship of parliamentary government, freedom to vote and extension of the right to vote, freedom of the press, divorce of secular from spiritual government, trial by jury, and so on' (Schumpeter 1954, p. 394).

continuous change: habit, repetitiveness, the myriad of 'mechanical' actions of everyday life.

The main point of differentiation between Schumpeter and traditional marginalist theory concerned the theory of interest. Schumpeter criticised the theory developed by his professor Böhm-Bawerk, who 'defines interest as the premium of present goods over future goods' (ibid., p. 329), and opposed this theory with a different, 'dynamic' approach: 'The essential phenomenon is the interest deriving from credit which serves for the creation of new industries, new forms of organisation, new techniques, new consumption goods' (ibid., p. 355). In the static system, according to Schumpeter, the money market plays only a secondary, passive role, while it becomes an active player only within the process of economic development.

This thesis was developed in the *Theory of Economic Development*. The first edition of this famous work – a massive volume in German, prolix and rich in disquisitions on historiography and methodology – was published in 1912, with a second edition in 1926; its popularity is mainly due to the much shortened English edition, published in 1934.

The dichotomy between statics and dynamics was substituted in this work with a dichotomy between theory of the circular flow and theory of development. The circular flow corresponds to the stationary state, in which the economy reproduces itself, period after period, without structural change; Schumpeter also admitted in this context a purely quantitative growth, from which changes in production technologies and consumers' tastes were excluded by definition.

Development, by contrast, is characterised by change. The role of active agent in the process of change is attributed to the producer, while consumers follow passively and 'are educated by him if necessary' (Schumpeter 1912, p. 65). Having recalled that 'to produce means to combine materials and forces within our reach' (ibid.), Schumpeter noted that 'development in our sense is then defined by the carrying out of new combinations' (ibid., p. 66), namely 'the introduction of a new good', 'the introduction of a new method of production', 'the opening of a new market', 'the conquest of a new source of supply of raw materials or half-manufactured goods' and 'the carrying out of the new organisation of any industry, like the creation of a monopoly position . . . or the breaking up of a monopoly position' (ibid.).

The introduction of new productive combinations is the work of the *entrepreneurs*, who are such only insofar as they make innovative choices. That of the entrepreneur is a key category: as the originator of change, the entrepreneur generates capitalistic development (while within the classical economists' approach it is the process of development that generates the drive to change); his motivation is not that of the *homo oeconomicus* but rather 'the dream and the will to found a private kingdom . . . the will to conquer . . . the joy of creating, of getting things done, or simply of exercising one's energy and ingenuity' (ibid., p. 93).

Alongside the entrepreneur in the process of development Schumpeter extolled the role of the banker, considered equally necessary. This thesis stemmed from two crucial assumptions in the Schumpeterian model. In conformity to traditional marginalist theory, to which Schumpeter adhered, in equilibrium there are no unused resources on which entrepreneur-innovators can rely. Thus entrepreneurs can accomplish their innovations only if they have at their disposal some *ad hoc* purchasing power with which they are able to draw the resources required to start new productive processes from 'old' firms (that is, from the set of traditional productive activities) and from consumers. Such purchasing power is created *ex novo* by the banks: thus, the innovative and executive capacity of entrepreneurs needs to be accompanied by the far-sightedness and ability of the bankers to evaluate aright the potentialities of new initiatives. Bankers too, like entrepreneurs, have to accept the challenge of uncertainty (and the consequent risks of losses and failures) that accompanies anything that is new.

Entrepreneurs set on innovation apply to bankers who, if they decide to finance the innovation, agree to the loan and thus create the means of payment with which entrepreneurs can enter the markets for productive resources. By assumption, in equilibrium all available productive resources are already utilised; as a consequence, the additional demand cannot be satisfied by an increase in supply. Thus, there is an increase in prices, which automatically reduces the purchasing power of consumers and traditional firms. The inflationary process allows new firms, financed by banks with newly created means of payment, to draw productive resources from their traditional uses. This is a theory of *forced saving*: an element common to various theories developed within the Austrian school and connected to the idea that the economy tends to full employment. (Monetarist theories maintaining that private investments are crowded out by public expenditure, developed in the 1950s and 1960s as a reaction to Keynesian policies, are but variants of the theory of forced saving.)

The trade cycle is linked to the process of development. The phases of expansion take place when the innovation is imitated by a swarm of new firms attracted by the temporary profits realised by the entrepreneur-innovator. The phases of recession arrive when repayment of the loans provokes credit deflation; furthermore, if firms are able to pay back the banks, it is thanks to sale on the market of products obtained with new technologies, but this exerts a downward pressure on the demand for, and prices of, the old products, which leads to bankruptcy for firms that have remained anchored to old production technologies, and especially those most directly hit by competition from the new products; thus, those who fail to keep pace by adapting to the innovations are expelled from the market.

If innovations were uniformly distributed over time, taking place now in one sector of the economy, now in another, the phases of expansion and recession would concern different sectors in different periods of time, while on average development would follow a regular path for the economy as a whole. However, according to Schumpeter the development process is discontinuous. In fact, innovation implies a break in the traditional way of proceeding: in other words, the barriers represented by the force of tradition must be overcome in order to implement the innovative change, and such barriers are easier to overcome the more widespread the change is within the economy. Thus innovations do not constitute a regular flow over time but appear as grouped in swarms. Schumpeter's trade cycle theory, like Marx's, is thus characterised by the endogenous nature – that is, internal to the theory – of the relationship between cycle and development. Within both theories, the situation at the end of a cycle must be different from the situation at the beginning because of technological change, which plays an essential part in the cyclical movement of the economy.

The basic model of development theory presented in the 1912 book did not change in substance in the ponderous work on *Business Cycles* (1939) but was further developed with analysis of market forms other than perfect competition, the simultaneous presence of short, long and very long cycles, the fifty-year cycle having to do with *epoch-making innovations* that affect the whole of the productive system such as railways, with the transport revolution, electricity, or information technology in our own times.

15.4   The Breakdown of Capitalism

In *Capitalism, Socialism and Democracy* (1942) Schumpeter maintained that capitalism cannot survive and is destined to be supplanted by socialism. However, unlike Marx, Schumpeter saw this not as a triumphal march of human progress but rather as an advance on the road to decadence.[2]

---

[2] Schumpeter (1946, pp. 103–8) summarised the theses of his 1942 book and proposed that 'free men' react to the tendencies therein illustrated, which risk leading to the 'decomposition' of society and the victory of 'centralised and authoritarian statism',

Schumpeter's thesis had already taken shape before the Great Crisis:[3] it had nothing to do with the stagnation theories based on the dissolution of investment opportunities, which were taken up and developed by Hansen (1938) after Keynes, but rather looked back to Weber's (1904–5) view of capitalism as an all-embracing rationalisation process affecting both productive activity and culture. According to Schumpeter, there is a contradiction inherent to capitalistic development: economic stability requires incessant development, but this creates growing difficulties for political stability. Beyond a certain point such difficulties make the breakdown of capitalism inevitable.

The core of Schumpeter's argument is the connection between economic development and destruction of the politico-social foundations of capitalism. The connection has two aspects: on the positive side, growth of an opposition to capitalism associated mainly with the spread of rationalistic ways of thinking and the swelling ranks of intellectuals; on the negative side, the weakening of capitalism's 'protective strata', consisting mainly of the ranks of small and average entrepreneurs, faced with the growth of the big bureaucratised firms. The former aspect concerns what the Marxist tradition considers the super-structure of capitalistic societies, the latter the structure; the two aspects interact in the process of social transformation.[4]

Bureaucratisation of the economy hinders both the innovative action of entrepreneurs and the 'creative destruction', i.e. bankruptcy of slow-moving firms, which frees resources for the innovating firms and functions as continuous natural selection of the ranks of firm owners and managers. Bureaucratisation is the result of changes in dominant market forms through a process of industrial concentration that implies, among other things, transformation of the activity of technological innovation into routine. (Much the same had already been argued by Karl Renner and Rudolf Hilferding, leading representatives of Austrian socialism and companions of Schumpeter's at Vienna University.)

with a 'moral reform' drawing on the corporative principles of the encyclical *Quadragesimo Anno* of Pope Pius XI.

[3] The central thesis of the book had already been foreshadowed by Schumpeter in 1928 (pp. 385–6): 'Capitalism, whilst economically stable, and ever gaining in stability, creates, by rationalising the human mind, a mentality and a style of life incompatible with its own fundamental conditions, motives and social institutions, and will be changed, although not by economic necessity and probably even at some sacrifice of economic welfare, into an order of things which it will be merely matter of taste and terminology to call Socialism or not.'

[4] Schumpeter followed Weber in rejecting Marxian materialism, according to which the evolution of the superstructure is mainly determined by what happens within the structure of human societies; the causal relation was not however inverted but left room for recognition of a complex interdependence between the two aspects.

The Schumpeterian theory of market forms stands out distinctly from the traditional marginalist theory, given its intrinsically dynamic character. Against 'the traditional [static] conception of the *modus operandi* of competition', which leads to the so-called law of the one price, Schumpeter (1942, pp. 84–5) opposed

the competition from the new commodity, the new technology, the new source of supply, the new type of organization (the largest-scale unit of control for instance) – competition which commands a decisive cost or quality advantage and which strikes not at the margins of the profits and the outputs of the existing firms but at their foundations and their very lives. This kind of competition is as much more effective than the other as a bombardment is in comparison with forcing a door ... [It] acts not only when in being but also when it is merely an ever-present threat.

Competition, we see, is associated with the freedom of entry of new innovative firms into the market. This means attributing little importance to the barriers to competition stemming from market differentiation, upon which Chamberlin (1933) insists. It also foreshadows a radical critique of anti-monopolistic policies based on the number of firms active in the market.

The process of industrial concentration also generates drastic change in the social structure: 'The perfectly bureaucratized giant industrial unit not only ousts the small or medium-sized firm and "expropriates" its owners, but in the end it also ousts the entrepreneur and expropriates the bourgeoisie as a class which in the process stands to lose not only its income but also what is infinitely more important, its function' (ibid., p. 134).

Economic and social transformations are accompanied by equally radical changes in culture and ideology: 'capitalism creates a critical frame of mind which, after having destroyed the moral authority of so many institutions, in the end turns against its own; the bourgeois finds to his amazement that the rationalist attitude does not stop at the credentials of kings and popes but goes on to attack private property and the whole scheme of bourgeois values' (ibid., p. 143). Intellectuals favour the spread of critical attitudes towards capitalist society, and in particular an attitude of rejection towards the heroic role of the entrepreneur and that basic institution of capitalism that is private property; hence the 'decomposition' (ibid., p. 156) of capitalistic society.

15.5   The Path of Economic Science

With *Epochs in the History of Doctrines and Methods* (1914) and the *History of Economic Analysis*, left unfinished and published posthumously in

1954, Schumpeter provided a reconstruction of the path followed by economic science.

According to Schumpeter (ibid.),

Scientific analysis ... is not simply progressive discovery of an objective reality ... Rather it is an incessant struggle with creations of our own and our predecessors' minds and it "progresses", if at all, in a criss-cross fashion, not as logic, but as the impact of new ideas or observations or needs, and also as the bents and temperaments of new men, dictate.

In studying the zigzag path of economic science, Schumpeter focused attention on theories and analytical tools, leaving aside visions or ideologies, or 'systems of political economy'. Indeed, it is only when we succeed in isolating the analytical aspect in economic enquiries from the elements of vision and ideology that we can speak of "'scientific progress" between Mill and Samuelson' in 'the same sense in which we may say that there has been technological progress in the extraction of teeth between the times of John Stuart Mill and our own' (ibid., p. 39). The analytical work also includes elaborating a conceptual apparatus for the representation of reality, and indeed this latter aspect comes before the stage of construction of formal models.

Schumpeter identified in the chain physiocrats-Smith-John Stuart Mill-neoclassical theory the dominant line of development in economic research, while the Ricardo-Marx line was considered a deviation along which sight is lost of the central role played by demand and supply in the determination of equilibrium and of the fact that the issue of income distribution in essence concerns determination of the prices of productive factors. Schumpeter also criticized the notion of *homo oeconomicus*:

The conscious will of the individual, fleeing from pain and seeking satisfaction, is the scientific nucleus of this strictly rationalist and intellectualist system of philosophy and sociology which, unsurpassed in its baldness, shallowness and its radical lack of understanding for every thing that moves man and holds together society, was with a certain justification already an abomination to the contemporaries and to an even larger extent to later generations in spite of all its merits.[5]

The Austrian economist was implicitly suggesting here the possibility of a different – and more attractive – view of the economic agent, namely the active figure of the entrepreneur-innovator (and of the banker) on which his own theory of economic development relied. As was the case with many theoreticians, so too for Schumpeter

[5] Schumpeter 1914, p. 87; cf. also p. 97 and pp. 177–8.

reconstruction of the history of economic thought was in a sense part of his theoretical contribution, in the twofold sense of clarifying its methodological and conceptual foundations through contrasts and analogies while stressing the innovative qualities marking it out from the whole of the previous tradition.

16   Piero Sraffa

16.1   First Writings: Money and Banking

Piero Sraffa (1898–1983) is one of the leading intellectuals of the twentieth century not only for his strictly economic contributions but also for his influence on others, from Antonio Gramsci to Ludwig Wittgenstein. In the field of economic sciences, Sraffa's cultural project was an extremely ambitious one: to expose the weak points of the marginalist approach and at the same time to re-propose the classical approach of Adam Smith, David Ricardo and, in certain respects, Karl Marx.

Piero Sraffa was born in Turin, the son of a professor of commercial law and subsequently Dean of the Bocconi University in Milan, and studied in Parma, Milan and Turin, where he attended the classical lyceum and then the faculty of Law. From March 1917 to March 1920 he did his military service; in November 1920 he graduated with a dissertation on *L'inflazione monetaria in Italia durante e dopo la guerra (Monetary Inflation in Italy during and after the War)*, discussed with Luigi Einaudi.[1]

[1] Luigi Einaudi (1874–1961), a pragmatic liberal, professor of public finance at Turin as from 1902 and member of the Senate as from 1919, withdrew from public life under Fascism and became Governor of the Bank of Italy in 1945, minister for the budget in 1947 and president of the Italian Republic (1948–55). It is worth recalling here his controversy with Croce on the relationship between economic and political liberalism (cf. Croce and Einaudi 1957). Einaudi and Croce agreed on the fact that economic liberalism cannot be an absolute tenet, unlike political liberalism, but only a practical rule. However, Einaudi stressed the instrumental role of liberalism in favouring the diffusion of economic power (which otherwise would be concentrated in the hands of the State or of the political elite). The fact remains that no one could call himself a liberal if his liberalism is confined to the most widespread *laissez faire* in the economic arena. Though holding conservative views, Einaudi thus opened the way to the development of a reformist or socialist liberalism, like that of Piero Gobetti, Carlo and Nello Rosselli and the political movement 'Justice and Freedom' (Giustizia e libertà). As a student at the D'Azeglio Lyceum and a relative of the Rosselli brothers, Sraffa was involved in this cultural climate and, though oriented towards Gramsci's Marxism, always had very good relations with many protagonists of the democratic streams of anti-fascism.

The degree dissertation (Sraffa 1920) proposed some original ideas. In analysing inflation, it considered the diverse evolution of different price indexes, connected to the different viewpoints of the various social groups such as workers and entrepreneurs. Recourse to a general price index (as in the quantity theory of money, but more generally in all theories that conceive of money simply as a veil, with no influence on real variables) is misleading precisely in that it obscures the central role of social conflicts in economic life.[2] This point would underlie Keynes's (1930) criticism of the quantity theory of money. Moreover, Sraffa distinguished between stabilising the internal and the external value of money, or in other words between stabilising the average level of domestic prices or the exchange rate. The two coincide, according to the traditional theory of the gold standard; however, the distinction becomes essential when considering either short-run problems or inconvertible paper money systems and was therefore relevant to the policy choices of the time. Keynes did not use it in *Indian Currency and Finance* (1913) but did bring it into his *Tract on Monetary Reform* (1923), having in the meantime (in August 1921) met Sraffa.[3]

16.2   Criticism of Marshallian Theory

Sraffa's interest in theoretical issues probably developed when he became lecturer at the University of Perugia in November 1923. Sraffa thus developed a radical critique of the Marshallian theory of the equilibrium of the firm and the industry, in a long article published in Italian in 1925, 'Sulle relazioni fra costo e quantità prodotta' ('On the Relations between Cost and Quantity Produced'), which entered into the debate on the *laws of returns* sparked off by John Harold Clapham (1873–1946).

Marshallian theory singled out three cases: constant, increasing or decreasing returns, according to whether the average unit cost remains constant, decreases or increases when the quantity produced increases. Clapham (1922) maintained that the three categories are 'empty

---

[2] Sraffa (1932) developed one of his critiques of Hayek along similar lines. According to the theory of forced savings utilised by Hayek, a period of inflation may correspond to a more rapid accumulation of capital than is justified by the basic parameters of the economy, but the system then automatically goes back to its long-period equilibrium through a deflationary process. Sraffa (1932, p. 110) stressed that the re-establishment of a situation of monetary equilibrium does not bring each individual economic agent back to the initial conditions.

[3] Sraffa's early publications (1922a, 1922b) addressed monetary and banking issues and testify to his personality as an all-round economist, in whom the dominant interest for pure theory was accompanied by a solid knowledge of the institutional details and by exemplary analyses of specific real-world issues.

economic boxes', impossible to fill with concrete examples of real industries.[4] Sraffa (1925) argued that the problem of the 'empty boxes' does not concern how to apply the three categories to real situations but rather stems from insurmountable theoretical difficulties within the theory of firm and industry equilibrium, resulting from a conceptual confusion: in classical political economy the law of decreasing returns was associated with the problem of rent (that is, with the theory of distribution), while the law of increasing returns was associated with the division of labour, or in other words general economic progress (that is, with the theory of production). Marshall tried to put these two laws on the same plane, co-ordinating them in a single law of non-proportional returns, so as to express costs as a function of the quantity produced, for firm and industry alike. We thus get a supply curve for each product, to be set against the corresponding demand curve deduced from the law of decreasing marginal utility.

However, as Sraffa showed, this meant transposing increasing and decreasing returns to an ambit different from the original ones, and in turn this made it difficult to apply the justifications originally used to account for the variations in costs in the new ambit. In particular, decreasing returns are connected to changes in the proportions of factors of production, while increasing returns stem from expanding production and increasing division of labour. Decreasing returns occur when a factor of production is scarce. Now, unless we identify the industry with all the firms using a scarce factor, variations in average cost associated with increased production in the industry under consideration will be of the same order of magnitude as variations in costs simultaneously experienced by other industries using the same factor of production. The *ceteris paribus* assumption that underlies

---

[4] Clapham's article brought on a further spate of articles, first of all by Pigou (1922), paladin of a line of Marshallian orthodoxy. The debate went on with contributions by, among others, Dennis Robertson (1924), Allyn Young (1928), Lionel Robbins (1928), Gerald Shove (1928), Joseph Schumpeter (1928) and Roy Harrod (1930). Allyn Young (1876–1929) stressed the importance of increasing returns; his influence on the development of economic thought was often indirect; for instance, the books by Knight (1921) and Chamberlin (1933) began as doctorate dissertations under his supervision. Gerald Shove (1887–1947), Marshall's pupil, notwithstanding the few pages he had published, was an influential member of the Cambridge school. Lionel Robbins (1898–1984) dominated the London School of Economics (where he was a professor from 1929) in the central decades of the twentieth century; a supporter of Hayek against Keynes, he participated as a protagonist in the policy debates of the period; from 1960 he was chairman of the *Financial Times*; his best known work is *Nature and Significance of Economic Science* (1932), famous for his definition of economics ('economics is the science which studies human behaviour as a relationship between ends and scarce means which have alternative uses': ibid., p. 16), but he was also the author of important works in the history of economic thought.

partial equilibrium analysis is thus violated: prices of other goods change and the demand curve shifts.

As for increasing returns, they cannot concern the individual firms, since otherwise firms would go on expanding until they reached a size incompatible with the assumption of competition. Nor can they concern various industries at the same time; otherwise the *ceteris paribus* clause would be breached once again. Hence the category of economies of production external to the individual firm but internal to the industry: an unrealistic category, though, certainly not utilisable as a general assumption. In conclusion, the Marshallian construction cannot comply with the requirement of logical consistency except by recourse to unrealistic *ad hoc* assumptions, which obviously constitute inadequate foundations for a theory designed for general interpretative application.

16.3   Imperfect Competition and the Critique of the Representative Firm

Sraffa's 1925 Italian paper was followed by a much shorter article in the *Economic Journal* (Sraffa 1926), the first half of it consisting of a summary of the Italian article, while the second half elaborates an original line of research: a theory of imperfect competition, which has the advantage of being compatible with the cases of increasing and constant returns as well while embodying realistic features suggested in Marshall's writings. The idea is that, as a consequence of market imperfections, within every industry each firm is confronted with a specific, negatively sloped demand curve, even when many firms are simultaneously present in the industry, while according to the traditional theory of competition in this case each firm should be faced with a horizontal demand curve. However, Sraffa stressed the limits of this approach, since it ignores the possibility of new firms entering the industry, thus neglecting competition in the classical sense of the term, consisting of the shifting of capital from one sector to another in pursuit of the maximum returns. Thus Sraffa did not share in the enthusiasm for imperfect competition raging in the 1930s, turning, rather, to the classical notion of competition, which constituted the basis for the line of research that led to his 1960 book on *Production of Commodities by Means of Commodities*.

Sraffa's radical departure from the traditional framework of the theory of the firm and the industry was evident in his contributions to the symposium on 'Increasing Returns and the Representative Firm' published in the *Economic Journal* in March 1930. The conclusion of these brief contributions was a clear-cut break with the then mainstream views: 'Marshall's theory ... cannot be interpreted in a way which makes it logically self-consistent and, at the same time, reconciles it with the facts it sets out to explain'; thus, 'I think ... that [it] should be discarded' (Sraffa 1930, p. 93).

Here Sraffa's criticism was levelled against Robertson's (1930) evolutionary version of the Marshallian theory, based on the concept of the firm's life cycle, which Marshall had employed in an attempt to make increasing returns compatible with the firm's competitive equilibrium. Like a biological organism, the firm goes through successive stages of development, maturity and decline; the representative firm is half-way through the process of development and thus at a stage of increasing returns to scale. As Marshall himself pointed out, a concept of this type, that sees the expansion of firms depending on the life cycle of entrepreneurial capacities, may be plausible in the case of directly family-run concerns but cannot apply to modern joint stock companies.

Thus biological analogies prove a false exit to the blind alley Marshallian analysis had got into, hemmed in by the contradiction between increasing returns and competitive equilibrium. Sraffa had an easy task in pointing out the *deus ex machina* nature of the biological metaphors, which cannot fill in the gaps in logical consistency intrinsic to these analytic structures: 'At the critical points of his argument the firms and the industry drop out of the scene, and their place is taken by the trees and the forest, the bones and the skeleton, the water-drops and the wave – indeed all the kingdoms of nature are drawn upon to contribute to the wealth of his metaphors' (Sraffa 1930, p. 91).

16.4 Cambridge: Wittgenstein and Keynes

Sraffa's 1926 paper had considerable impact. Keynes was thus able to offer him a job as lecturer at Cambridge University; after Gramsci's imprisonment and the threats he himself received as an anti-fascist, Sraffa decided to move to England, where he lived from 1927 until his death in 1983. There Sraffa developed his research along three lines connected in one great cultural design: the work on the critical edition of Ricardo's writings, entrusted to him by the Royal Society at the initiative of Keynes in 1930; research in the field of the theory of value, which was to lead to *Production of Commodities by Means of Commodities*; and a collateral interest in the development of Keynesian theory. Moreover, in Cambridge Sraffa made the acquaintance of the Austrian philosopher Ludwig Wittgenstein (1889–1951), on whom Sraffa was to have a significant influence, specifically on the shift from the logical atomism of the *Tractatus* (1921) to the mature views of the *Philosophical Investigations*, published posthumously in 1953.

Between Wittgenstein's initial and final positions there was a clear change. With drastic simplification, let us focus attention on the methodological results that are of more direct interest to us. The *Tractatus* argued that there was a correspondence between the world and the elements that constitute it (the 'facts') on the one hand and our representation of the world (whose constituent elements are the 'thoughts', expressed in 'propositions') on the other. On this basis Wittgenstein argued that it is possible to build a logical, axiomatic set of propositions, each describing a 'fact' while together they describe the world, or rather, if not all the world, all that can be described in a rational form. On that for which no rational description can be provided (sentiments, religious beliefs, aesthetic judgements, etc.), said Wittgenstein, 'one must be silent'.

However, under Sraffa's influence, in the *Philosophical Investigations* Wittgenstein abandoned the idea of language as 'mirroring' the world and the idea of the 'unspeakable' and developed a new theory. There is not just one type of language, Wittgenstein (1953, p. 21) asserted, 'but there are *countless* kinds: countless different types of use of what we call "symbols", "words", "sentences". And this multiplicity is not something fixed, given once for all; but new types of language, new language-games, as we may say, come into existence, and others become obsolete and get forgotten.' In general, 'the meaning of a word is its use in the language' (ibid., p. 33). However, words do not correspond to simple elements of reality, and these simple elements cannot be rigorously defined; nor is it possible to produce a general theory of language. These theses are demonstrated with a series of examples of 'language games', ideal models that focused attention on particular aspects of the real language, presenting them as the general language of a group of people.

We do not know whether Sraffa agreed with the point of arrival of Wittgenstein's reflections. Perhaps we may perceive Sraffa's political interests behind his preference for a theory open to recognise the role of social factors (the environment in which the 'linguistic game' takes place), of rules and conventions, as well as a methodological choice, namely the rejection of all-embracing theories that pretend to describe any and all aspects of the world, starting from its elementary constituting elements and the choice, rather, of flexibility in theoretical constructions, aiming in each case at the specific problem under consideration.

After Gramsci and Wittgenstein, a third protagonist of twentieth-century culture to have fecund exchange with Sraffa was John Maynard Keynes, fifteen years older and a great help to Sraffa on various occasions: from publication of his early writings to the invitation to move to Cambridge and entrustment of the task of preparing the critical edition of Ricardo's writings. The only publication Sraffa signed jointly was with Keynes: both keen bibliophiles, in 1938 they edited the reprint of an extremely rare booklet, *An Abstract of a Treatise on Human Nature* (Hume 1740), complete with a learned introduction containing decisive proof of its attribution to Hume rather than to Adam Smith as was generally supposed. Sraffa also took care of the Italian edition (1925) of Keynes's *Tract on Monetary Reform*.

More relevant to our immediate concern is the cultural exchange in the field of economic theory. Four episodes may be recalled in this respect: the likely influence on Keynes of the distinction, proposed by Sraffa in his graduate thesis, between monetary policy aimed at stabilising the level of domestic prices or the exchange rate; Sraffa's participation in the debates that stimulated Keynes's transition from the *Treatise on Money* to the *General Theory*; his critical contribution (Sraffa 1932) on Hayek's theory, from which Keynes derived the theory of own interest rates that is at the centre of the analysis in chapter 17 of the *General Theory*; and, finally, a suggestion by Keynes, recalled by Sraffa (1960, p. vi) in his preface to *Production of Commodities by Means of Commodities*: 'when in 1928 Lord Keynes read a draft of the opening propositions of this paper, he recommended that, if constant returns were *not* to be assumed, an emphatic warning to that effect should be given'. The point Keynes intervened on is of fundamental importance, since the absence of an assumption on returns constitutes a crucially distinctive feature of Sraffa's book, implying among other things abandonment of the marginalist notion of equilibrium; thus it seems quite likely that his discussions with Keynes played an important role in the development of Sraffa's ideas.

16.5   The Critical Edition of Ricardo's Writings

The difficulties economists such as Robertson (in the 1930 symposium) and Hayek (in the 1932 controversy) had in understanding just what Sraffa was aiming at reveal the extent to which the marginalist approach had encroached on the classical tradition in the first half of the twentieth century – hence the need for the rediscovery of the classical approach, based on the notion of the surplus, which Sraffa pursued with his critical edition of Ricardo's works, busying at it for more than a quarter of a century.

When Sraffa began his work the most commonly accepted interpretations were that of Marshall (1890, appendix i), who saw Ricardo as a somewhat imprecise and unilateral precursor of modern theory (since he took account of the cost of production, i.e. supply, but not of demand, in the determination of prices), and that of Jevons (in the preface to the second edition of the *Theory of Political Economy*), who considered Ricardo responsible for perniciously diverting economics from the path of true science. For either interpretation, there was no reason to waste time on Ricardo's works. At most, one might recall his theory of rent as forerunner of the principle of decreasing marginal productivity or his theory of international trade based on the principle of comparative costs.

Sraffa's critical edition of Ricardo's *Works and Correspondence* is unanimously recognised as a model of philological rigour. It was above all for this quality that in 1961 Sraffa was awarded the gold medal of the Swedish Academy of Sciences: an honour that among the economists had also been accorded to Keynes and Myrdal and that may be considered as an anticipation of the Nobel Prize, awarded for economics only from 1969 on. The writings published in this edition, together with the apparatus of notes and, above all, Sraffa's introduction to the first volume, restored Ricardo – and through him the whole classical approach to political economy – to a central position in economic theory, freeing interpretation of his thought (in substance, as illustrated in Chapter 7) from the accretions of misleading marginalist readings. Sraffa stressed in particular the importance of the notion of the surplus and of the conception of the economic system as a circular flow of production and consumption. The size of the surplus (the Smithian problem of the wealth of nations and the division of labour), its distribution among the various social classes (the problem on which Ricardo focused attention in his *Principles*) and its utilisation in unproductive consumption or accumulation constituted the issues upon which the classical economists focused their analyses, 'in striking contrast – as Sraffa 1960, p. 93, pointed out – with the view presented by modern theory, of a one-way avenue that leads from "Factors of production" to "Consumption goods"'.

16.6   Production of Commodities by Means of Commodities

As we saw in Chapter 7, the analytic representation Ricardo offered had a weak point in the assumption that relative prices are proportional to the quantity of labour required for the production of the various commodities. In *Production of Commodities by Means of Commodities* Sraffa came up with a solution to the problem framed in terms of the classical conception. There is therefore a close link between the critical edition of Ricardo's writings and the theoretical research Sraffa himself was engaged in.

In analogy to the line of enquiry followed by classical economists, Sraffa put at the centre of his analysis an economic system based on the division of labour, in which the product of each sector does not correspond to its requirements for means of production (inclusive of the means of subsistence for the workers employed in the sector). Each sector taken in isolation is not able to continue its activity but needs to obtain from other sectors in the economy its own means of production in exchange for at least part of its product. We thus have a web of exchanges. As Sraffa showed, the problem of the exchange ratios (of prices) is connected to the problem of income distribution between workers, capitalists and landlords and constitutes what in the classical tradition was called the problem of value.

Value, therefore, does not stem from the subjective appreciation of each good but from the objective element of the difficulty of production (technology) together with the relationship that connects among them sectors and social classes within the economy. Moreover, Sraffa's analysis is based on assumptions (the law of the one price; division into the social classes of workers, capitalists and landowners; a uniform rate of profits) that mirror the fundamental characteristics of capitalism.

When commodities are at one and the same time products and means of production, the price of one commodity cannot be determined independently of the others nor the set of relative prices independently of income distribution between profits and wages. We must consider income distribution and the determination of relative prices simultaneously. This was precisely the line of enquiry developed by Sraffa in his 1960 book.

In the preface Sraffa stressed that his analysis of the relations connecting prices and distributive variables did not require the assumption of constant returns to scale. However, Sraffa added that, 'as a temporary working hypothesis', 'anyone accustomed to think in terms of the equilibrium of demand and supply may be inclined ... to suppose that the argument rests on a tacit assumption of constant returns in all industries' (Sraffa 1960, p. v). Thanks to the assumption of constant returns, analysis of the relationship between relative prices and income distribution may be considered as part of a marginalist model of general economic equilibrium, in which the initial endowments of productive factors are given in such a way as to be compatible with the final demand of economic agents. In this way, thanks to the possibility of 'translating' it into a particular case of the marginalist analysis, Sraffa's analysis may serve as the foundation for an internal criticism of logical inconsistency of the traditional marginalist theories of value and distribution. As a matter of fact, however, the assumption that equilibrium prices correspond to the equality between supply and demand which characterised marginalist economic theory is absent from Sraffa's exposition.[5]

Let us now illustrate the various steps in Sraffa's analysis. As a first step, Sraffa (1960, p. 3) showed that in a system of production for mere subsistence, 'which produces just enough to maintain itself' and where 'commodities are produced by separate industries and are exchanged for one another at the market held' at the end of the production period, 'there is a unique set of exchange values which if adopted by the market restores the original distribution of the products and makes it possible for the process to be repeated; such values spring directly from the methods of production'.

If the economic system under consideration is able to produce a surplus, also 'the distribution of the surplus must be determined through the same mechanism and at the same time as are the prices of commodities' (Sraffa 1960, p. 6). If the wage can exceed subsistence level, relative prices and one or other of the two distributive variables are jointly determined, once the technology and the other distributive variable are known; the higher the wage is, the lower will be the rate of profits. 'The key to the movement of relative prices consequent upon a change in the wage lies in the inequality of the proportions in which labour and means of production are employed in the various industries'. Indeed, 'if the proportions were the same in all industries no price-changes could ensue', while 'it is impossible for prices to remain unchanged when there is inequality of "proportions"' (ibid, pp. 12–3).

Sraffa (1960, pp. 18–33) also constructed a particular analytical tool, namely the 'Standard commodity', thanks to which he was able to solve the Ricardian problem of an invariable measure of value, after having aptly redefined it. Ricardo had in fact attributed two meanings to the notion of a standard measure of value, which must not be confused: that of having invariable value (in relation to the complex of the means of production necessary to obtain it) when changes occur in the distribution of income, the technology remaining unaltered; and that of having invariable value when technology changes (cultivation of ever less fertile lands, technological progress). Sraffa solved the former problem

---

[5] On this point and on the interpretation of Sraffa's work, cf. Roncaglia (1975, 2009b).

with the 'Standard commodity': a composite commodity (i.e. a set of commodities taken in particular proportions) so determined that the aggregate of its means of production has the same composition as it. Thus, in the Standard system – the abstract economic system the product of which consists of a certain quantity of Standard commodity – and under the assumption that wages are included in the costs of production, it is possible to determine the rate of profits as a ratio between two physically homogeneous quantities: the surplus, i.e. the difference between product and means of production, and the means of production advanced by the capitalists. Coming to the second problem – invariance in the face of changes in technology – labour embodied retains significance as a broad but imperfect indicator of the difficulty of production, but there is also the risk of bringing metaphysical or subjectivist nuances into play within the economic discourse (labour as toil and trouble). Sraffa thus appears to suggest a reinterpretation of Marx that frees him from a metaphysical notion of labour as absolute value, that is, as a substance embodied in the commodities that univocally characterises their difficulty of production.

The analysis of prices of production is completed with the case of joint products and, within this category, fixed capital goods and scarce or non-reproducible means of production such as land. The book closes with a chapter on the choice between economically alternative methods of production in relation to variations in the rate of profits and with four appendices including the 'References to the literature', where Sraffa explicitly associated his analysis with that of the classical economists.

16.7   Critique of the Marginalist Approach

While advancing a theory of production prices within the framework of the classical approach, Sraffa's book also offered the tools for a critique of the foundations of the marginalist theory of value and distribution. Preliminarily, however, we need to clear the path of a misunderstanding, namely interpretation of Sraffa's contribution as a general equilibrium analysis conducted under the assumption of constant returns to scale, in which it would have been possible to explain prices by focusing attention on production costs – the supply side – and dropping the demand side. Sraffa explicitly rejected– three times, in the preface to his book – the idea that his analysis would require the assumption of constant returns. 'No question arises as to the variation or constancy of returns. The investigation is concerned exclusively with such properties of an economic system as do not depend on changes in the scale of production or in the proportions of "factors".' 'This standpoint, which is that of the old classical economists . . ., has been submerged and forgotten since the advent of the "marginal" method' (Sraffa 1960, p. v). We can, however, utilize the analytical results reached with regard to prices of production for an internal criticism of logical inconsistency of the marginalist theory of value and distribution by transposing them into the marginalist conceptual framework.

The results in Sraffa's book that can be directly used as the foundation for a critique of the marginalist theories of value and distribution concern the average period of production and the choice of techniques. The average period of production had been propounded by Böhm-Bawerk (1889) as a measure of the capital intensity of production. Sraffa showed that, depending as it does on the rate of profits, it cannot be used to measure capital in the ambit of an explanation of the rate of profits taken as the price of this factor of production. The difficulty had already been sensed by Wicksell (1901–6), but modern exponents of the Austrian school, including Hayek (1931), were later to return to the notion of the average period of production.[6]

With regard to the choice between alternative techniques of production when the rate of profits changes, Sraffa (1960, pp. 81–7) pointed out the possibility of a *reswitching of techniques*; in other words, a given technique that proves the most advantageous for a given rate of profits may be superseded by another technique when we raise the rate of profits but may once again be preferable when the rate of profits rises still higher. The implication is that, however the capital intensity of the two techniques (or in other words the ratio between the quantities utilised of capital and labour) is measured, the general rule that the marginalist theory of value rests on remains contradicted. This rule takes the distributive variables, wage rate and rate of profits, as prices of the corresponding factors of production determined by the law of demand and supply, so that the quantity of capital employed in production should diminish (and the quantity of labour increase) as the rate of profits rises (and the wage consequently falls). With the reswitching of techniques, violation of the marginalist rule is unavoidable: if the rule

---

[6] Harrod (1961), in a review of Sraffa's book, persisted in defending the Austrian theory of value by recalling that for any level of the rate of profits we may univocally define the average period of production, though in the presence of compounded interest. Sraffa (1962) replied that this fact is not sufficient, since here we fall into a logical vicious circle: the rate of profits must be known in order to determine the average period of production to be utilised, as a measure of the capitalistic intensity of production, in determining the rate of profits.

holds when one technique gives way to another with a rising rate of profits, the contrary occurs when from the second technology the economy turns again to the first as the rate of profits rises yet higher. This criticism gave rise to widespread debate,[7] while the crucial question of its relevance received relatively scant attention. It applies not only to the aggregate production function but also to all those cases in which, while acknowledging the fact that capital is a collection of heterogeneous means of production, the rate of profits is still interpreted as the price of a factor of production capital, however it be defined (aggregate of value, waiting, average period of production). In particular, Sraffa's critique undermines the very foundations of the idea – crucial to marginalist macroeconomic theory – of an inverse relationship between real wage rate and employment, such that a competitive labour market in a closed economy would automatically tend towards full employment equilibrium, since the decline in real wages brought about by unemployment would prompt an increase in the labour-capital ratio and hence, given the endowment of capital, an increase in the quantity of labour employed. Sraffa's critique not only rejects the idea of the existence of equilibrium (optimal) values for the distributive variables, wage rate and rate of profits but also sides with Keynes's critique in denying the existence of an automatic tendency of competitive labour markets towards full employment.[8]

---

[7] More or less simultaneously with the publication of Sraffa's book, Garegnani (1960) developed a direct critique of some of the main theoretical contributions in the marginalist tradition. Publication of Sraffa's book was then followed by lively debate. An initial skirmish (Harrod 1961; Sraffa 1962) has already been recalled in the previous footnote. A second clash began with Samuelson's 1962 attempt to depict the aggregate production function as a 'parable' not betraying the essential characteristics of a market economy and by Levhari's (1965) attempt to show that the problems raised by Sraffa (such as the possibility of the reswitching of techniques) referred only to the single industry and not to the economic system as a whole. These propositions were immediately refuted by Garegnani (1970), Spaventa (1968) and Pasinetti (1966); Samuelson 1966 and Levhari (with Samuelson, 1966) were themselves to recognise the erroneousness of their theses. Pasinetti (1969) then criticised the recourse on the part of Solow (1963, 1967) to the Fisherian notion of the rate of return, considered as index of the quantity of capital definable independently of the profit rate and thus utilisable for explaining the latter.

[8] Incidentally, this means that the so-called structural reforms insisted upon in the past few years by the so-called Washington consensus, aiming at reducing workers' bargaining power, are certain to affect income distribution, while the effects on employment may turn out to be positive or negative depending on circumstances (and Keynesian theory indicates that negative effects are more likely).

We may add that Sraffa's revival of the classical approach appears to be compatible with the Keynesian approach. Abandoning the approach to the determination of equilibrium prices and quantities based on the demand-supply mechanism leaves us free to consider the determination of prices and the determination of quantities as separate analytical issues, which opens the way to a Keynesian determination of the levels of production and

16.8   The Sraffian Schools

Sraffa's contributions were followed by many works: research into the history of economic thought, contributing to a reconstruction of the classical approach and of its differences with respect to the marginalist approach, debate over the theory of capital and the critiques of the marginalist approach in the different fields of economic research and analytical development and transposition of Sraffa's analysis of prices of production into rigorous mathematical terms. We then have at least three more general attempts at reconstruction of political economy that, for the sake of clear exposition, we will associate with the names of the three leading representatives of the classical approach: Smith, Ricardo, Marx.

Pasinetti's (1960, 1965, 1975, 1981) 'Ricardian' reconstruction begins with the post-Keynesian theory of distribution (Pasinetti 1962), connecting income distribution between wages and profits to the level of investments, once the saving propensities of workers and capitalists and the growth rate are given. Subsequently, there is the development of the theory of vertically integrated sectors (Pasinetti 1973). This is the background for an analysis of 'the conditions under which it [the economy] may grow and benefit by exploiting all its potential possibilities' (Pasinetti 1981, p. 25). Specifically, in any vertically integrated sector the 'natural' rate of profits – which differs from sector to sector – must be such as to ensure an amount of profits equal to the 'equilibrium' value of investments, that is, to the amount of investments required for expanding productive capacity at a rate equal to 'the rate of population growth' plus 'the rate of increase of per capita demand for each consumption good' (1981, p. 130). In order to account for the changes over time in the structure of demand, Pasinetti drew on 'Engel's law', thus avoiding any reference to subjective elements such as utility maps and consumers' preferences. The increase in per capita income and demand corresponds in equilibrium to the increase in per capita product due to technical progress (which can proceed at different speeds in different sectors).

In this context the notion of equilibrium assumed a normative meaning, connected as it was to the assumption of full employment of the available labour force and of productive capacity. In other words,

employment based on the notion of effective demand; moreover, Sraffa's (1960, p. 33) reference to the influence of the interest rate on the rate of profits hinted at the importance of monetary and financial factors for the evolution of the real economy (in other words, to the non-neutrality of money), i.e. to one of the main tenets of the Keynesian approach. Cf. Roncaglia and Tonveronachi, 2015.

Pasinetti's analysis focused on what should happen to ensure full employ-ment, not on the actual behaviour of an economic system tied to specific institutions.[9]

Garegnani's (1981, 1984) 'Marxian' reconstruction located the analytical core common to classical economists, to Marx and Sraffa, in the set of relations concerning production prices and distributive variables analysed in Sraffa 1960: wage rate, national product and technology are the data utilized for determining the distributive shares for profits and rents and the relative prices. As a separate logical stage other issues may then be considered, such as determination of the wage rate, product and technology. However, while within the analytical core 'general quantitative relations of sufficiently definite form can be postulated', outside the core 'relations in the economy are so complex and variable according to circumstances, as to allow not for general quantitative relations of sufficiently definite form'.[10]

A 'Smithian' interpretation of the central aspects of classical poli-tical economy was developed by Paolo Sylos Labini (1954, 1956, 1972, 1974, 1976, 1984, 2000), who brought to the centre of the programme for reconstruction of classical political economy the role of market forms in their interaction with accumulation and techno-logical change. This meant bringing to the centre of the analysis a Smithian causal chain that goes from changes in the division of labour (i.e. technological changes) to changes over time in market forms, and hence in the pace of accumulation, and so, together with aspects concerning public policy and the politico-institutional setting, to income distribution. In this way, the relations connecting production prices and income distribution which constituted the core of Sraffa's analysis maintained their role as central pillar of economic theorising, but the main object of the analysis is rather the wealth of nations, the factors determining its development over time and in different countries, and in particular the distribution of income and wealth among different groups of economic agents. In other words, in order to re-propose a classical interpretation of the development of the economic systems in which we live it is not sufficient to build on the analysis developed by Sraffa in *Production of Commodities by*

[9] On the limits of this approach (the normative character of the analysis, the exogenous nature of technical progress and the exclusion from the analysis of the role of market forms and of monetary and financial factors as well as the role of 'short period' elements in 'long period' evolution) cf. Roncaglia 1990a, pp. 207–9.

[10] Garegnani (1990, pp. 123–4). For a critique of this distinction, cf. Roncaglia (1990a, pp. 209–11, and 1990b).

Means of Commodities – neither in the sense of gradually extending a basic formal model nor in the sense of gradually extending a restricted analytical nucleus of causal relations.

The variety of these developments testifies to the vitality and attractiveness of the research project started by Sraffa.

17 The Age of Disgregation

17.1 From One Side of the Atlantic to the Other

The field that this chapter should cover is enormous. Rather than embarking on a wide-ranging but incomplete survey, only the main lines of research will be explored.

After the end of the Second World War the focal centre of economic culture shifted from Europe to the United States. Many had moved there, escaping racial or political persecutions. The wealth of a country that had won the war without experiencing within its territory the devastation it entailed constituted another important advantage. The Fulbright grant programme, for instance, financed study in American universities for many young European economists as well as visiting professorships. Moreover, research activity was supported (and to some extent directed to specific issues) by an extensive network of foundations (such as the Cowles Foundation or the Rand Corporation) and by military programmes started in wartime and continued in the cold war period.

Only recently has this latter aspect received the attention it deserves (Mirowski 2002, 2012). Together with a more practical leaning of American culture, the immediate issues raised by the war contribute to explaining some differences between the European cultural climate and the economic culture that gradually made its way from the United States to conquer the world, albeit – as we shall see – amidst many variants and never with complete success.

Though remaining within the conceptual framework of the marginalist tradition (the one-way avenue leading from scarce resources to the satisfaction of human needs and desires), the focus of US economic culture shifted from the analysis of society to the analysis of decisions, and from parametric to strategic, game-theoretic analysis of general equilibrium (i.e. from assuming the independence of each individual's decisions from those of all the other individuals to considering their interdependence).

Hence the importance attributed to the notion of the rational economic agent, which constitutes both the main pillar and the week point of the theoretical construction. Hence, too, the drive to bring within the scope of economic science, conceived as analysis of rational choice, all aspects of human life – the so-called imperialism of economics.

Built in an axiomatic way, the notion of rationality implied adhesion to the utilitarian foundations of the marginalist tradition.[1] We will therefore take it, in the next section, as the starting point for our analysis of the paths recently followed by economic science: an analysis made more complex by the exponentially growing number of economic researchers active in universities and research centres. The trend towards professionalization of economics, already felt in Marshall's times, became dominant and imposed on economic research scientific criteria typical of those stages that Kuhn (1962) christened 'normal science': internal consistency and coherence with the basic axioms of the dominant tradition and a strict attitude of closure towards whatever did not fit into this tradition. Hence the growing importance of what came to be called the mainstream, a dominant approach combining idolatry for mathematical models based on a one-dimensional view of the economic agent with a strong penchant for liberalism in policy.

17.2   The New Foundations: General Equilibrium and Expected Utilities

Two elements – one more general, the other more specific – need be stressed here: choice of the problem of individual decisions as the starting point of economics and von Neumann's role. The first element is probably attributable to the military interest in scientific (objective) formulation of decisional problems; the second to the brilliance of the Hungarian mathematician but also to his varied activities as consultant during and after the war (including his participation in the Manhattan Project for the development of the atomic bomb and in the development of the first computers).

Born in Budapest and an emigrant to the United States in the early thirties, in 1933 John von Neumann (1903–1957) became the youngest member of the Institute for Advanced Studies at Princeton, where Albert Einstein was one of his colleagues. Author of a celebrated model of balanced growth (von Neumann 1937), as from 1940 alongside his

---

[1] Quite different would have been the implications, for instance, of a generic reference to the good sense of the *pater familias*, a notion that by itself would not have sufficed for the construction of utility functions.

consultant activities he worked with Oskar Morgenstern (1902–1977)[2] on a book, *Theory of Games and Economic Behaviour* (1944), which had a strong influence on developments in economic research in the United States.

This work relied on axiomatic analysis. It provided a systematic treatment of n-person zero-sum games and broad introductory analysis of non-zero-sum games. It also relied on the notion of expected utility, which constitutes an extension of the problem of consumer's choice between alternative uses of scarce resources. Each act of choice may have not one certain univocal outcome but a multiplicity of possible outcomes; the agent then needs to evaluate both the utility and the probability of each outcome, thus obtaining the expected utility stemming from his/her choice as an average of the utilities of the different outcomes weighted with their probabilities.

In order to analyse expected utilities, von Neumann and Morgenstern (1944, pp. 26 ff.) introduced a system of postulates, which in substance correspond to completeness, continuity and transitivity of the agent's preferences (if I prefer *A* to *B* and *B* to *C*, then I also have to prefer *A* to *C*) and of the probability of the different outcomes; moreover, each preference relation is considered independent of other events (absence of external effects). The set of postulates ensures that probabilities and utilities – hence, expected utilities – retain the properties of mathematical expectations. Moreover, both utilities and probabilities are considered measurable (numerable).[3] Hence, assuming the agent to have complete information, we can determine the decisions (the solutions of the system) corresponding to a 'rational behaviour' that maximizes expected utility.

The game-theory approach, in which each agent tries to take into account other agents' decisions, enables us to move on from analysis of the isolated agent (Jevons's Robinson Crusoe) to analysis of the agent's choices in the presence of other agents, and so to analysis of the general

---

[2] Morgenstern had migrated from Vienna to Princeton in 1938 for political reasons.

[3] The assumption of a regular (complete, transitive and continuous) ordering of preferences in itself implies ordinal utility functions; von Neumann and Morgenstern obtain cardinal utility functions thanks to the assumption of an arithmetical average of utilities weighted with the probabilities of the outcomes (I owe this point to Aldo Montesano). The preference ordering can be obtained (ibid, p. 18 note) by questioning individual agents; such data are held to be reproducible (ibid, p. 24: this means, although the authors do not make it explicit, that individual preference systems are stable over time).

Von Neumann and Morgenstern (1944, p. 17) consider utility as a natural phenomenon, objectively measurable, following in this the marginalist pre-Pareto tradition: 'Even if utilities look very unnumerical today, the history of the experience in the theory of heat may repeat itself', as happened (in different ways) for the theory of light, of colours and of radio waves.

equilibrium of an economy in which agents interact. Under perfect competition, this does not imply substantial differences from the analysis conducted by Walras and his successors; however, von Neumann and Morgenstern attribute great importance to the role of coalitions, i.e. games in which the possibility of cooperation is admitted, while subsequent research focused on non-cooperative games, in particular under conditions of incomplete information. Simplifying, we may say that general economic equilibrium analysis focused on market interdependency, while von Neumann and Morgenstern – and by and large the broad flows of research to which they opened the way – focused attention on a rational economic agent's choices.

Declaredly in the wake of von Neumann and Morgenstern (1944), an important contribution was provided by Savage with his *Foundations of Statistics* (1954), which retained the expected utility notion and provided a fully axiomatic treatment of it, integrating it with the subjective view of probability proposed by De Finetti and Ramsey; the *Foundations* have since been seen as the basis of modern inferential statistics.

The analytical results of this research are important but cannot be considered to constitute the crowning moment of the general equilibrium research programme started by Walras. So much can be learnt from the developments of the traditional Walrasian approach (hence under the assumptions of perfect competition and absence of combinations), based on the axiomatic method and on the use of topology: the results concerning the demonstration of the existence of solutions for the general equilibrium model (Wald 1936, Nash 1950, Arrow and Debreu 1954, Debreu 1959)[4] are accompanied by negative results concerning uniqueness and stability of equilibrium. Reformulation of the problem in terms of decision theory opened the way to circumvent these issues, as well as the limits of the assumption of convex preference sets, the unrealism of which is evident especially when applied to

---

[4] In the early 1950s, Gerard Debreu (1921–2004, Nobel Laureate in 1983) was a colleague of Arrow at the Cowles Commission at Chicago and then remained in America as professor first at Yale and then at Berkeley. In Debreu 1959 and in other works the general economic equilibrium model is extended to take account of 'dated' commodities (a barrel of corn available at a given date is different from a barrel of corn available at a different date) and 'contingent commodities' (the same commodity, an umbrella for instance, is considered as a different commodity depending on the 'state of nature', for instance, whether it is a sunny day or it rains); it is also possible to translate contingent markets into markets for insurance certificates concerning the different possible 'states of nature' (assuming that the set of all possible states of nature may be univocally defined, with each state of nature fully specified – an untenable assumption, as recalled in Section 16.4 with reference to Wittgenstein).

production technologies.[5] These limits are in any case ignored in the systematic presentations of economic theory, beginning with the one that constituted for generations the reference point, Samuelson's *Foundations of Economic Analysis* (1947).[6]

Another negative result concerned the impossibility of extending the consistency of the system of choices from the individual to society. Kenneth Arrow (1921–2017, Nobel Laureate 1972) in *Social Choice and Individual Values* (1951) proposed the *impossibility theorem*, according to which no decisional procedure exists such as to satisfy simultaneously two requirements: first, to guarantee the transitivity of social choices among three or more alternatives (if *A* is preferred to *B* and *B* is preferred to *C*, *A* too is preferred to *C*); second, to satisfy some requirements of democracy expressed in formal terms: for instance, if one of the alternatives goes up in an individual's ranking, while all other individuals' rankings remain unchanged, that alternative cannot go down in ranking for society as

---

[5] Let us recall that increasing returns are incompatible with the assumption of competition. The attempts in recent years to introduce local concavities in production sets correspond to the quest for relatively untried fields of enquiry rather than to a real understanding of the crucial importance of this limit of general equilibrium analysis. For a survey of the results reached in various fields by research on general equilibrium models, cf. Mas-Colell *et al.* (1995).

[6] In a new 1983 edition, the 1947 text was re-proposed without modifications, with the addition of new material at the end. We find there, in the context of an illustration of input-output systems, some references to Sraffa's analysis and to the capital theory criticisms discussed in Chapter 16. The references in Samuelson's book, however, imply a misinterpretation of Sraffa's analysis and a reductive evaluation of the weight of the criticism stemming from it to the marginalist theory of value and distribution. In fact Samuelson, assimilating Sraffa's analysis to Leontief's, interpreted it erroneously as a general equilibrium model within which the assumption of constant returns to scale (explicitly ruled out by Sraffa in his 1960 book) allows for the determination of relative prices without consideration of the demand side. Moreover, as far as the criticism is concerned, Samuelson reduced it (following in this a presentation of the criticism by Joan Robinson, 1953, and thus preceding the publication of Sraffa's book) to a critique of the aggregate notion of capital utilised in aggregate production functions (such as the famous Cobb-Douglas, which constitutes the foundational pillar of Solow's theory of growth, to be discussed in Section 17.3: 'the *simpliste* J.B. Clark parable of a platonic capital stuff', as Samuelson called it, 1947, p. 568 of the 1983 edition): hence a critique considered valid but not applicable to the 'general' marginalist model. Thus the fact that Sraffa's critique concerned not only and not so much the aggregate notion of capital as also and mainly the impossibility of demonstrating the existence in general of an inverse relation between real wage rate and employment remained out of the scene, though such an inverse relationship is essential for the existence of the marginalist equilibrating mechanism leading to full employment (the invisible hand of the market), which, as we shall see in Section 17.3, remained the foundational pillar of mainstream macroeconomics. From here followed a separation between a 'lowbrow theory', which utilises the aggregate supply function, and a 'highbrow theory', the general equilibrium one, endowed with internal consistency but devoid of definite results and within which the simplistic parables obtainable through the aggregate production function are out of place.

a whole. In other words, though relying on complete and transitive individual ordering of preferences, we cannot obtain a complete and transitive social ordering of preferences.[7]

Axiomatic general economic equilibrium theory has been considered by many as the frontier of basic research in the field of economics and as a compulsory reference for any economic enquiry, or in other words as a programme for the reduction of the whole of economic theory to a central core: a precise set of axioms from which, with the addition of further assumptions that may change from case to case, we can deduce a series of theorems constituting a complete representation of economic reality or at least of everything in economic reality that is capable of scientific expression. As a matter of fact, the results of this research (multiplicity of equilibriums, non-demonstrability of stability, impossibility to drop the axioms of convexity of production sets) make it impossible to utilize general equilibrium models directly in the analysis of real-world issues. References to general equilibrium analysis commonly cover recourse to simplified – one-commodity, one-representative-agent – models, by now prevailing in mainstream macroeconomics, or, in other fields of enquiry, recourse to the Marshallian *ceteris paribus* clause opening the way to partial equilibrium analysis. The problem of the contradiction between requirement of realism and requirement of logical consistency thus raises its head once again.

Beginning in the 1970s, research within the general economic equilibrium approach focused on the limits set to the optimal functioning of the market by different circumstances. Thus, the impossibility of fully specifying all aspects of an agreement gave rise to the so-called *principal-agent problem*, that is, the possibility that the person who accepts responsibility for a certain task (the agent) utilises the margins of freedom of action available in his/her own interest rather than in the interest of the person who entrusts him/her with the task (the principal). A vast literature discusses the problem of designing incentive structures such as to induce the agent to adopt the principal's interests as her/his own. Analogous is the case of asymmetric information, i.e. the fact that different agents are endowed with different information sets; this is utilised for instance in explaining the mechanisms of adverse selection by which the bad commodity squeezes the good

---

[7] Notwithstanding Arrow's negative result, the analytical tools of the theory of rational agents' decisions have been utilised to study the behavior of electors, politicians and bureaucrats thus originating the field of enquiry of public choice. The main exponent of this stream is James Buchanan.

commodity out of the market due to the different availability of information between seller and buyer.[8] Quite often, though, these models fall in the category of partial equilibriums due to the simplifications obtained through *ad hoc* assumptions. However, without simplifications it is practically impossible to get meaningful results from the analysis. Thus, interest in general equilibrium theory has drastically declined in recent years.

17.3 Behavioural Paradoxes and Behavioural Economics

Debate on von Neumann and Morgenstern's work mainly concerned the assumption of rationality underlying the system of axioms. In this respect we can distinguish two streams: rationality understood in a descriptive sense, as a characteristic perhaps not perfectly present in all agents but nevertheless endowed with sufficient general validity, so that the theory based on it can contribute to our interpretation of the real world (and the failure to adopt rational behaviour constitutes an imperfection of the agent); and rationality understood as a prescriptive norm, i.e. the behaviour that agents should adopt in order to obtain optimal results.[9]

The two interpretations, the normative and the descriptive one, constitute a useful distinctive element for the various positions present in the subsequent debate, involving psychologists and economists. The distinction is adopted by Savage, after a debate in which he and Friedman were opposed to Allais, Baumol and Samuelson, who supported a descriptive interpretation of the axioms. In this respect, Maurice Allais (1911–2010, Nobel Laureate 1988) found some counterexamples: when submitted to a few persons – high-ranking economists and probability scholars, among them Savage, hence persons one may

---

[8] George Akerlof's (b. 1940, Nobel Laureate 2001; cf. Akerlof 1970) example is that of the used-car market: the buyer is unable to evaluate exactly the conditions of the used car offered for sale, and it is likely that if the price demanded is the average one for a car of that age, the specific car offered for sale is of an inferior quality compared to the average one. The cases to which this theory is applicable are numerous: from selection among loan applications to selection among potential insurance clients and selection among workers for hire.

[9] This dichotomy differs from the one concerning the ambit of positive science and the normative ambit of ethics proposed by Friedman 1953: even in its 'normative' meaning, von Neumann and Morgenstern's theory is 'objective', in the sense that its results automatically stem from the assumptions of the theory without recourse to any value judgment. Like Savage, von Neumann and Morgenstern considered their axioms as at the same time an abstract but realistic representation of human behavior and as a norm for rational decision making. For a history of behavioural economics, cf. Heukelom 2014.

assume to be capable of rational reasoning – their choices were quite often different from those prescribed by the von Neumann-Morgenstern theory.[10] If we interpret expected utility theory as describing the agents' behaviour, then the 'Allais paradox' in itself constitutes destructive criticism of this theory, showing that rational agents violate its postulates. (An analogous critique, aimed at the postulate of independence of individual preference sets, considering not risk aversion but aversion to uncertainty, was proposed by Daniel Ellsberg (b. 1931) in 1961.) According to the normative interpretation, though, violations of the postulates may be interpreted as a deviation of individual agents from the optimal choice path, which remains the one described by the theory.

Such developments intersect with the parallel developments in mathematical and experimental psychology, concerning the two aspects – normative and descriptive – of decision theory. These research fields also received substantial funding, partly connected to military research.[11] In this context, research on decisional processes developed at the University of Michigan, in the Institute for Social Research founded in 1947 and mainly staffed by psychologists, followed in 1949 by the Mathematical Psychology Group, the Mental Health Research Institute in 1955 and the Human Performance Center in 1958. Ward Edwards (1927–2005), stimulated by the von Neumann-Morgenstern work, proposed a fusion of mathematical and experimental psychology, giving rise to the field of *behavioural decision theory* (the title of his influential 1961 article). Expected utility analysis was interpreted as a theory of measurement and as the basis for an understanding of the behaviour of the rational agent when confronted with uncertainty.

According to subjective probability theory, proposed by De Finetti and taken up by Savage, each agent has her/his own evaluation – not necessarily a correct one – of probabilities and outcomes (i.e. of expected utility) of events, and this evaluation determines the agent's choices. Errors in the agent's behaviour consist in violations of her own system of preferences and probabilities and may be attributed to causes such as the scarcity of time, decision taken under stress and the like. A different problem, specifically considered by Kahneman and Tversky in the 1970s, concerned the fact that agents systematically make 'wrong' decisions,

---

[10] For an account of Allais's experiments, conducted by mail (with Savage and others) or at the occasion of international conferences such as the one held in Paris in May 1952, cf. Heukelom 2014, pp. 44 ff. For an illustration, cf. Allais 1953.

[11] Mirowski 2002 and Heukelom 2014 provide various examples in this respect.

differing from those considered optimal by decision theory, as a consequence of their incapacity for rational reasoning.

Amos Tversky's (1937–1996) work at the end of the 1960s focused on verification of the transitivity axiom, a necessary condition for the existence of an ordinal scale of utility. Of course, each violation of the axiom may be attributed to a change in the agent's preferences; however, when this justification becomes recurrent, it must be considered *ad hoc*. Daniel Kahneman (b. 1934, Nobel Laureate 2002), on the other hand, studied how agents deviate from the rational norm of behaviour and was convinced that human beings often commit cognitive errors. The issue thus became how to simplify and reorganize the decisional problem so that even an unsophisticated agent would be able to tackle and solve it. Collaboration between Kahneman and Tversky began along this line of research at the end of the 1960s, leading to what is known as *prospect theory*.[12] This theory took as reference an S-shaped utility curve, defined by considering the distance from the *status quo*: due to risk aversion, the loss (disutility) corresponding to a negative deviation from the status quo is greater than the gain (utility) stemming from a positive deviation of equal magnitude. Kahneman and Tversky concluded that expected utility theory interpreted as a descriptive theory is falsified by this result.

These conclusions opened the way to what may be called *behavioural paternalism*: economic agents are sufficiently but not fully rational; the scientist engaged in a human engineering programme, and more specifically in efforts to improve their decisional processes, is better able to locate the optimal choices and to point them out to the agents.[13]

Kahneman and Tversky's theory differed from the mainstream less than the theory developed by Herbert Simon (1916–2001), who stressed the distance between the mainstream notion of rationality and the agents' actual behaviour. Simon (1957, 1979) proposed the notion of *bounded rationality*, abandoning the assumptions of a predefined set of alternative actions among which to choose, of knowledge of the outcomes of the different actions and of a given utility function to be maximised. Confronted with a multiplicity of objectives, it is reasonable to adopt a *satisficing behaviour*, aiming at reaching an acceptable result for each of

---

[12] Cf. for instance Kahneman and Tversky 1979.
[13] Experimental economics as originated by Vernon Smith (b. 1927, Nobel Laureate in 2002) mainly concerns the behavior of the markets, which according to Smith function well, in the sense that they show convergence to what mainstream theory indicates. The techniques of experimental economics, widely utilised in the past couple of decades, may in any case be utilised regardless of Vernon Smith's free market views.

the different objectives, rather than maximising a function that embodies all of them, adequately weighted.

Relative to the notion of rationality we then have a series of specifications. The first, already implicit in von Neumann-Morgenstern's work and in the subsequent debate, concerns the distinction between rationality understood as internal consistency of the system of choices, or as systematic pursuit of self-interest on the part of the agent. We then have the distinction between *substantive rationality*, understood as the pursuit of a personal interest defined in an objective way, i.e. independently of the individual's own choices, and *instrumental rationality*, when the agent pursues a target however it is chosen; on many counts this distinction is connected to, but does not coincide with, the first one. Within a new field of research, *neuroeconomics*, some authors suggested the need to consider as distinct fields of thinking the short and the long period, the latter being more rational-dominated, the former more sentiment-dominated (McClure *et al.* 2004). Both neuroeconomics, and the bioeconomics that preceded it, rely in their analyses of the agents' behaviour on the assumption of rational behaviour, considered as the result of a natural process of evolutionary selection (cf. for instance Vromen 2007).

Another recent stream of research aims to extend the von Neumann-Morgenstern utility functions to include in them aspects such as the importance for the agent of identities (sex, religion, nationality and so on): the choices implying adhesion to or refusal of the identity entail positive or negative effects both for the agent concerned and (externalities) for other agents (Akerlof and Kranton 2000). Multiple equilibriums may derive from this, depending on the values of the parameters. The assumption that the outcomes of the choices may be measured on a one-dimensional scale remains in any case essential, since it allows for addition to or subtraction from the utility directly expected from the act of choice the utility indirectly stemming from the strengthening or weakening of the identity: precisely the assumption that, as we saw in Chapter 8, John Stuart Mill criticised with respect to Bentham's utilitarianism.

Finally, in the most recent stage, a series of interdisciplinary research, with the collaboration of anthropologists, psychologists and economists, tend to render endogenous the formation of preferences (see the important work by Henrich *et al.*, *Foundations of Human Sociality*, 2004). This research implies superseding the original von Neumann-Morgenstern approach; hence the tendency to exclude it from the field of economics, or at least from the field of mainstream economics.

17.4   The 'Lowbrow Theory': Macroeconomics and Growth Theory

General economic equilibrium and expected utility theories were taken up by mainstream US economic culture as reference as far as pure theory was concerned. However, various problems remained open, and in particular questions regarding the analytical background for the formulation of policy strategies: macroeconomics, monetary theory, public finance.

In these fields, the Great Depression of the 1930s and the diffusion in that context of Keynesian-type policies of income and employment support gave rise to a dilemma: on the one hand, the pure theory of competitive equilibrium implies full employment of productive resources, labour included; on the other hand, actual experience brought forcibly to attention the issue of unemployment as a possible or, better, all too probable prospect. How could mainstream economists reconcile these two things?

As Sraffa (1930, p. 93) had suggested in a different context, when theory and reality clash, we can forego neither realism nor internal consistency in the theory: we should, rather, abandon the (neoclassical or marginalist) approach that had led to such an irresolvable conflict.

However, the US mainstream followed different paths, such as a dichotomy between long and short periods. In the long period and under competitive conditions the pure theory would retain full validity, including the full employment thesis.[14] In the short period, on the other hand, the adjustment processes leading to equilibrium may be assumed not to be able to exercise their full effects, so that a situation of unemployment would be possible;[15] in this context Keynesian policies may help insofar as they accelerate convergence to the equilibrium position. Alternatively, assumptions other than free competition were adopted, in particular concerning the labour market, where the presence of trade unions may impede reduction in real wages towards the equilibrium value notwithstanding the presence of unemployment.[16]

---

[14] As a matter of fact, the abstract theory to which reference is made is not the pure theory of general economic equilibrium, but a simplified version of it with only one commodity and one representative agent, utilised in order to maintain the thesis of existence and stability of a full employment equilibrium.

[15] Among the instances of this line of research we may include instances of mismatch between the qualities of labour demanded and supplied (too many philosophers, too few plumbers) that cannot be overcome in the short period.

[16] This second road coincides with the first one if we assume that the trade unions are able to impede the reduction in real wages only for a limited time span.

Both roads allowed for separation between micro- and macroeconomics: the realm of pure theory from a dusty but more realistic field of research, or in other words the optimal realm of perfect competition from the actual world of market imperfections. In any case, in the field of macroeconomics, too, theorising was to rely on the requirement of equilibrium between supply and demand in simplified general equilibrium models describing the working of interrelated markets.

Thus, in a 1937 article John Hicks (1904–1989, Nobel Laureate 1972) proposed the so-called IS-LL scheme, which translated Keynes's theory into the more traditional terms of a simplified general economic equilibrium model, with the presence of three markets: for goods, money and bonds (though the latter plays only a purely passive role). The goods market is in equilibrium when supply, i.e. production, is equal to aggregate demand (which, under the simplifying assumption of a closed economy with no government expenditure and no taxes, corresponds to demand for consumption and investment goods). This happens when savings, which are an increasing function of income, are equal to investments, which are considered a decreasing function of the rate of interest. The money market is in equilibrium when the supply of money (determined by the monetary authorities) is equal to the demand of money (for transactions, which is an increasing function of income, and speculative demand, considered a decreasing function of the rate of interest). In this model, commonly utilised for illustrating fiscal and monetary policies in support of employment, the traditional adjustment mechanism leading to full employment does not come into play because, quite simply, the labour market is not considered.

In two articles dated 1944 and 1963, Franco Modigliani (1918–2003, born in Italy, eventually emigrating to the United States to escape racial persecution, Nobel Laureate 1985) extended the IS-LL scheme to consider the labour market, too. In it, changes in the wage rate bring labour demand and supply into equilibrium, thus ensuring full employment. The 'Keynesian' (persistent unemployment) result is then arrived at by introducing some obstacles hindering the free operation of the labour market, connected to the trade unions' bargaining power, which determines the downward rigidity of wages. In this way, Keynesian theory is presented as a particular case of marginalist theory: the case in which full employment equilibrium cannot be reached, because the labour market is not a competitive market. We thus have the *neoclassical synthesis*, a synthesis between the neoclassical theory of value and Keynes's theory of employment, which for decades dominated macroeconomics teaching all over the world.

Whenever the trade unions are able to exert some market power, public intervention aiming at reducing unemployment can lead to an increase in the rate of growth in money wage rates, which in turn generates an increase of inflation. The trade-off between unemployment and rate of inflation, known as the Phillips curve (Phillips 1958), represents, according to neoclassical synthesis economists, the set of possible economic policy choices.

There are some variants of the neoclassical synthesis. The first was originated by Robert Clower (1926–2011) and Axel Leijonhufvud (b. 1933), who interpreted Keynes's as a disequilibrium theory, whose microfoundations are to be found not in the Walrasian approach but rather in the Marshallian and Wicksellian ones, taking into account the problems of information diffusion and intertemporal coordination of real economies.[17]

The second line of research is the so-called new Keynesian economics. Joseph Stiglitz (b. 1943, Nobel Laureate 2001) and others tried to locate the origin of unemployment in different kinds of market failures, related to the lack of certain elements that should characterise a perfectly competitive state. We thus have models based on *menu costs* (costs of adjusting prices that induce firms to adjust to changes in demand through changes in levels of production and hence of employment rather than through prices), *insider-outsider* models (in which those already employed enjoy a margin of market power that they use to get higher wages at the expense of higher employment levels), *efficiency wages* models (in which firms prefer to avoid reductions in money wages in order to retain experienced workers, presumably more efficient than potential new employees) – and the list might go on. Unemployment is thus explained through *ad hoc* assumptions of quite dubious generality, on the sandy theoretical foundations of one-commodity, one-representative agent models and/or partial equilibrium models with their inverse relationship between real wages and unemployment (a relationship that, as recalled previously, cannot be deduced from a general equilibrium model and that was the object of destructive criticism on the part of Sraffa and others).

The third line of research concerned extension of the neoclassical synthesis to the field of monetary theory. James Tobin (1918–2002,

---

[17] Cf. Clower 1965, Leijonhufvud 1968. However, the models by Barro and Grossman (1971) and Malinvaud (1977) were formulated in Walrasian terms, with prices and money wages fixed and transactions taking place at disequilibrium prices, bringing about rationing of either demand or supply, and hence a 'classical' unemployment provoked by downward wage rigidity or a 'Keynesian' unemployment provoked by insufficient effective demand.

Nobel Laureate 1981) explained demand for money as a portfolio choice on the part of a rational economic agent in the presence of risk. Modigliani and Miller (1958) showed that, under conditions of perfect competition and absence of uncertainty, the different sources of finance (bank loans, issue of new shares or bonds, profits not distributed to the shareholders) are equivalent for the firms.[18]

Among those who showed faith in the equilibrating powers of the market and hostility to state intervention in the economy, and thus to Keynesian theories and policies even in the watered-down version of the neoclassical synthesis, the Chicago or monetarist school was prominent. Milton Friedman (1912–2006, Nobel Laureate 1976), the recognised leader of this school, took on and developed the theses of the old quantity theory: in the long if not in the short run, the equilibrium level of income depends on 'real' factors such as resource endowments, technology and preferences of economic agents; the velocity of circulation of money is considered a stable function of the rates of return of various kinds of assets (money, bonds, goods, human capital).[19] Friedman maintained that the money supply can influence income and employment only in the short run; in the long run it influences the general price level: the Phillips curve, negatively sloped in the short period, becomes vertical in the long period.[20]

Moreover, Friedman criticised monetary and fiscal policy measures, not only because their efficacy is limited to the short period, but also because the short period effects are uncertain and may well be negative. Indeed, economic policy measures are subject to three kinds of lags and uncertainties, arising over: evaluation of the situation in which to intervene; transition from such evaluation to choice of policy measures and their application; and, finally, the very impact of the policy adopted.

A still more extreme thesis was proposed by *rational expectations* theoreticians. In a 1972 article, Robert Lucas (b. 1937, Nobel Laureate 1995) combined the assumption of markets in continuous equilibrium with that of rational expectations, originally formulated by Muth (1961, p. 194), according to which 'expectations ... are essentially the same as

---

[18] This line of research also includes Fama's (1970) thesis holding that with efficient capital markets the prices of financial assets correspond to the equilibrium values determined by the 'real' factors of the economy and the CAPM (capital asset pricing models), which has dominated the theory of finance over the past few decades. This line of research yielded a few Nobel prizes: apart from Modigliani and Tobin, the other Nobel laureates were Harry Markowitz (b. 1927), Merton Miller (1923–2000) and William Sharpe (b. 1934) in 1990 and Robert Merton (b. 1944) in 1997. However, the outcomes of the 2007–8 financial crisis should suggest greater caution in this respect.

[19] Cf. in particular Friedman 1956.   [20] Cf. Friedman 1968; Phelps 1967.

the predictions of the relevant economic theory', so that economic agents learn to take account of public intervention in the economy, discounting its effects beforehand. Thus, for instance, deficit public expenditure, which is not financed by a simultaneous increase in taxation, adopted to stimulate aggregate demand, is counterbalanced by a reduction in private consumption resulting from the decision to put aside savings to pay the taxes that will sooner or later have to be introduced to pay the public debt with which public expenditure is financed. In this context, the Phillips curve proves vertical also in the short run: expansionary monetary and fiscal policy interventions can only produce an increase in the rate of inflation, not in the level of employment.[21] Only policy measures unforeseen by economic agents (policy shocks) may have an impact, albeit temporary, on the real variables.

The only kind of economic policy admitted by rational expectations theoreticians is policy designed to reduce the natural rate of unemployment, i.e. the rate of unemployment corresponding to equilibrium in the presence of frictions in the working of the market that cause some unemployment. We thus have the so-called *supply-side policies*, consisting, for instance, in facilitating worker mobility from one job to another or ensuring that the qualifications with which the labour force is endowed correspond to the economic system's requirements or reducing fiscal pressure, since increase in income net of taxes is accompanied, in equilibrium, by an increase in the amount of sacrifice (namely, productive effort) that economic agents are ready to make, and hence by an increase in accumulation and growth.

The neoclassical synthesis also embraces a theory of growth. The history of these developments began with a 1939 article in which Roy Harrod (1900–1978) used Keynes's approach to define the *warranted rate of growth*, which corresponds to continuous equality between growth rate of productive capacity and growth rate of aggregate demand. Harrod's model is based on three equations: the first defines savings as a function of income, the second follows accelerator theory in setting investments equal to the product between change in income and capital-output ratio, and the third expresses the Keynesian condition of

---

[21] This theory presupposes that all economic agents share the same model of the way the economy functions: the neoclassical one-commodity model, in which an inverse relationship between real wage rate and employment holds, so that, under competitive conditions, a stable full employment equilibrium is obtained. In a multi-commodity model, the uniqueness and stability of such an equilibrium cannot be proved. The rational expectations assumption applied to a model of this kind would thus give quite different results – in fact, everything becomes possible, and Keynesian uncertainty once again becomes relevant.

equilibrium between aggregate supply and demand as equality between savings and investments. Substitution in the third equation of the expressions for savings and investments defined by the first two equations makes the 'warranted' rate of growth equal to the ratio between propensity to save and capital-output ratio.

Harrod, moreover, stressed the instability of the actual growth rate as soon as it diverges from the warranted rate: the knife-edge problem, as it came to be called. Whenever actual growth is higher than warranted growth, productive capacity lags behind. This implies an increase in investments, hence in aggregate demand, in the following period, which generates new increases in the growth rate. Conversely, if the actual growth is lower than that corresponding to the warranted rate, investments will be reduced and the consequent decrease in aggregate demand will bring about a further slowing down of growth.

An increase in unemployment may take place when the actual growth rate corresponds to the warranted one, but the latter is lower than the natural rate of growth, equal to the rate of growth of productivity plus the rate of population growth. Different mechanisms were then proposed in support of a tendency of the two growth rates to converge. According to the Malthusian approach, adjustment takes place through the growth rate of the population, which falls when increasing unemployment brings down the wage rate. According to Kaldor (1956), when unemployment grows, the wage falls, and since the workers' propensity to save is lower than the capitalists', the average propensity to save increases, corresponding to an increase in the warranted growth rate. Finally, according to the neoclassical approach developed by Robert Solow (b. 1924, Nobel Laureate 1987), the fall in wages brought about by increasing unemployment leads firms to adopt production techniques that use relatively more labour; thus the capital-output ratio falls; once again, this corresponds to an increase in the warranted growth rate.

These equilibrating mechanisms are not, however, without defects. For instance, it is dubious whether in present-day conditions population growth depends on the wage level, according to an inverse relation, as required by the Malthusian approach. The Kaldorian theory requires that increase in unemployment provoke a change in distributive shares in favour of profits, while in general during a crisis or a depression profits may well decrease more than wages. Finally, Sraffa's 1960 critique and the ensuing debate showed that the capital-labour ratio cannot be considered as an increasing function of the wage. We thus return to Harrod's original thesis, a typically Keynesian one: growth in a capitalistic economy is intrinsically unstable, and full employment is far from being guaranteed by automatic market adjustment mechanisms.

Solow's theory of growth mentioned previously, despite its basic weakness, stimulated various streams of research. Solow (1956) introduced exogenous technical progress into the original model. A rich stream of empirical research followed, seeking to determine the relative contribution of capital, labour and technical progress to economic growth in different countries. Such works identified technical progress with the *residuum*, that is, with that part of income growth that is not justified by increase in labour and capital inputs; this means failing to explain the major component of economic growth. After some attempts at reducing the size of the residuum by including accumulation in *human capital* alongside accumulation in fixed capital, a new stream of research was opened by Romer (1986), connecting technical progress to income growth by introducing increasing returns or learning-by-doing mechanisms.[22] This stream of research has unstable foundations: increasing returns are incompatible with competitive equilibrium of individual productive units, except for the case of economies of scale external to individual firms but internal to the industry (that is, to the economic system as a whole, in the 'one-commodity world' formalised in endogenous growth models); as Sraffa had already remarked in his 1925 and 1926 articles, this is a very specific case.[23]

In opposition to the reinterpretation of Keynes's theory proposed by the neoclassical synthesis and to the monetarist critiques, there was

---

[22] *Learning-by-doing* phenomena, discussed in Arrow (1962), appear when unit cost of production decreases as experience is acquired, which means in proportion to the cumulated amount of product. These effects should not be confused with the connection between growth of production and technical progress (a dynamic form of increasing returns to scale), which goes under the name of *Verdoorn's law* (cf. Verdoorn 1949); it may be associated with investments in new machinery, generally more efficient than the machinery already in use.

[23] Let us recall here two other lines of research: one, at the boundaries with economic statistics, originated by Simon Kuznetz (1901–1985, Nobel Laureate in 1971), looking for empirical regularities in the process of economic growth; and another, at the boundaries with economic history, originated by Walt Rostow (1916–2003), with his theory of 'stages of economic development' (cf. Rostow 1960). We then have various other research lines, quantifying qualitative variables such as democracy, corruption or the good functioning of public administration or the administration of justice in order to study empirically their relationship with the rate of growth of the different national economies; obviously, the results of these studies depend on the way the qualitative variables under consideration are translated into one-dimensional quantitative variables. Cf. for instance Acemoglu and Robinson 2006, combining empirical analysis of democracy with a theoretical analysis conducted on the lines of the public choice school tradition and utilising aggregate growth theory.

a decided reaction on the part of some post-Keynesians, exponents of the 'new Cambridge school' such as Richard Kahn, Nicholas Kaldor and Joan Robinson (see Chapter 14), together with American economists like Sidney Weintraub (1914–1983), Hyman Minsky (1919–1996) and Jan Kregel (b. 1944), who stress the importance of uncertainty, expectations and their volatility.[24]

Instead of the simultaneous equilibrium of the various markets, post-Keynesian economists proposed a sequence of cause and effect relations: speculative demand for money affects the interest rate; this in turn, together with expectations, affects the level of investments; and in turn investments, through the multiplier, determine income and employment. Thus the influence exercised by monetary and financial markets on income and employment was stressed, in opposition to the thesis of the neutrality of money accepted in the classical and marginalist traditions. Moreover, various post-Keynesian economists maintained that the supply of money is endogenous: that is, the quantity of money (in particular bank money) in circulation is not rigidly controlled by the monetary authorities but depends at least in part on the decisions of other agents.[25]

17.5   The New Theories of the Firm

In the first decades after the end of the Second World War, starting with Samuelson (1948) US economics textbooks adopted as main if not sole reference for theory of the firm the Marshallian theory in the version with U-shaped cost curves proposed by Viner. But other theories were also developed, within and outside of the marginalist tradition.

We owe the first of these theories to Ronald Coase (1910–2013, Nobel Laureate 1991), in an article published in 1937, the importance of which was only recognised much later (the Nobel Prize arrived fifty-four years later). Coase tackled the following problem: while within the market legally independent agents enter into relations with each other, within each firm organisational set-ups prevail based on 'command' – a hierarchy with centralised decision-making and control over their

---

[24] Cf. Harcourt 2006 for an attempt to delineate a unifying theoretical structure for the new Cambridge school, and Marcuzzo 2012 on some of the leading figures of the school.

[25] Minsky (1982) developed on this basis an 'endogenous' theory of financial crises, based on the notion of 'financial fragility'. This theory was utilised by Kindleberger (1978) in his historical investigation; Minsky's theory has also been continuously referred to in interpreting the most recent financial upheavals. Other lines of research within the post-Keynesian framework are the stock-flow analysis developed by Godley and Lavoie (2007) and the monetary circuit proposed by Graziani (2003) and others.

execution; what is it, then, that determines the boundary between these two different forms of organisation of economic life, market and command? In his article Coase stressed that market transactions have a cost for participants: it is necessary to collect information, search for a counter-party ready to trade and negotiate prices and the other conditions. In the absence of the firm, each worker would have to bargain to acquire a variety of inputs – the semi-finished products and raw materials he himself uses, his working tools, engineering services and so on – and then to sell the product, which in general will only be a semi-finished product or part of the final product. The firm drastically reduces the number of necessary transactions with a hierarchical decisional structure to obviate bargaining over all the aspects of the productive process. When the size of the firm grows, its internal organisation becomes increasingly complex and ever less efficient; once a certain point – corresponding to the optimal size of the firm – is passed, the costs of expanding relations based on command become higher than the costs of recourse to exchange, that is, to the market.[26]

Growth in firm size led to another problem: who controls the firms? In a book published in 1932, Adolf Berle (1895–1971) and Gardiner Means (1896–1988) identified in the public company and separation between owners and managers the characteristics of a new form of society, *managerial capitalism*, which substituted *competitive capitalism*, where small firms directly managed by their owners prevailed. With the rise of big firms organised as public companies, ownership is subdivided among many small shareholders; the managers of the firm acquire sufficient autonomy to assume responsibility for all decisions relative not only to the current life of the firms but also to strategic long-period choices.

Managerial capitalism also involved a shift in the firm's objectives: from profit maximisation, corresponding to the interests of the owners of the firms, to sales maximisation, which corresponds more closely to the interests of the firm's managers (Baumol 1959). Obviously, the managers have to consider the risk that they may be replaced if a new group of owners takes over the firm. The 'theory of managerial capitalism' developed by Robin Marris (1964) relied on this constraint.

Another stream of research concerned the market power of large firms. In two books, both published in 1956, Paolo Sylos Labini (1920–2005)

---

[26] Piore and Sabel 1984, on the other hand, maintained the determining influence of the institutional context in favouring the development of a system of large vertically integrated firms over a web of small and average firms.

and Joe Bain (1912–1991) developed a theory of oligopoly, considered as the general case, compared to which pure competition and monopoly constitute two polar extremes. Under oligopoly, the firms present in the market are partially protected from competition of potential entrants by a *barrier to entry*, which is not insurmountable (in which case there would be monopoly, while the case of no barriers at all corresponds to perfect competition). The proportions of such a barrier depend on a series of factors, including the minimal technologically optimal size of the most efficient plant, which requires the new firm to enter the market with a rather sizeable minimum production, which would not be able to find a market outlet at current prices (concentrated oligopoly). Then there is the expenditure on advertising necessary to impose the new trademark on the market (differentiated oligopoly). Defended by these barriers, firms already active in the market may enjoy profits well above the competitive level as well as a certain freedom of action.

According to some Keynesian economists (Josef Steindl, 1952; Alfred Eichner, 1976; Adrian Wood, 1975), firms exploit these margins of freedom and set product prices such as will generate a profit margin sufficient to finance the desired level of investments, since firms prefer to use internal sources of financing (profits not distributed as dividends to shareholders) rather than debt.[27]

Baumol and others (1982) then developed the *contestable markets* theory. Perfectly contestable markets are those for which there is no cost of entry or exit, so that no firm can enjoy extra profits, even temporary ones. Absence of exit costs allows new firms to adopt a hit-and-run strategy: enter the market, appropriate part of the extra profits, and exit before the dominant incumbent firms can adopt counter-measures. Exit costs mainly accrue over fixed capital goods that cannot be re-utilised once the activity for which they had been acquired has been abandoned – the 'sunk costs', as they are called.

The new theory of industrial organization made wide recourse to the mathematical tool of game theory. In the field of the theory of the firm, this approach aims at turning the structure of traditional theory upside down, deriving market forms from the behaviour of the firm rather than constructing a theory for each market form. In this field, as in macroeconomics, game theory provided an alternative to the idea that agents adopt a 'parametric' behaviour, implying choice of strategies assuming as given the behaviour of other agents; this gave way to the

---

[27] The 'Modigliani-Miller theorem' (1958), holding that under conditions of perfect competition and perfect knowledge the different sources of financing are equivalent, is considered inapplicable in the real world.

idea of a 'strategic' attitude, considering the reactions of each agent to the actions of others.[28]

We then have the evolutionary theories, proposed to explain the behaviour of the firm and the industry in the process of technological change. Richard Nelson and Sidney Winter (1982) considered the industry structure as the result not of a process of maximisation of profits or sales but of an evolutionary process. As in biology, recourse is proposed to mathematical stochastic models. The 'genes' of firms – which determine the identity of each of them, transfer from one to the other the main behavioural features and undergo mutations over time – consist of *routines*: standard procedures adopted by the firm in production, marketing, financial management and so on. In a market economy the routines that prevail, and thus determine the dominant features of firms, are the ones that ensure success.

While Coase's theory and the new theory of industrial organization are internal to the marginalist approach, the other theories briefly recalled in this section may, rather, be considered as open to, or more in line with, other approaches: the Classical one in the case of Sylos Labini's oligopoly theory; the Keynesian one for Steindl, Eichner and Wood; or the evolutionary one for Nelson and Winter.

17.6   Econometrics and A-theoretical Empiricism

The idea that economic issues are to be studied by analysing quantitative relations between different variables is old, dating back as far as William Petty's political arithmetic, for instance; although the subsequent centuries saw it superseded by the idea of political economy as a moral science, as maintained by Smith, Marshall and Keynes, it came to the fore once again in recent decades.

Wassily Leontief (1905–1999, Nobel Laureate 1973) developed input-output tables – a representation of the economy through matrixes: each column indicates the means of production utilised in a given sector distinguished by sector of origin; each row indicates the sector-by-sector destination of the product of a given sector (cf. Leontief 1941). Leontief's tables are a tool for empirical analysis, for instance, to study the differences in productive structures of the various countries or technical change. Moreover, statistical information organised in input-output tables has been used within linear programming, under the assumption

---

[28] For illustrations of these developments cf. Tirole 1988 (Jean Tirole (b. 1953) was Nobel Laureate in 2014).

of constant returns to scale in all sectors of the economy, to compute technical production coefficients (that is, the quantity of each means of production required for each unit of product) and thus to compute the quantity of gross output of the different sectors corresponding to a given set of net products. At the theoretical level, the system of determination of gross production levels thus arrived at turns out to be the dual (in the mathematical meaning of the term) of a system of determination of relative prices based on relative difficulties of production of the various commodities.[29]

Another tool of empirical analysis is the system of national accounting, developed by Richard Stone (1913–1991, Nobel Laureate 1984) among others, under the stimulus of Keynesian theory and the macroeconomic categories it used. The national accounting system offers a set of categories, defined in such a way as to be susceptible to precise statistical computation and to accord with the principles of double entry bookkeeping, which represent the working of the economic system as a web of flows of goods and money connecting different groups of economic agents. Initiated by the United Nations and placed under the direction of Stone, a system of national accounts (SNA) was devised (for the first time in 1953 and subsequently revised a number of times) to constitute a compulsory reference point for national statistic institutes.

Increasing availability of statistical information, sufficiently reliable and organised in well-defined categories, favoured development of applied economic research. But developments in statistical theory, and in particular inferential statistics (Savage 1954), also played an important role. These elements (and others including, in particular, advances in information technology) combine to account for the impetuous development of econometrics (from the Greek *metron*, 'measurement'): the science that aims at identifying quantitative relations among economic variables.

Rodolfo Benini (1862–1956), statistician, demographer and economist, was among the first (cf. Benini 1907) to utilise advanced statistical methods such as multiple regressions in economic analysis. Henry Moore (1869–1958) and his pupils (among them Paul Douglas (1892–1976) and Henry Schultz (1893–1938)) worked systematically on statistical estimates of economic relationships.

---

[29] Duality between price and quantity system lay at the centre of the model of homothetic growth proposed by von Neumann (1937), also based on the assumption of constant returns to scale; in addition, it stressed another correspondence – between profit rate and rate of growth.

Ambitious prospects for the newborn econometric science were evoked by Ragnar Frisch (1895–1973, Nobel Laureate in 1969), in his editorial for the first issue of *Econometrica* (Frisch 1933), the organ of the Econometric Society, founded in 1933. According to Frisch, econometrics constitutes the unification of statistics, economic theory and mathematics necessary 'for a real understanding of the quantitative relations in modern economic life'.

Contributions to the development of new econometric techniques came from economists grouped in the Cowles Commission, including Jacob Marshak (1898–1977), Jan Tinbergen (1903–1994, Nobel Laureate 1969), Tjalling Koopmans (1910–1985, Nobel Laureate 1975), Don Patinkin (1922–1997) and Lawrence Klein (1920–2013, Nobel Laureate 1980). Trygve Haavelmo (1911–1999, Nobel Laureate 1989), in an essay published in 1944, proposed estimation of econometric relations within a stochastic context, thus defending the econometric approach against the criticism that Keynes (1973, pp. 295–329) had levelled at the construction of macroeconomic models.

In the United States development of quantitative analysis received a boost through utilisation in support of the war effort during the Second World War, although mainly at the level of operational research, to solve planning problems in transport and suchlike. Modern econometrics, aiming at constructing large econometric models, only emerged in the immediate aftermath of World War II, at the Cowles Commission; the first econometric model of the US economy was devised by Klein. Increasing public intervention in the economy entailed the need to anticipate macroeconomic trends, thus favouring development of the new analytical methods. Cold War political tensions and expectations of a new Great Crisis in market economies when war expenditure dried up created an atmosphere in which the optimistic forecasts of the Cowles Commission economists came to constitute a crucial test for the new analytical techniques, soon to be widely adopted.

Noteworthy, too, were certain developments concerning methods of time series analysis, with the ARMA models (autoregressive moving average: cf. Box and Jenkins 1970), and with the VAR method (vector autoregressive: cf. Sims 1980, 1982), proposed as an alternative to traditional econometrics. The latter had come in for radical criticism; in particular Lucas (1976) had maintained that the structural parameters of macroeconomic models are subject to change when confronted with discretional economic policy measures, so that the models themselves cannot be used to predict the consequences of adopting policy measures. Moreover, econometric enquiries cannot verify (or reject) theories, since verification would simultaneously concern the theory itself and the auxiliary assumptions needed to translate it into an econometric model. Sims, on the other hand, proposed an a-theoretical econometrics, in which the structure of the model is not predetermined: econometric analysis is meant to specify case by case the most suitable model.[30] Thus, the distance between economic theory and econometrics widens, since economic theory seems to be losing the role of prompter of hypotheses to submit to econometric testing.

17.7   Evolutionary Theory and Institutionalism

The research streams extending the mainstream approach to new fields of analysis include a neo-institutionalist approach, which considers property rights and political institutions in general as the outcome of rational processes of choice in the presence of transaction costs (the importance of which had been stressed by Coase in 1937, as we saw previously when illustrating the issue of justifying the existence of a specific institution, the firm), asymmetrical information or 'principal-agent' problems, mentioned previously.

Of the main exponents of this line of research, we may recall Douglass North (1920–2015, Nobel Laureate 1993) and Oliver Williamson (b. 1932, Nobel Laureate 2009). Neo-institutionalism may be considered as yet another case of neoclassical synthesis: the problem of institutions, traditionally tackled with historical-sociological analyses, was brought within the field of the theory of rational behaviour of maximising economic agents, leading to spontaneous processes of self-organisation with outcomes often considered optimal (in the wake of the course steered by various authors including, notably, Hayek in the Austrian school). More generally, both neo-institutionalists and the institutionalists within the original tradition consider institutions as 'the complex of socially learned and shared values, norms, beliefs, meanings, symbols, customs, and standards that delineate the range of expected and accepted behaviour in a particular context' (Nelson 1995, p. 80).[31]

Confronted with static mainstream economic theory focused on the notion of equilibrium between supply and demand, some remnants of the

---

[30] In maintaining this theory, Sims is oblivious of the fact that conceptualisation, underlying the categories utilised for collecting statistical data, constitutes a stage of theorising.

[31] On the borderline between institutionalists and neo-institutionalists, Elinor Olstrom (1933–2012, Nobel Laureate 2009) studied the development of a variety of institutions designed to tackle the issues of sustainable utilisation of natural resources such as water and air, called commons due to their not being the object of private property.

earlier economic culture still present in the US resurfaced: the historical school, Marshall's persistent influence and Veblen's stress on institutions. We thus have two other lines of research taking their places outside the mainstream: evolutionary and institutionalist (the latter not to be confused with the neo-institutionalist stream discussed previously). In many ways these two lines of research are interconnected, so much so, indeed, as to be taken as inclusive the one of the other in surveys on their contributions (cf. Nelson 1995 on the evolutionary side and Hodgson 1988, 1998 on the institutionalist side).

The institutionalist school took up Thorstein Veblen's tradition, which enjoyed considerable success in the United States at the beginning of the twentieth century. In the wake of the German historical school, too, study of economic institutions and of the social structure, with even radical differences among countries, was opposed to abstract theory and the 'Ricardian vice', consisting in applying theory without due caution to direct interpretation of reality.[32]

We may also recall John Kenneth Galbraith (1908–2006) here; some of his works, such as *The Affluent Society* (1955) and *The New Industrial State* (1967), have attracted a vast readership. According to Galbraith, the paradigm of perfectly competitive equilibrium is wholly inappropriate for interpreting contemporary economies, the evolution of which is mainly determined by interaction among big players such as government bodies (especially the military), the major corporations and the trade unions. We may recall here the works on capitalism's structural changes, from Berle and Means (1932) on the shift from competitive to managerial capitalism up to Minsky (1993) on the shift from managerial to money-manager capitalism, dominated by finance.

The importance of the institutions was also stressed in works on the borderline between economics and economic history, such as Rosenberg and Birdzell (1986), analysing the differences between the various areas of the world to account for the faster pace of development of the Western

---

[32] Veblen (1899) advanced a passionate critique of the 'affluent society'. The birth of the American Economic Association owed much to Richard Ely (1854–1943), the founder of an institutionalist school at the University of Wisconsin, where John Commons (1862–1945) also taught. American institutionalism was then strengthened by the influx of Austrian and German scholars driven to exile by the Nazi regimes. This gave rise, among other things, to the New School for Social Sciences in New York. The revival of institutionalism in the aftermath of the Second World War led to the birth of new journals: the *Journal of Economic Issues* in 1961, published by the Association for Evolutionary Economics, and the *Journal of Evolutionary Economics* in 1991. Within the institutionalist approach we may also classify the French 'regulation' school (Robert Boyer, Michel Aglietta and others), active around the journal *Revue de la regulation*.

economies. Of the most recent lines in research, we may recall those concerning the 'varieties of capitalism', analysing the different institutional set-ups of the developed countries: the presence or absence of the welfare state, the dominant importance of the banks (Rhine capitalism) or the financial markets (Anglo-Saxon capitalism), greater or lesser flexibility of the labour market, the role of the public sector for the evolution of the productive structure (industrial policies, policies supporting basic and applied research) and so on: a wide range of issues, mostly tackled with recourse to historical-sociological-empirical analyses and avoiding recourse to mainstream theoretical models.[33]

Unlike the institutional approach, the evolutionary one mainly relied on the Marshallian tradition: not the tradition of U-shaped cost curves started by Pigou and Viner that, as we saw, dominates mainstream textbooks but the exoteric tradition aiming at translating the Darwinian evolutionary approach into the economics field, studying dynamical processes – mainly of a stochastic, non-deterministic kind – endowed with mechanisms able to induce systematic selection.[34]

We saw in Section 17.4 the first of these developments, namely Nelson and Winter's theory of the firm based on routines. Analyses of technological change then extended from the firm to the economy as a whole, with the notion of the 'technological paradigm' proposed by Dosi (1984; cf. also Dosi et al. 1988): a stage of progressive refinement of a consolidated technology is followed by a stage of radical change induced by an innovation with extensive impact on the whole economy (as in Schumpeter's 'long waves'). Various research in this field utilises the tools of stochastic analysis; other research focuses on the history of technology.

Within the evolutionary approach, the theory of repeated games (assuming the absence of coalitions) was utilised to analyse a notion of rationality more complex than the one adopted within mainstream theory, taking into account the possibility of interacting and evolving strategies, frequently on the basis of experiments in the form of computer tournaments, a tool often used due to the difficulties of

---

[33] See, for instance, the essays collected in Hall and Soskice (2001) and the extensive bibliography cited there.

[34] Nelson (1995, p. 54) stressed that such mechanisms may belong to Lamarkian evolutionary theory, where acquired characteristics can be inherited, more than to Darwinian evolutionary theory. As a matter of fact, the 'minimal concept' of a Darwinian population, constituting an object suitable for evolutionary analysis, 'features three ingredients: ... variations in individual character, which affects reproductive output, and which is heritable' (Godfrey-Smith 2009, p. 6). The majority of research presented as belonging to the evolutionary field does not satisfy these minimal requirements.

solving problems with more than two players mathematically.[35] In these tournaments each player is represented by a computer program, which may be equal to or different from those chosen by the other players; the computer then makes the different players interact according to the predetermined rules of the game. In a case that soon became a classic (Axelrod 1984), the players met in a series of direct encounters; as in the famous 'prisoner's dilemma', the choice not to cooperate gives a higher pay-off than cooperation, whatever the choice of the other player may be; but if both players decide not to cooperate, the result is worse than if both decide to cooperate. In the case of a non-repeated game, the equilibrium solution is the choice not to cooperate. In the case of repeated games, on the other hand, if each player recalls how the other behaved in previous encounters, cooperation may emerge. Indeed, the tournament experiments studied by Axelrod showed that in the spectrum between altruism and asocial selfishness the mechanism of economic (and social, in general) interactions rewards an intermediate position, the so-called 'tit for tat' strategy, in which the agent is ready to cooperate but reacts negatively to those who respond with non-cooperative behaviour, although ready to pardon anyone who returns to cooperation.

Like game theory, the mathematical technique of stochastic processes has also been used in the most recent debate both within the mainstream approach (for instance, in macroeconomics in real cycle models) and within heterodox approaches, in particular in pursuing evolutionary research lines. In the latter case, the outcome depends on the path randomly adopted (a case of 'path dependence'). In the now famous example of the typewriter (David 1985) as in Brian Arthur's theoretical contributions (cf. Arthur 1994), learning by doing or increasing returns to scale – that is, essentially, the presence of cumulative phenomena in the process of economic development – generate outcomes that depend on historical, even random, vicissitudes. A technique that for any reason is chosen more often than another in an initial stage – for instance, one keyboard arrangement rather than another or gasoline motors for cars rather than electric motors – is progressively favoured over the rival

---

[35] Within the traditional approach there were also various developments, such as use of the notion of *reputation* within the theory of industrial organisation and for some macroeconomic issues: if non-cooperative behaviour may be punished, but punishment has an immediate cost higher than pardon also for those who administer it, punishment may nonetheless be chosen systematically within a repeated game, since the reputation of non-acquiescence thus acquired will induce others into cooperation.

technique, up to the point at which 'lock-in' intervenes, i.e. the practical impossibility of changing the technological paradigm: a minimum initial advantage becomes insurmountable because of the presence of cumulative effects.

This type of phenomena, utilised in the field of research into technological change, also gave rise to what is known as the *new economic geography* (Krugman 1990), which aims to explain spatial concentration of specific productive activities. In substance, an initial random distribution of firms over the territory may evolve over time, driven by cumulative mechanisms due to increasing returns of localisation present in different productive sectors; the result is a progressive differentiation of the productive structure of different countries and regions, hence specialisation in the flows of international trade, with 'lock-in' phenomena in the geographical division of labour.

In all these cases, we are confronted with stochastic processes of a non-ergodic kind, in which it is not possible to invert the arrow of time, as can however be done in the case of ergodic processes. This distinction is used by Davidson (1994) in the context of the macroeconomic debate to distinguish the role played by time within the post-Keynesian approach and within mainstream theory.

Chaos theory, too, has been used both within mainstream theories and in support of evolutionary approaches that attribute a central role to uncertainty and history.[36] Chaos theories consider the temporal pattern of the variables under consideration extremely sensitive to the initial conditions: even a slight difference in such conditions brings out totally different patterns (according to a famous example, the flutter of a butterfly's wing in Peking may provoke a storm in New York). In the macroeconomic field, use of the mathematical tools of chaos shows how easy it is to obtain non-regular cyclical patterns in the economy. However, this analytical tool, whilst it allows us to criticise results previously arrived at on the basis of models consisting of linear equations, has not been greatly utilised to formulate positive explanations of production, prices and other phenomena.[37]

---

[36] Chaos theory is, in essence, a mathematical theory in which the pattern followed by a variable (or by a set of variables) is determined by non-linear differential equations. This theory has been applied to different research fields within the natural sciences, such as meteorology (which saw the birth of the theory of fractals, a fascinating theory for the beauty of the geometrical objects it produces, in which the dimensions of space vary continuously rather than by whole numbers: as yet a theory little applied to economic issues but which might prove useful, for instance, in criticising deterministic theories in macroeconomics).

[37] See, however, Goodwin 1990.

17.8   Economics and Ethics

Enquiry into the relation between economics and ethics is connected to the debate on rationality and the objectives of human action, drawing on the old debate between consequentialist and deontological ethics illustrated in Chapters 6 and 8. Consequentialism as a moral criterion would be very easy to apply if the utilities stemming from the different actions were computable in a univocal way, at least in principle; however, as John Stuart Mill stressed in his criticism of Bentham's views, this is not the case. This led to renewed interest in deontological ethics, especially with Rawls (1971).[38] The new consequentialism developing between the end of the 1970s and the beginning of the 1980s also broke any rigid connection with utilitarianism: see, for instance, Sen's contributions (1984, 2009), based on the distinction between rights, functions and capabilities. With the notion of capabilities in particular, Sen stressed that humans' needs differ, so that an equalitarian distribution of resources may not correspond – in general, indeed, does not correspond – to a criterion of justice: a handicapped person needs a greater income, and specific norms, in order to reduce his/her disadvantage compared with others. Thus, a richer and more complex view than that inherited from the neoclassical tradition entered the scene.

A similar line was followed in criticising the identification of economic development with simple quantitative growth of national income, implying the risk of ignoring the multiplicity of aspects that concur in determining the quality of life, in particular environmental aspects,[39] and of leaving out the relation between economic growth and civic development, which we will briefly consider later.

These aspects should not be confused with the debate on the limits to growth, which had greater resonance but also less substance. Malthus's conservative pessimism resurfaced in many writings over time, from Jevons's (1865) essay on coal to research on *The Limits to Growth*

---

[38] Rawls also originated a new development within welfare economics with his thesis on justice, according to which an equitable distribution of resources is that which would enjoy the consensus of all the agents involved before knowing which position each would occupy in it. On economics and ethics, cf. also Sen 2009.

[39] Critiques of 'growthmania' (cf. for instance Mishan 1967; Fuà 1993) revived attention to the different elements that comprise economic and social development. Thus indicators such as life expectancy at birth, infant mortality, education, income inequalities, political democracy and territorial disequilibria (which, in the context of the global economy, take the form of the terrible disequilibria between the North and the South of the world) acquire importance. Analyses of such indicators constitute a field of research in rapid development, beginning with the human development index constructed on the basis of Sen's theories by Ul Haq at Unctad and presented in an annual series of *Human Development Reports*.

prompted by the Club of Rome (Meadows *et al*. 1972), progressively acquiring greater attention for ecological issues. However, ecology within the classical tradition (environmental issues were already present in John Stuart Mill's *Principles* (1848)) has little to do with the fears, typical of the marginalist approach, of the limits to development set by impending exhaustion of natural resources. Rather, the problem concerns the set of interrelations between economic activity and the natural environment. The notion of *sustainable development* (Brundtland 1987) proposed a multi-dimensional view of economic growth, focusing attention on changes in technology and consumption patterns driven by policy interventions. Conversely, the theses on the limits to growth, in the context of a world economy characterised by dramatic problems of poverty and underdevelopment, have in some instances represented a conservative stance, analogous to that represented in other respects by the thesis concerning the alleged existence of an inverse relationship between rate of growth of the economy and some measure of equality in income distribution or, even worse, development of democracy and political freedoms.

Debate on these issues has followed different streams. In investigations into the dualism between the developed and developing countries, after a plethora of writings had maintained the most diverse theses, it clearly appears that neither inequalities in income distribution nor authoritarian political systems constitute prerequisites for sustained economic growth; on the contrary, we can maintain that progress in conditions of civic life (education, hygienic-sanitary conditions, morality and efficiency in public administration, law and order and the correct administration of justice, and on to the active involvement of citizens in political life in a context of democratic freedoms) constitutes a fundamental prerequisite for a socially sustainable development process.

Finally, we come to the stream of research on globalisation. Progress in information transmission associated with development in telecommunications and information technology, falling transportation costs, growing integration of financial markets in a single world market and large and increasing migration flows all lead to more direct ties between each country and the rest of the world. In this situation, the competition of economies with low labour costs exerts growing pressure on workers in the developed countries, especially the less skilled ones; the same holds for the competition between different fiscal or environmental regulatory systems.

The religious, political and social tensions that led to the collapse of State structures in various countries brought about epic migration flows, calling for policy responses able to integrate economic considerations with social, political and ethical elements. This is a challenge that appears to find economic culture unprepared, as it also appeared when confronted with the world financial and economic crisis of the past decade and even more so when confronted with the crisis of the euro area. Given this state of affairs, reflection on the basic characteristics of the different streams of economic research, and their alternating vicissitudes in our cultural history, is an ethical priority.

A Guide to the Literature

When, about fifty years ago, I asked Sylos Labini to be my thesis super-visor on a rather technical aspect (fixed capital) of Sraffa's then recent 1960 book, the first and unexpected advice I received was to read ('wholly, and with care') Smith's *Wealth of Nations*, Ricardo's *Principles* and Marx's *Capital* ('in particular Book Two'). As Sylos explained me, it would have been impossible for me to understand Sraffa's book without first studying what was behind it.

Immediately after graduating I went to Cambridge to study under Sraffa's supervision, and he asked me how Sylos's first-year economics lecture course was organised. It began with the neoclassical theory of the firm and employment and then the critiques (Sraffa's of the Marshallian U-shaped cost curves and Sylos's concerning the static character of the marginalist approach and its subjectivism) to conclude with Sylos's oligopoly theory and Keynes's theory of employment. 'First he corrupts the students, then he redeems them!', Sraffa commented; Sraffa too, however, had his students study in depth at least one of the great authors of the marginalist tradition. To me, he suggested Marshall's *Principles*.

These have proved very useful suggestions, and I gladly pass them on: both in their generic sense – in order to understand a theory we need study its cultural roots – and in their specific content – to begin with the giants of the history of economic thought. I can also confirm that the classical authors cannot be read in a hurry: we need patience, especially if we want to avoid reading the classics with the convenient but misleading lenses of contemporary theory. This means not only that we should try to consider the perspective of the author we are reading but also that some collateral reading is needed: economic history, history of culture, maybe a biography, some interpretative writings. On the basis of my own experi-ence, a good general rule is to devote at least twice as much time to these collateral readings as to perusal of the original text.

At that time, in Cambridge, I read Keynes's *General Theory* together with my friend Mario Tonveronachi. We found it very difficult. Mario worked ten years on his own interpretation (Tonveronachi 1983): what Keynes really aimed at was to demonstrate not only and not so much the instability of capitalism but especially, in that book, the possibility of equilibriums characterized by underutilization of available productive capacity and involuntary unemployment. Together with Mario's book (and the discussions with him), in the course of the years I have been helped in my understanding of Keynes by discussions with Jan Kregel and by his writings, in particular Kregel 1976, as well as study of Keynes's theory of probability (Roncaglia 2009a).

Thinking it over today, I believe I understand why Sylos and Sraffa did not suggest their students should read the *General Theory* (indeed Sraffa, who had a very high opinion of Keynes, gave the impression that he disliked it). The point is that, while my two masters tried in the first place to clarify the basic difference between the classical and marginalist traditions, Keynes presented his radically innovative contribution as belonging to the Marshallian tradition: a ploy to ease its acceptance (Keynes was mainly interested in policy choices to tackle unemployment, at the time a pressing issue, also for political reasons – to keep at bay Communism, Fascism and Nazism) but a risky strategy, since it opened the way to compromise with and assimilation into the marginalist tradition, as indeed happened with the neoclassical synthesis, with the result that Keynes's contribution was also sterilised in its policy implications. Keynes certainly needs to be studied with care but also with caution; in order to understand his viewpoint, it is useful to bear this strategy of his in mind as well as read some general introduction to his personality and thinking (such as Skidelsky 2010) and some of his contributions to the debate on his theory, for instance, Keynes 1937.

I realise that these few indications may have already exhausted the time available to the non-specialist reader, mainly interested in a better understanding of some issues but unwilling to devote the whole of her/his life to economics and the history of economic thought. Also, the reader may be led by curiosity and interests different from my own, and of course we are all happier reading what for one reason or another we find more interesting. I can say that Sraffa was glad to supervise my work on Torrens (1821) and was also glad when I decided to get down to serious study of Petty, whom I later discovered to be one of his favourite authors; but he never forced my reading choices – or if he did, it was done in such a subtle way that I did not realize it. In any case, I believe that every reader will make a better choice of any additional reading left to his/her own devices. In what follows, I will only indicate some possible reading paths, following the order of the chapters in this book.

On matters of method, there are many possible reading paths. One, perhaps having little to do with economics, at least directly, consists of comparing Smith's essay on the history of astronomy (in Smith 1795) with Kuhn's 1962 book on scientific revolutions. According to Schumpeter – who did not like Smith – that text is the best of the writings by the Scottish economist (Schumpeter 1954, p. 221); it would be interesting to verify, among Kuhn's papers, whether Schumpeter had any role in Kuhn's choice of the case to focus attention on, namely the shift from the Ptolemaic to the Copernican system: a theme suggested by Smith and which Schumpeter (1954, p. 389 n.) re-proposed.

The millennia preceding the naissance of political economy obviously constitute a vast territory. An interesting exercise might be to look up, in the Bible and other writings, the passages in which human labour is considered in its positive and negative aspects. Towards the end of this period, the text I like most is Serra 1613: wide-ranging in the wealth of themes it took up, a concise, difficult and stimulating text, not least because of the different connotations the concepts have since acquired.

William Petty is a strong personality, but his writings on economic issues are generally occasional, often pointing in different directions. It is not easy to infer a theoretical structure from them (as I tried to, Roncaglia 1977); one way to get an idea of the kind of work necessary to reconstruct the conceptual foundations of an author so distant in time would be to read the few pages of the *Dialogue of Diamonds* (in Petty 1899, pp. 624–30) and compare them with my interpretation, presented in summary in Section 3.4 or more fully in Roncaglia 1977, pp. 73–6 of the English translation.

Another striking personality who led an eventful life is Richard Cantillon. Together with his *Essay* (1755) it is worth reading Murphy's (1986) biography. A lively text offering much food for thought is Galiani 1770, opposing the spirit of system characterizing the physiocratic school. Then there are the writings of Locke, Mandeville, Quesnay or Turgot: in these as in other cases, my preferences (here, for Mandeville) cannot be taken to represent an objective ordering of importance.

Adam Smith is possibly the most outstanding of the authors discussed in this book, not only as an economist (Smith 1776) but also as a philosopher (Smith 1759). We can find pearls of wisdom in all his writings, still fresh today. The only advice I can give is to read as much of his writings as possible and take all the time they need. The volumes of the critical edition cited in the bibliography, with very good introductions also worth reading, are available in a paperback edition, at very low prices, in an anastatic Liberty Press reprint: in any library they would constitute a text to be consulted over the years and even from generation to generation.

Malthus's *Essay on Population* (1798) is better read in the first edition, shorter and livelier, than in the subsequent editions, where the many examples are suggestive but the digressions tend to obscure the main thesis. An interesting exercise could be to look into the writings of early nineteenth-century authors for the pages devoted to the possibility or impossibility of general over-production crises.

As far as Ricardo is concerned, the 1815 *Essay on Corn* and the 1817 *Principles* are compulsory reading (now in Ricardo, 1951–55, respectively in vol. 4, pp. 1–41, and in vol. 1), together with Sraffa's (1951) introduction – an absolute masterwork in the history of economic thought.

Economic debate was particularly lively in the first three decades of the nineteenth century. Torrens (1821) is very good for getting the flavour of the debate at the time on the theory of value. A persistent theme, already present in the Utopian literature (More 1516; Campanella 1602) but receiving concrete treatment only in this period and subsequently, concerns reduction in the length of the working day, possible in an egalitarian society; as far as I know, no history of this issue has been written; in pursuing it, one might well start with Patrick Colquhoun (1814) and Marx's son-in-law, Paul Lafargue (1880). Charles Babbage (1832) cannot be considered an interesting author for those focusing on the theory of value, but he is important for his dynamic analysis and the many indications he provided on technological and social change. By John Stuart Mill, rather than the *Principles* (1848) I would suggest the lively essays on liberty and on utilitarianism (Mill 1859, 1861), contributing original ideas still very relevant to present-day debate.

In the years of my university studies we were practically compelled to read all of Marx's major writings and some minor ones, too. Nowadays even reading – admittedly, no easy reading – *Capital* alone is uncommon. Let me recommend at least Book Two, for the plentiful food for thought it offers on a variety of economic issues. For those only interested in getting a quick idea of the development of Marx's thought, I would suggest the *Manifesto* (Marx and Engels 1848), the few pages of the preface to the *Critique of political economy* (Marx 1859), an elementary illustration of the themes discussed in *Capital* (Marx 1865) and, for the transition from capitalism to socialism and then to communism, the few pages of the *Critique of the Gotha programme* (Marx and Engels 1878).

Jevons's 1871 *Principles* are necessary reading for an understanding of the subjective approach. They may be read together with Schabas (1990), a readable biography and at the same time a well-argued interpretation of the thought of the founder of English marginalism.

Menger's *Principles* (1871) are prolix, but the first part, on goods and needs, usefully illustrates the serious conceptual problems hidden beneath the easy mathematics illustrating consumer equilibrium in today's textbooks. Weber (1904–5, 1922) is most certainly an author deserving serious study; however, he remains on the sidelines for today's economists – and this is certainly a pity. Wicksell is a profound theoretician; his *Lectures on Political Economy* (Wicksell, 1901–6) may be considered the best text (at least such was Sraffa's opinion) to get to grips with the theoretical structure of the marginalist approach; as a counter-balance to its logical rigour, one may read Gårdlund's (1956) truly fascinating biography, well illustrating Wicksell's progressive political stance. Hayek is a great polemist; his 1944 essay makes clear his influential viewpoint, shared by many conservative economists.

Walras is a difficult author, very little read in the original. An interesting exercise might be to look first into Walras (1874) and then into Pareto (1906) for the passages devoted to the stability of equilibriums.

Marshall's *Principles* (1890) are a basic but difficult read due to the recurring ambiguity between static equilibrium analysis and evolutionary views; it takes a lot of time, to be done – if you decide to venture on it – by keeping open in front of you the two volumes, text and notes, of the critical (variorum) edition of 1961.

Keynes has already been considered previously. By Schumpeter, the 1934 English version of his *Theory of Economic Development* makes easier reading than the original – far more prolix – 1912 German edition. An interesting and lively text, but, as in the case of Weber's writings, now considered external to the field of economics, is *Capitalism, Socialism, and Democracy* (Schumpeter, 1942).

That slim volume, Sraffa's *Production of Commodities by Means of Commodities* (1960), cannot be read in a hurry: it is necessary to ponder it line by line, with the help of the classics, particularly Ricardo, and possibly with the help of a commentary, such as Roncaglia 2009b.

I prefer to give no reading indications for the final chapter: they would be too many and are already included in the text and the footnotes. Allow me only to suggest two texts by my master, Sylos Labini (1956, 1984). Happy reading!

Bibliography

The year after the author's name indicates the original date of publication, except for pre-1500 writings. The original date of writing is occasionally indicated in square brackets. Page references in the text refer to the last of the editions cited below not in brackets. When this is not an English edition, the translation of the passages cited in the text is mine.

Acemoglu, D. and Robinson, J. A. 2006. *Economic origins of dictatorship and democracy*. Cambridge: Cambridge University Press.

Akerlof, G. 1970. 'The market for lemons', *Quarterly Journal of Economics* 84: 488–500.

Akerlof, G. and Kranton, R. 2000. 'Economics and identity', *Quarterly Journal of Economics* 115: 715–53.

Allais, M. 1953. 'Le comportement de l'homme rationnel devant le risque: critique des postulats et axiomes de l'école américaine', *Econometrica* 21: 503–46.

Andrews, P. W. S. 1993. *The economics of competitive enterprise. Selected essays*. ed. by F. S. Lee and P. E. Earl, Aldershot: Edward Elgar.

Anonymous [1581] 1893. *A discourse of the common weal of this realm of England*. New ed. by E. Lamond, Cambridge: Cambridge University Press; repr. 1929.

Aristotle 1977. *Politics*. With an English transl. by H. Rackham, The Loeb Classic Library, vol. 21, Cambridge (Mass.): Harvard University Press.

(Pseudo)Aristotle 1935. *The Oeconomica*. With an English transl. by G.C. Armstrong, London: Heinemann and Cambridge (Mass.): Harvard University Press.

Arrow, K. J. 1951. *Social choice and individual values*. New York: Wiley.
1962. 'The economic implications of learning by doing', *Review of Economic Studies* 26: 155–73.

Arrow, K. J. and Debreu, G. 1954. 'Existence of an equilibrium for a competitive economy', *Econometrica* 22: 265–90.

Arthur, B. 1994. *Increasing returns and path dependence in the economy*. Ann Arbor: University of Michigan Press.

Aspromourgos, T. 2009. *The science of wealth. Adam Smith and the framing of political economy*. Abingdon: Routledge.

Axelrod, R. 1984. *The evolution of cooperation*. New York: Basic Books.

Babbage, C. 1832. *On the economy of machinery and manufactures*. London: Charles Knight; fourth edn. 1835; repr. New York: M. Kelley, 1963.

Bacon, F. 1620. *Novum Organum*. London: Joannem Billium; repr. in *The works of Francis Bacon*, ed. by J. Spedding, R. Lesline Ellis, D. Demon Heath, vol. 4, London: Longman and Co. 1858.

    1626. *New Atlantis*. London: J.H. for W. Lee; repr. in F. Bacon, *'The advancement of learning' and 'New Atlantis'*. ed. by T. Case, Oxford: Oxford University Press, 1974.

Bailey, S. 1825. *A critical dissertation on the nature, measure and causes of value*. London: R. Hunter; repr. London: Frank Cass 1967.

Bain, J. S. 1956. *Barriers to new competition*. Cambridge (Mass.): Harvard University Press.

Baran, P. A. 1957. *The political economy of growth*. New York: Monthly Review Press.

Baran, P. A. and Sweezy, P. M. 1966. *Monopoly capital. An essay on the American economic and social order*. New York: Monthly Review Press.

Barone, E. 1908. 'Il ministro della produzione nello stato collettivista', *Giornale degli economisti* 2: 267–93 and 391–414. (English transl., 'The ministry of production in the collectivist state', in Hayek (ed.) 1935).

Barro, R. J. and Grossman, H. I. 1971. 'A general disequilibrium model of income and employment', *American Economic Review* 61: 82–93.

Barton, J. 1817. *On the conditions of the labouring classes*. London: John and Arthur Arch.

Baumol, W. J. 1959. *Business behaviour, value and growth*. New York: Harcourt & Co.

    1977. 'Say's (at least) eight laws, or what Say and James Mill may really have meant', *Economica* 44: 145–62.

Baumol, W. J., Panzar, J. C. and Willig, R. D. 1982. *Contestable markets and the theory of industry structure*. San Diego (Calif.): Harcourt Brace Jovanovich.

Beccaria, C. 1764. *Dei delitti e delle pene*. Livorno: Coltellini; repr. in F. Venturi (ed.), *Illuministi italiani. Tomo III. Riformatori lombardi piemontesi e toscani*, Milano-Napoli: Ricciardi, 1958, pp. 27–105.

    1804. *Elementi di economia politica*, in P. Custodi (ed.), *Scrittori classici italiani di economia politica*, Milano: Destefanis, vol. 18, pp. 17–356 and vol. 19, pp. 391–543.

Benini, R. 1907. 'Sull'uso delle formule empiriche nell'economia applicata', *Giornale degli economisti*, second series, 35: 1053–63.

Bentham, J. [1776]. 'Fragment on government', in *The works of Jeremy Bentham*, 9 vols., ed. by J. Bowring, Edinburgh and London: William Tait-Simpkin and Marshall & Co., 1843–59, vol. 1, pp. 221–95; repr. in *'A comment on the commentaries' and 'A fragment on government'*, ed. by J.H. Burns and H.L.A. Hart, London: Athlone Press 1977.

    [1787]. *Defence of usury*. Repr. in *Jeremy Bentham's economic writings*, 3 vols., ed. by W. Stark, London: Allen and Unwin with the Royal Economic Society, 1952, vol. 1, pp. 121–207.

Berg, M. 2005. *Luxury and pleasure in eighteenth century Britain*. Oxford: Oxford University Press.

Berle, A. A. and Means, G. 1932. *The modern corporation and private property*. New York: The Commerce Clearing House.

Bernstein, E. 1899. *Die Voraussetzungen des Sozialismus und die Aufgaben der Sozialdemokratie*. Stuttgart: Dietz. English transl., *Evolutionary socialism*, New York: Huebsch, 1909; repr. New York: Schocken, 1961.

Bible. *The Jerusalem Bible*. London: Darton, Longman and Todd, 1966.

Böhm-Bawerk, E. von 1889. *Kapital und Kapitalzins. Zweite Abteilung: Positive Theorie des Kapitales*. Innsbruck: Verlag der Wagner'schen Universitäts-Buchhandlung. English transl., *The positive theory of capital*, London: Macmillan, 1891.

1896. 'Zum Abschluss des Marxschen Systems', in O. von Boenigk (ed.), *Staatswissenschaftliche Arbeiten. Festgaben für Karl Knies*. Berlin: Haering. English transl., *Karl Marx and the close of his system*, London: Fisher Unwin, 1898.

Boisguilbert, Pierre le Pesant de 1695. *Le détail de la France*. Rouen: no publisher; repr. in Institut national d'études demographiques (INED), *Pierre de Boisguilbert or la naissance de l'économie politique*, 2 vols., Paris: Presses Universitaires de France, 1966.

Bortkiewicz, L. von 1906–7. 'Wertrechnung und Preisrechnung im Marxschen System', *Archiv für Sozialwissenschaft und Sozialpolitik* 23 (1906) n. 1 and 25 (1907) nn. 1–2. English transl., 'Value and price in the Marxian system', *International Economic Papers* 1952, 52: 5–60.

1907. 'Zur Berichtigung der grundlegenden theoretischen Konstruktion von Marx im dritten Band des "Kapital"', *Conrads Jahrbücher für Nationalökonomie und Statistik*, series 3, 34: 319–35. English transl., 'On the correction of Marx's fundamental theoretical construction in the third volume of *Capital*', in P. Sweezy (ed), *Karl Marx and the close of his system*. New York: Augustus M. Kelley, 1949.

Box, G. E. P. and Jenkins, J. M. 1970. *Time series analysis: forecasting and control*. San Francisco: Holden-Day.

Brundtland, G. H. (ed.) 1987. *Our common future* (Brundtland Report, World Commission on Environment and Development). Oxford: Oxford University Press.

Caldwell, B. 2004. *Hayek's challenge. An intellectual biography of F.A. Hayek*. Chicago: University of Chicago Press.

Campanella, T. [1602] 1964. *La città del sole*. Milano: Rizzoli.

Cantillon, R. 1755. *Essai sur la nature du commerce en général*. London: Fletcher Gyles. Repr. with English transl., *Essay on the nature of trade in general*, ed. by H. Higgs, London: Macmillan 1931; repr., New York: M. Kelley 1964.

Carlyle, T. 1888–89. *Works*. 37 vols., London: Chapman and Hall.

Chamberlin, E. 1933. *The theory of monopolistic competition*. Cambridge (Mass.): Harvard University Press.

Child, J. 1688. *Brief observations concerning trade and interest of money*. London: E. Calvert and H. Mortlock; repr. as *A discourse about trade*, London: A. Sowle, 1690.

Clapham, J. A. 1922. 'Of empty economic boxes', *Economic Journal* 32: 305–14.

Clark, J. B. 1899. *The distribution of wealth: a theory of wages, interests and profits*. New York: Macmillan.

Clower, R. W. 1965. 'The Keynesian counter-revolution: a theoretical appraisal', in F. H. Hahn and F. P. R. Brechling (eds.), *The theory of interest rates*. London: Macmillan, pp. 103–25.

Coase, R. H. 1937. 'The nature of the firm', *Economica* 4; repr. in R. H. Coase, *The firm, the market and the law*. Chicago: The University of Chicago Press 1988, pp. 33–55.

Colquhoun, P. 1814. *Treatise on the wealth, power and resources of the British Empire*. London: J. Mawman.

Comte, A. 1830–42. *Cours de philosophie positive*. 6 vols., Paris.

Croce, B. and Einaudi, L. 1957. *Liberismo e liberalismo*. ed. by P. Solari, Milano-Napoli: Riccardo Ricciardi editore.

Custodi, P. 1803. 'Notizie degli autori contenuti nel presente volume', in *Scrittori classici italiani di economia politica*, parte antica, tomo 1, Milano: Destefanis.

Darwin, C. 1859. *On the origin of species by means of natural selection*. London: Murray; sixth edn., 1872.

1871. *The descent of man, and selection in relation to sex*. London: Murray; second edn., 1874.

David, P. 1985. 'Clio and the economics of QWERTY', *American Economic Review, Papers and Proceedings* 75: 332–7.

Davidson, P. 1994. *Post Keynesian macroeconomic theory*. Aldershot: Edward Elgar.

Debreu, G. 1959. *Theory of value. An axiomatic analysis of economic equilibrium*. Cowles Foundation Monograph, n. 17, New Haven: Yale University Press.

De Finetti, B. 1930. 'Fondamenti logici del ragionamento probabilistico', *Bollettino dell'Unione matematica italiana* 9: 258–61.

De Finetti, B. 1931. *Probabilismo. Saggio critico sulla teoria delle probabilità e sul valore della scienza*. Napoli: Perrella.

1937. 'La prévision, ses lois logiques, ses sources subjectives', *Annales de l'Institut Henri Poincaré* 7: 1–68.

Defoe, D. 1719. *The life and strange surprizing adventures of Robinson Crusoe, of York, mariner*. 3 vols., London: W. Taylor.

De Quincey, T. 1821–22. 'Confessions of an English opium eater', *London Magazine*, Sept. 1821–Oct. 1822; repr. in volume form, 1822; second edn., 1856; repr. London: Grant Richards 1902.

1824. 'Dialogues of three templars on political economy', *London Magazine*; repr. in T. De Quincey, *Collected writings*, ed. by D. Masson, A. and C. Black, Edinburgh, vol. 9, repr. as *Political economy and politics*, New York: Augustus M. Kelley 1970, pp. 37–112.

1844. *The logic of political economy*. Edinburgh: William Blackwood and Sons; repr. in T. De Quincey, *Collected writings*, vol. 9, pp. 118–294.

Descartes, R. 1637. *Discours de la méthode*. Leyda: I. Maire. English transl., *Discourse on the method for conducting one's reason well and for seeking truth in the sciences*, Indianapolis: Hackett 1988.

D'Ippoliti, C. and Roncaglia, A. 2016. 'Heterodox economics and the history of economic thought', in T.-H. Jo and Z. Todorova, eds, *Advancing the frontiers of heterodox economics. Essays in honor of Frederick S. Lee*. Abingdon and New York: Routledge, pp. 21–38.

Dobb, M. 1928. *Russian economic development since the revolution*. London: Routledge.

1946. *Studies in the development of capitalism*. London: Routledge.

1955. *On economic theories and socialism*. London: Routledge.

1973. *Theories of value and distribution since Adam Smith*. Cambridge: Cambridge University Press.

Dosi G. 1984. *Technical change and industrial transformation*. London: Macmillan.

et al. 1988. *Technical change and economic theory*. London: Pinter.

Dunlop, J. T. 1938. 'The movement of real and money wage rates', *Economic Journal* 48: 413–34.

Edgeworth, F. Y. 1881. *Mathematical psychics. An essay on the application of mathematics to the moral sciences*. London: C. Kegan Paul; repr. San Diego: James and Gordon 1995.

1925. *Papers relating to political economy*. 3 vols., London: Royal Economic Society; repr. New York: Burt Franklin 1970.

Edwards, W. 1961. 'Behavioral decision theory', *Annual Review of Psychology* 12: 473–98.

Eichner, A. S. 1976. *The megacorp and oligopoly*. Cambridge: Cambridge University Press.

Ellsberg, D. 1961. 'Ambiguity, and the Savage axioms', *Quarterly Journal of Economics* 75: 643–69.

Fama, E. 1970. 'Efficient capital markets: a review of theory and empirical work', *Journal of Finance* 25: 383–417.

Ferguson, A. 1767. *An essay on the history of civil society*. Edinburgh: A. Kinkaid & J. Bell; repr. ed. by D. Forbes, Edinburgh: Edinburgh University Press 1966.

Feyerabend, P. 1975. *Against method. Outline of an anarchist theory of knowledge*. London: New Left Books.

Fisher, I. 1892. *Mathematical investigations in the theory of value and prices*. New Haven: Transactions of the Connecticut Academy of Arts and Sciences; repr. New York: A.M. Kelley 1965.

Flux, A.W. 1894. 'Review: K. Wicksell, *Über Wert, Kapital und Rente*; P.H. Wicksteed, *An essay on the coordination of the laws of distribution*', *Economic Journal* 4: 305–13.

Friedman, M. 1953. *Essays in positive economics*. Chicago: University of Chicago Press.

1956. 'The quantity theory of money. A restatement', in M. Friedman (ed.), *Studies in the quantity theory of money*. Chicago: University of Chicago Press, pp. 3–21.

1968. 'The role of monetary policy', *American Economic Review* 58: 1–17.

Frisch, R. 1933. 'Editorial', *Econometrica* 1: 1–4.

Fuà, G. 1993. *Crescita economica. Le insidie delle cifre*. Bologna: Il Mulino.

Galbraith, J. K. 1955. *The affluent society*. Boston: Houghton Mifflin.

1967. *The new industrial state*. Boston: Houghton Mifflin.

Galiani, F. 1751. *Della moneta*. Napoli: Giuseppe Raimondi; second edn. Napoli: Stamperia simoniana 1780; repr. Milano: Feltrinelli 1963. (English transl., *On money*, ed. by P. R. Toscano, Ann Arbor: University Microfilm International 1977).

1770. *Dialogues sur le commerce des blés*. Londres: no publisher; repr. ed. by F. Nicolini, Milano-Napoli: Ricciardi 1959; Italian transl., *Dialoghi sul commercio dei grani*, Roma: Editori Riuniti 1978.

Galilei, G. 1623. *Il Saggiatore*. Roma: Giacomo Mascardi e Accademia dei Lincei; repr. in *Opere*, Milano-Napoli: Ricciardi 1953, pp. 89–352.

Gårdlund, T. 1956. *Knut Wicksell, rebell l det nya riket*. Stockholm: Bonniers; English transl., *The life of Knut Wicksell*, Cheltenham: Edward Elgar 1996.

Garegnani, P. 1960. *Il capitale nelle teorie della distribuzione*. Milano: Giuffrè.

1970. 'Heterogeneous capital, the production function and the theory of distribution', *Review of Economic Studies* 37: 407–36.

1981. *Marx e gli economisti classici*. Torino: Einaudi.

1984. 'Value and distribution in the classical economists and Marx', *Oxford Economic Papers* 36: 291–325.

1990. 'Sraffa: Classical versus Marginalist analysis', in Bharadwaj, K. and Schefold, B. (eds.), *Essays on Piero Sraffa*, London: Routledge, pp. 112–41.

Genovesi, A. 1765–67. *Delle lezioni di commercio o sia d'economia civile*. 2 vols., Napoli: Fratelli Simone; repr. in *Scrittori classici italiani di economia politica*, ed. by P. Custodi, vols. 14–16, Milano: Destefanis, 1803.

Godfrey-Smith, P. 2009. *Darwinian populations and natural selections*. Oxford: Oxford University Press.

Godley, W. and Lavoie, M. 2007. *Monetary economics. An integrated approach to credit, money, income, production and wealth*. London: Palgrave Macmillan.

Godwin, W. 1793. *Enquiry concerning political justice, and its influence on moral and happiness*. London: G. G. and J. Robinson; repr. ed. by I. Kramnick, Harmondsworth: Penguin Books 1976.

1820. *Of population. An enquiry concerning the power of increase in the numbers of mankind, being an answer to mr. Malthus's essay on that subject*. London: Longman, Hurst, Rees, Orme and Brown.

Goodwin, R. M. 1967. 'A growth cycle', in C. H. Feinstein (ed.), *Socialism, capitalism and economic growth. Essays presented to Maurice Dobb*, Cambridge: Cambridge University Press, pp. 54–58.

1990. *Chaotic economic dynamics*. Oxford: Clarendon Press.

Gossen, H. H. 1854. *Entwickelung der Gesetze des menschlichen Verkehrs, und der daraus fliessenden Regeln für menschliches Handeln*. Brunswick: Vieweg; second edn. Berlin: Prager 1889. English transl., *The laws of human relations and the rules of human action derived therefrom*, ed. by N. Georgescu-Roegen, Cambridge (Mass.): MIT Press 1983.

Gray, J. 1825. *A lecture on human happiness*. Philadelphia: D. & S. Neall.

Graziani, A. 2003. *The monetary theory of production*. Cambridge: Cambridge University Press.

Haavelmo, T. 1944. 'The probability approach in econometrics', *Econometrica* 12 (Supplement): 1–118.

Hall, P. and Soskice, D. (eds) 2001. *Varieties of capitalism*. Oxford: Oxford University Press.

Hansen, A. 1938. *Full recovery or stagnation?*. New York: Norton.

Harcourt, G. C. 2006. *The structure of post-Keynesian economics. The core contributions of the pioneers*. Cambridge: Cambridge University Press.

Harrod, R.F. 1930. 'Notes on supply', *Economic Journal* 40: 232–41.

1939. 'An essay in dynamic theory', *Economic Journal* 49: 14–33.

1951. *The life of John Maynard Keynes*. London: Macmillan.

1961. 'Review of P. Sraffa, *Production of commodities by means of commodities*', *Economic Journal* 71: 78387.

Harvey, W. 1628. *Exercitatio anatomica de motu cordis et sanguinis*. Francoforti: G. Fitzeri. English transl., *The anatomical exercises*, ed. by G. Keynes, New York: Dover Publications 1995.

Hawtrey, R. G. 1919. *Currency and credit*. London: Longmans.

Hayek, F. von 1931. *Prices and production*. London: Routledge.

1932. 'Money and capital: a reply', *Economic Journal* 42: 237–49.

(ed.). 1935. *Collectivist economic planning*. London: Routledge.

1944. *The road to serfdom*. Chicago: Chicago University Press; repr. (with an introduction by M. Friedman) 1994.

1994. *Hayek on Hayek*, ed. by S. Kresge and L. Wenar, Chicago: University of Chicago Press.

Henrich, J. *et al.* (eds.), 2004. *Foundations of human sociality*. Oxford: Oxford University Press.

Heukelom, F. 2014. *Behavioral economics: a history*. Cambridge: Cambridge University Press.

Hicks, J. 1937. 'Mr. Keynes and the classics: a suggested interpretation', *Econometrica* 5: 147–59.

Hilferding, R. 1910. *Das Finanzkapital*. Wien: Wiener Volksbuchhandlung Ignaz Brand. English transl., *Finance capital: a study of the latest phase of capitalist development*, London: Routledge & Kegan Paul 1981.

Hirschman, A. 1977. *The passions and the interests*. Princeton: Princeton University Press.

1982. 'Rival interpretations of market society: civilizing, destructive, or feeble?', *Journal of Economic Literature* 20: 1463–84.

Hobbes, T. 1651. *Leviathan*. London: Andrew Crooke; repr. ed. by C. B. Macpherson, Harmondsworth: Penguin Books 1968, repr. 1987.

Hobson, J. 1902. *Imperialism: a study*. London: Nisbet.

Hodgskin, T. 1825. *Labour defended against the claims of capital or the unproductiveness of capital proved*. London: Knight and Lacey; repr. London: Hammersmith Bookshop 1964.

Hodgson, G.M. 1988. *Economics and institutions*. Cambridge: Polity Press.

1998. 'The approach of institutional economics', *Journal of Economic Literature*, 36: 166–92.

Hume, D. 1739–40. *A treatise of human nature*. 3 vols., London: John Noon; repr. Oxford: Clarendon Press 1978; repr. Bristol: Thoemmes 1990.

[1740] 1938. *An abstract of a treatise on human nature*. With an introduction and ed. by J. M. Keynes and P. Sraffa, Cambridge: Cambridge University Press.

1752. *Political discourses*. Edinburgh: A. Kincaid and A. Donaldson; repr. in *Essays: moral, political, and literary*, ed. by E. F. Miller, Indianapolis: Liberty Press 1987.

Huntington, S.P. 1996. *The clash of civilization and the remaking of the world order*. New York: Simon & Schuster.

Hutcheson, F. 1755. *A system of moral philosophy*. 3 vols., London: A. Millar.

Jevons, W. S. 1865. *The coal question*. London: Macmillan; repr. New York: Augustus M. Kelley 1965.

1871. *The theory of political economy*. London: Macmillan; second edn. 1879; repr. Harmondsworth: Penguin Books 1970.

1874. *The principles of science: a treatise on logic and scientific method*. London: Macmillan; second edn. 1877.

1881. 'Richard Cantillon and the nationality of political economy', *Contemporary Review*, January; repr. in R. Cantillon, *Essai sur la nature du commerce en général*, ed. by H. Higgs, London: Macmillan, 1931 (repr. New York: Kelley, 1964), pp. 333–60.

Kahn, R.F. [1929] 1983. *L'economia del breve periodo*. ed. by M. Dardi, Torino: Boringhieri; English edn., *The economics of the short period*. New York: St. Martin's Press 1989.

1931. 'The relation of home investment to unemployment', *Economic Journal* 41: 173–98; repr. in Kahn, 1972, pp. 1–27.

1972. *Selected essays on employment and growth*. Cambridge: Cambridge University Press.

Kahneman, D. and Tversky, A. 1979. 'Prospect theory: an analysis of decision under risk', *Econometrica* 47: 313–27.

Kaldor, N. 1942. 'Professor Hayek and the concertina effect', *Economica*. 9: 359–82.

1956. 'Alternative theories of distribution', *Review of Economic Studies* 23: 94–100.

1957. 'A model of economic growth', *Economic Journal* 67: 591–624.

1961. 'Capital accumulation and economic growth', in F. A. Lutz (ed.), *The theory of capital*, London: Macmillan, pp. 177–220.

1966. 'Marginal productivity and the macro-economic theories of distribution', *Review of Economic Studies* 33: 309–19.

Kalecki, M. 1943. *Studies in economic dynamics*. London: Allen & Unwin.

1971. *Selected essays on the dynamics of the capitalist economy*. Cambridge: Cambridge University Press.

1972. *Selected essays on the economic growth of the socialist and the mixed economy*. Cambridge: Cambridge University Press.

Kautilya [fourth century BC] 1967. *Arthaśāstra*. ed. by R. Shamasastri, Mysore: Mysore Printing and Publishing House.

Keynes, J. M. 1913. *Indian currency and finance*. London: Macmillan; repr. in J. M. Keynes, *Collected writings*, vol. 1, London: Macmillan 1971.

1919. *The economic consequences of the peace*. London: Macmillan; repr. in J. M. Keynes, *Collected writings*, vol. 2, London: Macmillan 1971.

1921. *A treatise on probability*. London: Macmillan; repr. in J. M. Keynes, *Collected writings*, vol. 8, London: Macmillan 1973.

1923. *A tract on monetary reform*. London: Macmillan; repr. in J. M. Keynes, *Collected writings*, vol. 4, London: Macmillan 1971. (Italian transl., ed. by P. Sraffa, *La riforma monetaria*, Milano: Fratelli Treves 1925).

1925. *The economic consequences of Mr. Churchill*. London: Hogarth Press; repr. in Keynes 1931, pp. 207–30 and in J. M. Keynes, *Collected writings*, vol. 9, pp. 272–94.

1930. *A treatise on money.* 2 vols., London: Macmillan; repr. in J. M. Keynes, *Collected writings*, vols. 5 and 6, London: Macmillan 1971.

1931. *Essays in persuasion.* London: Macmillan; repr. in J.M. Keynes, *Collected writings*, vol. 9, London: Macmillan 1972.

1933. *Essays in biography.* London: Macmillan; repr. in J. M. Keynes, *Collected writings*, vol. 10, London: Macmillan 1972.

1936. *The general theory of employment, interest and money.* London: Macmillan. (Repr. in J. M. Keynes, *Collected writings*, vol. 7, London: Macmillan 1973).

1937. 'The general theory of employment', *Quarterly Journal of Economics* 51: 200–23, repr. in Keynes 1973, vol. 14, pp. 109–23.

1940. *How to pay for the war.* London: Macmillan. (Repr. in J. M. Keynes, *Collected writings*, vol. 9, London: Macmillan 1972, pp. 367–439).

1973. *The General Theory and after.* In *Collected writings*, vols. 13 (*Part I: preparation*) and 14 (*Part II: defence and development*), ed. by D. Moggridge, London: Macmillan.

Keynes, J. N. 1891. *The scope and method of political economy.* London: Macmillan.

Kindleberger, C. P. 1978. *Manias, panics and crashes. A history of financial crisis.* New York: Basic Books.

Knight, F. H. 1921. *Risk, uncertainty and profit.* Boston: Hart, Schaffner & Marx; repr. Boston: Houghton Mifflin.

Kregel, J. A. 1976. 'Economic methodology in the face of uncertainty. The modelling methods of Keynes and the post-Keynesians', *Economic Journal* 86: 209–25.

Krugman, P.R. 1990. *Rethinking international trade.* Cambridge (Mass.): MIT Press.

Kuhn, T. S. 1962. *The structure of scientific revolutions.* Princeton: Princeton University Press; second edn. 1970.

Kula, W. 1958. *Rozwazania o historii.* Warszawa: Państwowe Wydawnictwo Naukowe. Italian transl., *Riflessioni sulla storia*, Venezia: Marsilio 1990. (English transl., *The problems and methods of economic history*, Aldershot: Ashgate 2001).

1970. *Miary i ludzie.* Warszawa: Państwowe Wydawnictwo Naukowe. English transl. *Measures and men*, Princeton: Princeton University Press.

Lafargue, P. 1880. 'Le droit à la paresse', *L'égalité*; repr. Paris: Maspero 1969. English transl., *The right to be lazy*, Chicago: C.H. Kerr 1989.

Lakatos, I. 1978. *The methodology of scientific research programmes. Philosophical papers.* Cambridge: Cambridge University Press.

Lange, O. 1936–37. 'On the economic theory of socialism', *Review of Economic Studies* 4: 53–71 and 123–42.

Leijonhufvud, A. 1968. *On Keynesian economics and the economics of Keynes.* London: Oxford University Press.

Lenin (Vladimir Ilyich Ulianov) 1916. English transl., *Imperialism, the highest stage of capitalism*, London: Junius 1996.

Leontief, W. 1941. *The structure of the American economy, 1919–1939.* New York: Oxford University Press; second edn. 1951.

Levhari, D. 1965. 'A nonsubstitution theorem and switching of techniques', *Quarterly Journal of Economics* 79: 98–105.

Levhari, D. and Samuelson, P. 1966. 'The nonswitching theorem is false', *Quarterly Journal of Economics* 80: 518–19.

List, F. 1841. *Das nationale System der politischen Oekonomie.* Stuttgard: J.G. Cotta. English transl., *The national system of political economy*, ed. by S. S. Lloyd, London: Longmans, Greene and Co. 1909.

Lloyd, W. F. 1837. *Lectures on population, value, poor laws and rent.* London; repr. New York: A.M. Kelley 1968.

Locke, J. 1690. *Two treatises of government.* London: Awnsham and John Churchill; critical edn., ed. by P. Laslett, Cambridge: Cambridge University Press 1960; edn. quoted, London: J.M. Dent (Everyman's Library) 1975.

1692. *Some considerations on the consequences of the lowering of interest, and raising the value of money.* London: A. and J. Churchill; repr. in *Locke on money*, 2 vols., ed. by P.H. Kelly, Oxford: Clarendon Press 1991.

Longfield, M. 1834. *Lectures on political economy.* Dublin: R. Milliken & Son.

1835. *Three lectures on commerce, and one on absenteeism.* Dublin: William Curry, Junior & Co.

Lucas, R.E. 1972. 'Expectations and the neutrality of money', *Journal of Economic Theory* 4: 103–24.

1976. 'Econometric policy evaluation: a critique', in K. Brenner and A. M. Meltzer (ed.), *The Phillips curve and labor markets*, Amsterdam: North Holland, pp. 19–46.

Luxemburg, R. 1913. *Die Akkumulation des Kapitals. Ein Beitrag zur ökonomischen Erklärung des Imperialismus.* Berlin: Paul Singer. Italian transl., *L'accumulazione del capitale*, Torino: Einaudi 1960; repr. 1968. English transl., *The accumulation of capital*, London: Routledge 2003.

Machiavelli, N. [1513] 1960. *Il principe.* Milano: Feltrinelli. English transl., *The prince*, ed. by R. M. Adams, New York: Norton 1992.

Maifreda, G. 2012. *From oikonomia to political economy.* Farnham: Ashgate.

Malinvaud, E. 1977. *The theory of unemployment reconsidered.* Oxford: Basil Blackwell.

Malthus, T. R. 1798. *An essay on the principle of population as it affects the future improvement of society.* London; second edn., 1803; critical edn., ed. by P. James, Cambridge: Cambridge University Press 1989.

Malthus, T. R. 1800. *An investigation of the cause of the present high price of provisions.* London: J. Johnson.

1820. *Principles of political economy.* London: John Murray; second edn., London: William Pickering 1836; repr. New York: Augustus M. Kelley 1964.

Mandeville, B. 1714. *The fable of the bees, or private vices, public benefits.* London: J. Roberts; critical edn., ed. by F. B. Haye, Oxford: Clarendon Press 1924; repr. Indianapolis: Liberty Press 1988.

Mann, T. 1901. *Buddenbrooks. Verfall einer Familie.* München: Fisher.

Marcuse, H. 1956. *One-dimensional man.* Boston: Beacon Press.

Marcuzzo, M. C. 2012. *Fighting market failure.* London: Routledge.

Marris, R. 1964. *The economic theory of 'managerial' capitalism.* London: Macmillan.

Marshall, A. 1872. 'Mr. Jevons's *Theory of political economy*', *Academy*, 1 April; repr. in Marshall 1925, pp. 93–100.

Marshall, A. and M. P. 1879a. *The economics of industry*. London: Macmillan. (Italian transl., *Economia della produzione*, Milano: Isedi 1975).

1879b. *The pure theory of foreign trade. The pure theory of domestic values.* Cambridge: Privately printed.

1890. *Principles of economics*. London: Macmillan; eighth edn., 1920; critical edn., ed. by C. W. Guillebaud, 2 vols., London: Macmillan 1961.

1892. *Elements of economics of industry*. London: Macmillan.

1919. *Industry and trade*. London: Macmillan.

1923. *Money, credit, and commerce*. London: Macmillan; repr., Fairfield: Augustus M. Kelley 1991.

1925. *Memoirs*. ed. by A.C. Pigou, London: Macmillan.

1926. *Official papers*. ed. by J.M. Keynes, London: Macmillan.

1996a. *The correspondence of Alfred Marshall economist*. ed. by J. K. Whitaker, 3 vols., Cambridge: Cambridge University Press.

1996b. *Official papers of Alfred Marshall. A supplement*. ed. by P. Groenewegen, Cambridge: Cambridge University Press.

Marx, K. [1844] 1932. *Ökonomisch-philosophische Manuskripte aus dem Jahre 1844*. In *Karl Marx – Friedrich Engels Historisc-kritische Gesamtausgabe*, ed. by V. Adoratskij, Berlin: Marx-Engels Gesamtausgabe (MEGA). English transl., 'Economic and philosophical manuscripts', in K. Marx, *Early writings*, ed. by T. B. Bottomore, London: C.A. Watts & Co. 1963, pp. 61–219.

1847. *Misère de la philosophie. Réponse à la philosophie de la misère de M. Proudhon.* Paris: A. Frank, and Bruxelles: C. G. Vogler. English transl., *The poverty of philosophy*, Moscow: Foreign Languages Publishing House 1962.

1859. *Zur Kritik der Politischen Ökonomie*. Berlin: Dietz. English transl., *Contributions to the critique of political economy*, London: Lawrence & Wishart 1970; passages quoted from Marx and Engels 1959, pp. 83–7.

[1865] 1898, *Value, price and profit*, ed. by E. Marx Aveling. Chicago: Charles Kerr & Company co-operative.

1867–94. *Das Kapital*. 3 vols., Hamburg: O. Meissner. English transl., *Capital*, London: Dent 1946 (for vols. 1 and 2) and Harmondsworth: Penguin Books 1976, repr. 1986 (for vol. 3).

1905–10. *Theorien über den Mehrwert*. ed. by K. Kautsky, Stuttgart: Dietz. English transl., *Theories of surplus-value*, Moscow: Foreign Languages Publishing House and London: Lawrence and Wishart, Part 1, 1963; Part 2, 1969; Part 3, 1972.

Marx, K. and Engels, F. [1845] 1888. 'Feuerbach', appendix to Engels F., *Ludwig Feuerbach*, Stuttgard: Dietz. English transl., 'Theses on Feuerbach', in Marx and Engels 1959, pp. 283–6.

[1845–46] 1932. *Die Deutsche Ideologie*. Berlin: Marx-Engels Gesamtausgabe (MEGA). English transl., *The German ideology*, London: Lawrence and Wishart 1939; passages quoted from Marx and Engels 1959, pp. 287–302.

1848. *Manifest der Kommunistischen Partei*. London: J.E. Burghard, Bildungs-Gesellschaft für Arbeiter. (Italian transl., *Manifesto del partito comunista*, Torino: Einaudi, fourth edn. 1966.) English transl., 'Manifesto of the Communist Party', in Marx and Engels 1959, pp. 43–82.

1878. 'Kritik des Gothaer Programms', *Die Neue Zeit*, n. 18. English transl., 'Critique of the Gotha programme', in Marx and Engels 1959, pp. 153–73.

Mas-Colell, A., Whinston, M. D. and Green, J. R. 1995. *Microeconomic theory*. New York: Oxford University Press.

McCloskey, D. 1985. *The rhetoric of economics*. Madison: University of Wisconsin Press.

McClure, S. M., Laibson, D. I., Loewenstein, G., Cohen and J. D. 2004. 'Separate neural systems value immediate and delayed monetary rewards', *Science* 306: 503–7.

McCormick, T. 2009. *William Petty*. Oxford: Oxford University Press.

McCulloch, J.R. 1825. *The principles of political economy*. Edinburgh: William and Charles Tait, and London: Longmans and Co..

1845. *The literature of political economy*. London: Longman, Brown, Green and Longmans; repr., Fairfield: Augustus M. Kelley 1991.

Meadows, D. H., Meadows, D. L., Randers, D. L. and Beherens, W. W. III 1972. *The limits to growth*. New York: New American Library.

Menger, C. 1871. *Grundsätze der Volkswirtschaftslehre*. Wien: Braumuller; second edn., ed. by K. Menger, 1923. English transl., *Principles of economics*, New York: New York University Press 1981.

1883. *Untersuchungen über die Methode der Sozialwissenschaften und der politischen Oekonomie insbesondere*. Berlin: Dunker & Humblot. English transl., *Problems of economics and sociology*, Urbana: University of Illinois Press 1963; repr. as *Investigations into the method of the social sciences with special reference to economics*, New York: New York University Press 1985.

Menger, C. 1884. *Die Irrthümer des Historismus in den deutschen Nationalökonomie*. Wien: Hölder; Italian transl., *Gli errori dello storicismo*, Milano: Rusconi 1991.

Mill, J. 1821. *Elements of political economy*. London: Baldwin, Cradock and Joy; repr. in J. Mill, *Selected economic writings*, pp. 203–366.

1843. *A system of logic*. 2 vols., London: John W. Parker.

Mill, J. S. 1844. *Essays on some unsettled questions of political economy*. London: John W. Parker; second edn., 1874; repr. Clifton: Augustus M. Kelley, 1974.

Mill, J. S. 1848. *Principles of political economy*. London: John W. Parker.

1859. *On liberty*. London: J.W. Parker. Repr. Northbrook (Ill.): AHM Publishing Co. 1947.

1861. 'Utilitarianism', *Fraser's Magazine* 64: 383–4; repr. in J. S. Mill and J. Bentham, *Utilitarianism and other essays*, A. Ryan ed., London: Penguin Books 1987, pp. 272–338.

Minsky, H. P. 1982. *Can 'it' happen again? Essays on instability and finance*, Armonk (N.Y.): Sharpe.

1993. 'Schumpeter and finance', in S. Biasco, A. Roncaglia and M. Salvati (eds.), *Market and institutions in economic development*. Houndmills: Macmillan, pp. 103–15.

Mirabeau (Victor Riqueti, marquis de) 1756. *L'ami des hommes*. Avignon: no publisher.

Mirowski, P. 2002. *Machine dreams. Economics becomes a cyborg science*. Cambridge: Cambridge University Press.

2012. *Science-Mart. Privatizing American science.* Cambridge (Mass.): Harvard University Press.

Mises, L. von 1920. 'Die Wirtschaftsrechnung im Sozialistischen Gemeinwesen', *Arkiv für Sozialwissenschaft und Sozialpolitik* 47: 86–121. (English transl. in Hayek (ed.) 1935).

Mishan, E. J. 1967. *The costs of economic growth.* London: Staples Press.

Modigliani, F. 1944. 'Liquidity preference and the theory of interest and money', *Econometrica* 12: 45–88.

1963. 'The monetary mechanism and its interaction with real phenomena', *Review of Economics and Statistics* 45 (Supplement): 79–107.

Modigliani, F. and Miller, M. 1958. 'The cost of capital, corporation finance and the theory of investment', *American Economic Review* 48: 161–97.

Moggridge, D. E. 1992. *Maynard Keynes. An economist's biography.* London: Routledge.

Montchrétien, A. de 1615. *Traité de l'oeconomie politique.* Paris; critical edn., ed. by F. Billacois, Genève: Droz 1999.

More, T. 1516. *Utopia.* Louvain: T. Martens. English transl., *Utopia*, in *The complete works of St. Thomas More*, vol. 4, ed. by E. Surtz and J. H. Hexter, New Haven: Yale University Press 1965; repr. 1979.

Murphy, A. E. 1986. *Richard Cantillon: entrepreneur and economist.* Oxford: Clarendon Press.

Muth, J. F. 1961. 'Rational expectations and the theory of price movements', *Econometrica* 29: 315–35.

Nash, J. F. 1950. 'Equilibrium points in N-person games', *Proceedings of the National Academy of Sciences* (USA) 36: 48–9.

Neisser, H. 1932. 'Lohnhohe und beschäftigungsgrad in Marktgleichgewicht', *Weltwirtschaftliches Archiv* 36: 415–55.

Nelson, R. 1995. 'Recent evolutionary theorizing about economic change', *Journal of Economic Literature* 33: 48–90.

Nelson, R. and Winter, S. 1982. *An evolutionary theory of economic change.* Cambridge (Mass.): Harvard University Press.

Neumann, J. von 1937. 'Über ein ökonomisches Gleichungssystem und eine Verallgemeinerung des Brouwerschen Fixpunktsatzes', in K. Menger (ed.), *Ergebrisse eines mathematischen Kolloquiums, 1935–36*, vol. 8, pp. 73–83, Wien: Deuticke. English transl., 'A model of general economic equilibrium', *Review of Economic Studies* 13 (1945): 1–9.

Neumann, J. von and Morgenstern, O. 1944. *Theory of games and economic behaviour.* Princeton: Princeton University Press; second edn. 1947; third edn. 1953.

Ortes, G. 1790. *Riflessioni sulla popolazione delle nazioni in rapporto all'economia nazionale.* Firenze: no publisher, repr. in P. Custodi (ed.), *Scrittori classici italiani di economia politica*, Parte moderna, vol. 24, Milano: Destefanis 1804, pp. 5–111.

Owen, R. 1813. *A new view of society.* London: Cadell and Davies; repr. in R. Owen, *Report to the county of Lanark. A new view of society.* Harmondsworth: Penguin Books 1970, pp. 85–198.

1820. *Report to the county of Lanark.* Lanark, 1 May; repr. in Owen 1857–58, vol. 2, pp. 261–310; repr. in R. Owen, *Report to the county of Lanark. A new view of society*, pp. 199–270.

1857–58. *The life of Robert Owen, written by himself.* 2 vols., London: Effingham Wilson; repr. Fairfield: Augustus M. Kelley 1977.

Pantaleoni, M. 1889. *Principii di economia pura.* Firenze: G. Barbera; second edn. 1894. English transl., *Pure economics,* London: Macmillan 1898.

1898. 'Dei criteri che devono informare la storia delle dottrine economiche', *Giornale degli economisti,* 4 novembre, repr. in Pantaleoni 1925, pp. 211–45.

Pareto, V. 1896. 'La courbe de la répartition de la richesse', in *Recueil publié par la Faculté de Droit de l'Université de Lausanne à l'occasion de l'Exposition nationale de 1896,* pp. 373–87. Italian transl., *La curva di ripartizione della ricchezza,* in M. Corsi (ed.), *Le diseguaglianze economiche,* Torino: Giappichelli 1995, pp. 51–70.

Pareto, V. 1896–97. *Cours d'économie politique.* 2 vols., Lausanne: F. Rouge.

1901–2. *Les systèmes socialistes.* 2 vols., Paris: Giard et Briére; second edn. 1926.

1906. *Manuale di economia politica.* Milano: Società editrice libraria; repr. Roma: Bizzarri 1965.

1916. *Trattato di sociologia generale.* 2 vols., Firenze: Barbera; repr. Roma: Bizzarri 1964.

Pasinetti, L. 1960. 'A mathematical formulation of the Ricardian system', *Review of Economic Studies* 27: 78–98 (repr. in Pasinetti 1974).

1962. 'Rate of profit and income distribution in relation to the rate of economic growth', *Review of Economic Studies* 29: 267–79 (repr. in Pasinetti 1974).

1965. 'A new theoretical approach to the problems of economic growth', *Academiae Pontificiae Scientiarum Scripta Varia,* n. 28: 571–696.

1966. 'Changes in the rate of profits and switches of techniques', *Quarterly Journal of Economics* 80: 503–17.

1969. 'Switches of technique and the "rate of return" in capital theory', *Economic Journal* 79: 508–31.

1973. 'The notion of vertical integration in economic analysis', *Metroeconomica* 25: 129.

1975. *Lezioni di teoria della produzione.* Bologna: Il Mulino. English transl., *Lectures in the theory of production,* London: Macmillan, 1977.

1981. *Structural change and economic growth.* Cambridge: Cambridge University Press.

Perrotta, C. 2004. *Consumption as an investment: I. On the fear of goods from Hesiod to Adam Smith.* Abingdon: Routledge.

Petty, W. 1662. *A treatise of taxes and contributions.* London: N. Brooke; repr. in Petty 1899, pp. 1–97.

1690. *Political arithmetick.* London: Robert Clavel and Henry Mortlock; repr. in Petty 1899, pp. 233–313.

1691a. *The political anatomy of Ireland.* London: D. Brown and W. Rogers; repr. in Petty 1899, pp. 121–231.

1691b. *Verbum sapienti.* In appendix to W. Petty 1691a; repr. in Petty 1899, pp. 99–120.

1899. *Economic writings.* ed. by C. Hull, 2 vols., Cambridge: Cambridge University Press; repr. New York: Augustus M. Kelley 1963.

1927. *Papers.* 2 vols., ed. by H. Lansdowne, London: Constable.

Phelps, E. S. 1967. 'Phillips curves, expectations of inflation and optimal unemployment over time', *Economica* 34: 254–81.

Phillips, A. W. 1958. 'The relationship between unemployment and the rate of change of money wage rates in the United Kingdom, 1861–1957', *Economica* 25: 283–99.

Pigou, A.C. 1912. *Wealth and welfare.* London: Macmillan; new ed., *The Economics of Welfare*, London: Macmillan 1920.

1922. 'Empty economic boxes: a reply', *Economic Journal* 32: 458–65.

1927. *Industrial fluctuations.* London: Macmillan.

1933. *The theory of unemployment.* London: Macmillan.

1950. *Keynes's General Theory: a retrospective view.* London: Macmillan.

Piore, M. and Sabel, C. 1984. *The second industrial divide.* New York: Basic Books.

Plato 1930. *The republic.* Books 1–5 (vol. 1), with an English transl. by P. Shorey, The Loeb Classic Library, London: Heinemann and Cambridge (Mass.): Harvard University Press.

Poitras, G. 2000. *The early history of financial economics, 1478–1776.* Cheltenham: Edward Elgar.

Popper, K.R. 1934. *Logik der Forschnung.* Wien: Springer. enlarged English edn., *The logic of scientific discovery*, London: Hutchison 1959.

1945. *The open society and its enemies.* 2 vols., London: Routledge and Kegan Paul; fifth edn., 1966.

1969. *Conjectures and refutations.* London: Routledge and Kegan Paul.

Postlethwayt, M. 1751–55. *Universal dictionary of trade and commerce.* London: W. Strahan.

Pownall, T. 1776. *A letter from Governor Pownall to Adam Smith, L.L.D. F.R.S., being an examination of several points of doctrine, laid down in his 'Inquiry in to the nature and causes of the wealth of nations'.* London; repr. New York: Augustus M. Kelley 1967; repr. in Smith 1977, pp. 337–76.

Proudhon, P.-J. 1840. *Qu'est-ce que la propriété?*. Paris: Brocard. English transl., *What is property?* Cambridge: Cambridge University Press 1994.

Quesnay, F. 1758–59. *Tableau économique.* Paris (first edn., 1758; second edn., 1759; third edn., 1759). Repr. with an English transl. in M. Kuczynski and R. L. Meek, *Quesnay's tableau économique*, London: Macmillan and New York: Kelley 1972.

Radcliffe Report 1959. Committee on the working of the monetary system, *Report*, London: HMSO.

Ramsey, F. P. 1931. *The foundations of mathematics.* London: Routledge and Kegan Paul.

Raphael, D. D. 2007. *The impartial spectator. Adam Smith's moral philosophy.* Oxford: Clarendon Press.

Ravix, J. and Romani, P.-M. eds. 1997. *Turgot. Formation et distribution des richesses.* Paris: Flammarion.

Rawls, J. 1971. *A theory of justice.* Cambridge (Mass.): Harvard University Press.

Reinert, S. A. 2011. *Translating empire. Emulation and the origins of political economy.* Cambridge (Mass.): Harvard University Press.

Remak, R. 1929. 'Kann die Volkswirtschaftslehre eine exakte Wissenschaft werden?', *Jahrbucher für Nationalökonomie und Statistik* 131: 703–36.

Ricardo, D. 1951–55. *Works and correspondence.* 10 vols., ed. by P. Sraffa, Cambridge: Cambridge University Press (vol. 11, *Indexes*, 1973).

Rickett, W. A. 1985–98. *Guanzi.* 2 vols., Princeton: Princeton University Press.

Robbins, L. 1928. 'The representative firm', *Economic Journal* 38: 387–404.

1932. *An essay on the nature and significance of economic science.* London: Macmillan.

Robertson, D. 1915. *A study of industrial fluctuations.* London: P.S. King & Son; repr., London School of Economics and Political Science 1948.

1924. 'Those empty boxes', *Economic Journal* 34: 16–30.

1926. *Banking policy and the price level. An essay in the theory of trade cycle.* London: King and Son.

1930. 'The trees of the forest', *Economic Journal* 40: 80–89.

Robinson, J. 1933. *The economics of imperfect competition.* London: Macmillan; second edn. 1969.

1953. 'The production function and the theory of capital', *Review of Economic Studies* 21: 81–106.

1956. *The accumulation of capital.* London: Macmillan; third edn. 1969.

Romer, P. 1986. 'Increasing returns and long-run growth', *Journal of Political Economy* 94: 1002–37.

1990b. 'Is the notion of long-period positions compatible with classical political economy?', *Political Economy* 6: 103–11.

2009a, 'Keynes and probability: an assessment', *European Journal of the History of Economic Thought* 16: 485–510.

Roncaglia, A. 1975. *Sraffa e la teoria dei prezzi.* Roma-Bari: Laterza; second edn., 1981. English transl. *Sraffa and the theory of prices*, Chichester: Wiley 1977.

1977. *Petty: la nascita dell'economia politica.* Milano: Etas Libri. English transl. *Petty. The origins of political economy*, Armonk: Sharpe 1985.

1990a. 'Le scuole sraffiane', in Becattini (ed.), *Il pensiero economico: temi, problemi e scuole.* Torino: Utet, pp. 233–74. English transl., 'The Sraffian schools', *Review of Political Economy* 1991, 3: 187–219.

1990b. 'Is the notion of long-period positions compatible with classical political economy?', *Political Economy* 6: 103–11.

2005a. *The wealth of ideas.* Cambridge: Cambridge University Press.

2005b. *Il mito della mano invisibile.* Roma-Bari: Laterza.

2009a, 'Keynes and probability: an assessment', *European Journal of the History of Economic Thought* 16: 485–510.

2009b, *Piero Sraffa.* Houndmills: Palgrave Macmillan.

2015. 'Institutions, resources and the common weal', in M. Baranzini, C. Rotondi and R. Scazzieri eds. *Resources, production and structural dynamics.* Cambridge: Cambridge University Press, pp. 259–78.

Roncaglia, A. and Tonveronachi, M. 2015. 'Post-Keynesian, post-Sraffian economics: an outline', in D. Papadimitriou (ed.), *Contributions to economic theory, policy, development and finance. Essays in honor of Jan A. Kregel.* Houndmills: Palgrave Macmillan, pp. 40–64.

Rosenberg, N. and Birdzell, L.E. 1986. *How the West grew rich.* New York: Basic Books.

Rossi, E. 1946. *Abolire la miseria.* La fiaccola; repr. ed. by P. Sylos Labini, Roma-Bari: Laterza 1977.

Rostow, W. W. 1960. *The stages of economic growth*. Cambridge: Cambridge University Press.

Russell, B. and Whitehead, A. N. 1910–13. *Principia mathematica*. 3 vols., Cambridge: Cambridge University Press.

Samuelson, P.A. 1947. *Foundations of economic analysis*. Cambridge (Mass.): Harvard University Press.

1948. *Economics*. New York: Mc Graw Hill.

1962. 'Parable and realism in capital theory: the surrogate production function', *Review of Economic Studies* 29: 193–206.

1966. 'A summing up', *Quarterly Journal of Economics* 80: 568–83.

Savage, L. J. 1954. *The foundation of statistics*. New York: Wiley.

Savary, J. 1675. *Le parfait negociant*. Paris: Louis Billaine; repr., Düsseldorf: Verlag Wirtschaft und Finanzen 1993.

Say, J. B. 1803. *Traité d'économie politique*. Paris: Deterville. English transl., *A treatise on political economy*, New Brunswick and London: Transaction Publishers 2000.

Schabas, M. 1990. *A world ruled by numbers*. Princeton: Princeton University Press.

Schumpeter, J. 1908. *Das Wesen und der Hauptinhalt der theoretischen Nationalökonomie*. München-Leipzig: Duncker & Humblot. Italian transl., *L'essenza e i principi dell'economia teorica*, Roma-Bari: Laterza 1982.

1912. *Theorie der wirtschaftlichen Entwicklung*. München-Leipzig: Duncker & Humblot; second edn. 1926; third edn. 1931; fourth edn. 1935. English edn. *The theory of economic development*. Cambridge (Mass.): Harvard University Press 1934; repr. New York: Oxford University Press 1961.

1914. 'Epochen der Dogmen- und Methodengeschichte', in *Grundriss der Sozialökonomie*, Tübingen: Mohr, first part, pp. 19–124. English transl., *Economic doctrine and method: an historical sketch*. London: Allen & Unwin and New York: Oxford University Press.

1928. 'The instability of capitalism', *Economic Journal* 38: 361–86.

1939. *Business cycles. A theoretical, historical and statistical analysis of the capitalist process*. 2 vols., New York and London: McGraw Hill; repr., Philadelphia: Porcupine Press 1982. (Partial repr. ed. by R. Fels, New York and London: McGraw Hill 1964.)

1942. *Capitalism, socialism and democracy*. New York: Harpers & Bro.; second edn. 1947; third edn. 1950; fourth edn. 1954; fifth edn. 1976; repr. London: Routledge 1994.

1946. 'L'avenir de l'entreprise privée devant les tendences socialistes modernes', in *Comment sauvegarder l'entreprise privée*, Editions Association Professionelle des Industriels, Canada, pp. 103–08.

1954. *History of economic analysis*. ed. by E. Boody Schumpeter, New York: Oxford University Press.

1970. *Das Wesen Des Geldes*, ed. by F.K. Mann. Göttingen: Vanderlök & Ruprecht; English transl., *Treatise on money*. Aalten: Wordbridge, 2014.

Sen, A. 1984. *Resources, values and development*. Oxford: Basil Blackwell.

1991. *Money and value: on the etics and economics of finance*. Roma: Edizioni dell'Elefante.

2009. *The idea of justice*. London: Allen Lane.

Senior, W. N. 1827. *An introductory lecture on political economy*. London: J. Mawman.

1836. *An outline of the science of political economy*. London: W. Cloves and Sons.

1837. *Letters on the Factory Act*. London: B. Fellowes.

Serra, A. 1613. *Breve trattato delle cause che possono far abbondare li regni d'oro, e argento, dove non sono miniere. Con applicatione al Regno di Napoli*. Napoli: L. Scorriggio; repr., Düsseldorf: Verlag Wirtschaft und Finanzen GmbH 1994. English transl., ed. by S. Reinert. *A short treatise on the wealth and poverty of nations*. London: Anthem Press, 2011.

Shove, G. F. 1928. 'Varying costs and marginal net products', *Economic Journal* 38: 258–66.

Simon, H. A. 1957. *Models of man*. New York: Wiley.

1979. *Models of thought*. New Haven: Yale University Press.

Sims, C. A. 1980. 'Macroeconomics and reality', *Econometrica* 48: 1–48.

1982. 'Policy analysis with econometric models', *Brookings Papers on Economic Activity*, n. 1: 107–64.

Sismondi, S. de 1819. *Nouveaux principes d'économie politique, ou De la richesse dans ses rapports avec la population*. Paris: Delaunay; second edn., Paris: Treuttel et Würst 1827. English transl., *New principles of political economy*. New Brunswick (N.J.): Transaction Publishers 1991.

Skidelsky, R. 1983. *John Maynard Keynes. Hopes betrayed. 1883–1920*. London: Macmillan.

1992. *John Maynard Keynes. The economist as saviour, 1920–1937*. London: Macmillan.

2000. *John Maynard Keynes. Fighting for Britain, 1937–1946*. London: Macmillan.

2010. *Keynes. A very short introduction*. Oxford: Oxford University Press.

Smith, A. 1759. *The theory of moral sentiments*. London: A. Millar; critical edn., ed. by D.D. Raphael and A.L. Macfie, Oxford: Oxford University Press 1976.

1776. *An inquiry into the nature and causes of the wealth of nations*. London: W. Strahan and T. Cadell; critical edn., ed. by R.H. Campbell and A.S. Skinner, Oxford: Oxford University Press 1976.

1795. *Essays on philosophical subjects*. London: T. Cadell and W. Davies; critical edn., ed. by W.P.D. Wightman and J.C. Bryce, Oxford: Oxford University Press 1980.

1977. *Correspondence*. ed. by E. C. Mossner and I. S. Ross, Oxford: Oxford University Press.

1978. *Lectures on jurisprudence*. ed. by R. L. Meek, D. D. Raphael and P. G. Stein, Oxford: Oxford University Press.

1983. *Lectures on rhetoric and belles lettres*. Ed. by J. C. Bryce, Oxford: Oxford University Press.

Solow, R.M. 1956. 'A contribution to the theory of economic growth', *Quarterly Journal of Economics* 79: 65–94.

1957. 'Technical change and the aggregate production function', *Review of Economics and Statistics* 39: 312–20.

1963. *Capital theory and the rate of return*. Amsterdam: North Holland.

1967. 'The interest rate and transition between techniques', in C.H. Feinstein (ed.), *Socialism, capitalism and economic growth. Essays presented to Maurice Dobb*, Cambridge: Cambridge University Press, pp. 30–9.

Spaventa, L. 1968. 'Realism without parables in capital theory', in *Récherches récentes sur la fonction de production*, Centre d'études et de récherches universitaire de Namur, p. 15–45.

Spence, W. 1807. *Britain independent of commerce*. London: T. Cadell and W. Davies.

Sraffa, P. 1920. *L'inflazione monetaria in Italia durante e dopo la guerra*. Milano: Scuola tipografica salesiana. English transl., 'Monetary inflation in Italy during and after the war', *Cambridge Journal of Economics* 1993, 17: 7–26.

1922a. 'The bank crisis in Italy', *Economic Journal* 32: 178–97.

1922b. 'Italian banking today', *Manchester Guardian Commercial. The reconstrucion of Europe*, 7 December, n. 11: 675–76.

1925. 'Sulle relazioni fra costo e quantità prodotta', *Annali di economia* 2: 277–328. English transl., 'On the relations between cost and quantity produced', *Italian Economic Papers*, 1998, 3: 323–63.

1926. 'The laws of returns under competitive conditions', *Economic Journal* 36: 535–50.

1930. 'A criticism' and 'A Rejoinder', in 'Symposium on increasing returns and the representative firm', *Economic Journal* 40: 89–93.

1932. 'Dr. Hayek on money and capital' and 'A rejoinder', *Economic Journal* 42: 42–53, 249–51.

1951. 'Introduction', in Ricardo D., 1951–55, vol. I, pp. xiii–lxii.

1960. *Production of commodities by means of commodities*. Cambridge: Cambridge University Press.

1962. 'Production of commodities: a comment', *Economic Journal* 72: 477–79.

Stackelberg, H. von 1933. 'Zwei kritische Bemerkungen zur Preistheorie Gustav Cassel', *Zeitschrift für Nationalökonomie* 4.

Steindl, J. 1945. *Small and big business. Economic problems of the size of firms*. Oxford: Basil Blackwell; new Italian edn., *Piccola e grande impresa. Problemi economici della dimensione dell'impresa*, Milano: Franco Angeli 1991.

1952. *Maturity and stagnation in American capitalism*. Oxford: Basil Blackwell; repr. New York: Monthly Review Press 1976.

1990. *Economic papers, 1941–88*. London: Macmillan.

Steuart, J. 1767. *An inquiry into the principles of political oeconomy*. 2 vols., London: A. Millar and T. Cadell; critical edn., ed. by A. S. Skinner, Edinburgh and London: Oliver and Boyd 1966.

Stewart, D. 1794. 'Account of the life and writings of Adam Smith LL. D.', *Transactions of the Royal Society of Edinburgh* 3: 55–137; repr. in Smith 1795 (1980), pp. 269–332.

Sweezy, P. 1942. *The theory of capitalist development*. NewYork: Monthly Review Press; repr. 1968.

Sylos Labini, P. 1954. 'Il problema dello sviluppo economico in Marx ed in Schumpeter', in G.U. Papi (ed.), *Teoria dello sviluppo economico*, Milano: Giuffrè. English transl., 'The problem of economic growth in Marx and Schumpeter', in Sylos Labini 1984, pp. 37–78.

298   Bibliography

1956. *Oligopolio e progresso tecnico*. Milano: Giuffrè; fourth edn. Torino: Einaudi
    1967. English transl., *Oligopoly and technical progress*, Cambridge (Mass.):
    Harvard University Press 1962; second edn., 1969.
1972. *Sindacati, inflazione e produttività*. Roma-Bari: Laterza. English transl.,
    Trade unions, inflation and productivity, Westmead: Saxon House 1974.
1974. *Saggio sulle classi sociali*. Roma-Bari: Laterza.
1976. 'Competition: the product markets', in Wilson and Skinner (eds.),
    pp. 200–32.
1984. *The forces of economic growth and decline*. Cambridge (Mass.): MIT Press.
2000. *Sottosviluppo. Una strategia di riforme*. Roma-Bari: Laterza. English
    transl., *Underdevelopment. A strategy for reform*, Cambridge: Cambridge
    University Press 2001.
Tagliacozzo, G. (ed.) 1937. *Economisti napoletani dei sec. XVII e XVIII*. Bologna:
    Cappelli.
Tarshis, L. 1939. 'Changes in real and money wages', *Economic Journal* 49: 150–4.
Thomas Aquinas 1265–73. *Summa theologiae*. repr. in 5 vols., Roma 1962.
Thompson, W. 1824. *An inquiry into the principles of the distribution of wealth most
    conducive to human happiness*. London: Longman, Hurst, Rees, Orme, Brown
    and Green-Wheatley and Adlard.
Thornton, H. 1802. *Enquiry into the nature and effects of the paper credit of Great
    Britain*. London: Hatchard; repr. ed. by F. Hayek, London School of
    Economics, 1939.
Thünen, J. H. von 1826–50. *Der isolierte Staat in Beziehung auf Landwirtschaft und
    Nationalökonomie*. Part one, Hamburg: Perthes 1826; Part two, Rostock:
    Leopold 1850; Part three, Rostock: Leopold 1850 and 1863. English transl.
    of Part one, *Isolated state*, ed. by P. Hall, Oxford: Pergamon Press 1966.
Tirole, J. 1988. *The theory of industrial organization*. Cambridge (Mass.): MIT Press.
Tonveronachi, M. 1983. *J. M. Keynes. Dall'instabilità ciclica all'equilibrio di sottoc-
    cupazione*. Roma: NIS.
Tooke, T. 1838–57. *History of prices, 1793–1856*. 6 vols., London: Longman,
    Orme, Brown, Green & Longmans.
Tooke, T. 1844. *An inquiry into the currency principle*. London: Longman, Brown,
    Green & Longmans; repr., Series of reprints of scarce works in political
    economy, n. 15, London School of Economics and Political Sciences 1959.
Torrens, R. 1808. *The economists refuted*. Dublin: LaGrange and London: S.A. Oddy.
    1815. *An essay on the external corn trade*. London: J. Hatchard.
    1817. 'A paper on the means of reducing the poors rates and of affording
    effectual and permanent relief to the labouring classes', *The Pamphleteer*
    n. 20: 509–28.
    1818. 'Strictures on Mr. Ricardo's doctrine respecting exchangeable value',
    Edinburgh Magazine, Oct., pp. 335–38.
    1821. *An essays on the production of wealth*. London: Longman, Rees, Orme,
    Brown, & Longmans.
    1835. *Colonization of South Australia*. London: Longman, Rees, Orme, Brown
    & Green.
Tugan-Baranovsky, M. J. 1905. *Theoretische Grundlagen des Marxismus*. Leipzig:
    Dunker & Humblot.

Turgot, A.-R.-J. [1759]. 'Éloge de Vincent de Gournai', *Mercure de France*; repr. in Ravix and Romani 1997, pp. 123–53.

[1766]. *Réflexions sur la formation et la distribution des richesses*. Publ. in 1769–70 in *Ephémérides du citoyen* with changes introduced by DuPont de Nemours; original text in Schelle, 1913–23, vol. 2, pp. 533–601; repr. in Ravix and Romani 1997, pp. 157–226.

Veblen, T. 1899. *The theory of the leisure class*. New York: Macmillan.

1904. *The theory of business enterprise*. New York: Charles Scribener's Sons.

Verdoorn, P. 1949. 'Fattori che regolano lo sviluppo della produttività del lavoro', *L'industria* 1: 3–10.

Viner, J. 1931. 'Cost curves and supply curves', *Zeitschrift für Nationalökonomie* 3: 23–46.

1937. *Studies in the theory of international trade*. New York: Harper.

1991. *Essays on the intellectual history of economics*. ed. by D.A. Irwin, Princeton: Princeton University Press.

Vromen, J. J. 2007. 'Neuroeconomics as a natural extension of bioeconomics: the shifting scope of standard economic theory', *Journal of Bioeconomics* 9: 145–67.

Wakefield, E. G. 1829. *A letter from Sydney, the principal town of Australasia*. London: Joseph Cross.

1833. *England and America*. 2 vols., London: R. Bentley.

Wald, A. 1936. 'Über einige Gleichungssysteme der Mathematischen Ökonomie', *Zeitschrift für Nationalökonomie* 7: 637–70. English transl., 'On some systems of equations of mathematical economics', *Econometrica* 19 (1951): 368–403.

Walras, L. 1867. 'La Bourse et le crédit', in *Paris guide, par les principaux écrivains et artistes de la France, deuxième partie*, Paris: Librairie Internationale, pp. 1731–51; repr. in Auguste et Leon Walras, *Oeuvres économiques complètes, vol. 7, Mélanges d'économie politique et sociale*, Paris: Economica 1987, pp. 180–200.

1874. *Eléments d'économie politique pure*. Lausanne: Corbaz; second part, 1877; second edn. 1889, third edn. 1896, fourth edn. 1900, 'definitive' edn. 1926. English transl. of the 1926 edn., ed. by W. Jaffé, *Elements of pure economics*, London: Irwin Inc. 1954; repr. London: Allen & Unwin 1965.

1880. 'La Bourse, la spéculation et l'agiotage', *Bibliothèque Universelle et Revue Suisse* n. 5 (March): 452–76 and n. 6 (April): 66–94.

1896. *Études d'économie sociale. Théorie de la répartition de la richesse sociale*. Lausanne: Corbaz; repr. Paris: Economica 1990.

1898. *Études d'économie politique appliquée. Théorie de la production de la richesse sociale*. ed. definitive ed. by G. Leduc, Lausanne: P. Rouge and Paris: F. Pichon 1936; repr. Paris: Economica 1992.

Weber, M. 1904–5. 'Die protestantische Ethik und der Geist des Kapitalismus', *Archiv für Sozialwissenschaft und Sozialpolitik* 20–21; second edn. in *Gesammelte Aufsätze zur Religionssoziologie*, Tübingen: Mohr 1922. English transl., *The protestant ethic and the spirit of capitalism*, London: Allen & Unwin 1930.

1922. *Wirtschaft und Gesellschaft*. 2 vols., Tübingen: Mohr. English transl., *Economy and society*, New York: Bedminster Press 1968.

Whately, R. 1831. *Introductory lectures on political economy*. London: B. Fellowes; second edn. 1832.

Wicksell, K. 1893. *Über Wert, Kapital, und Rente*. Jena: G. Fischer. English transl., *Value, capital and rent*, London: Allen & Unwin 1954.

1898. *Geldzins und Güterpreise bestimmenden Ursachen*. Jena: G. Fischer. English transl., *Interest and prices*, London: Macmillan.

1900. 'Om gränsproduktivitaten såsom grundval för den nationalekonomiska fördelningen', *Ekonomisk Tidskrift* 2: 305–37. English transl., 'Marginal productivity as the basis for distribution in economics', in K. Wicksell, *Selected papers on economic theory*, London: Allen & Unwin 1958, pp. 93–121.

1901–6. *Forelasningar i nationalekonomi*. 2 vols., Stockholm-Lund: Fritzes-Berlingska. English transl., *Lectures on political economy*, 2 vols., London: Routledge and Kegan Paul 1934–35.

Wicksteed, P. H. 1894. *An essay on the co-ordination of the laws of distribution*. London: Macmillan; repr. ed. by I. Steedman, Aldershot: Edward Elgar 1992.

1910. *The common sense of political economy*. London: Macmillan; repr. ed. by L. Robbins, 2 vols., London: Routledge 1933.

Wilson, T. 1572. *A discourse uppon usurye*. Londini: Rychardi Tottelli; repr. ed. by R. H. Tawney, London: Bell 1926; repr. London: Frank Cass 1963.

Wittgenstein, L. 1921. 'Logisch-philosophische Abhandlung', *Annalen der Naturphilosophie*, 14: 185–262. English edn. with revisions and the German text, *Tractatus logico-philosophicus*. London: Kegan Paul 1922.

1953. *Philosophische Untersuchungen*. (with English transl., *Philosophical investigations*). ed. by G. E. M. Anscombe and R. Rhees, Oxford: Blackwell; repr. 1972.

Wood, A. 1975. *A theory of profits*. Cambridge: Cambridge University Press.

Xenophon 1923. *Memorabilia and Oeconomicus*. ed. E. Capps, T.E. Page and W.H.D. Rouse, Loeb Classic Library, London: Heinemann and New York: Putnam's Sons.

Young, A. 1928. 'Increasing returns and economic progress', *Economic Journal* 38: 527–42.

Zeuthen, F. 1933. 'Das Prinzip der Knappheit, technische Kombination und ökonomische Qualität', *Zeitschrift für Nationalökonomie* 4: 1–24.

Author Index

Subject Index

absolute value, 37, 68, 101–2
abstinence, 118, 124, 125, 159
accumulation, 23, 63, 66, 67, 84, 95–7,
    107, 134, 142, 159, 170, 173, 234
aggregate demand, 83, 84, 142, 171, 196,
    207, 211, 254, 257, 258
agriculture, 12, 23, 31, 40, 46, 48,
    49, 50, 52, 66, 95, 97, 109, 111,
    124, 134, 142
alienation, 76, 126, 128
allocation of resources, 150, 167
American Economic Association, 177, 194,
    267
analytic statements, 2, 3
anarchist theory of knowledge, 5
Arthasastra, 14
artisans, 46, 50, 65, 134, 135
astronomy, 5, 59, 275
asymmetric information, 248
asymmetries in economic policy, 212
Austrian school, 153–66, 221
avances annuelles, fonciéres, primitives, 50
axiomatic analysis, 244–9

balance of payments, 25, 56, 200
balance of trade, 23, 25, 32, 56, 105, 200,
    212
banking, 103–4, 221
banking school, 103
Bank of England, 95, 112
beggar-my-neighbour policies, 211
benevolence, 55, 56, 62
Bible, 14, 30
bilateral monopoly, 152, 155
biology, 263
blood, circulation of the, 11, 32
bourgeoisie, 97, 127, 132, 158, 224
British Economic Association,
    182, 192
budget constraint, 150, 155, 171
Bullionists, 22
business cycles, 134–5, 162, 165, 174, 213,
    214, 221–2

Cambridge equation, 193
Cambridge school, 162, 193, 213, 214,
    215, 229, 260
cameralists, 22
capital
    circulating and fixed capital, 101, 110,
        111
    constant and variable capital, 133, 136,
        137
capitalism, 23, 31, 43, 127, 129, 135, 139,
    142, 159, 195, 201, 222–4, 268
cardinal utility, 176, 245
central banking, 104, 204
chaos theory, 270
chemistry, 11
Church, as *corpus mysticum*, 18
Church Fathers, *see* Patristic thought
circular flow, 234
Colbertism, 40, 49
colonies, 23, 59, 75, 89–90, 112
commerce, 17, 19, 43, 65, 212
commodity fetishism, 128, 129
Communism, 125, 126, 127, 132, 140, 163
comparative costs, comparative advantage,
    105, 110, 183
comparative statics, 172, 219
compensation, theory of, 88, 107
competition
    competition of capitals, 71, 84, 106, 145
    free competition, 71, 170
    imperfect competition, 197, 215, 230
    monopolistic competition, 198
    perfect competition, 73, 155, 176, 187,
        190, 262
competitive view, 6
complacibilitas, 22, 155
consequentialist ethics, 91, 122, 123, 150,
    271
consumer's surplus, 197
consumption, 15, 33, 47, 54, 85, 123, 144,
    150, 157, 166, 167, 168, 174, 196,
    207, 208, 220, 257, 272; *see also*
    luxury consumption, subsistence

Made in the USA
Las Vegas, NV
23 August 2022

53854918R00177